HOUSE & GARDEN'S
Party Menu
Cookbook

COMPILED AND EDITED BY
José Wilson

SIMON AND SCHUSTER   New York

SBN 671-21508-6
Library of Congress Catalog Card Number: 73–7702
Designed by Irving Perkins
Manufactured in the United States of America
By The Maple Press Company, York, Pennsylvania

1   2   3   4   5   6   7   8   9   10

Contents

Introduction

Here is a book of imaginative, realistic ways to feed family and friends and have time to enjoy them too. There are 126 menus for inspiration and 593 superb recipes from some of the best cooks in the world. All the menus are well planned with food that looks good, tastes good and, very important, much of it can be prepared ahead of time. "The most delicious food possible, with a minimum of time and trouble in the making" is what editor José Wilson had in mind as she selected each recipe. You'll find ideas for super breakfasts to small dinners, low-calorie meals to big parties with little price tags, plus organizing and preparation tips, techniques, and encouragements. The recipes are choice ones from the many that have appeared recently in the pages of *House & Garden*. Probably there are some you meant to clip and didn't, and now you have them here in easy reference form.

Food and drink editor of *House & Garden* for fifteen years, José Wilson, now a contributing editor, is Manager of the James Beard Cooking Classes, has several books to her credit, and is an accomplished cook herself. We wish to thank her for the planning and editing of this book and also to thank these distinguished cooks, hosts and hostesses, and restaurants for allowing us to publish their excellent recipes: Mrs.

Ralph Bailey, Mrs. Jack Baker, Ruth Conrad Bateman, James A. Beard, Iris Brooks, Helen Evans Brown, Philip S. Brown, Elizabeth Burton, Giorgio Cavallon, Ruth Ellen Church, Craig Claiborne, John Clancy, Onalee Cooke, Mrs. John Sherman Cooper, Mrs. Wyatt Cooper, Lelia Carson Cox, Julie Dannenbaum, Eloise Davison, Star Duwyenie, Mrs. David Evins, Edward Fields, Vittoria Graham, Peggy Harvey, Alex D. Hawkes, Nika Hazelton, Mary Moon Hemingway, Jerome Hill, Cathrine Hindley, Stanley Kunitz, Leon Leanides, Dione Lucas, Vice Admiral William J. Marshall, Tatiana McKenna, Dina Merrill, Kay Shaw Nelson, Yoshie Okamoto, Richard Olney, Elisabeth Ortiz, Lou Seibert Pappas, Paula Peck, Kathleen Winsor Porter, Mrs. Jule Rabó, Mrs. Julian Robinson, Mrs. John Robson, Harry Rogers, Mrs. Archibald B. Roosevelt, Jr., Elaine Ross, Myra Waldo, Betty Wason, Mrs. George Y. Wheeler II, Countess Margaret Willaumez, Milton Williams, José Wilson, Elena Zelayeta, Manoir de Vaumadeuc, Grand Véfour.

MARY JANE POOL, EDITOR-IN-CHIEF
House & Garden Magazine

Breakfast Parties

Whether you prefer to call it breakfast or brunch (the latter word seems to have fallen into linguistic ill repute lately), there's no denying that a late-morning party has become very much a part of the relaxed, informal American way of entertaining, especially on a holiday or weekend. Often, it's easier to snare guests for late breakfast, apt to be a rather casual drop-in and sit-around affair, than for a more formal lunch.

For the hostess who is her own cook, a breakfast party offers a flexible and comparatively inexpensive way to entertain a large group of friends—and it really doesn't matter too much how many show up, as breakfast menus can be stretched or shortened with ease. The menu is usually one that can either be cooked on the spot or done ahead of time. Seldom does it involve complicated dishes that take a long time to cook.

According to the season, the hour, the day and the appetites of the guests, the food can range from something as simple as fresh fruit in champagne, an omelette and some good rolls with honey and jam to a rather elaborate buffet with all kinds of dishes kept hot on warming trays or in chafing dishes in an updated version of the English hunt breakfast. In either case, the food should be satisfying but on the light side, usually with fruit in some form, either fresh, poached or baked, and an easy-to-eat main course. Here you can choose from an enormous number of

9

suitable dishes, perhaps a variation on the familiar eggs and bacon routine, some favorite standbys like chicken hash, kedgeree, finnan haddie, or rather more involved productions—a mushroom roll or brook trout sauté meunière.

Drinks for a breakfast party are no problem; anything that is light and refreshing will do very well. In the hard-liquor category, drinks with fruit juice bases are the most suitable, variations on the Bloody Mary and other vodka drinks, sours, or, if you're feeling rather more adventurous, those marvelous New Orleans concoctions, the Suissesse and the Sazerac. Aperitifs, with their delicate fruit and herb flavors, are always a good choice, either on the rocks or as a long, tall drink with chilled club soda. Then there are all the lovely wine concoctions—sangria, kir, spritzers, champagne punch—and, of course, the wines that go with the meal itself, which should again be light and cool—chilled white wine, champagne, vin rosé, or Beaujolais.

Breakfast for Four Light Eaters

A tempting succession of flavors for people who don't really eat breakfast—or for one of those hot summer mornings when sustenance is needed but the appetite must be coaxed.

MENU

Papaya with Lime
Oeufs sur le Plat
Toasted English Muffins with Prosciutto Butter
Hot or Iced Café au lait

OEUFS SUR LE PLAT

Preheat the broiler to very hot. Melt 4 tablespoons of butter in a shallow metal au gratin dish. Break in 4 eggs and cook over moderate heat for about 30 seconds, or until the white is just beginning to set. Tilt the dish and baste with the butter.

Place under the broiler for about 1 minute, pulling the dish out and basting the eggs with butter every few seconds until the white is completely set. Sprinkle with salt and freshly ground pepper and serve immediately.

PROSCIUTTO BUTTER

> 1 cup prosciutto
> ½ cup unsalted butter, softened

Remove the fat from the prosciutto and grind or chop very, very finely. Beat the ground prosciutto with the butter until it is a smooth paste. Pack into a small crock and chill.

As a variation, Westphalian ham or smoked salmon can be substituted for the prosciutto.

A Pre-Ski Breakfast for Four

An energy-giving breakfast before setting out for the slopes, with a taste of honey on the grapefruit and a high-protein course to follow.

MENU

Honeyed Grapefruit
Italian Ham and Eggs
Hot Coffee or Hot Chocolate

HONEYED GRAPEFRUIT

Halve two large pink grapefruit, remove the seeds, and cut into sections. Dribble a tablespoon of honey over each half and heat under the broiler until the honey bubbles.

ITALIAN HAM AND EGGS

> 8 thin slices protein toast
> 8 thin slices lightly sautéed ham
> 8 poached eggs
> 1½ to 2 cups Mornay sauce (see page 58)
> Grated Parmesan cheese

Place the toast on a flameproof dish and top each piece with a slice of ham and a poached egg. Cover with Mornay sauce, sprinkle with grated Parmesan cheese, and put under the broiler to glaze. Serve two eggs per person.

A Hearty Winter Breakfast for Six

The spiciness of powdered ginger to bring out the flavor of melon and the unusual touch of chopped apple in the pancakes are the elements that make this simple country-style breakfast out of the ordinary.

MENU

Melon with Ginger
Canadian Bacon or Country Sausage Cakes
Apple Pancakes with Warm Maple Syrup
Coffee

APPLE PANCAKES

> 2 cups all-purpose flour
> 1 teaspoon salt
> 2 teaspoons sugar
> 2 teaspoons double-acting baking powder
> ½ teaspoon cinnamon
> 3 eggs, lightly beaten

2 cups milk
¼ cup melted butter
1 large tart apple, peeled and finely chopped
¼ cup vegetable oil

Sift together into a bowl the flour, salt, sugar, baking powder, and cinnamon. Make a well in the center and pour in the eggs and milk. Mix lightly to blend—the batter will be lumpy. Stir in the butter. Just before cooking, stir in the chopped apple. Heat a griddle or heavy skillet until a drop of water flicked on it sizzles and evaporates instantly. Lightly grease the griddle with the vegetable oil; continue to grease when necessary. Pour on the batter to form cakes about 4 inches in diameter. Cook until small bubbles form on surface, then turn and cook until other side is golden brown. Stack on a heated plate, serve immediately. Makes about 18–20.

A Simple but Special Breakfast for Four

Make sure your guests have adventurous palates, for the unusual combinations of flavors in this meal are not for the staunch advocates of bacon and eggs as the only way to start the day. If you like, you can omit the lentils in the kedgeree.

MENU

Grilled Bacon and Banana Rolls
Fish Kedgeree with Mango Chutney
Toast
Grapefruit or Bitter Orange Marmalade

GRILLED BACON AND BANANA ROLLS

6 bananas
6 large slices bacon

Peel the bananas and cut bananas and bacon slices in half. Wrap pieces of bacon around the banana halves. Secure with toothpicks if desired. Broil for about 7 minutes, turning often, until the bananas are quite soft and the bacon crisp.

FISH KEDGEREE
[ELISABETH ORTIZ]

½ cup lentils (optional)
1 cup raw rice
1 clove garlic
4 tablespoons unsalted butter
1 tablespoon pungent curry powder
1 pound cooked salmon, finnan haddie, or any white fish, flaked
3 hard-cooked eggs, the whites chopped, the yolks sieved
Salt, freshly ground black pepper
¼ teaspoon cayenne pepper, or to taste
3 tablespoons finely chopped parsley

Cook the lentils until tender in boiling salted water, drain, and set aside. Cook the rice in salted water with the garlic until tender. Drain, set aside, and remove garlic. Heat the butter in a large, heavy frying pan and sauté the curry powder gently for 1 or 2 minutes, being careful not to let it burn. Add the lentils, rice, fish, chopped egg whites, salt, pepper, and cayenne. Mix gently and cook until heated through. Transfer to a warm platter and sprinkle with the egg yolks and parsley. Serve with mango chutney.

Mexican Almuerzo for Six

Although the Mexicans, like other Latin Americans, eat an early-morning meal of sweet breads with café con leche (coffee with milk) or hot chocolate, known as *desayuno*, they also have another, later breakfast, or *almuerzo*, similar to our brunch. Taken anywhere from 9 A.M. to 11 or 11:30, *almuerzo* is a much heartier meal of fruit or fruit juices, egg dishes, beans, and tortillas. For a Mexican-inspired breakfast party you might start, if you wish, with a drink such as a tequila sour or tequila screwdriver, and serve Mexican beer with the main dish.

MENU
[ELISABETH ORTIZ]

Platter of Tropical Fruits—Papaya, Pineapple, Mango, Cherimoya

or

Pitchers of Fruit Juices
Huevos en Rabo de Mestiza
Tortillas   Frijoles Refritos
Buñuelos
Café de Olla

HUEVOS EN RABO DE MESTIZA

- 2 poblano chiles or green bell peppers
- 4 tablespoons olive oil
- 1 onion, finely chopped
- 1½ pounds tomatoes, peeled, seeded, and mashed
  Salt, freshly ground pepper to taste
- ½ teaspoon sugar
- 6 slices Monterey Jack, Cheddar, or similar cheese
- 6 eggs

Roast peppers over gas flame or electric burner, wrap in a damp cloth for ½ hour, peel, remove stems, seeds, and veins, and cut into strips. Heat the oil in a skillet and sauté the peppers, being careful not to let them brown. Add onion and continue cooking until it is transparent. Add tomatoes, salt, pepper, and sugar. When the tomatoes have cooked down, place slices of cheese on top and continue cooking for a few minutes. Slide eggs on top of sauce and cheese, cover, and cook for a few minutes, then turn off heat and let stand until white is cooked.

VARIATION: Make the rabo with hard-cooked eggs and pour heavy cream over the dish while the egg halves warm in the sauce.

TORTILLAS (see page 300)

FRIJOLES REFRITOS (see page 299)

BUÑUELOS

> 2 eggs
> 1 cup milk
> 1 teaspoon salt
> 1 teaspoon baking powder
> 2 tablespoons sugar
> 4 cups flour
> ¼ cup melted butter
> Sugar and cinnamon or ground cloves

Beat eggs thoroughly. Whisk milk into eggs. Sift dry ingredients and add gradually to the egg-milk mixture, then add melted butter. Turn on to a lightly floured board and knead very gently until the dough is smooth. Roll out as thin as possible and cut into 2- to 3-inch squares or circles the size of small or large tortillas. Fry in very hot deep fat or oil (370°) until delicately browned, turning as the first side puffs up. Roll in sugar and cinnamon, or in sugar and ground cloves, and serve as cookies. Makes about forty 3-inch squares.

CAFÉ DE OLLA

Heat 6 cups water, ½ cup dark brown sugar, a 2-inch piece of stick cinnamon, and 6 whole cloves in a saucepan or heat-proof coffee pot, stirring until the sugar dissolves. Add 6 tablespoons regular-grind dark-roast coffee and bring to a boil. Simmer for a minute or two. Stir, cover and leave on the range in a warm place until the grounds settle. Strain into coffee cups.

A Fish Breakfast for Six

Breakfasters seem to fall into two camps—those who love all kinds of fish for breakfast, be it smoked black cod, kippers, or sautéed trout, and those who can't face anything finny in the morning. For the first group, this is a simple and simply delicious menu.

MENU

Turkish Grapes and Yoghurt
Fish Filets with Bacon and Green Onion
Melbaed English Muffins
Marmalade

TURKISH GRAPES AND YOGHURT
[HELEN EVANS BROWN]

> 2 cups seedless grapes
> 1 cup water
> 2 tablespoons honey
> 1 cup yoghurt

Cook grapes in water and honey until tender. Reduce syrup, pour over grapes and serve warm, with chilled yoghurt as a sauce.

FISH FILETS WITH BACON AND GREEN ONION
[PHILIP S. BROWN]

> 3 slices bacon, finely chopped
> 6 fish filets (sole, haddock, cod, trout, etc.)
> 1 teaspoon salt
> ¾ teaspoon freshly ground black pepper
> 3 green onions, finely chopped
> 1 tomato, peeled, seeded, and finely chopped

Sauté the bacon for 3 to 4 minutes and drain on absorbent paper. Arrange the filets on buttered foil or a greased broiling rack. Salt and pepper them. Combine the bacon with the onion and tomato, and spoon over the filets. Broil 4 to 5 inches from the broiling unit for 3 to 4 minutes, depending on the thickness of the filets.

17

MELBAED ENGLISH MUFFINS
[JAMES A. BEARD]

Thinly slice 6 English muffins, as if you were making Melba toast. Toast and butter them, then put in a 300° oven until crisped.

After-the-Holidays Breakfast for Six

Once Thanksgiving is over, there need be no problem about using up leftover turkey and stuffing, because it can be turned into a sensational hash for a weekend breakfast. As the melon is already saturated with Rhine wine, you might serve more of the same wine, chilled, with the hash.

MENU

Parke's Cantaloupe in Rhine Wine

Turkey Hash

Baking Powder Biscuits   *Fruit Preserves*

PARKE'S CANTALOUPE IN RHINE WINE
[ELAINE ROSS]

    3 small ripe cantaloupes
    1 bottle Rhine wine
    30 to 36 grapefruit sections, fresh or canned

Peel the cantaloupes, cut in half crosswise, and scoop out the seeds. Marinate the melon in the wine for several hours in the refrigerator, turning the melon occasionally. Set each melon half in a dessert bowl. Fill melon halves with grapefruit sections, spoon a little wine over them and serve immediately.

TURKEY HASH
[JAMES A. BEARD]

    1 onion, coarsely chopped
    1 green pepper, coarsely chopped
    4 tablespoons butter
    2 tablespoons oil
    2 cups or more diced cold turkey
    1 cup cold stuffing, if available, or 1 cup diced cooked potatoes
      Dash Tabasco sauce
    ½ teaspoon freshly ground black pepper
      Cream or hot water
    ¼ cup blanched almonds
    1 cup pitted Greek olives
    5 eggs
    ¼ cup grated Parmesan cheese

Sauté the onion and green pepper in the butter and oil for 3 or 4 minutes. Add the turkey and stuffing or potatoes and press down into pan. Add Tabasco and pepper, mix all ingredients well, press again, and cook over medium heat. If the mixture seems too dry, add some cream or hot water and let it cook down a bit. Add almonds and olives and correct the seasoning.

Beat eggs lightly, mix with half the cheese and pour gently over the hash. Sprinkle remaining cheese on top. Cook until eggs are just set. If you wish, you may run the pan under the broiler to brown for a minute, but be careful the eggs do not overcook and burn.

BAKING POWDER BISCUITS
[KATHLEEN WINSOR PORTER]

    2 cups flour
    ½ teaspoon salt
    4 teaspoons baking powder
    4 heaping tablespoons vegetable shortening
    ¾ cup milk

Preheat oven to 450°. Sift dry ingredients. Add shortening and cut in with knife and fork (or pastry cutter). Add milk slowly to make a soft dough. Roll out on a lightly floured board until about ½ inch thick. Cut with biscuit cutter and lay on baking pan coated with a thick layer of shortening. Bake for 12 to 15 minutes, or until golden. Makes about 2 dozen.

Emergency Sunday Breakfast for Eight

If on the spur of the moment you invited guests from a Saturday night party to come for breakfast next morning and then find you haven't a thing in the refrigerator, this breakfast can literally be put together from what the corner delicatessen has to offer. The only exception might be staples such as onions, which you'd probably have on hand anyway.

To start, you could serve Bloody Marys and similar vodka drinks or, for those who like it, tiny glasses (chill them in the freezer) of icy-cold vodka with the smoked salmon and sturgeon.

MENU

Platter of Smoked Salmon and Sturgeon Garnished with Sliced
Bermuda Onion, Lemon Wedges and Capers
Chive-Cheese Scrambled Eggs
Selection of Bake-and-Serve Hot Breads: Brioches, French
Loaves, Croissants, Rolls with Sweet Butter and Preserves
Applesauce Brûlée

CHIVE-CHEESE SCRAMBLED EGGS
[EDWARD FIELDS]

16 eggs
½ cup milk
¼ pound chive cream cheese
1 teaspoon salt
¼ teaspoon coarsely ground black pepper
¼ pound butter
2 large onions, sliced and sautéed in butter

Put half the eggs, milk, cheese, salt, pepper, and 1 tablespoon butter in an electric blender. Whirl until foamy and pour into a large bowl. Repeat with the remaining eggs, milk, cheese, salt, pepper, and 1 tablespoon butter.

Melt 1 tablespoon butter over medium heat in a large skillet or in an electric fry pan. Pour half the contents of the bowl into the pan and cook, stirring constantly with the flat of a fork, until the eggs have reached the desired consistency. Transfer eggs to a chafing dish. Clean skillet, melt remaining butter and repeat with remaining egg mixture. Add to chafing dish and serve immediately. Serve onions separately.

APPLESAUCE BRÛLÉE

> 4 cups applesauce, flavored with a little grated nutmeg and cinnamon
> 1 pint commercial sour cream, chilled
> ½ to ¾ cup light brown sugar, sieved

Fill eight individual custard cups ⅔ full of applesauce. Spread sour cream evenly on top. Generously sprinkle with brown sugar, making sure to cover all the sour cream. Put custard cups on broiler pan or cookie sheet and put under hot broiler for 1 to 3 minutes, until the sugar has melted and caramelized; watch carefully to see that it does not burn.

Summer Breakfast in the Garden for Eight

A late-late breakfast that is light, but satisfying enough to stand in for lunch—in which case you might serve a refreshing fruity, Alsatian wine, which would complement the delicate flavors of the chicken and cantaloupe and the mushroom roll.

MENU

Cantaloupe with Chicken and Water Chestnuts
Mushroom Roll
White Asparagus Spears with Vinaigrette Sauce
Hot Rolls
Golden Compote

The Wine

Sylvaner or Traminer

CANTALOUPE WITH CHICKEN AND WATER CHESTNUTS
[ELAINE ROSS]

    4 small cantaloupes
    5 cups white meat of chicken, cut in bite-size pieces
    ⅓ cup sliced water chestnuts
    ¾ cup sour cream
    ¼ cup mango chutney (remove mango pieces first and chop finely)

Halve melons and remove seeds. With a ball cutter, scoop a couple of melon balls from each cavity. Combine chicken and water chestnuts. Mix sour cream and chutney, add to chicken, and toss lightly. Heap in melon cavities and garnish with melon balls.

MUSHROOM ROLL
[JULIE DANNENBAUM]

        Oil
    1½ pounds mushrooms
     6 eggs, separated
    ¼ pound butter, melted
        Salt, freshly ground pepper
     2 tablespoons lemon juice
     4 or 5 whole mushrooms, fluted
        Butter, lemon juice
        Chopped parsley

Oil a 10″ x 15″ jelly-roll pan, line with wax paper, and oil the paper.

Wipe the mushrooms clean with a damp cloth. Chop the mushrooms finely and wring them in a cloth to remove excess moisture. Beat egg yolks until fluffy and combine with the chopped mushrooms, melted butter, ½ teaspoon salt, ¼ teaspoon pepper and lemon juice. Beat egg whites until soft peaks form, then carefully fold in the mushroom mixture. Pour into the prepared pan and smooth flat with a rubber spatula. Bake in a 350° oven for 15 minutes. Cool, carefully turn out onto a sheet of wax paper, and peel off the wax paper on the top. Roll up with the aid of the wax paper underneath and put on a long narrow board or platter (put roll on the board or platter on the paper and then cut the paper away).

Sauté the fluted mushrooms in butter over high heat, sprinkling them with lemon juice, salt, and pepper. Arrange on top of the roll. Sprinkle with chopped parsley and serve with hot melted butter. The roll is good hot or cold and may be prepared in advance and then reheated—wrap it loosely in foil and warm through on platter over simmering hot water.

WHITE ASPARAGUS SPEARS WITH VINAIGRETTE SAUCE

Use the canned giant white asparagus. Drain well and arrange 3 stalks on each individual plate, then pour on vinaigrette sauce and sprinkle with a little chopped chives or parsley.

GOLDEN COMPOTE
[ELAINE ROSS]

       5 large nectarines
       5 large freestone peaches
     ⅔ cup sugar
     1 cup water
     1 2-inch piece of vanilla bean
    18 preserved kumquats, drained

Scald the nectarines and peaches, slip off the skins, and cut the fruit in half, discarding the pits. Place the sugar and water in a saucepan and bring to a boil, stirring constantly until the sugar is dissolved. Reduce the heat, add the vanilla bean and the nectarines. Cover and simmer for about 5 minutes, or until the fruit is just tender. Do not overcook. With a slotted spoon, remove the fruit and set aside. Cook the peaches in the same way. In a large, shallow oven-to-table baking dish, arrange the nectarines, cut side up, around the edge of the dish. Place a kumquat in the depression of each nectarine half. Arrange the peach halves, cut side down, inside the circle of nectarines, and place the remaining kumquats in the center. Pour any remaining syrup over fruit. Bake, uncovered, in a preheated 425° oven for 25 minutes, basting every 5 minutes. Serve hot, cold, or at room temperature.

Country Breakfast for Eight to Ten

This is a good expandable menu for a fall weekend when you might still have house guests and the unexpected addition of friends who decide to drive out and see you on Sunday morning. The ham will serve up to sixteen people, the spoon bread is filling, and you can easily add a few more relishes and hot breads. You might welcome the arrivals with a cocktail of cider spiked with applejack, or straight cider for those who prefer it.

MENU

Cinnamon Glazed Ham

Southern Spoon Bread

Applesauce Beet Ring   *Preserved Watermelon Rind*

Corn Relish

Marmalade Coffee Cake

Hot Rolls   *Brioches*   *Fruit Preserves*

CINNAMON GLAZED HAM
[ELAINE ROSS]

> 7- to 8-pound cooked ham, scored on top
> ¾ cup cider
> ½ cup sugar
> 1½ teaspoons cinnamon
> 1½ tablespoons prepared mustard

Place the ham in a shallow baking pan and pour the cider into the pan. Mix the remaining ingredients to a paste, spread over the top of the ham, and bake in a preheated 375° oven for 1 hour, basting every 15 minutes. Add more cider if the liquid evaporates.

SOUTHERN SPOON BREAD (see page 293)

APPLESAUCE BEET RING
[ELAINE ROSS]

> 1 1-pound can sliced or julienne beets
> 1 tablespoon gelatin
> 2 cups applesauce, homemade or ready-made
> 1 to 2 teaspoons prepared horseradish
>   Fresh horseradish, optional

Drain the beets, reserve the liquid, and chop the beets very finely. Pour ¼ cup of the reserved beet juice into a small saucepan, sprinkle the gelatin on top, and let it soak for 5 minutes. Heat and stir constantly until the gelatin dissolves. Let it cool for 5 minutes, then gradually stir in the beets. Add 1 cup of the applesauce and 1 to 2 teaspoons of the horseradish, to taste. Rinse a 4-cup ring mold with cold water, pour in the beet mixture, and chill in the refrigerator until set. Run the tip of a small sharp knife around the edges of the mold to loosen the jelled ring. Dip the bottom of the mold in hot water for a few seconds. Turn the ring out onto a serving platter. Spoon the remaining applesauce into the center of the ring. If desired, slice paper-thin curls of fresh horse-radish with a vegetable peeler and place them over the applesauce in the center of the ring.

MARMALADE COFFEE CAKE
[ELAINE ROSS]

> 2⅓ cups all-purpose flour
> 5 teaspoons baking powder
> 1 cup plus 4 teaspoons sugar
> 2 eggs, separated
> ¾ cup milk
> 4 tablespoons butter, melted
> 1 teaspoon vanilla
> 2 tablespoons orange marmalade
> 1 teaspoon cinnamon

Sift 2 cups of the flour, the baking powder and ¾ cup of the sugar into a mixing bowl. Beat the egg yolks lightly in another bowl. Add the milk, 2 tablespoons butter, and vanilla, and stir until blended. Pour over the dry ingredients and mix lightly. Beat the egg whites until stiff, but not dry, and fold into the batter with the marmalade. Spread the batter evenly in a well-greased 9″ x 12″ pan.

Place the remaining ⅓ cup flour, ⅓ cup sugar, 2 tablespoons melted butter, and the cinnamon in the bowl in which the batter was mixed. Scrape down any batter clinging to the sides of the bowl. Rub all the ingredients together with your fingertips until the mixture forms crumbs. Sprinkle this crumb mixture over the batter. Bake in a preheated 350° oven for 25 minutes.

Chafing Dish Breakfast Buffet for Twelve

In a variation on the English hunt breakfast, set up the whole meal on a buffet table or sideboard, and let guests help themselves. This is a good way to cope with weekend guests who may wander downstairs at different hours, as only the scrambled eggs need to be served when cooked; the rest can stand. It isn't necessary to have four chafing dishes. Once cooked, the chipped beef, chicken and scallops, and chicken livers can be kept warm on a hot tray—or you could use electric skillets as well as chafing dishes.

MENU

Berries Rafraîchis
Chipped Beef Coco Palms
Brandied Chicken Livers
Scrambled Eggs Escoffier
Chicken and Scallops Victoria

Hot Toast   *Toasted English Muffins*   *Brioches*

Honey   *Bitter Orange Marmalade*   *Fruit Preserves*

BERRIES RAFRAÎCHIS
[ELAINE ROSS]

½ cup sugar
½ teaspoon cinnamon
½ cup water
½ cup red Burgundy wine
1 tablespoon lemon juice
1 pint currants, stemmed
1 pint strawberries
1 pint blueberries
1 pint raspberries

Mix the sugar and cinnamon in a saucepan. Add the water, bring to a boil and cook until the sugar dissolves, stirring constantly. Remove from the heat, add the wine and lemon juice, and cool. Spoon the currants, strawberries, and blueberries gently into a serving bowl. Scatter the raspberries on top, and pour the wine mixture over fruit. Chill for several hours before serving.

CHIPPED BEEF COCO PALMS
[RUTH CONRAD BATEMAN]

  ¼ cup butter
  ¼ pound dried beef, chipped or shredded
  ¼ cup flour
  2 cups half-and-half (milk and cream)
     Freshly ground pepper to taste
  ⅓ cup coarsely chopped water chestnuts
  ½ soft avocado, peeled and diced
  1 teaspoon lemon juice
     Hot toast or toasted English muffins

Melt butter in blazer pan of chafing dish over direct heat. Add beef and sauté lightly. Stir in flour until well blended, then gradually whisk in half-and-half. Stir continuously until sauce boils and thickens. Set over hot water and add a few grindings of pepper, the water chestnuts, and avocado. Add lemon juice and a little salt, if needed. Serve hot over toast or English muffins, split and toasted. Serves 4.

BRANDIED CHICKEN LIVERS
[RUTH CONRAD BATEMAN]

  ¼ pound fresh mushrooms, trimmed
  5 tablespoons butter
  1 minced shallot or 2 chopped green onions
  1 teaspoon lemon juice
     Salt, freshly ground pepper, nutmeg to taste
  1 pound chicken livers
     Flour
  3 tablespoons brandy
  1 cup cream
     Pinch thyme
     Minced parsley
  4 slices crisp hot toast or toasted English muffins

Wipe mushrooms with damp paper towels and slice lengthwise. Heat 1½ tablespoons butter in blazer pan of chafing dish over direct heat. Add shallot and mushrooms. Cook, shaking pan occasionally, 2 to 3 minutes. Season with lemon juice, salt, a few grindings of pepper, and a dash of nutmeg. Remove to a small bowl. Quarter livers; blot with paper towels, and dust lightly with flour. Heat rest of butter in blazer and sauté livers until richly browned, but still moist inside. (If your chafing dish is small, brown in several batches or you will have too much moisture in pan for good browning and flaming.) Warm brandy and pour over livers. Light and spoon pan juices over livers until flames die. Set blazer in hot water pan and add mushrooms and cream. Season with salt, pepper, a little more nutmeg, and the thyme. Heat, stirring occasionally, until sauce is richly colored and slightly thickened. Add the parsley. Serve over crisp hot toast or toasted English muffins. Serves 4.

SCRAMBLED EGGS ESCOFFIER
[RUTH CONRAD BATEMAN]

This Escoffier method of scrambling eggs may be varied by adding sautéed mushrooms, smoked salmon, ham or bacon bits, foie gras, anchovy paste, grated cheese, sour cream, or fresh chopped herbs.

　6 tablespoons butter
　6 eggs
　½ cup heavy cream
　　Salt, freshly ground pepper
　1 tablespoon fines herbes (equal parts chopped parsley, chives, tarragon, and chervil)

Heat 3 tablespoons butter in chafing dish over flame. Beat eggs lightly, stir in cream, and season with salt, a few grindings of pepper, and the herbs. Pour into chafing dish and set over hot water pan. Cook, stirring occasionally with a wooden spoon in long strokes across the pan, not around and around, until the eggs are lightly cooked, but still soft and moist. Cut up the remaining 3 tablespoons butter and stir into the eggs. Serve with brioches or toast. Serves 4.

CHICKEN AND SCALLOPS VICTORIA
[RUTH CONRAD BATEMAN]

> 2 tablespoons butter
> ½ cup sliced mushrooms
> ½ pound bay or sea scallops
> 1 tablespoon flour
> 1 cup light cream
> 1½ cups cooked chicken, in bite-size pieces
> ½ teaspoon salt
>   Freshly grated nutmeg, cayenne pepper to taste
> 2 tablespoons sherry
> 2 egg yolks
> ½ teaspoon lemon juice
>   Toast Cups

Heat butter in blazer directly over heat. Add mushrooms and cook a few minutes. Blot scallops dry on paper towels. If sea scallops are used, halve them. Bay scallops should be left whole. Add scallops to pan and toss to coat them with butter. Sprinkle in flour, stirring continuously, then gradually blend in cream. Add chicken and season with salt, nutmeg, cayenne, and sherry. Set blazer in hot water pan. Cover and heat about 10 minutes. Beat egg yolks lightly; stir in a few spoonfuls of the hot sauce, then stir back into dish. Add lemon juice, cover and heat about 5 minutes longer. Do not allow to boil. Serve in Toast Cups (see below). Serves 4.

TOAST CUPS

Trim crusts from thinly sliced white bread. Spread both sides with soft butter and press into muffin cups. Bake in a 300° oven until crisp.

Sunday Breakfast for Twenty or More

This breakfast party for a crowd is rather elastic in timing. It can extend over several hours, with guests dropping in between noon and three o'clock.

If you're giving this party outdoors, you might set up games like croquet so early arrivals can have a glass of champagne and the first course, amuse themselves, and then have an omelette afterward.

For the omelette bar, small stoves or burners, either electric or propane gas, can be arranged on a long table with all the makings and fillings. If you are an expert at making omelettes (it takes only about thirty seconds for each one), turn out your own. Otherwise, get someone in to help.

Have enormous coolers (an old or new copper wash boiler filled with ice, for instance) to hold champagne and white wine and a bottle of crème de cassis for those who might prefer a kir—white wine tinged with cassis.

MENU
[JAMES A. BEARD]

Prosciutto with Figs or Melon
Omelettes with a Choice of Fillings
Cold Sliced Steak with Mustards
Baked Tomatoes with Sautéed Mushrooms
French Bread   Small Brioches
Butter   Cream Cheese
Strawberries Glacé

The Wine

Champagne, Pouilly Fumé or California Pinot Chardonnay

PROSCIUTTO WITH FIGS OR MELON

If figs are in season, arrange them on platters, peeled, and well wrapped with prosciutto slices. Lacking prosciutto, you can substitute paper-thin slices of Smithfield ham or good Genoa salami. If figs are not available, serve wedges of cantaloupe or other melon in its prime. The accessories: small plates, forks, and pepper grinders.

OMELETTES

Gauge about 2½ eggs per omelette. For each 2½ eggs add about 1 teaspoon of water, a little salt, and a dash of Tabasco. The egg mixture for a dozen or a dozen and a half omelettes can be prepared ahead. Have butter ready for the pans and warm plates waiting to receive the finished omelettes. Offer 2 hot fillings, 1 warm, and 1 cold. Keep hot and warm fillings in chafing dishes or on a hot tray, the cold filling in a bowl. Make omelettes according to the method you prefer. The following are some suggested fillings:

RATATOUILLE

>   3 medium onions, thinly sliced
>   ½ cup olive oil
>   3 cloves garlic, finely chopped
>   1 eggplant, cubed
>   5 small zucchini, thinly sliced
>   1 green pepper, seeded and cut into thin strips
>   2 cups canned Italian plum tomatoes
>   2 teaspoons salt
>   1 teaspoon freshly ground black pepper
>   2 tablespoons chopped fresh basil or 2 teaspoons dried basil

Sauté onions in oil until limp. Add garlic, eggplant, zucchini, and green pepper, and cook over high heat until wilted. Add the tomatoes, mix well, and bring to a boil. Simmer until the vegetables have cooked down and most of the liquid has evaporated. Add seasonings and cook down for another 5 minutes. Correct the seasoning. Keep filling just tepid.

FRESH TOMATOES WITH ONION

>   6 tablespoons butter
>   6 tablespoons finely chopped onion
>   12 ripe tomatoes, peeled, seeded and chopped
>   1 tablespoon fresh tarragon, finely chopped
>   1 teaspoon salt
>   ½ teaspoon freshly ground black pepper

Melt the butter in a skillet, add the onion, and cook until just wilted. Add the tomatoes, bring to a boil, and reduce the heat. Simmer until cooked down and blended with the onion. Add seasonings and let the mixture simmer for 5 to 6 minutes. Keep quite hot.

CURRIED CHICKEN

> 1½ cups Béchamel sauce (see page 418) made with chicken broth
> 1 cup heavy cream
> 2 tablespoons curry powder
> 1 tablespoon turmeric
> 1 tablespoon chopped chutney
> Salt, freshly ground pepper to taste
> ¼ teaspoon Tabasco sauce
> 2 cups cooked diced chicken (mostly dark meat)

Make a rather thick Béchamel sauce and add the heavy cream, curry powder, and turmeric. Simmer for 8 to 9 minutes over low heat, stirring constantly. Add the chopped chutney and simmer for 2 more minutes. Add seasonings. Finally, add the chicken and heat through. Keep hot. Serve a dollop of chutney with each curried omelette, if desired.

PESTO

> ½ cup olive oil
> 1½ cups fresh basil leaves
> 3 large cloves garlic
> ½ cup pine nuts
> 1 cup parsley sprigs
> ½ cup grated Romano cheese
> Salt to taste

Combine first 6 ingredients in an electric blender and blend to a smooth paste. Add 1 teaspoon salt or more, to taste. Serve at room temperature.

COLD SLICED STEAK WITH MUSTARDS

Broil thick sirloin steaks to taste—as they are to be served cold, remove from the broiler while still on the rare side—and cool. Serve on carving boards and slice fairly thin. Accompany with mustards of varying degrees of hotness and pungency—American, English, Dijon, German.

BAKED TOMATOES WITH SAUTÉED MUSHROOMS

　2 pounds mushrooms, coarsely chopped
　1 clove garlic, finely chopped
　¾ pound butter
　3 tablespoons olive oil
　　Salt, pepper
　12 firm, ripe tomatoes (or 1 per person)
　12 mushroom caps (or 1 per person)
　　Additional butter

Sauté the chopped mushrooms and garlic in the butter and oil over low heat for 1 hour or more, or until they are quite dark. Season with salt and pepper to taste. Remove tops from the tomatoes and scoop out seeds and some of the flesh. Fill shells with the cooked mushrooms. Sauté mushroom caps in butter over rather high heat for just 3 minutes. Top each tomato with a cap. Arrange in a buttered baking dish and add about ¾ cup water. Bake in a 350° oven for 15 to 20 minutes, or until just heated through. Makes 12 servings.

NOTE: If you wish to double or triple the recipe, use 3 to 4 pounds mushrooms.

STRAWBERRIES GLACÉ

　4 cups sugar
　1 quart ripe strawberries

Combine 2 cups of the sugar and 2 cups water, and boil until the syrup spins a thread. Add strawberries and remaining sugar. When sugar has blended, cook for 18 minutes, or until the berries are still whole but nicely glazed. Allow to cool. Serve with French bread, brioches, cream cheese, and butter. Double or triple recipe according to number of guests.

Luncheon Parties

With the faster pace of life today, the old leisurely luncheon party often gets lost in the shuffle. People are more apt to say, "Come to dinner," than "Do come for lunch." Yet luncheons have a very definite place of their own in the entertaining pattern. They are more relaxed than a dinner, more sociable than a buffet, more fun to give than a supper.

A middle-of-the-day party makes good sense on many counts. On weekends it provides a chance to see friends who live too far away to face the drive home after dinner, or to entertain friends with whom you have afternoon plans in common—a matinee or a sports event. In midweek it can be an unhurried opportunity to catch up with old friends in town for the day, or even business friends who would undoubtedly prefer the relief of a quiet lunch at home to lunch in a noisy restaurant. A series of small lunches with a limited guest list of no more than four or six can be a most civilized and easy way to entertain different groups of people who really like to sit and talk to each other. In fact, as many hostesses have found, you can make a reputation with a string of parties like that even if you're not the world's greatest cook.

The very informality and simplicity of a luncheon party makes it less taxing and nerve-wracking, for it is perfectly permissible to serve something as uncomplicated as a soup, an omelette and salad, and a fresh fruit dessert, without feeling you have short changed your guests. Generally speaking, the menu for lunch is lighter and shorter than for dinner, the food less ambitious.

There's one exception to the rule about light food, though. According to James Beard, one of America's most accomplished hosts, many of the heavy, hearty dishes we tend to think of as evening fare, such as cassoulet, feijoada, bollito misto, are really better served at midday. They are just too burdensome for the digestion to be eaten late at night. Save them, says he, for lunch on a good brisk day, so everyone has a chance to work off the effects afterward.

It's also legitimate, if the rest of the meal is light, to end it with a really luscious dessert, all chocolate or cream, the kind of thing that would be just too much after an elaborate dinner. Many people crave, now and then, a taste of something sinfully rich, and they enjoy it all the more if they feel they can afford to indulge themselves. For those who set their face against any kind of high-calorie dessert, though, be sure to have a second choice of fresh fruit, or sherbet. Always take your guests into account when you plan menus. An all-woman luncheon usually calls for less caloric food than a weekend or holiday party when men are also involved. Very few men get a kick out of being served a weight-watcher's salad or an amusing little casserole.

Another pleasant thing about a luncheon is that it goes just about anywhere—including in the kitchen. Many of the best luncheons of all are those at which the guests sit around the kitchen table sipping an aperitif and talking to the hostess as she puts the meal together, or the outdoor kind that are all the fun of a picnic, with everyone helping himself from big platters of hors d'oeuvres, French family-style, while a chicken roasts in the oven or a fish simmers gently on the stove.

Like any meal, luncheon goes better with wine, but see that it is light and refreshing, a chilled white or rosé, or a light red, not the big red wine that leads to an afternoon of stupor and somnolence.

Omelette Luncheon for Four

One of the easiest of all luncheons—and the most popular with many people—is an omelette and a salad, with a luscious dessert. In this menu, the accent is French, the omelette, created at the Grand Véfour restaurant in Paris for actress Madeleine Renaud, something special. The ethereal chocolate dessert, named for a French music-hall star, comes from Manoir de Vaumadeuc restaurant in Brittany.

A light white wine would be good with the omelette or, if you prefer, an imported hard cider from France or England.

MENU

Omelette Madeleine Renaud
French Mushroom Salad
Crusty French Rolls or Croissants
Fondant Colette Renard

The Wine

Mâcon Blanc or Pouilly Fuissé or American Pinot Chardonnay

OMELETTE MADELEINE RENAUD
[RESTAURANT GRAND VÉFOUR]

    5¼-ounce tunnel-shaped can mousse de foie gras
4 tablespoons butter
2 tablespoons olive oil
8 eggs
    Salt, cayenne pepper to taste
2 tablespoons heavy cream

Remove the mousse de foie gras from the can. Cut into ¼" cubes. Gently heat in the oil and half the butter in a skillet until heated through but not hot. Beat the eggs. Add the seasonings. Heat the remaining butter in a large skillet. When very hot, pour in the eggs and reduce the heat. When the eggs are firm on bottom, lift the edges to allow the liquid egg to seep under.

As soon as the omelette is done, slip two or three tiny bits of butter under the omelette to help loosen it from the pan. When slightly browned on bottom, fold in half with a spatula and turn it onto a heated platter. Cut the omelette down the center, but not all the way through.

37

Fill the slit with the heated foie gras cubes. Lightly pour the heavy cream over the omelette. Serve immediately.

FRENCH MUSHROOM SALAD
[KAY SHAW NELSON]

    ½ pound mushrooms
    2 tablespoons minced fresh chives
    3 tablespoons chopped fresh parsley
    ½ cup olive oil
    2 tablespoons tarragon vinegar
    ¼ teaspoon dry mustard
    ¼ teaspoon paprika
      Salt, freshly ground pepper to taste

Wash and dry mushrooms. Cut off tough stem ends. Slice thickly. Mix with chives and parsley in a bowl. Combine remaining ingredients; mix well. Pour over mushrooms. Marinate 1 hour.

FONDANT COLETTE RENARD
[RESTAURANT MANOIR DE VAUMADEUC]

    1 square bitter chocolate
    3 tablespoons milk
  1½ cups confectioners' sugar
    1 teaspoon instant coffee
    5 tablespoons butter
    4 eggs, separated

Melt the chocolate in the milk over low heat. Add the sugar with the instant coffee while stirring. Add the butter and stir until glossy and smooth. Remove from heat and cool until slightly thickened. Add the egg yolks, one at a time, beating well. Beat the egg whites until stiff and fold into the chocolate mixture. Pour into a well-buttered 8″ ring mold. Set mold in a pan of boiling water and bake in a 375° oven for 25 to 30 minutes.

Allow to cool in the mold (as this is a type of soufflé, it will shrink and fall as it cools). To unmold, run a spatula around the edges and invert on a serving dish. Serve with custard sauce flavored with 1 teaspoon instant coffee, or with partly melted vanilla ice cream, and sprinkle top with halved almonds or other nuts.

Simple Spring Luncheon for Four

A delicious progression of natural flavors, with a touch of the exotic in the bean sprout salad (which is also good with roast pork), makes this a perfect menu for the switchover from winter to spring eating. You can use the same wine to steam the mussels that you serve with the luncheon.

MENU

Mussels Steamed in White Wine, Garlic-Toasted French Bread
Broiled Squab Chickens
Bean Sprout Salad
Papaya Sherbet

The Wine

Muscadet or California Fumé Blanc

MUSSELS STEAMED IN WHITE WINE
[JAMES A. BEARD]

   2 quarts mussels
   6 cloves garlic, finely chopped
   1 small onion, chopped
   4 sprigs parsley
   1 cup white wine
     Finely chopped parsley
     Melted butter
     Garlic-toasted French bread

Wash and beard the mussels. Place them in a large kettle with the garlic, onion and parsley. Add the white wine, cover and place over medium heat until the mussels open. Discard those which do not open. Serve in large soup plates with finely chopped parsley, melted butter, and garlic-toasted French bread.

BROILED SQUAB CHICKEN
[JAMES A. BEARD]

Squab chickens average around a pound each. They are readily available in most communities, although in some places they must be ordered in advance from the butcher.

For each serving, split one chicken and rub well with garlic and soy sauce. Broil, bone side up, for about 9 minutes. Turn, salt and pepper to taste, and broil, skin side up, for 7 minutes. Remove from broiler.

BEAN SPROUT SALAD
[HELEN EVANS BROWN]

  ½ pound bean sprouts
  ½ cup thinly sliced celery
  2 tablespoons minced green onion
  1 teaspoon grated fresh or preserved ginger (optional)
  ½ cup mayonnaise
  2 tablespoons soy sauce
  1 teaspoon curry powder
  1 teaspoon lemon juice
    Slivered toasted almonds (optional)

Combine bean sprouts with celery, green onions and ginger. Make a dressing with the mayonnaise, soy sauce, curry powder, and lemon juice. Mix gently with the bean sprouts, arrange on lettuce and, if you wish, sprinkle with almonds.

PAPAYA SHERBET
[LOU SEIBERT PAPPAS]

>   1 large ripe papaya
>   1 cup orange juice
>   Juice of 1 lime (about 2 tablespoons)
>   ¼ cup honey
>   2 egg whites

Peel and halve papaya. Scoop out seeds and dice fruit. Put in blender container with orange juice, lime juice, and honey. Purée until smooth. Pour into an ice cube tray and freeze until just solid. Remove from freezer and turn into a mixing bowl. Beat with an electric mixer, starting at low and gradually increasing to high speed, until smooth and slushy. Beat egg whites until soft peaks form and fold into the papaya mixture. Turn into a plastic container, cover, and freeze until firm. Makes about 1 quart.

Quick Luncheon for Four

A speedy menu for the day when you have to whip up a meal at the last minute. Spinach may be substituted for the sorrel, though the flavor will not be as unusual—it's well worth growing this deliciously bitter green just for the satisfaction of making sorrel soups and purées. Serve a very simple white wine with this meal.

MENU

Eastern Shore Crab Meat
Sorrel Frittata
Hearts of Lettuce with French Dressing
Lemon Cream

The Wine

California Chablis

EASTERN SHORE CRAB MEAT
[ELAINE ROSS]

 1 egg
 3 tablespoons mayonnaise
 1½ teaspoons prepared mustard
 1½ teaspoons dried fines herbes
 ½ teaspoons minced fresh parsley
   Salt to taste
 1 pound lump crab meat, picked over

Beat the egg lightly and stir in the mayonnaise, mustard, and seasonings. Pour over the crab meat and toss lightly. Divide mixture between 4 large scallop or clam shells. Bake in a preheated 400° oven for 12 to 15 minutes, or until bubbling.

SORREL FRITTATA
[ALEX D. HAWKES]

 2 cups coarsely chopped sorrel
 2 tablespoons butter
 1 tablespoon finely chopped green onion tops
 6 large fresh eggs
   Salt and freshly ground black pepper
 3 tablespoons freshly grated Parmesan or Romano cheese

Cook the coarsely chopped sorrel by plunging it into a small quantity of lightly salted boiling water, mix through, and cook uncovered for about 1 minute, or until thoroughly wilted but still crisp in texture. Drain very thoroughly, patting dry in paper towels. In an oven-proof skillet, melt the butter and sauté the onion tops, stirring often, until they are soft. Beat eggs, add the drained sorrel, salt and pepper to taste, and turn into the skillet. Cook slowly until bottom of omelette is set. Then sprinkle with cheese and run under broiler until puffed and lightly browned. Serve immediately from skillet.

LEMON CREAM
[KAY SHAW NELSON]

    4 eggs, separated
    ½ cup sugar
    ½ cup white wine
      Juice of 2 lemons
      Grated rind of ½ lemon

Beat the egg yolks with the sugar in the top of a double boiler. Add the wine, lemon juice, and rind. Cook over hot water, beating vigorously, until mixture thickens. Remove from the stove and cool. Beat the egg whites until stiff, but not dry. Fold into the wine mixture. Spoon into serving dishes. Garnish with whole strawberries, if desired.

Summer Weekend Luncheon for Four

The appeal of this meal is in the lovely green flavor of fresh herbs, which flourish in the summer months. Rocket, a peppery, pungent salad green, sold in Italian markets as rugula, is very easy to grow, in fact it thrives on cutting. The young, fresh leaves have a flavor somewhat reminiscent of horseradish and they should be used in salads with caution, unless you are addicted to this particular taste. The chicken breast rolls may be cooked indoors, or on the outdoor grill, whichever you prefer. A lightly chilled Beaujolais would be pleasant with this luncheon menu.

MENU

Eggs Meulemeester

Chicken Breast Rolls

Green Rocket Salad

Mangoes Flambé

The Wine

Beaujolais Brouilly or Fleurie

EGGS MEULEMEESTER
[KAY SHAW NELSON]

      6 hard-cooked eggs
    ½ pound (about 10) cooked and shelled large shrimp
    ¾ cup light cream
      1 tablespoon chopped fresh parsley
      2 teaspoons minced chervil
      2 teaspoons sharp mustard
    ½ cup grated Parmesan cheese
        Salt, freshly ground pepper to taste
        Butter

Peel the eggs and cut them into shreds. Cut the shrimp into bite-size pieces. Combine the eggs and the shrimp with the cream, parsley, chervil, mustard, and ⅓ cup of the cheese. Season with salt and pepper. Spoon into a shallow baking dish. Sprinkle with the remaining cheese and dot with butter. Bake in a preheated 400° oven until the mixture is heated through and golden on top, about 10 minutes.

GRILLED CHICKEN BREAST ROLLS
[RICHARD OLNEY]

      4 chicken breasts, boned
      1 heaping tablespoon chopped fines herbes (parsley, chervil, chives, tarragon)
      1 tablespoon finely chopped shallot
        Small pinch crumbled oregano
      3 to 4 ounces mushrooms, finely chopped
        Juice of ½ lemon
      3 tablespoons olive oil
        Coarsely ground pepper
        Salt

Remove the skin from the breasts and trim them neatly, making certain that no fragments of bone remain. Each is composed of 2 muscles known as the filet and the filet-mignon. They are connected only by a fragile membrane except at 1 edge. Open them out so that the opened breast is vaguely heart shaped, and flatten with the side of a large knife. Mix the fines herbes, shallot, oregano, mushrooms, lemon juice, olive oil, and pepper to taste on a platter. Spread the chicken breasts out on the platter. Marinate 1 hour, gently turning them around and over 2 or 3 times. Salt the inside surface of each filet lightly, spread it well with the chopped vegetables from the marinade, and roll it up, holding it together with toothpicks. Salt outsides lightly and broil, or grill breasts on a preheated grill 10 to 12 minutes, turning every 2 or 3 minutes. Baste colored surfaces regularly, adding more olive oil to marinade if necessary.

GREEN ROCKET SALAD
[ALEX D. HAWKES]

    1 bunch rocket (rugula)
    1 bunch watercress
    1 medium head romaine lettuce
    ¼ cup peanut or soy oil
    ¼ cup virgin olive oil
    3 tablespoons or more fresh lemon juice
      Drained feta cheese to taste
      Salt and freshly ground black pepper

Rinse and gently pat dry the rocket and watercress. Leave in as large pieces as manageable. Thoroughly rinse the romaine, and tear into bite-size pieces. Pat dry and chill all greens, wrapped in plastic or a paper towel, for an hour or so. Prepare a dressing by thoroughly combining in a bowl the 2 oils, with lemon juice to taste. Crumble in the drained feta cheese, gently mix, and correct seasoning. Arrange chilled salad greens in a bowl, and pour over the dressing. Toss gently and serve at once.

MANGOES FLAMBÉ
[DINA MERRILL]

    1 large ripe mango or 1-pound, 3-ounce can mango slices in syrup
      (available at gourmet food stores)
    ¼ cup cognac
    ¼ cup orange marmalade or apricot preserves
      Vanilla ice cream

Peel the mango and slice off the flesh. Either dice or cut the flesh into slices and reserve any juice. If canned mangoes are used, drain and reserve ¼ cup syrup. Place prepared fruit in a heat-proof serving bowl. Warm and ignite the cognac and pour over fruit. Combine ¼ cup reserved juice (if additional juice is needed, use orange juice) with the marmalade or preserves and mix into fruit. Spoon over vanilla ice cream.

Spring Luncheon for Four to Six

A superb, elegant luncheon for weekend entertaining. You can make the brioche dough the night before, and leave it overnight in the refrigerator. The soufflé mixture may be made in the morning, then the egg whites beaten and folded in just before serving time so the soufflé can bake while the first part of the meal is being eaten. With the exquisitely rich lobster dish have a fine white Burgundy.

MENU

Artichokes Vinaigrette
Brioche Ring with Lobster in White Wine Sauce
Soufflé Sarah Bernhardt

The Wine

Corton-Charlemagne or Puligny-Montrachet

BRIOCHE RING WITH LOBSTER IN WHITE WINE SAUCE
[JAMES A. BEARD]

BRIOCHE RING

> 1 package active dry yeast
> ¼ cup warm water (105° to 110°)
> 1½ cups all-purpose flour, sifted
> 1 teaspoon sugar
> 1½ teaspoons salt

2 large eggs
½ cup butter, softened
Egg wash

Dissolve the yeast in the warm water. Combine the sifted flour, sugar, and salt with the eggs and the yeast mixture, and beat well by hand or in an electric mixer having a dough hook. When the dough is smooth, beat in the butter a tablespoon at a time until it is thoroughly blended. Form the dough into a ball and slash it across the top. Put into a buttered bowl. Cover with a towel, and put in a warm, draft-free place to rise until doubled in bulk.

When it has risen, either punch down and divide the dough into 2 pieces to use at once, or punch down and store in the refrigerator until ready to bake.

If you form the ring at once, butter a 9½" x 2" ring mold well. Roll the 2 pieces of dough out between the floured palms of your hands. Fit the rolls into the ring so that the ends of both pieces meet and are evenly joined or form a ring on a baking sheet. Let it rise until doubled in bulk.

If you are using chilled dough, punch down and shape into a roll long enough to fit into the well-buttered ring mold. Let it rise until it has doubled in bulk.

Brush the dough well with egg wash, and bake at 375° for about 25 minutes, or until well browned and cooked through. This brioche is particularly good served warm. Makes 1 ring.

This recipe is excellent when making a small amount of brioche.

LOBSTER IN WHITE WINE SAUCE

    3 tablespoons butter
    3 tablespoons flour
   ⅔ cup hot chicken, clam, or lobster broth
   ½ cup white wine
    1 teaspoon salt
   ¼ teaspoon Tabasco sauce
    1 teaspoon dried tarragon, crushed, or 1 tablespoon fresh tarragon, chopped
    2 tablespoons tomato paste
    1 cup heavy cream
    2 egg yolks
    2 cups lobster meat, cut into bite-size pieces
    1 brioche ring, warm
    1 tablespoon chopped parsley

To prepare the sauce, melt the butter in a heavy saucepan over medium-high heat, blend in the flour, and allow it to cook for a few minutes. Gradually stir in the hot broth and the white wine. Continue stirring until the mixture thickens. Season to taste with salt, Tabasco, and tarragon, making certain the tarragon gives a definite flavor (add more if necessary). Stir in the tomato paste, and simmer the sauce for 3 to 4 minutes. Remove from the heat. Mix together the cream and egg yolks, and add a little sauce to this mixture. Stir this into the sauce. Heat until it is well thickened, but do not allow it to boil. Heat the lobster pieces in a little butter or white wine and add to the sauce. Taste for seasoning. Spoon the lobster mixture into the center of the warm brioche ring, and sprinkle with parsley. Serve at once.

NOTE: If you are cooking fresh lobsters for the lobster meat, you will need 2 or 3 1½-pound lobsters. The broth from the cooking may be reduced and used for the sauce. If you wish, cook an extra lobster and reserve the claws to use as a garnish for the ring.

SOUFFLÉ SARAH BERNHARDT
[JAMES A. BEARD, ADAPTED FROM ESCOFFIER]

   ½ cup Curaçao liqueur
  12 almond macaroons
    3 tablespoons butter

3 tablespoons flour
1 cup milk
⅓ cup sugar
5 egg yolks
1½ teaspoons vanilla
7 egg whites
¼ teaspoon salt
1½ cups crushed strawberries, fresh or frozen, flavored with Curaçao

Pour the Curaçao over the macaroons and allow them to soak up the liqueur. Melt the butter in a saucepan, add the flour, and cook until bubbling. Remove from heat and add the milk and sugar. Return to heat and cook, stirring constantly, until thick and smooth. Set aside to cool.

Beat the egg yolks and add to the cooled mixture with the vanilla. The mixture should be the consistency of mayonnaise. If it is too thin, return to heat and cook over low heat, stirring vigorously until thickened.

Beat the egg whites with the salt until stiff but not dry. Mix about one third of the whites into the yolk mixture. Then fold in remaining egg whites very lightly. Pour half the mixture into a buttered 1½-quart soufflé dish sprinkled with sugar. Add half of the macaroons, then add the remaining soufflé mixture. Place the remaining macaroons around edge of dish.

Bake the soufflé in a 375° oven for about 25 minutes, or until well-risen and delicately brown on top. Do not overcook. It should be moist in the center. Serve with the crushed strawberries flavored with Curaçao.

Soup and Salad Luncheon for Six

Soup and salad doesn't have to mean something from a can—it can be really fine eating if you make the soup yourself from good fresh vegetables, and serve an unusual kind of salad such as brains gribiche (should your guests be turned off by what the British term "offal," you may substitute shrimp). If you feel a dessert is needed, have whatever fresh seasonal fruit is best—pears, peaches, nectarines, berries. As the main course is a salad, wine is contraindicated, but you could serve an inexpensive white jug wine.

MENU

Gardener's Chowder
Brains Gribiche
Miniature Cheese Rolls
Fresh Fruit

The Wine

California Mountain White Chablis

GARDENER'S CHOWDER
[IRIS BROOKS]

> 3 leeks, white part only, thinly sliced
> 4 tablespoons pork sausage or bacon fat
> 1 cup each cut green beans, green limas, peeled and sliced tomatoes
> ½ cup each peeled and diced eggplant, diced carrot, kernel corn, and sliced okra
> ¼ cup sweet red pepper or pimiento, cut into julienne strips
> ¼ cup each chopped green pepper and celery
> 2½ cups brown stock or 2 10½-ounce cans beef bouillon
> 1 cup evaporated milk, undiluted
> 2 tablespoons butter, melted
> 2 tablespoons cornstarch
> Thyme, marjoram, salt, pepper to taste

Sauté the leeks in the fat until limp in a small skillet. Turn contents of the pan into a large soup kettle and add all the vegetables and the stock or bouillon. Bring to a boil over high heat. Cover and simmer 30 minutes. Add the milk and ⅔ cup water and let soup cook, uncovered, 20 minutes more. Blend the butter and cornstarch with ½ cup water and add to soup to thicken it slightly. Add seasonings, then simmer 10 minutes more, stirring occasionally.

BRAINS GRIBICHE
[IRIS BROOKS]

 3 pairs calves' brains
½ lemon
 1 thick slice onion, stuck with 1 clove
 2 leafy stalks celery
   Few sprigs parsley
 1 small bay leaf
 4 peppercorns
½ teaspoon salt
   Iceberg lettuce leaves
   White radishes, cut into fans

Thoroughly rinse the brains and let stand 15 minutes in cold water to firm them. Put into a large saucepan just enough water to cover brains and squeeze the lemon juice into it, adding the rind, onion, celery, parsley, bay leaf, peppercorns, and salt. Bring to a boil, then reduce heat and drop brains carefully into the bubbling liquid. Cover and poach about 15 minutes. Remove the brains and blanch immediately in cold water. Carefully remove membrane and blood vessels. Cut each pair in half and refrigerate immediately under a weighted plate. When thoroughly chilled and firm, serve on lettuce leaves, garnished with radish fans. Serve with Sauce Gribiche (see below).

SAUCE GRIBICHE

 3 hard-cooked eggs
 1 teaspoon Dijon mustard
½ teaspoon salt
⅛ teaspoon pepper
1½ cups olive or salad oil
½ cup white wine vinegar
⅓ cup chopped sour gherkins
 1 teaspoon each minced parsley, chives, fresh tarragon, and chervil

Separate the egg yolks from the whites and mash them to a smooth paste in a small bowl with the mustard, salt, and pepper. As in preparing mayonnaise, beat in a bit of the oil briskly, alternating with a small amount of vinegar, to make a smooth, thick dressing. Finally chop the egg whites and add with the remaining ingredients. Blend together thoroughly. Chill. Makes 2½ cups.

MINIATURE CHEESE ROLLS
[ELAINE ROSS]

> 1 package granular yeast
> 1 cup warm water
> 1½ teaspoons seasoned salt
> 1 tablespoon brown sugar
> 2 tablespoons vegetable shortening
> 1½ ounces Tilsit cheese, coarsely grated
> 3 tablespoons heavy cream
> 2¼ cups all-purpose flour
> Fine bread crumbs

Dissolve the yeast in the warm water in a mixing bowl. Add the salt, sugar, shortening, cheese, and cream and stir until mixed. Add the flour and beat with a wooden spoon until the dough leaves the spoon and the sides of the bowl clean. Cover and set in a warm place to rise for 1¼ hours, or until the dough doubles in bulk.

Generously grease 36 tiny muffin tins and dust them with fine bread crumbs. Place a rounded teaspoon of dough in each tin, and let rest for 15 minutes. Bake in a preheated 375° oven for 20 minutes. Remove from the tins immediately and serve hot, or reheat before serving. Makes 3 dozen miniature rolls.

Quick Luncheon for Six

You don't have to spend the whole morning in the kitchen to serve a superb luncheon, as this menu proves. The actual cooking schedule for everything is only about 20 minutes, although the veal escalopes do take some ahead-of-time preparation. Belgium and Holland, where white asparagus is grown, take credit for the unusual first course. There the asparagus is served with a dipping sauce of chopped eggs mollet (with runny yolks), melted butter, chopped parsley, salt and pepper, which is usually mixed to taste by each diner—you can follow this procedure if you like. If fresh asparagus isn't in season, you could use the Belgian white asparagus, imported in cans or jars. With the veal you might have a Swiss white wine.

MENU

Asparagus, Flemish Style
Veal Cordon Bleu
Purée of Green Beans
Baked Cherry Tomatoes
Pineapple Sherbet with Fresh Pineapple

The Wine

Fendant or Neuchâtel

ASPARAGUS, FLEMISH-STYLE
[KAY SHAW NELSON]

2 pounds fresh asparagus
6 eggs, cooked 5 to 6 minutes and shelled and chopped
¾ cup melted butter
¾ cup chopped fresh parsley
   Salt, freshly ground pepper to taste

Wash the asparagus in running water, cut off the tough stem ends, and remove any large scales. Put in a large skillet and cover with boiling salted water. Cook, uncovered, over moderate heat until tender, a few minutes. Carefully remove from the water with tongs and drain. In the meantime, combine chopped eggs, butter, parsley, salt and pepper. Spoon over asparagus and serve.

VEAL CORDON BLEU
[PHILIP S. BROWN]

> 2 pounds veal escalopes, cut in 12 pieces
> Salt, pepper
> 6 thin slices cooked ham
> 6 thin slices Swiss cheese
> Flour
> 2 eggs, slightly beaten
> 1½ cups fine dry bread crumbs
> 8 tablespoons butter
> 3 tablespoons lemon juice
> 2 tablespoons minced parsley
> 1 tablespoon minced chives

Season the escalopes with salt and pepper. Place a slice of ham and one of cheese on each of 6 escalopes, trimming them to escalope size. Top with the other veal slices, and pound the edges together lightly. Dredge these little sandwiches in flour, dip in the egg, then coat completely and thickly with bread crumbs and refrigerate, uncovered, for at least an hour. Sauté them in 4 tablespoons butter for about 5 minutes on each side, until they are a nice golden brown. Arrange them on a heat-proof platter and put in a 325° oven for 5 to 10 minutes. Add the remaining 4 tablespoons butter to the pan, along with the lemon juice, parsley, and chives, heat gently, and pour over the meat.

PURÉE OF GREEN BEANS
[MRS. DAVID EVINS]

> 3 pounds young, tender green beans
> Salt
> ½ cup milk
> 1 to 2 tablespoons butter
> ¼ cup heavy cream
> Freshly ground pepper
> Nutmeg

Cook the beans in boiling salted water for about 10 minutes, until just tender. Drain and cut in small pieces. Purée the beans with milk in the blender a little at a time. When all have been puréed, add the butter, cream, salt, pepper, and nutmeg to taste.

NOTE: For additional flavor, sauté 1 onion in a little butter until soft but not brown. Purée in the blender with the beans.

BAKED CHERRY TOMATOES
[MRS. DAVID EVINS]

Put about 24 cherry tomatoes in a baking dish with 4 tablespoons butter, salt, and 1 teaspoon sugar. Bake in a 350° oven for 8 to 10 minutes, shaking the pan occasionally so the tomatoes turn in the butter.

PINEAPPLE SHERBET WITH FRESH PINEAPPLE

Cut a ripe pineapple into six wedges (include the leafy top) and trim off the core. Slice off the flesh and cut into bite-size pieces. When ready to serve, arrange the flesh on the pineapple rind and put a scoop of pineapple sherbet at either end. The idea is to eat a spoonful of sherbet and a mouthful of pineapple. If you like, you can marinate the pineapple pieces in a little kirsch first.

Vegetable Luncheon for Six

A rather pleasant change from the usual meat, fish, or poultry is a summer luncheon based on vegetable and fruit dishes. If you are entertaining vegetarians, you could serve this, omitting the bacon on the broccoli timbale and using milk rather than chicken stock for the sauce Mornay. A light, summery white wine goes well with the timbale.

MENU

Stuffed Cherry Tomatoes
Broccoli Timbale Mornay
Hot Rolls
Peaches, Melon, and Blueberries

The Wine

California Chenin Blanc or Johannisberg Riesling

STUFFED CHERRY TOMATOES
[ALEX D. HAWKES]

> 24 firm unblemished cherry tomatoes
> 1 large (8-ounce) package cream cheese, softened
> ⅓ cup finely chopped walnuts
> ⅛ teaspoon grated lemon or lime rind
> ½ cup finely chopped fresh watercress
> Salad dressing (see recipe below)
> Salt and freshly ground black pepper to taste
> Fresh watercress sprigs for garnish

Using a sharp knife, cut off top of each rinsed cherry tomato, then carefully scoop out pulp and seeds and discard. Turn tomato shells upside down on a plate to drain. Thoroughly blend together softened cream cheese, walnuts, grated lemon or lime rind, chopped watercress, and enough salad dressing to make a firm paste. Season well with salt and freshly ground black pepper. Carefully fill tomato shells, cover with wax paper or aluminum foil, and chill for an hour or so. Serve garnished with crisp watercress.

SALAD DRESSING

> 1 teaspoon salt
> 2 rounded teaspoons dry mustard
> 3 teaspoons flour
> 4 tablespoons sugar

2 large eggs
⅔ cup cider vinegar
1 cup light cream or sour cream
Salt and freshly ground black pepper

Mix all dry ingredients together in a bowl, then add the eggs and mix thoroughly. Gradually add the vinegar and the cream, mixing with a wire whisk or an electric beater to remove all lumps. Cook in a nonstick heavy saucepan or in the top of a double boiler over boiling water, stirring constantly, until the dressing becomes thick. Season to taste with salt and freshly ground black pepper. Cool and refrigerate. Makes 2½ cups.

BROCCOLI TIMBALE MORNAY
[RUTH CONRAD BATEMAN]

2 pounds fresh broccoli (or 2 packages frozen)
1 cup dry French bread crumbs, packed
½ cup minced onion
5 tablespoons butter
¾ cup grated aged Swiss cheese
5 eggs
1 cup milk
Salt, freshly ground black pepper, nutmeg
Sauce Mornay (see recipe below) or Hollandaise sauce (see page 420)
2 to 3 slices crisp-cooked bacon, crumbled

Trim and cook broccoli in boiling salted water until tender. Drain, chop, and measure 3 cups. Butter a 6-cup mold or soufflé dish well and coat with 3 to 4 tablespoons of the bread crumbs. Cook onion slowly in 2 tablespoons butter until soft and golden, but not brown. Combine onion, cheese, and remaining crumbs. Beat in eggs, one by one, with a wooden spoon. Heat milk just to boiling with remaining butter and slowly beat into egg mixture. Fold in broccoli and salt, pepper, and nutmeg to taste. Pour into mold and set in pan of hot water. Bake in a 325° oven for 35 to 40 minutes, or until timbale is puffed and knife inserted in center is clean when removed. Remove from water. Allow to stand about 5 minutes. Loosen carefully around edges with knife and invert on warm serving plate. Top with a little of the sauce and sprinkle with crumbled bacon. Serve remaining sauce separately.

SAUCE MORNAY

> 4 tablespoons butter
> 4 tablespoons flour
> 1½ cups chicken stock or consommé
> ½ cup cream
> ¼ cup freshly grated Parmesan cheese

Melt butter and stir in flour. Heat chicken stock or consommé and gradually blend in with a whisk. Blend in cream and cook over low heat, stirring constantly, until sauce boils and thickens. Simmer 2 to 3 minutes longer. Stir in Parmesan cheese. Makes 2 cups.

PEACHES, MELON, AND BLUEBERRIES
[ELAINE ROSS]

> 2 pounds slightly underripe peaches
> ½ cup sugar
> ¼ cup ruby port
> 1 large cantaloupe
> 1 cup blueberries

Scald the peaches and slip off the skins. (If the skins do not slip off easily, peel the peaches.) Slice the fruit into a saucepan, add the sugar and wine, and cook, covered, for about 5 minutes, or until just tender. Scoop out as many melon balls as possible and add to the hot peaches. Gently stir in the blueberries, cool, and chill.

Curry Luncheon for Six

For a spring or summer luncheon, the piquancy of a spicy curry tempts the palate, and a cool yoghurt and cucumber salad, with the fresh sweetness of green grapes, is a good counterpoint. A hot lime pickle and a milder mango chutney are really all you need with the curry, though you might serve other traditional accompaniments, if you wish. Cold beer is the best drink.

MENU

Trinidad Shrimp Curry

Steamed Rice *Mango Chutney* *Lime Pickle*

Turkish Cucumber Salad

Lemon Ice and Melon Balls

The Drinks

Chilled imported or domestic beer

TRINIDAD SHRIMP CURRY
[ELISABETH ORTIZ]

1½ teaspoons each of turmeric, coriander, and cumin seeds
1 teaspoon mustard seed
2 bay leaves
1½ teaspoons black peppercorns
½ teaspoon hot red dried peppers
3 tablespoons each oil and butter
2 pounds large, raw shrimp, shelled
2 large onions, finely chopped
1 clove garlic, crushed
4 tomatoes, peeled and chopped
1 tablespoon lime juice
½ teaspoon sugar
Salt to taste
1 tablespoon chopped lime pickle (optional)
Cooked white rice

Grind the turmeric, coriander, cumin, and mustard seeds with the bay leaves, peppercorns, and dried hot peppers in a mortar. Set aside. Heat 1 tablespoon each of the oil and butter in a skillet and cook the shrimp until they are pink all over, about 5 minutes. Remove the shrimp and keep warm.

Add the remaining oil and butter to the skillet and sauté the onions until tender and lightly browned. Add the garlic and the ground spices, and cook, stirring, for 2 or 3 minutes longer. Add the tomatoes, lime juice, sugar, salt, and the chopped lime pickle, if desired. (This is very hot.) Cover and cook for ½ hour over very low heat, adding a little stock or water if necessary. The sauce should be quite thick. Add the shrimp and cook for 5 minutes longer without allowing the sauce to do more than barely simmer. Serve surrounded by rice.

TURKISH CUCUMBER SALAD
[ALEX D. HAWKES]

>   2 cups plain yoghurt
> ¼ teaspoon mashed garlic
>   1 tablespoon distilled white vinegar
> 1½ teaspoons salt
>   1 tablespoon light olive oil
>   1 tablespoon finely chopped green onion tops
>   1 teaspoon finely minced fresh mint leaves
> 1½ cups peeled, seeded, finely diced cucumber
>   1 cup halved seedless green grapes

In a large bowl, whip the yoghurt with rotary beater or fork until it is very smooth. Thoroughly blend in the garlic, vinegar, salt, olive oil, onion tops, and mint leaves. Gently fold in the cucumber dice and grapes, reserving a few halves for garnish. Refrigerate for at least 1 hour, and serve well chilled, garnished with a few grape halves.

LIME ICE AND MELON BALLS
[JAMES A. BEARD]

>   1 honeydew melon
> ½ bottle dry white wine or champagne
> ⅔ cup sugar
>   2 cups water
> ½ cup lime juice (fresh)
>   Green food coloring

Halve the melon and, using a melon ball cutter, cut it into balls. Place balls in a bowl and cover with wine or champagne. Refrigerate to chill.

Simmer the sugar and water for about 10 minutes. Add the lime juice and cool. Color with a bit of green food coloring and pour into a freezing tray. Freeze until firm. Remove from the freezer and turn the mixture into a bowl. Beat until light and frothy. Return to the freezer tray and refreeze.

To serve, place a scoop of the lime ice in each dish and surround with the melon balls.

Weekend Summer Luncheon for Six

A delightful menu for weekend guests that is relatively easy on the cook, as half the preparation can be done ahead. If smoked trout is not available, you could substitute smoked whitefish. You might have a white wine with the smoked fish, and continue with the same wine for the main course.

MENU

Smoked Trout with Horseradish Cream
Veal Birds Fontanges
Watercress-Mushroom Salad
Currant Ice

The Wine

Chablis or American Pinot Chardonnay

SMOKED TROUT WITH HORSERADISH CREAM
[PHILIP S. BROWN]

Arrange two filets of trout per serving on lettuce leaves and serve the horseradish cream in a bowl.

HORSERADISH CREAM

    1 cup sour cream
    ½ cup fresh horseradish, grated
    1 tablespoon Dijon mustard
    1 teaspoon salt
    1 tablespoon grated lemon rind

Combine the ingredients and blend well. Allow to stand in the refrigerator for an hour or more before using.

VEAL BIRDS FONTANGES
[PHILIP S. BROWN]

    1 pound finely ground veal
    ¼ pound bacon, finely ground
      Salt, pepper to taste
    1 egg
    1 tablespoon chopped chives
    2 pounds veal escalopes, cut in 12 pieces
    3 tablespoons butter
    ¼ cup cognac
    1 tablespoon tomato paste
    1 teaspoon meat glaze or Bovril
    1 tablespoon flour
    1 cup veal or chicken stock
    ¼ cup dry white wine
    1 bay leaf
      Pea purée (see recipe below)

Mix together very thoroughly the ground veal, bacon, salt and pepper, egg, and chives, and spread evenly on the escalopes. Roll them up, tie with string, and brown all over in the butter. Heat the cognac slightly, ignite, and pour over the veal birds. When the flames die out, remove the meat, and add the tomato paste, meat glaze, and flour to the pan, stirring to blend. Add the stock and white wine, bring to a boil, reduce heat, replace the veal birds, add the bay leaf. Cover and simmer for 30 to 40 minutes. Remove strings, arrange the birds on a bed of pea purée (see below), and strain the gravy over them.

PEA PURÉE

>   3 cups shelled fresh peas (or 2 packages frozen peas)
>   2 tablespoons butter
>   2 tablespoons flour
>   Salt, pepper
>   ¼ cup sour cream

Cook peas in boiling water until soft. Drain well and put through a food mill or force through a sieve. Melt butter, stir in flour, and cook until quite brown. Add the peas, salt and pepper to taste, and sour cream, and heat thoroughly.

WATERCRESS-MUSHROOM SALAD
[KAY SHAW NELSON]

>   2 cups washed watercress
>   2 cups sliced mushrooms
>   ½ cup sliced radishes
>   ⅓ cup French dressing

Arrange watercress in the center of a plate. Cover with mushrooms and radishes mixed together. Pour dressing over vegetables.

CURRANT ICE
[NIKA HAZELTON]

>   1 quart fresh currants, washed, with stems removed
>   1 teaspoon unflavored gelatin
>   1 cup sugar
>   Juice of ½ lemon
>   ⅛ teaspoon salt

Set refrigerator control to coldest setting. Put the currants and 2 cups of water in a saucepan. Bring to a boil, then simmer 5 minutes, or until the currants are soft. Force through a fine sieve. Sprinkle gelatin on ¼ cup water and let stand 5 minutes. Add remaining ingredients and mix well. Bring the sieved currants to a boil and pour over the gelatin mixture. Stir until the gelatin and sugar are completely dissolved. Cool and freeze in a refrigerator tray until firm, but not frozen hard. Put in a cold bowl and beat with rotary beater until fluffy. Return to tray and freeze again.

Cold Luncheon for Six

A menu for the dog days, when food has to be really tempting. Both the seviche and the Circassian chicken are light, refreshing, and sufficiently unusual to pique the most jaded appetite. The cassis (a black currant liqueur) ice cream is also an out-of-the-ordinary taste. Choose a white wine from the Loire.

MENU

Seviche

Circassian Chicken

Cassis Ice Cream

The Wine

Muscadet or Quincy

SEVICHE
[PHILIP S. BROWN]

6 filets of sole or similar white fish, cut in thin diagonal strips
1 cup fresh lime or lemon juice
1 orange, peeled and thinly sliced
1 medium sweet red onion, thinly sliced and separated into rings
2 tablespoons canned green chilis, peeled and finely chopped
2 tablespoons capers
½ to ⅔ cup olive oil
Salt, freshly ground black pepper
Chopped cilantro for garnish

Cover fish strips with lime or lemon juice and refrigerate for 2 hours. Drain well. Combine the orange, onion, chilis, capers, and oil and pour over the fish strips, season to taste, tossing lightly. Garnish with chopped cilantro.

CIRCASSIAN CHICKEN
[JAMES A. BEARD]

> 3 quarts water
> 4-pound chicken, cut in pieces
> 1 onion
> 1 carrot
> 1 bunch parsley
> 1 teaspoon salt
> ½ teaspoon freshly ground black pepper
> 2 cups walnut meats
> 1 tablespoon paprika
> 3 slices white bread

Bring water to the boil and add the chicken, onion, carrot, parsley, salt and pepper. Simmer gently until very tender. Skim the broth and let the chicken cool in the liquid. When cool, remove the chicken pieces and take the meat from the bones. Discard the bones, skin and gristle and dice the chicken meat.

Place the walnut meats in the blender and blend until finely ground. Remove; mix with the paprika. Press in fine cheesecloth to extract the reddened nut oil. Reserve the nuts and the oil.

Cook the chicken stock down a little until it is quite rich. Cool. Soak the bread slices in a little of the broth and then squeeze them dry. Combine the bread and ground nuts and place in the blender. Blend until smooth, adding 1 cup chicken broth, a little at a time, until the mixture is a paste.

Arrange the chicken on a serving platter and spread with the nut paste. Sprinkle the red oil over the top. Or mix half of the paste into the chicken, top with the rest of the paste.

CASSIS ICE CREAM
[JAMES A. BEARD]

    2 cups black currant preserves
    1 cup crème de cassis
    Juice of 1 lemon
    ½ teaspoon vanilla
    2 cups light cream
    2 cups heavy cream
    ½ teaspoon salt
    Currant preserves blended with cassis, if desired

Put the preserves in the blender and purée with some of the cassis. Add the lemon juice, the remaining cassis, and the vanilla. Mix the light and heavy cream with the salt and stir in the currant mixture. Pour into an ice cream freezer and freeze. Serve with currant preserves blended with cassis, if you wish.

International Luncheon for Six

An Italian first course, Caribbean vegetable, and French dessert combine with a cosmopolitan poached sole entrée in a menu that is an intriguing progression of tastes—from salty to sweet. A white Burgundy or American Pinot Chardonnay would complement the sole beautifully.

MENU

Fried Mozzarella with Anchovy Sauce
Sole Poached in Vermouth and Madeira
Steamed Rice   Stewed Cucumbers in Orange Sauce
Pear Flan

The Wine

Meursault or Pinot Chardonnay

FRIED MOZZARELLA WITH ANCHOVY SAUCE

1 pound mozzarella cheese
½ cup flour
2 eggs, lightly beaten
½ cup dry, fine fresh bread crumbs
2 tablespoons unsalted butter
Anchovy Sauce (see recipe below)
Parsley

Cut mozzarella into ¼-inch slices. Dip each slice of cheese into flour, then the egg, and finally the crumbs. Melt butter in skillet. Sauté cheese for about 2 minutes on each side or until nicely browned. Add more butter if necessary. Serve immediately with Anchovy Sauce, garnished with parsley.

ANCHOVY SAUCE

8 tablespoons unsalted butter
4 anchovy filets, finely chopped
1 tablespoon finely chopped Italian parsley
2 teaspoons lemon juice
Freshly ground black pepper

Melt butter and stir in anchovies, parsley, lemon juice, and pepper to taste. Keep warm until served.

SOLE POACHED IN VERMOUTH AND MADEIRA
[JEROME HILL]

Butter
½ cup blanched slivered almonds
½ cup dry vermouth
½ cup Madeira
3 pounds sole or flounder filets
Salt, ground white pepper

Melt 2 tablespoons butter in a small skillet over medium heat. Add almonds and sauté, stirring constantly, until golden brown, about 2 to 3 minutes. Pour off the butter, reserve the almonds.

Bring the vermouth and Madeira to the simmering point in a large enameled skillet over medium heat. Sprinkle filets with ½ teaspoon salt and a little pepper, add to skillet 2 or 3 at a time and poach for 2 minutes on one side. Then with a broad spatula turn the filets and poach 2 or 3 minutes longer, or until fish is opaque and firm to the touch. As filets are poached, remove to a large platter and keep hot in a 250° oven. When all are cooked, measure the accumulated juices from the platter and pour back into the skillet. Stir in an equal amount of melted butter.

Transfer the fish to a serving platter. Scatter the reserved almonds over the fish, spoon a small amount of butter sauce over the top, and pass the remaining sauce in a sauceboat.

STEWED CUCUMBERS IN ORANGE SAUCE
[ELISABETH ORTIZ]

> 3 cucumbers, 8 inches long
> 3 tablespoons butter
> 1 tablespoon flour
> 1 cup orange juice, strained
>   Salt and freshly ground pepper
> 1 teaspoon grated orange zest

Peel cucumbers and cut in half lengthwise. Scoop out seeds with a spoon. Slice crosswise in ½" slices. Drop into boiling salted water and cook for 5 minutes. Drain, and place in a warmed serving dish.

Melt butter in a small saucepan. Stir in flour and cook without allowing flour to take on any color for 1 or 2 minutes. Add orange juice and cook, stirring, until smooth and thickened. Season to taste with salt and pepper. Add zest, mix thoroughly, and pour over cucumbers.

PEAR FLAN
[JAMES A. BEARD]

> 4 egg yolks, lightly beaten
> 2 tablespoons sugar
> 1 cup light cream
>   Eau de vie de poire (pear brandy)
>   Pinch salt

3 pears, peeled, cored, and halved, or 6 halves canned pears
   Simple syrup (1 cup water boiled with 1 cup sugar)
1-pound jar pure apricot preserves
1 baked 9″ flan shell

Combine the egg yolks and sugar in the top of a double boiler or heavy pan. Heat the cream separately to the boiling point. Warm the egg mixture with a little of the cream, and then combine the two. Stir over medium heat or hot water until the mixture coats a wooden spoon or spatula. Add 3 tablespoons pear brandy and the salt and stir well. (Do not overcook, or the custard will curdle.) Transfer this pastry cream to a bowl to cool. Chill until ready to use.

Poach pear halves in simple syrup until they are just tender. Drain and pour some pear brandy into each half. (If you use canned pears, add pear brandy to each half.) Chill.

Put apricot preserves in a heavy saucepan and bring to the boiling point, stirring with a wooden spoon. Allow to simmer for 2 minutes and then force through a rather fine strainer. Keep warm.

Spoon a thin layer of chilled pastry cream in the bottom of the flan shell. Arrange the poached pears on top. Spoon the warm apricot glaze over the pears and cool. Serve with or without sweetened whipped cream.

Provençal Luncheon for Six

The flavors of Provence, in the ratatouille, herbed steak, and a sherbet made with crème de cassis, a black currant liqueur, combine in a delicious menu for spring or fall. An appropriate red wine would be a Châteauneuf-du-Pape from the southern part of the Rhône valley, near Avignon.

MENU

Ratatouille Crêpes
Sirloin Steak Provençal
Tossed Green Salad with Tiny Black Niçoise Olives
Hot French Bread
Raspberry Sherbet Cassis

The Wine

Châteauneuf-du-Pape

RATATOUILLE CRÊPES
[ELAINE ROSS]

  12 6″ crêpes (see page 425)
   1 green pepper, seeded and cut into julienne strips
   1 small eggplant, peeled and cut into ¾″ cubes
   2 medium zucchini, sliced ⅛″ thick
     Salt, pepper
  ¼ cup olive oil (more if needed)
   3 medium-size onions, chopped
   2 cloves garlic, mashed
   2 1-pound cans whole, peeled tomatoes, coarsely chopped
     Freshly grated Parmesan cheese
   3 tablespoons minced parsley

Make crêpes and cover them until needed. Place the green pepper, eggplant, and zucchini in a bowl, sprinkle with 1 teaspoon salt, and leave for 1 hour. Drain off any juices that may have accumulated. Heat oil in a heavy skillet, brown drained vegetables lightly, and remove them to a bowl. Add a bit more oil if necessary and sauté the onions over fairly low heat until tender, but not brown. Add the garlic and tomatoes, cook together for 3 minutes, and add salt and pepper to taste. Pour off half the mixture and reserve. Combine the remaining tomato-onion mixture, the reserved vegetables, Parmesan cheese to taste, and the parsley in a large, heavy saucepan or Dutch oven. Cover and simmer this ratatouille over low heat for 10 minutes, then uncover and cook for an additional 15 minutes, stirring occasionally.

Spread the crêpes, speckled side up, on a board or working surface. Place a portion of ratatouille on the center of each crêpe, roll up the crêpes, and place them, seam-side down and in a single layer, in a shallow baking dish that can come to the table. Shortly before serving time, heat the filled crêpes in a preheated 375° oven for 15 to 20 minutes. Purée and reheat the reserved tomato-onion mixture and pass this sauce separately with additional cheese.

SIRLOIN STEAK PROVENÇAL
[LOU SEIBERT PAPPAS]

¼ cup butter, softened
2 teaspoons minced parsley
½ teaspoon crumbled tarragon
2 cloves garlic, minced
½ teaspoon grated lemon zest
1½ teaspoons lemon juice
2- to 2½-pound top sirloin steak
Salt and freshly ground pepper

Blend softened butter well with parsley, tarragon, garlic, lemon zest, and lemon juice. Broil sirloin steak, turning to brown both sides, and seasoning with salt and pepper, until rare. Transfer to a carving board and spread with herb butter. Cut into individual servings or slice thinly and serve on hot French bread.

RASPBERRY SHERBET CASSIS
[ELAINE ROSS]

2 packages frozen red raspberries
¼ cup crème de cassis

Defrost the raspberries just long enough to break them up into chunks. Place the contents of 1 package in the blender with 2 tablespoons cassis. Blend at low speed until the mixture is smooth. Stir down frequently. Repeat with the remaining berries and cassis. Freeze for 6 hours, or until firm.

Fall Luncheon for Six

The richness of the main dish dictates a light and appetite-provoking soup, a fruit dessert, and a voluptuous German white wine.

MENU

Tomato Lemon Consommé
Sautéed Sweetbreads with Virginia Ham and Cream
Green Beans with Slivered Toasted Almonds
Ho's Cobbler

The Wine

Wehlener Sonnenuhr "Auslese"

TOMATO LEMON CONSOMMÉ
[MARY MOON HEMINGWAY]

1 cup beef consommé
2 cups tomato juice
2 cups orange juice
½ cup lemon juice
   Celery salt
   Chopped chives

Blend consommé and juices together and season with celery salt. If too strong, add more consommé. Serve hot or cold garnished with chopped chives.

SAUTÉED SWEETBREADS WITH VIRGINIA HAM AND CREAM
[JAMES A. BEARD]

3 pairs sweetbreads
12 squares fried toast
12 small slices Virginia ham

12 large mushroom caps
Flour
Salt, freshly ground black pepper to taste
¼ teaspoon nutmeg
3 eggs, lightly beaten
1½ to 2 cups bread crumbs
6 to 8 tablespoons butter
¼ cup armagnac or Calvados brandy, warmed
1½ to 2 cups heavy cream
¼ teaspoon Tabasco sauce
Chopped parsley

Soak the sweetbreads in ice water for 20 minutes. Plunge into salted water, bring to a boil, and simmer for 5 minutes. Plunge again into ice water. When cool, remove the tubes and particles of fat. Weight down the sweetbreads for 2 hours. (Use a chopping board or flat plate with cans of food on top.) Cut the sweetbreads into even "cutlets."

Prepare the fried toast, heat the slices of ham, and sauté the mushroom caps. Dip the sweetbreads into flour seasoned with salt, freshly ground pepper, and nutmeg, then dip in the beaten egg and finally in the crumbs. Heat the butter in a large skillet until it is bubbling. Add the sweetbreads and let them brown nicely on both sides. Salt and pepper them. Pour the armagnac or Calvados over them and flambé. Place a slice of ham on each square of toast and follow with a slice of sweetbread. Keep hot while you prepare the sauce.

Blend 2 tablespoons flour with the butter left in the skillet, adding a little more butter if the mixture is too floury. Gradually stir in the cream. Add the Tabasco. Stir over low heat until nicely thickened. Correct the seasoning. Spoon over the sweetbreads and ham and top with mushroom caps. Garnish with parsley.

HO'S COBBLER
[STAR DUWYENIE]

½ cup butter
1 cup flour
1 cup sugar
1 teaspoon baking powder
½ cup milk
2 cups canned blackberries with juice

Preheat the oven to 375°. Melt butter in a large baking dish. Sift flour, sugar, and baking powder into a bowl. Add milk and mix well. Heat blackberries in their juice. Pour the batter over the melted butter. Do not stir. Pour hot blackberries over batter. Do not stir. Bake until batter creeps to the top of the baking dish and forms a brown crust, about 30 minutes.

Hearty Fall Luncheon for Six

Certain dishes, such as pot-au-feu, bouillabaisse, cassoulet, choucroute garnie, and other great regional specialties of the cuisine bourgeoise, are really better for luncheon than for dinner or supper, because by their very nature they are hardly foods to sleep on. Eaten at noon or one o'clock, there's the rest of the day to work them off. With the classic peasant pot-au-feu you really need nothing more than plenty of French bread, a robust red wine, and a very simple dessert.

MENU

Pot-au-Feu

Hot French Bread

Baked Custard Americana

The Wine

Côtes du Rhône or California Petite Sirah

POT-AU-FEU
[ELISABETH ORTIZ]

   4 pounds chuck roast or bottom round
   3 quarts beef stock, approximately
      Bouquet garni (3 sprigs parsley, bay leaf, ½ teaspoon thyme, 12 peppercorns, bruised, tied in cheesecloth)
   2 medium onions, each stuck with a clove

6 carrots, scraped and cut into quarters
2 stalks celery, cut into 2" pieces
3 medium white turnips, peeled and quartered
3 parsnips, peeled and quartered
6 small leeks, well washed
  Salt to taste
2 pounds marrow bones, cut into about 12 pieces
1 small head cabbage

Put the beef in a large pot or soup kettle, and add enough stock to cover the meat by about 3 inches. Add the bouquet garni to the pot with the onions, 3 carrots, and the celery. Bring to a boil, skim off all the scum, reduce the heat so that the surface of the liquid barely moves, and cook at this slow simmer for 2½ hours, skimming periodically.

Remove the beef, strain the broth, and discard the cooked vegetables. If there is a great deal of fat, skim off most of it. Rinse out the pot, return the beef to it with the broth, turnips, parsnips, leeks, and remaining carrots. Season to taste with salt, and simmer, partly covered, for ½ hour, at which time both meat and vegetables should be done. Add the marrow bones 5 minutes before the end of the cooking time.

In the meantime wash the cabbage, remove any discolored leaves, trim the stalk end, and blanch in boiling water. Cut into 6 wedges and cook separately in stock for 15 minutes.

At serving time, remove the bones, scrape out the marrow, and keep it warm. Slice the beef and set it on a warmed platter surrounded by the vegetables and cabbage wedges. Add the marrow to the soup. Serve the soup with the meat and vegetables separately, either at the same time or as two courses, accompanied by hot French bread, sour pickles, coarse salt, mustard, and horseradish sauce (see below).

HORSERADISH SAUCE

1 4-ounce bottle grated horseradish or ½ cup grated fresh horse-radish, lightly packed
1 teaspoon sugar
½ teaspoon dry mustard
  Salt to taste
1 cup sour cream

Mix all ingredients thoroughly together. When using fresh grated horseradish, also add 2 tablespoons lemon juice. Makes about 1½ cups.

BAKED CUSTARD AMERICANA
[RUTH CONRAD BATEMAN]

> 2 cups milk
> 3 eggs
> 6 tablespoons sugar
> ¼ teaspoon salt
> 1 teaspoon vanilla extract
> Grated nutmeg (or shaved chocolate, coconut, chopped nuts)

Heat milk until film forms on top. Beat eggs, sugar, and salt lightly until just mixed. Gradually whisk in milk until blended. Add vanilla. Strain. Set 6 custard cups or a larger baking dish in shallow pan on oven rack. Fill dishes with custard and sprinkle with nutmeg or one of the other toppings. Fill pan with hot water to ½ depth of custards. Bake in a 325° oven for 25 to 30 minutes, or until knife, inserted near edge, is clean when removed, but center is still quivery. Remove custards from water bath, cool, and chill.

FLAVORINGS: Nutmeg or mace and vanilla are traditional custard flavors. Try grated orange or lemon peel, a little dark rum, a drop of almond extract with the vanilla, diced candied ginger, raisins, instant coffee.

Country Luncheon for Six

If you live in a part of the country where you can get wild pigeons, and dry (not sweet) cider, so much the better. Otherwise, use the commercially raised squab and either imported hard cider or red wine. Drink a light red or a dry rosé wine.

MENU

Herb Cream Soup
Braised Pigeons or Squab
Ragoût of Vegetables
Buttered-Rum Apples

The Wine

Tavel Rosé or California Grenache Rosé or Zinfandel

HERB CREAM SOUP
[KAY SHAW NELSON]

2 tablespoons butter
6 green onions, with tops, chopped
¾ cup shredded lettuce
½ cup shredded spinach
3 tablespoons chopped parsley
½ cup watercress
2 teaspoons sugar
6 cups chicken stock
Salt, pepper to taste
1 cup light cream
Chopped chives (optional)

Melt the butter in a large saucepan and sauté the green onions until tender. Add the lettuce, spinach, parsley, and watercress. Simmer, covered, for 10 minutes. Add the sugar, chicken stock, salt, and pepper and simmer, covered, 30 minutes longer, stirring occasionally. Add the cream and bring to a boil. Remove at once from the heat. Garnish with chopped fresh chives, if desired.

BRAISED PIGEONS IN CIDER
[MRS. JULIAN ROBINSON]

  6 plump pigeons (or squab)
  2 tablespoons beef fat
  ½ pound button mushrooms
  3 to 4 slices well-cured bacon
  1 pound small white onions, peeled and left whole
  2 bay leaves
  1 twig thyme
    Salt and freshly ground black pepper
 12 meatballs (see recipe below)
 1¼ cups dry cider (or beer or red wine)
  2 tablespoons cornstarch
  1 teaspoon Dijon mustard

Cut the pigeons in half and sauté until brown in the beef fat. Remove and set aside. Wash and dry button mushrooms and cut in half lengthwise. Chop the bacon coarsely and fry with the onions in the remaining fat, adding the mushrooms after a few minutes. Line the bottom of a cast-iron casserole with the bacon, onion, and mushroom mixture, and arrange the pigeon halves on top with bay leaves, thyme, and salt and pepper to taste. Sauté the meatballs and arrange around the pigeons, adding 3 tablespoons cider. Cover and cook in a 350° oven for 2 hours. Add ¾ cup cider, cover, and cook for 1 more hour. If you are using squab, braise for only 1 hour altogether. Mix the remaining cider, cornstarch, and Dijon mustard until smooth, and pour over the pigeons. Return to the oven for 10 minutes to allow the sauce to thicken.

This dish can be cooked the day before and allowed to mature in its juices. When ready to serve, reheat slowly.

VEAL AND PORK MEATBALLS

  ½ pound finely ground veal
  ½ pound finely ground pork
  1 cup bread crumbs
  1 egg
    Salt and freshly ground black pepper

Thoroughly mix together ground veal, pork, bread crumbs, egg, and salt and pepper to taste. Shape into balls 1″ in diameter.

RAGOÛT OF VEGETABLES
[MRS. JULIAN ROBINSON]

¼ cup chopped bacon
1 large onion, thinly sliced
2 tablespoons beef fat
2 tablespoons flour
2 cups stock
3 pounds mixed vegetables in season—carrots, celery, parsnips, kohlrabi, leeks, onions, peas, potatoes, etc.—cleaned and sliced, or diced
Bouquet garni
Salt
Freshly ground black pepper
4 tablespoons wine vinegar

Sauté the bacon and onion in the beef fat until lightly browned. Add flour and cook until golden. Add the stock and stir until it boils. Add vegetables, bouquet garni, salt and pepper to taste and gently simmer until vegetables are tender, stirring occasionally to prevent sticking. Add wine vinegar and correct seasoning.

BUTTERED-RUM APPLES
[ELAINE ROSS]

2 tablespoons butter
¼ cup sugar
2 tablespoons light rum
¼ cup honey
2 tablespoons evaporated milk
6 medium apples, peeled, cored, and cut into eighths
Sour cream

Place the butter, sugar, rum, honey, and evaporated milk in a sauce-pan. Bring to a rolling boil, stirring constantly. Add the apples, mix well to coat each piece with the syrup, and pour into a shallow baking dish or pie plate. Bake, covered, in a 350° oven for 20 minutes, or until just tender. Remove the cover, raise the heat to 425°, and bake for 40 to 50 minutes, basting every 10 minutes, until the sauce is thickened and the apples golden. Serve warm or at room temperature with sour cream passed separately.

Casserole Luncheon for Six

This is an easy meal to prepare, for both the casserole and the orange custard bake at the same oven temperature, for about the same length of time. A fruity Alsatian wine would be a good choice with the shrimp dish.

MENU

Old-Fashioned Charleston Shrimp Casserole
Zucchini in Tomato Sauce
Orange Custard

The Wine

Sylvaner or Traminer

OLD-FASHIONED CHARLESTON SHRIMP CASSEROLE
[NIKA HAZELTON]

    8 slices firm white bread, crusts trimmed, torn into crumbs
    1 cup dry white wine
    1 cup good quality medium sherry
  ¼ cup butter, softened
    1 teaspoon salt
  ¼ to ½ teaspoon nutmeg
  ¼ teaspoon pepper
    2 pounds cooked shrimp, shelled and deveined

Soak the bread crumbs in the wine and sherry in a deep bowl. Mash in the butter with a fork to make a paste. Beat in the salt, nutmeg, and pepper. Add the shrimp and mix well. Turn into a buttered 1½-quart casserole. Bake uncovered in a preheated 350° oven about 40 minutes, or until top is crusty and golden.

NOTE: In the Tidewater country, this dish is also made with oysters or crabmeat.

ZUCCHINI IN TOMATO SAUCE
[JAMES A. BEARD]

   3 tablespoons olive oil
   1 clove garlic, finely chopped
   2 1-pound, 13-ounce cans Italian plum tomatoes
   1 teaspoon salt
   1 teaspoon sugar
  ½ teaspoon finely ground black pepper
   3 tablespoons tomato paste
12 small zucchini, peeled
   2 tablespoons chopped basil

Heat the olive oil, add the garlic and cook 3 minutes. Add tomatoes and bring to a boil. Simmer slowly for 20 to 25 minutes, stirring occasionally. Add salt, sugar, pepper, and tomato paste and simmer again for 10 minutes. Add the zucchini and cook until just pierceable (about 15 minutes). Stir in the chopped basil.

ORANGE CUSTARD
[JAMES A. BEARD]

5 eggs
⅓ cup sugar
1 cup orange juice
1 cup heavy cream
1 tablespoon Grand Marnier liqueur

Beat the eggs and add the sugar. Beat in the orange juice and finally add the cream and Grand Marnier, mixing well with a wire whisk. Pour the mixture into a baking dish and bake in a 350° oven for about 50 minutes, or until the custard is set.

Fall or Winter Luncheon for Six

A menu of surprises—the unusual hors d'oeuvre, the stuffed lamb chops, a lusciously creamy dessert—that you might serve to weekend guests or to visiting relatives. Have a good red Bordeaux or Cabernet Sauvignon with the chops.

MENU

Turkish Leek and Onion Hors d'Oeuvre

Lamb Chops Eleanore

Potato Soufflé   *Carrots Russe*

Watercress Salad

Tipsy Pudding

The Wine

A Saint-Emilion—Château Ausone or Château Nenin—
or a vintage California Cabernet Sauvignon

TURKISH LEEK AND ONION HORS D'OEUVRE
[NIKA HAZELTON]

  12 leeks
  ½ cup olive oil
  2 cups dry white wine
  4 cups black olives, pitted and sliced
    Boiling water
  3 large onions, quartered

Trim tough outer leaves from the leeks and remove all but 2 inches of the green part. Cut into 4″ to 5″ pieces. Wash thoroughly to remove all the sand nestling between leaves. Heat half the olive oil in a large, deep skillet and sauté the leeks for 3 minutes. Add 2 cups water and the wine. Simmer, covered, over lowest possible heat for 15 minutes, or until leeks are barely tender. Cover olives with boiling water and let stand for 2 minutes. Drain. Add olives to the leeks and simmer 5 minutes. Drain the leeks and olives and arrange on a serving dish. Heat the remaining oil in the skillet and cook the onions in it until soft and golden. Arrange the onions on top of the leeks and olives. Chill before serving.

LAMB CHOPS ELEANORE
[MRS. JOHN ROBSON]

    6 chicken livers
    ½ pound mushrooms
    5 tablespoons butter
       Salt, freshly ground black pepper
    1 tablespoon finely chopped parsley
    6 double-rib lamb chops
       Chopped parsley

Trim and finely chop the chicken livers and mushrooms. Sauté them over low heat in 2 tablespoons of the butter, stirring frequently, without letting them brown. Season with salt and pepper to taste and add the parsley. Trim fat from the lamb chops and slit them to make a pocket. Stuff them with the chicken liver mixture. Heat remaining butter in a heavy casserole, add the chops, and sear them over high heat on both sides. Cover the casserole and bake the chops in a 350° oven for 25 minutes, or until tender. Or skewer the chops to close the pockets and broil them on both sides until they are brown and crisp. Arrange the chops on a heated platter, pour the juices over, and sprinkle with parsley.

POTATO SOUFFLÉ
[NIKA HAZELTON]

    3 cups hot mashed potatoes
    ¾ cup hot milk or light cream
    ½ cup grated Swiss cheese
    4 tablespoons butter
    2 tablespoons minced parsley
    4 eggs, separated
       Salt, pepper to taste

While the mashed potatoes are still hot, beat in the hot milk or cream, cheese, butter, and parsley. Beat the egg yolks until thick and lemon-colored. Beat the egg whites until stiff. Beat the egg yolks into the potato mixture and fold in the beaten egg whites. Season with salt and pepper. Pile lightly in a buttered 1½-quart baking dish. Bake in a preheated 400° oven 15 to 20 minutes, or until puffed and golden.

CARROTS RUSSE
[HELEN EVANS BROWN]

> 3 cups diced carrots
> 1 cup yoghurt
> 1 tablespoon minced parsley
> 1 tablespoon minced chives
>   Salt, pepper to taste

Cook carrots until barely tender. Drain and dress with yoghurt, parsley, and chives. Season to taste.

TIPSY PUDDING
[JAMES A. BEARD]

> 40 lady fingers
> ½ cup cognac mixed with ¼ cup water
> ¼ cup or more raspberry jam
> 1½ cups Brandied Custard Sauce (see recipe below)
>   1 cup toasted blanched almonds
>   1 cup heavy cream, whipped
>   2 tablespoons powdered sugar
>   1 tablespoon cognac

Dip the lady fingers in the cognac-water mixture and arrange a layer of about 20 in a serving dish. Spread layer with half the raspberry jam, cover with remaining lady fingers, spread with remaining jam, cover with custard sauce, and chill. Just before serving, stud surface with the almonds and serve with whipped cream, sweetened with powdered sugar and flavored with 1 tablespoon cognac.

BRANDIED CUSTARD SAUCE

    1 cup milk
    1 cup heavy cream
    6 egg yolks
    ½ cup sugar
    ¼ cup brandy
    ½ teaspoon vanilla

Heat the milk and cream to the boiling point. Beat the egg yolks and sugar together lightly over low heat in a heavy enameled pan, a stainless-steel pan, or in the top of a glass double boiler over hot, but not boiling, water. Gradually add the hot milk and cream and stir vigorously. Heat the brandy in a small pan to the boiling point to volatilize the alcohol. Continue stirring the custard mixture until it coats a wooden spoon or spatula. Do not overcook or let it get too hot or it will curdle. Add the brandy and vanilla, cook gently for another moment or two, then remove to a bowl and cool. Makes 2½ to 3 cups.

Seafood Luncheon for Six to Eight

Italian fish stores usually carry squid, and you can often buy it ready-cleaned and prepared for cooking. Omit the squid, if you can't get it, and use another type of seafood, such as clams or crabmeat. All you need with the risotto is a salad and hot bread for those who like it. Drink a light white Italian wine.

MENU

Venetian Seafood Risotto

Salad of Marinated Artichoke Hearts, Green Beans, and Tiny Black Olives

Hot Italian Bread

Delicate Almond Soufflé, Mandarine Sauce

The Wine

Verdicchio or Soave

VENETIAN SEAFOOD RISOTTO
[PAULA PECK]

  1 pound squid
  3 pounds mussels
 3½ cups fish stock or clam juice
  ½ cup mussel juice (approximately)
  ¼ teaspoon powdered saffron
   Salt to taste
  ½ cup unsalted butter
  ½ cup olive oil
  2 cups Italian short-grain rice
 1½ cups chopped onion
  4 cloves garlic, finely minced
  1 cup dry white wine
 1½ pounds raw, shelled, cleaned shrimp, cut into ½" pieces
  ¾ cup chopped parsley

Squid, contrary to general opinion, is easily cleaned. The outer, thin, dark membrane should be entirely rubbed off. Then pull out all the contents of the center of the squid and cut off the tentacles, unless you want to add them to the risotto. They may be used if they are carefully washed under running water. Remove the cellophane-like blade and bit of intestine in the center of the squid. Rinse inside of squid under cold water. You then will have a clean, tube-like cylinder. Cut all squid into ¼" slices and reserve.

Rinse the mussels very well (or soak them for an hour or two) to get rid of the outer sand. Then open the mussels with a small, pointed paring knife (because the shells are thin, they are much easier to open than either clams or oysters; simply insert the knife tip at the point where the shells are joined and pry them apart), holding them over a bowl to catch as much juice as possible. You should have about ½ cup. If there is a small hairy beard in some of the mussels, remove it (a scissors works well for this). Remove mussel meat from shell and place in refrigerator until needed.

Cover squid with fish stock or clam juice and ½ cup juice from the mussels. Simmer until tender, about 30 to 40 minutes. Drain squid. Reserve squid and liquid separately. Add powdered saffron to stock (if not powdered, crumble with your fingers before adding). Season liquid with salt. Place in a saucepan and simmer over very low heat.

Melt butter and oil in a 3- to 4-quart heavy pot. When bubbly, add rice. Stir briskly so that all the rice is coated with fat, but do not allow it to brown. As soon as fat again begins to bubble, stir in onion and garlic and sauté until they soften. (You may cut down on the amount of butter and oil, if you wish, although it makes a very succulent risotto.)

Add wine, all at once, raise heat as high as possible. Stir constantly until wine has almost evaporated. Add ¾ of the simmering stock. Cover pot, allow to cook very slowly for about 10 minutes. Stir rice. If it appears to be becoming dry, add remaining liquid. Otherwise, allow to cook, covered, a little longer. Check again. Stir. Add remaining liquid. Allow to cook slowly until all liquid is absorbed and rice is just tender.

Add squid, raw mussels, and shrimp to rice. Stir. Cover pot and allow to cook slowly for about 5 minutes, or until shrimp are just tender, but not overcooked. The mussels cook even more quickly, but a bit of overcooking won't hurt them, as it would the shrimp. Stir in chopped parsley and serve.

DELICATE ALMOND SOUFFLÉ
[MRS. DAVID EVINS]

    Butter
    Sugar
2 tablespoons cornstarch
2 cups cold milk
8 eggs, separated
1 cup sugar
¼ teaspoon salt
1 teaspoon almond extract
1 teaspoon vanilla extract
¼ cup ground almonds
    Mandarine Sauce (see recipe below)

Butter a 2-quart soufflé dish well and dust it with sugar. Put cornstarch in a saucepan and slowly add milk, stirring until smooth. Bring to a boil over medium heat, stirring frequently, and boil 1 minute. Combine egg yolks, ½ cup sugar, and salt, and beat until thick and light. Slowly pour in milk mixture, stirring briskly. Cool 10 to 15 minutes. Add almond and vanilla extracts.

Beat egg whites until soft peaks form. Gradually add remaining sugar and continue to beat until stiff, glossy peaks form. Fold gently and thoroughly into egg yolk mixture. Pour into prepared soufflé dish. Set in shallow pan with 1 inch of hot water. Sprinkle top of soufflé with ground almonds. Bake in a 325° oven for 60 to 65 minutes.

MANDARINE SAUCE

1 tablespoon butter or margarine
1 tablespoon cornstarch
½ cup sugar
¼ teaspoon salt
1½ cups tangerine juice
2 tablespoons grated tangerine zest
2 tangerines, peeled and sectioned, all membranes cut away
2 tablespoons apricot brandy

Melt butter in a heavy saucepan. Stir in cornstarch, sugar, and salt. Slowly add the tangerine juice and stir until smooth. Cook, stirring, over medium heat until sauce boils and is thick and clear. Add tangerine zest, tangerine sections, and apricot brandy and stir until blended. Serve warm. Makes about 1½ cups.

Summer Luncheon for Eight

In the months when sun-ripened tomatoes are in season, take advantage of it by making a fresh tomato soup for weekend guests. This would be a savvy menu for Saturday or Sunday, because none of the dishes has to be served right away; they can all be held until the guests are ready to eat. Have carafes of an inexpensive white wine with the pie.

MENU

Fresh Tomato Soup
Deep Dish Chicken and Artichoke Pie
Baked Pears Beauchamp Place

The Wine

California Chablis or Mâcon Blanc

FRESH TOMATO SOUP
[CRAIG CLAIBORNE]

        12 tablespoons butter
         2 tablespoons olive oil
         1 large onion, thinly sliced (about 2 cups)
         2 sprigs fresh thyme or ½ teaspoon dried
         4 basil leaves, chopped, or ½ teaspoon dried basil
            Salt, freshly ground black pepper
       2½ pounds fresh, ripe tomatoes, cored, or 1 2-pound, 3-ounce can
            Italian tomatoes
         3 tablespoons tomato paste
        ¼ cup flour
       3¾ cups fresh or canned chicken broth
         1 teaspoon sugar
         1 cup heavy cream
            Croutons for garnish (see recipe below)

Heat 8 tablespoons butter and the oil in a heavy kettle. Add onion, thyme, basil, salt and pepper to taste. Cook, stirring, until onion is wilted. Add tomatoes and tomato paste, blend. Simmer 10 minutes.

Put the flour in a small mixing bowl and add about 5 tablespoons chicken broth, stirring to blend. Stir this paste into the tomato mixture. Add the remaining broth and simmer 30 minutes, stirring frequently all over the bottom of the kettle to make certain that the soup does not stick, scorch, or burn.

Put the soup through the finest possible food mill or sieve. Return it to the heat and add the sugar and cream. Simmer, stirring occasionally, for about 5 minutes. Add the remaining butter, swirling it around in the soup. Garnish with croutons.

CROUTONS

Preheat the oven to 400°. Rub both sides of 8 slices crusty, day-old French or Italian bread with 1 large split garlic clove, then brush generously with about 8 teaspoons olive oil. Place on a baking sheet and bake until golden, turning once if necessary.

DEEP DISH CHICKEN AND ARTICHOKE PIE
[LOU SEIBERT PAPPAS]

6 split chicken breasts
½ teaspoon salt
2 tablespoons butter
1 clove garlic, minced
½ cup chicken broth
8 canned artichoke bottoms
¾ cup dry white wine
2 tablespoons cornstarch
3 tablespoons sour cream
Salt and pepper to taste
⅛ teaspoon nutmeg
Pastry for a double crust pie or 1 large package pastry mix
4 ounces sliced smoked tongue, cut in strips
4 hard-cooked eggs, cut in eighths
1 cup shredded Gruyère or Samsoe cheese
1 egg white, lightly beaten

Season chicken breasts with salt and sauté in 1 tablespoon butter on both sides. Add garlic. Pour in chicken broth, cover, and simmer 15 minutes, or until tender. Remove from broth and let cool. Remove skin and bones and cut meat into strips ½ inch wide and about 1 inch long. Reserve broth for sauce.

Quarter artichoke bottoms and sauté on both sides in the remaining tablespoon of butter. Bring the reserved chicken broth to a boil with the wine and stir in a paste of cornstarch blended with sour cream. Stir constantly until thickened. Season with salt, pepper, and nutmeg.

Roll out half the pastry into a circle 14 inches in diameter and place in a 9-inch round, 2½-inch deep pan (with removable bottom or spring-release sides). Arrange the chicken strips, artichoke bottoms, tongue, and egg wedges on pastry. Pour on wine sauce and sprinkle with cheese. Cover with remaining pastry and pinch edges of pastry together to seal. Make a hole in the center of pastry for steam to escape and brush with lightly beaten egg white. Bake in a 425° oven for 15 minutes; reduce temperature to 350° and bake 20 minutes longer. Cool slightly on a rack. Remove sides of pan. Serve warm or at room temperature.

BAKED PEARS BEAUCHAMP PLACE
[ELAINE ROSS]

For each serving:
  1 ripe Bartlett pear or other juicy variety
  2 tablespoons raspberry syrup
  1 small scoop butter pecan ice cream
  ½ teaspoon finely chopped pecans

Peel and core the pear and place it in a small heavy saucepan. Pour the raspberry syrup over the pear, turning the fruit in the syrup to coat all sides. Bake, uncovered, in a preheated 350° oven for 40 minutes, or until the fruit is tender and has acquired a rosy blush. (While the fruit is baking, turn it in the juices every 10 minutes and baste it. Should the pear seem dry, cover the pan.) Leave the pear in its juices for 2 hours or more, basting occasionally. Shortly before serving time, place the pear upright in a custard cup or ramekin and heat it for 10 to 12 minutes in a 350° oven. Reduce the pan juices over high heat until thickened and pour over the hot pear. Place the ice cream in a small egg cup or tiny ramekin and sprinkle with the chopped nuts. Put the pear and ice cream on a dessert plate and serve immediately.

Dinner Parties

Within the last few years the dinner party seems to have become less a meal than a status symbol. Maybe it is the influence of those proliferating little "gourmet" groups, where hostesses vie with each other in the presentation of new or esoteric dishes, and hosts discuss in infinite, endless detail the nuances of wine. The simple, straightforward dinner has given way to the culinary *tour de force*, and people who once thought nothing of asking a few friends in for a meal now go into a spin at the idea of exposing their lack of Cordon Bleu expertise. That's all a lot of nonsense. No one can be expected to compete with some *haute cuisine* temple where dozens of *sous-chefs* scurry around skimming stocks, stirring sauces, and rolling out pâte feuilletée. A dinner doesn't succeed or fail by its strict adherence to Escoffier. All that is really required is a well-balanced menu, with good food and wine that will be conducive to a flow of talk and an atmosphere of well-being.

When you plan a dinner party, keep it within your scope and abilities. Don't try to do too much, have too many courses. An elegant sufficiency of food is better any day than a groaning table and (silently) groaning guests. Three courses is all you should attempt, preferably two of them things you can either do ahead or put together very quickly at the last minute.

Never, ever, attempt a dish for the first time, even if it sounds fool-proof. By the law of averages, something is bound to go wrong. Try it out on your family at least once, so you have a pretty good idea of timing and any possible pitfalls, before serving it to guests. If you do occasionally get the urge to show off your kitchen talents with a tricky dish like *quenelles de brochet* with sauce nantua, make sure the other courses don't require as much attention. Unless you have two ovens, avoid menus where you have to juggle two dishes that need to be cooked at different temperatures. Simple first courses that can be made up ahead of time and stashed in the refrigerator are life-savers, because ten to one you're going to find something that needs your attention just when you're about to get the food on the table.

Often, it's a smart idea to serve the first course in the living room. Clams Rockefeller, which can be served on a small plate with an oyster fork, or hot consommé, to be sipped from a demitasse, are the kind of things that are easy to eat away from the table. This not only gives you a breathing space before the guests sit down, but also helps to break up any lingering over cocktails. And if you want your guests to do justice to the dinner, keep away from all those little cocktail nibbles that surfeit without satisfying. If you like to have something with cocktails, tiny olives, raw vegetables, or salted nuts will do, but don't spin the cocktail hour out so long that everyone becomes so faint and famished they'll fill up with whatever is at hand.

While it is fairly simple to figure out what to have for lunch or supper, constructing a dinner menu is rather more challenging. Obviously, you are not going to commit some gross culinary stupidity like having a cream soup, chicken with a cream sauce, and a baked custard—all pale, rich, and bland. Beyond that, though, you should try to devise a menu that is provocative to the palate, with contrasts of texture, taste, and temperature. If the main course is a suavely sauced capon, lead in with something *al dente* and assertive, like vegetables vinaigrette, or oysters or clams on the half shell, and toss crunchy toasted almonds or a few pine nuts into the vegetable you serve with it. After a heavy main course, bring on a light dessert—a soufflé made with egg whites alone, a brisk sherbet, poached fruit. Should you, on the other hand, serve a clear soup, roast meat, a vegetable and salad, you can afford to end with a creamy, delectable torte, frozen mousse, or French pastry.

Even if you aren't the greatest whiz in the kitchen, don't let that intimidate you into staying in a safe but uninspiring rut of steak or roasts and a baked potato. Roasts are perfectly sound choices for a dinner party, but they can take a more imaginative accompaniment—a purée of chestnuts, an onion quiche, or a spinach pie—and if you really don't want to venture beyond potatoes, make them pommes Anna or Chantilly or Byron, or purée them with celery root.

A touch of the unexpected makes a meal more dashing. It can be something as easy as adding grated raw carrot to steamed rice, a pinch of curry powder to oyster soup, putting slivers of prosciutto in a dish of broccoli or a handful of nasturtium leaves and flowers in a green salad. Originality must, of course, be guided by good sense, but if you want your dinner parties to be looked forward to, it pays to be innovative.

Black Tie Dinner for Six

A small but elegant dinner for a few friends before a vernissage or a first night doesn't have to be complicated, but the food must be rather special. Nothing is more spectacular and festive than a whole filet of beef, and while this is always an expensive piece of meat, there is no bone, no waste, and the rich sauce customarily served with the filet stretches it nicely. You'll find half a pound per person an ample allowance for all but the greediest of trenchermen. This is the time to bring out your finest red Burgundy or Bordeaux.

MENU

Consommé Bellevue

Filet of Beef Alsatian, Sauce Périgueux

Tiny Green Beans

Purée of Celery Root and Potatoes

Salad of Bibb Lettuce and Julienne of Endive
with French Dressing, Sprinkled with Chopped Chives

Frozen Honey Soufflé

The Wine

Red Burgundy, a Grand Cru, such as Musigny or Bonnes Mares,
or a red Bordeaux, a first growth from St. Emilion or the Médoc,
such as Château Ausone or Château Margaux

CONSOMMÉ BELLEVUE
[IRIS BROOKS]

> 4 cups homemade or canned chicken broth, skimmed of all fat
> 2 cups clam broth or bottled clam juice
> 1 teaspoon celery salt
>   Generous pinch of cayenne pepper
> ¼ cup heavy cream

Mix the chicken and clam broths in a saucepan and season with the celery salt and cayenne. Bring to a boil, then reduce heat and simmer for 10 minutes to blend the flavors.

Meanwhile, whip the cream until stiff and season it lightly with salt. Ladle the hot soup into heated soup plates or cups and top each serving with a tablespoon of salted whipped cream.

FILET OF BEEF ALSATIAN, SAUCE PÉRIGUEUX
[PHILIP S. BROWN]

> 3½-pound beef tenderloin
> 6 to 8 thin slices of Virginia or Westphalian ham
>   Pâté de foie gras
> ½ cup strong beef stock
>   Meat glaze
>   Truffles, chopped
>   Pastry to envelop meat
>   Egg yolk, beaten with 1 tablespoon water
>   Périgueux Sauce (see page 420)

Trim both ends of beef and cut it three-fourths of the way through in six or eight evenly spaced slices. Insert a thin slice of cooked ham, which has been spread with pâté de foie gras, into each cut. Reshape the filet and tie it well, then roast in a 375° oven for about 15 minutes, basting frequently with beef stock. Remove from the oven, brush with meat glaze, and let cool somewhat before spreading the filet with a thin layer of pâté de foie gras and rolling it in chopped truffles. Now roll out puff paste or pie pastry about ⅛" thick and large enough to cover the meat. Wrap the meat, tuck in the ends, and paste down with cold water. Put on a baking sheet, brush with egg yolk beaten with a tablespoon of water, and prick the dough well with a fork. Bake in a 400° oven until the crust is nicely browned. To serve, cut through the existing slices and pass Périgueux Sauce.

PURÉE OF CELERY ROOT AND POTATOES

> 2 pounds celery root
> Salt, freshly ground black pepper
> 4 tablespoons butter
> 1 to 1½ cups chicken stock or water
> 5 large hot boiled potatoes
> 1½ cups milk, hot

Peel the celery root, cut in ½″ slices, and blanch in boiling salted water 5 minutes. Drain and put in a heavy saucepan with 2 tablespoons butter, enough stock or water to barely cover, and salt and pepper to taste. Cover and boil slowly for 20 to 30 minutes, until tender. Drain, reserving liquid for soup, etc.

Put the boiled potatoes and celery root in bowl of an electric mixer and break up with a fork. Turn on at a low speed and beat, gradually increasing speed, until smooth. Add milk, 2 tablespoons butter, and salt and pepper to taste and increase speed gradually, beating until fluffy. Add light cream if necessary.

FROZEN HONEY SOUFFLÉ
[DIONE LUCAS]

> 2 cups heavy cream
> ½ cup honey
> Grated rind of 1 lemon, 1 orange, 1 lime
> Pinch of salt
> ½ teaspoon almond extract
> ½ cup chopped toasted almonds

Beat the cream until slightly thick. Gradually fold in the honey and beat until well blended. Add citrus rinds, salt, and almond extract. Put in an ice cream freezer and turn until thick.

Tie a band of oiled wax paper around a 6″ soufflé dish. Fill with the frozen mixture and cover the top with the almonds. Freeze for 2 hours. When set and firm, remove the paper and serve.

Saturday Night Dinner for Six

Although this menu will enrapture the palates of the most critical guests, it is actually fairly easy to organize, as two of the main courses can be prepared ahead.

If you want to serve more than one wine, a young fruity Muscadet from the Loire would be a good balance to the pungent sauce on the shrimp. The lamb, of course, calls for a fine red wine, such as a château-bottled Bordeaux or a vintage California Cabernet Sauvignon. Be sure to provide enough to drink with the cheese, and leave the Brie or Camembert at room temperature until it reaches soft, creamy perfection.

MENU

Shrimp in Avocado with Mustard Sauce
Roast Saddle of Lamb
Potatoes Anna   Broccoli with Prosciutto
Brie or Camembert with French Bread, Sweet Butter
Strawberry Singapore

The Wines

A young Muscadet; a château-bottled Médoc,
Pomerol, or St. Emilion of a good year; or a vintage Cabernet
Sauvignon from California

SHRIMP IN AVOCADO WITH MUSTARD SAUCE
[CRAIG CLAIBORNE]

    36 raw shrimp in the shell
        Salt to taste
     1 lemon slice
    ½ bay leaf
     2 sprigs parsley
     1 stalk celery, cut into thirds

  10 peppercorns
  ½ teaspoon dried thyme
  1 tablespoon Dijon or Dusseldorf mustard
  1 teaspoon anchovy paste
  3 tablespoons lemon juice
  ¾ cup olive oil
  1 tablespoon fresh chopped tarragon or dill or
     ½ teaspoon dried tarragon or dill
  2 tablespoons capers
  3 ripe avocados
     Lemon wedges

Place the shrimp in a saucepan and add boiling water to cover. Add salt, lemon slice, bay leaf, parsley, celery, peppercorns and thyme. Bring to a boil and cook 4 to 6 minutes, depending on the size of the shrimp. Drain and chill. Peel shrimp and remove intestinal vein. Place the mustard and anchovy paste in a mixing bowl and add the lemon juice. Beat with a wire whisk, adding the oil a little at a time. Add salt to taste, tarragon or dill, and capers. Pour over shrimp. Marinate 1 or 2 hours.

Leave the shrimp in the marinade until just before you are ready to sit down to dinner, as avocado discolors quickly once it is cut.

Peel and halve the avocados. Remove and discard pits. Fill the cavity of each half with shrimp and serve with lemon wedges.

ROAST SADDLE OF LAMB
[JAMES A. BEARD]

The saddle is sometimes called the double loin or double rack. The best saddles are cut from the loin. Ask the butcher to remove all excess fat and the long, flat flank sections. The saddle should then be rolled and tied so that it looks trim. Rub well with freshly ground pepper, a little salt, and a bit of rosemary. Place on a rack and roast in a 325° oven, allowing about 12 minutes per pound, until the internal temperature has reached 135°. Salt again just before removing from the oven. Let stand for 10 minutes in a warm place before carving.

Remove the strings which hold the roast together and with a sharp knife cut the meat in long, thinnish slices parallel to the spine. Run the point of the knife along the bone to loosen the slices. Repeat on the other side. Turn the roast over and remove the small filets on the underside. Slice them in rounds. Serve each person a long slice and one or two of the small slices from the filet, with some of the pan juices.

POTATOES ANNA
[TATIANA McKENNA]

    8 medium Idaho potatoes
    ½ pound butter, melted
       Salt, freshly ground black pepper

Peel and slice potatoes into even rounds. Put in salted ice water until ready to use. Generously butter two 8″ pie plates. Dry the potatoes thoroughly and arrange them in the pie plates in a circle with the rounds overlapping. Pour melted butter over each layer, salting lightly and peppering generously. Continue until dishes are full. Preheat oven to 400° and bake potatoes until crusty and brown. Invert on round platters and cut like a pie.

BROCCOLI WITH PROSCIUTTO
[STAR DUWYENIE]

    2 bunches broccoli
       Salt
    4 tablespoons butter
    2 tablespoons olive oil
    3 cloves garlic
    8 slices prosciutto, cut into thin strips
    1 cup fresh bread crumbs, optional

Cook broccoli in salted water until almost tender. Drain and set aside. Heat 3 tablespoons butter and olive oil and sauté the garlic until golden. Discard the garlic. Sauté prosciutto in garlic-flavored butter. Add broccoli and cook, covered, until tender, turning occasionally. Add more butter if necessary. Put broccoli and prosciutto on a heated platter. If desired, brown bread crumbs in remaining butter and sprinkle over broccoli.

STRAWBERRY SINGAPORE
[DIONE LUCAS]

2 packages strawberry gelatin
4 tablespoons plain gelatin
1 tablespoon lemon juice
2 cups whole strawberries
¾ cup long-grain rice
1 quart plus 1 cup milk
½ teaspoon salt
¾ cup sugar
2 teaspoons vanilla
1 cup heavy cream

Dissolve the strawberry gelatin as directed on the package and add 2 tablespoons plain gelatin and the lemon juice. Stir over ice until on the point of setting, then stir in the strawberries. Rinse a small shallow bombe mold with cold water, fill with the strawberry mixture and put to set in the refrigerator. Meanwhile, make the rice cream. Cook the rice, milk, salt and sugar over low heat until soft and creamy. Rub through a fine strainer and add the vanilla. Soften the remaining plain gelatin in ¼ cup water and stir into the hot rice until thoroughly dissolved. Stir over ice until mixture is lukewarm. Beat the heavy cream over ice until stiff and mix into the cooled rice. Fill a lightly oiled ring mold with the rice cream and chill until well set—at least 2 hours. Unmold on a cold, flat serving dish, unmold the strawberry mixture and put in the center of the ring. This dish may be made with other berries and fruits with appropriate gelatin flavor.

International Dinner for Six to Eight

A truly mixed-up meal this, for the soup comes from Jamaica, the gigot from Provence, the spinach pie from Greece, and the dessert from Switzerland, yet such is the fellowship of the cuisines of the world that the menu is a serendipitous balance of flavors and textures. The accompanying wine, while red, might be a Rioja from Spain, a Rhône from France, an Italian aged Chianti, or a California varietal.

MENU

Jamaican Cream of Pumpkin Soup
Gigot Provençal
Spanakopita
Swiss Apple Tart with Cream

The Wine

Marqués de Riscal or Côte Rôte or Chianti Riserva
or Cabernet Sauvignon

JAMAICAN CREAM OF PUMPKIN SOUP
[ELISABETH ORTIZ]

    2 tablespoons butter
    2 large onions, finely chopped
    2 pounds pumpkin, peeled and cut in chunks
    4 cups chicken stock
      Salt, freshly ground black pepper to taste
    1 cup light cream
      Dash hot pepper sauce

Heat the butter and sauté the onion until transparent. Put the onion, pumpkin and stock in a saucepan and simmer, covered, until pumpkin is tender. Cool slightly and put through a food mill or purée for a few seconds in the electric blender. Return to saucepan, season to taste with salt and pepper, and add the cream and hot pepper sauce. Reheat gently before serving.

GIGOT PROVENÇAL
[JAMES A. BEARD]

    1 leg of lamb, 5 to 6 pounds
   18 to 20 anchovy fillets
    4 cloves garlic, cut in thin slices
      Rosemary
      Salt, pepper

Make small incisions in the gigot with a sharp knife. Alternately insert anchovy filets and garlic slices. Rub the meat lightly with rosemary, salt and freshly ground pepper.

Roast on a rack in a shallow pan at 325°. For pink lamb, which is lamb at its best, allow 15 to 18 minutes per pound, or roast until the meat thermometer registers 135°.

SPANAKOPITA (SPINACH PIE)
[LOU SEIBERT PAPPAS]

> 2 bunches spinach
> 1 bunch Swiss chard
> 1 bunch parsley
> 1 bunch green onions
> 6 leaves fresh mint
> 1 tablespoon salt
> Freshly ground pepper
> 1½ teaspoons uncooked rice
> ⅔ cup olive oil
> 3 eggs, slightly beaten
> ½ pound feta cheese, crumbled
> ½ pound filo (approximately)
> Cinnamon

Wash the spinach, Swiss chard, parsley, green onions, and mint. Dry as thoroughly as possible and chop finely. Spread out on a towel and let stand at room temperature for several hours to dry completely. Put greens in a large mixing bowl with the salt, pepper to taste, rice, 2 table-spoons of the olive oil, beaten eggs, and crumbled cheese, and toss together.

Spread 6 sheets of filo with oil and line a 10″ by 14″ baking pan, one sheet on top of the other, letting filo come up the sides of the pan. Spread tossed mixture over the dough and sprinkle lightly with cin-namon. Trim off excess filo around pan edges. Spread 6 more sheets of filo with oil and place on top of the mixture. Cut through the top layers of filo (down to the filling), making 2½″ squares. Bake in a preheated 350° oven for 1 hour, or until greens are tender. Finish cutting into squares and serve hot or cool. Makes about 24 pieces.

SWISS APPLE TART WITH CREAM
[NIKA HAZELTON]

  1¼ cups flour
    2 egg yolks
       Sugar
       Grated rind of 1 lemon
   ½ cup butter, softened and cut into small pieces
   6 cups peeled, cored, and sliced apples (approximately)
   ½ teaspoon nutmeg
   ½ cup heavy cream
   ½ cup blanched almonds, slivered

Sift flour onto a baking board or into a large bowl. Make a well in the middle. Put 1 egg yolk, 1 tablespoon sugar, lemon rind and butter into well. Stir together with a fork. Work dough with floured hands until all ingredients have blended together and dough is smooth. Pat dough with fingers into bottom and sides of a 9″ pie plate. Crimp sides with a fork. Chill for at least 2 hours.

Place apples on top of chilled dough in slightly overlapping circles. Sprinkle with ½ cup sugar and nutmeg. Bake in a 350° oven for 15 minutes. Beat together the remaining egg yolk, cream, and almonds, and drip over fruit. Continue baking for 20 minutes, or until dough is golden brown, fruit tender. Serve warm.

Weekend Dinner for Four

For a special dinner party, duck with an apricot glaze is an interesting departure from the usual canard à l'orange or aux pêches, and the barley casserole an unexpected accompaniment. The tartness of asparagus vinaigrette makes a good gambit for the richness of the duck. A red Rhône or Loire wine would go well with the main course.

MENU

Asparagus Vinaigrette
Duck with Apricot Glaze
Barley-Mushroom Casserole
Leafy Endive Salad Vivian
Jamaican Baked Bananas

The Wine

Côte Rôtie or Chinon

ASPARAGUS VINAIGRETTE
[DIONE LUCAS]

    2 pounds asparagus
    1 teaspoon salt
    ½ teaspoon freshly cracked black and white pepper
    ½ teaspoon crushed garlic
    ¼ teaspoon sugar
    ½ teaspoon dry mustard
      Dash of Worcestershire sauce
      Dash of Tabasco sauce
    3 tablespoons tarragon vinegar
   10 tablespoons oil
    2 tablespoons thick cream
    1 finely chopped hard-cooked egg
    2 teaspoons freshly chopped parsley

Trim the asparagus neatly and scrape off the scales. Tie securely with string. Put in bottom of a double boiler, tips uppermost, and add boiling salted water halfway up stalks. Cover with inverted top of double boiler and cook for about 15 minutes (do not overcook). Drain well. Make the vinaigrette sauce by shaking the remaining ingredients in a screw-topped jar. Pour the vinaigrette sauce over the asparagus tips.

DUCK WITH APRICOT GLAZE

>   1 pound dried apricots
> 1½ cups dry sherry
>   Rind of 2 lemons, thinly sliced
>   Juice of 2 lemons
>   ⅓ cup apricot liqueur
>   ⅓ cup Curaçao liqueur
>   1 cup honey
>   2 5-pound ducks with giblets
>   Salt to taste
>   2 tablespoons flour

Cook the apricots according to the directions on the package, sub-stituting 1 cup sherry for the water. Place the lemon rind in a saucepan and cover with boiling water. Simmer 5 minutes. Drain well. Place 1 cup of the stewed apricots and lemon juice in a blender with the apricot liqueur, Curaçao, and honey. Blend well. Pour into a saucepan and use as a glaze for basting the ducks.

Place the remaining stewed apricots and the lemon rind in the cavities of the ducks. (Reserve the giblets.) Truss the ducks and place on a rack in a baking pan. Sprinkle with salt and brush with the apricot glaze. Roast in a 350° oven for about 1½ to 2 hours. Baste the ducks every 15 minutes with the glaze. Prick the birds with a fork several times during baking to allow fat to drain off.

Meanwhile cover the reserved giblets with cold water and simmer for 1 hour. When the ducks are nicely browned and tender (the legs should be easy to move), remove to a warm serving platter. Skim off the fat from the roasting pan. Place over medium heat and sprinkle in the flour. Add the remaining ½ cup sherry and scrape up all bits of brown from pan. Add the remaining apricot glaze and enough cooking liquid from the giblets to make a gravy. Strain the gravy into a sauce dish and serve with the ducks.

BARLEY-MUSHROOM CASSEROLE
[KAY SHAW NELSON]

    1 ounce dried mushrooms
    1 cup pearl barley, washed
      Salt, freshly ground pepper
    ½ teaspoon caraway seeds
    3 tablespoons butter
    2 cloves garlic, crushed
    2 tablespoons chopped fresh dill or parsley

Soak the mushrooms in lukewarm water to cover for 20 minutes. Drain; press water out. Chop.

Put the barley in 3 cups boiling water seasoned with ½ teaspoon salt and the caraway seeds. Cook, covered, until barley is tender and the liquid has been absorbed, about 40 minutes. Melt the butter in a skillet, add the garlic, ½ teaspoon salt, pepper to taste, and mushrooms, and sauté 4 minutes. Mix into barley. Spoon into a well-buttered shallow baking dish. Sprinkle dill or parsley over the top. Bake in a 350° oven for 20 minutes.

LEAFY ENDIVE SALAD VIVIAN
[ALEX D. HAWKES]

    1 large bunch leafy endive (if unavailable, substitute chicory or
      escarole)
    2 hard-cooked eggs, coarsely mashed
    2 teaspoons finely minced chives
    ¼ cup light olive oil
    ¼ cup salad oil
      Red wine vinegar to taste
    3 tablespoons coarsely chopped ripe olives
      Salt and freshly ground black pepper

Rinse the leafy endive thoroughly to remove all grit. Tear into bite-size pieces, pat dry, and chill wrapped in plastic or paper towel for an hour or so. Thoroughly combine remaining ingredients and chill slightly. Arrange endive leaves in salad bowl, pour over the well-blended dressing, toss gently but well.

107

JAMAICAN BAKED BANANAS
[ALEX D. HAWKES]

> 4 tablespoons canned or freshly grated coconut
> 4 firm ripe bananas
> 4 tablespoons butter
> ½ teaspoon ground allspice
> 3 tablespoons light or dark rum, preferably Jamaican

Lightly toast grated coconut on baking sheet in a 250° oven, stirring occasionally, until it is pale brown and just crispy to the taste. Peel bananas and place in shallow oven-proof serving dish or individual dishes. Preheat oven to 375°. Dot bananas with butter and sprinkle with allspice. Bake until nicely browned and fork-tender, about 8 to 10 minutes, basting frequently with butter. Pour rum over during last few minutes of baking, and baste frequently, until done. Serve sprinkled with hot toasted coconut.

Simple Spring Dinner for Eight

A relatively easy menu for a largish dinner party, for one of those evenings when you don't feel like spending all your time in the kitchen. The first course and dessert can be made ahead, and the main dish partly prepared beforehand and assembled at the last minute, while the noodle soufflé bakes. A white wine from the Loire or a lightly chilled red Beaujolais would be a pleasant choice to accompany the creamy capon.

MENU

Coupe Charleston
Breast of Capon with Artichoke Hearts and Mushrooms
Noodle Soufflé
Lettuce Hearts with French Dressing
Strawberry Sorbet

The Wine

Muscadet or Sancerre, or lightly chilled Fleurie or Julienas

COUPE CHARLESTON
[MARY MOON HEMINGWAY]

2 tablespoons blue cheese, crumbled
3-ounce package cream cheese
½ teaspoon grated onion
1 teaspoon Worcestershire sauce
1 teaspoon salt
Dash freshly ground black pepper
2 tablespoons lemon juice
2 cups tomato juice
2 egg whites, stiffly beaten

Cream together the cheeses. Add the onion, Worcestershire sauce, salt, pepper, and lemon juice. Mix in tomato juice, blending smoothly. Pour into a freezing tray and freeze until all but the center is firm. Remove, break up in a bowl, and beat with chilled beaters until smooth. Fold immediately into the egg whites. Freeze and serve in hollowed, drained, cold tomatoes.

BREAST OF CAPON WITH ARTICHOKE HEARTS AND MUSHROOMS
[MILTON WILLIAMS]

    1 quart water
    4 large capon breasts
    2 stalks celery
    1 small onion, quartered
      Salt, freshly ground white pepper
   16 large mushrooms
    2 tablespoons butter
    ¼ onion, grated
      Juice of 1 lemon
    ½ cup dry sherry
    2 teaspoons cornstarch
    1 cup heavy cream
      Seasoning salt
    1 teaspoon chicken stock base
    ⅛ teaspoon dill weed
    ⅛ teaspoon dry mustard
    2 14-ounce cans small artichoke hearts
      Chopped parsley, chives or paprika

Put the water, capon breasts, celery, onion, 2 teaspoons salt, and ½ teaspoon white pepper in a large saucepan and bring to a boil. Reduce heat, cover, and simmer for about 25 minutes, or until the capon is tender. Strain the broth, cool, and reserve. Skin and bone the breasts, and when cool, cut each into 8 slices.

Wash and slice the whole mushrooms. Sauté in the butter, and add the grated onion and lemon juice. Add 1½ cups of the strained broth and the sherry and simmer for 5 minutes. Mix the cornstarch and cream and stir into the simmering broth mixture. Continue stirring until it thickens to consistency of a thin gravy. Add seasoning salt and pepper to taste, chicken stock base, dill weed, and dry mustard. At this point the sauce may be set aside, the surface covered with buttered wax paper, and gently reheated just before serving time.

Drain the artichoke hearts. Just before serving, add the artichokes hearts and capon slices to the sauce just long enough to heat through. Garnish with chopped parsley, chives, or paprika.

NOODLE SOUFFLÉ
[MILTON WILLIAMS]

¼ pound unsalted butter
1 pint sour cream
Juice of 1 lemon
3-ounce package cream cheese
3 tablespoons sugar
4 eggs
1½ quarts water
1 teaspoon salt
8 ounces broad noodles
Butter

Beat butter, sour cream, lemon juice, cream cheese, sugar, and eggs in an electric mixer, starting at medium speed and then turning to high speed when the ingredients are well mixed.

Bring the water and salt to a boil and cook the noodles for 6 to 8 minutes. Drain and fold into the beaten mixture. Butter a 1½-quart soufflé dish and pour in the noodle mixture. Bake in a 350° oven for 1 hour, until golden-brown on top. Serve immediately.

STRAWBERRY SORBET
[JAMES A. BEARD]

3 pints fresh strawberries, hulled and cleaned
2 cups sugar
Juice of 3 oranges
Juice of 3 lemons
⅓ cup Grand Marnier liqueur

Combine the strawberries with the sugar and orange and lemon juices in the blender and blend until smooth. Add the Grand Marnier and pour into two freezer trays. Freeze until the mixture is partially frozen. Transfer to a large bowl and beat until mushy. Return to trays and freeze until firm.

Dinner by the Pool for Six or Eight

In a summer mood, this elegant dinner stresses the delights of seafood—
a creamy chilled clam bisque and poached salmon with mayonnaise
flavored and colored by spinach and fresh herbs from the garden or
market. As a whole salmon will easily serve 18 to 20 guests, if you want
to enlarge the party all you have to do is double or triple the other recipes. Leftover salmon is no problem. It can always be served cold for
lunch next day, turned into an ethereal soufflé or mousse, or potted
(mashed with melted butter and grated nutmeg) as a sandwich filling.
An excellent Moselle would be the thing to serve with both soup and
fish.

MENU
[JAMES A. BEARD]

Cold Clam Bisque

Water Biscuits

Cooled Salmon with Green Mayonnaise

Tiny New Potatoes Tossed with Butter, Parsley and Mint

Tomatoes Stuffed with Smothered Cucumbers

Finger Sandwiches of Thin, Buttered Brown Bread

Homemade Peach Ice Cream with Peaches in Bourbon

The Wine

A Moselle—Wehlener Sonnenuhr or Bernkasteler Doctor

COLD CLAM BISQUE

½ cup rice
4 cups clam broth
1 pint cherrystone or razor clams

3 tablespoons butter
Salt, pepper
1½ cups heavy cream
Finely chopped parsley and chives

Cook the rice in the clam broth for 45 to 50 minutes, or until it is very soft. Whirl in a blender or put through a fine sieve. Purée clams in blender, or chop very fine. Combine rice-broth mixture, clams, and butter. Heat to boiling, reduce heat, and simmer for 5 minutes. Season to taste with salt and pepper. Cool. Combine with heavy cream and chill thoroughly. Serve in cups set in a bed of crushed ice. Sprinkle soup with chopped parsley and chives and serve with water biscuits.

COOLED SALMON WITH GREEN MAYONNAISE

1 pint white wine
1 onion stuck with 2 cloves
1 teaspoon thyme
12 peppercorns
1 tablespoon or more salt
Whole salmon weighing 9 to 10 pounds
1 lemon, cut into thin slices
Several sprigs parsley

Combine the wine, 3 cups water, onion, thyme, peppercorns, and salt in a fish cooker or deep pan large enough to accommodate the salmon. Bring to a boil and simmer for 20 minutes. Measure the cleaned salmon at the thickest point, and place on a triple-layered piece of cheesecloth, leaving ends long enough to use as handles in lifting the fish. Lower the fish into the liquid. It should be completely covered.

Bring to a boil, reduce the heat, and simmer. Allow 10 minutes per inch of measured thickness. Remove the fish and allow to cool. Just before serving, arrange on a platter or plank and remove the skin. Arrange lemon slices down the middle of the fish, and garnish with lemon wedges or rounds and parsley. The fish should be barely cold when eaten. Allow about ½ pound salmon per serving. Serve with Green Mayonnaise (see below).

GREEN MAYONNAISE

> 1 cup chopped cooked spinach, well drained
> 1 tablespoon each chopped parsley, tarragon, chives
> 2 cups mayonnaise
> 1 teaspoon Dijon mustard
> Salt to taste

Wash spinach well and cook until just wilted. Do not overcook. Chop very fine and combine with the chopped herbs. Fold into the mayonnaise with the mustard. Let stand for 2 hours and taste for salt. Makes about 3 cups.

NEW POTATOES

Leave skins on tiny new potatoes, or peel a thin band of skin from around them lengthwise. Boil, drain, and toss with plenty of butter, finely chopped parsley, and fresh chopped mint.

TOMATOES STUFFED WITH SMOTHERED CUCUMBERS

> 6 to 8 large ripe tomatoes
> Salt
> 4 medium-size cucumbers
> 4 tablespoons mayonnaise
> 3 tablespoons yoghurt
> 1½ teaspoons finely chopped dill or 1 teaspoon dill weed
> Finely chopped parsley and fresh dill

Slice off the tops of the tomatoes and scoop out the seeds and most of the flesh. Salt insides and invert on a rack or on paper towels to drain. Chill while preparing the cucumbers.

Peel and seed the cucumbers, cut into long, thin strips, and salt well. Refrigerate for 1 hour. Drain thoroughly and run water over them; drain again. Combine with the mayonnaise, yoghurt, and dill, and blend thoroughly. Allow to mellow for 2 hours. Just before serving, fill tomatoes with the chilled cucumber mixture, and top with the chopped parsley and dill. Serve with the salmon.

THIN BROWN BREAD SANDWICHES

Spread very thin slices of rye or whole wheat bread with sweet butter, remove crusts, and cut into fingers.

HOMEMADE PEACH ICE CREAM

    1 quart cream
    1 cup milk
    1 cup sugar
    1 tablespoon vanilla extract
    2 cups finely crushed fresh peaches
    ¼ teaspoon salt

Combine all ingredients in a large bowl and blend well. Taste for flavor. Transfer to an ice cream freezer. Pack freezer with ice and coarse salt, using about 6 parts ice to 1 part salt, and turn until mixture is frozen. Remove dasher from container, and pack container in additional ice and salt. If you do not have an ice cream freezer, buy a good brand of peach ice cream.

PEACHES IN BOURBON

For each serving, slice 1 large peach, and sprinkle with 2 teaspoons sugar and 1 tablespoon bourbon. Spoon over the ice cream. Top with whipped cream for greater embellishment.

Summer Dinner in the City for Six

Those who by choice or necessity spend summer in the city need not forgo the pleasures of outdoor dining. You can give this informal picnic-style dinner on the terrace, or move it into the park (where you might be going for a concert or play). For a movable feast, dry ice or an insulated picnic bag with canned refrigerant will keep the sherbet at serving temperature—it should not be frozen solid, but a little on the soft side. Wine also may be kept chilled in an insulated bag or a styrofoam ice chest.

The pâté may be made a day or so in advance, but the game hens should be roasted near the time of the party, so they will be barely cooled when eaten.

Champagne or a Kir (a drop or two of crème de cassis in a glass of champagne or white wine) would be a perfect aperitif, and the wine might be an Italian or California white.

MENU
[JAMES A. BEARD]

Pâté of Vitello Tonnato

Hot Toast or Melba Toast and Butter

Roast Rock Cornish Game Hens with Tarragon

Potato and Hearts of Palm Salad

Chilled Cherry Tomatoes

French Bread

Orange Sherbet

The Wine

Chilled Verdicchio or California Chenin Blanc

PÂTÉ OF VITELLO TONNATO

 2½ pounds veal from leg or shoulder
  3 cloves garlic, crushed
  1 veal knuckle bone
  1 onion, stuck with 2 cloves
   Salt, freshly ground pepper to taste
   Dried or fresh basil
   7-ounce can tuna in oil, finely shredded
  1 tablespoon chopped parsley
   Capers
  1 envelope unflavored gelatin
  1 can beef bouillon, undiluted
   Anchovy filets

Make small incisions in the veal and insert the garlic. Place in a deep saucepan with the bone, onion, salt, and pepper, 1 teaspoon dried basil or a sprig of fresh basil, and enough water to come halfway up the meat. Boil for 5 minutes, skimming off any scum that rises to the surface. Reduce heat and cover. Simmer until the veal is tender and cooked through—it should not be falling to pieces. Remove veal and cook stock down by half. When the veal is partially cooled, remove all fat and put the meat through a meat grinder, using the finest blade. Combine with the tuna, 1 teaspoon dried basil or 1 tablespoon chopped fresh basil, the parsley, and 1 tablespoon capers. Blend well, moistening with a small amount of reduced, strained stock. Spoon mixture into a terrine or casserole. Cool and chill. Dissolve gelatin in ¼ cup cold water. Heat the bouillon to boiling, mix with the dissolved gelatin, and stir until blended. Cool until thick and syrupy, then spoon a thinnish layer of this aspic over the pâté. Decorate top with anchovy filets and capers. Serve with hot toast and butter.

ROAST ROCK CORNISH GAME HENS WITH TARRAGON

    6 Rock Cornish game hens
    1 lemon, cut in half
      Fresh tarragon
    ½ pound butter
      Salt, pepper to taste

Rub the interior of the birds with the cut lemon and fill with sprigs of fresh tarragon. Chop enough tarragon leaves to make ¼ cup. Add to ¼ pound of the butter, softened, blend well, and rub the birds with this mixture. Season with salt and pepper. Melt the remaining butter for basting. Place the birds on their sides on a rack in a roasting pan and roast for 15 minutes at 350°. Turn on other side, baste well with pan juices and melted butter, and roast for another 15 minutes. Test for doneness. Turn birds on their backs and roast until tender, about another 10 minutes. They should not be overcooked. Allow birds to cool a little before serving, in case your guests prefer to eat the birds with their fingers rather than a knife and fork.

NOTE: For a darker skin, heat 5 tablespoons butter and 3 tablespoons oil in a heavy skillet, and brown birds on all sides. Transfer to rack and roast as above, basting often.

POTATO AND HEARTS OF PALM SALAD

    24 (approximately) tiny new potatoes in their jackets, well scrubbed
       Olive oil
       Wine vinegar
       Salt, pepper to taste
     2 1-pound cans hearts of palm
    ¼ cup chopped parsley
    ¼ cup finely cut scallions or more, to taste
       Salad greens
       Hard-cooked eggs, sliced

Boil the potatoes in salted water until just pierceable. Cool slightly. Peel, slice thickly into a bowl, and add a little oil and vinegar. Salt and pepper to taste. Allow potatoes to cool in this marinade; they will probably absorb most of it. Cut the hearts of palm into ½″ slices, using 1 good-size stalk for each service. Combine 8 tablespoons olive oil, 3 to 4 tablespoons wine vinegar, 1 teaspoon salt (or more, to taste), 1 teaspoon freshly ground pepper, the parsley and scallions to make a sauce. When the potatoes are almost cool, combine with the hearts of palm and the scallion sauce. Toss lightly and allow to mellow for 2 to 3 hours before serving. Serve on fresh salad greens, and decorate with sliced eggs and additional cut scallions. For a park picnic, pack the salad in a covered plastic bowl and put into an insulated bag.

ORANGE SHERBET

This should be served softly frozen, not hard. Freezing will take about 20 minutes in an ice cream freezer and 2 to 3 hours if you use ice trays in the refrigerator freezing compartment.

     1 cup sugar
    ½ cup lemon juice
     4 cups frozen orange juice, thawed but undiluted
    ½ cup bitter orange marmalade
    ½ cup Grand Marnier liqueur

Cook 1 cup water and the sugar together until they come to a boil. Add the lemon juice and combine with the thawed orange juice. Fold in the marmalade and the Grand Marnier and freeze in an ice cream freezer or in ice trays.

If you are using ice trays, remove the sherbet when barely frozen, beat well with a fork and return to the freezing compartment. Repeating this process will improve the sherbet, or you may prefer to incorporate 2 to 3 tablespoons of heavy cream to give it a smoother texture.

A Hearty Country Dinner for Six

This is a good menu for a weekend dinner, after the day has been spent outdoors at a football game or just walking in the crisp fall air.

Country hams may be ordered by mail from farms and smokehouses in various parts of the country, such as New York State, New England, Pennsylvania, the South and the Middle West, and some of the better meat and specialty food stores carry them. These hams are usually heavily smoked and have a rich, old-fashioned flavor, and they come with cooking instructions. They may or may not need to be boiled before being baked.

A whole ham will, of course, feed many more than six, but there should never be any problem using up leftovers in sandwiches, as a cold meat for luncheon, or in all kinds of dishes from a ham and bean casserole to jambon persillé. A fruity white wine is best with ham, preferably an Alsatian or Rhine wine or a similar American wine—this could also be drunk with the first course of clams Rockefeller, unless you prefer to serve them as an appetizer with cocktails.

MENU

Clams Rockefeller
Baked Country Ham, Sauce à la Crème
Squash Soufflé   Braised Leeks
Salad of Endive and Grated Beets with a Mustardy French Dressing
Apple and Orange Tart

The Wine

Alsatian Riesling or Sylvaner; a German wine
from the Rheingau—Schloss Johannisberger or Schloss Vollrads;
an American Johannisberg Riesling

CLAMS ROCKEFELLER
[ELIZABETH BURTON]

½ cup very finely minced onions
3 tablespoons butter
2 cups very finely puréed cooked spinach
1 large garlic clove, crushed
½ cup finely crumbled cooked bacon
1 tablespoon lemon juice
  Salt, black pepper, cayenne pepper
1 to 2 tablespoons dry sherry or white wine
36 raw clams on the half shell
1 cup fresh white bread crumbs
½ cup melted butter

Cook the onions in the butter until tender and translucent but not browned. Scrape into a mixing bowl. Beat in the spinach, garlic, and bacon. Add lemon juice, salt and pepper to taste, and wine. Be sparing with the salt, as the clams are salty to begin with. The mixture should hold its shape softly in a spoon. If it is too liquid, beat in a tablespoon or two of the bread crumbs. Spread mixture over the clams on the half shell and sprinkle with bread crumbs and melted butter.

At serving time, arrange on a broiler pan with the surface of the bread crumbs about 4 inches from the broiler and leave for several minutes, or until clams are bubbling and crumbs lightly browned. Serve at once.

BAKED COUNTRY HAM, SAUCE À LA CRÈME
[JAMES A. BEARD]

Whole ham, 10 to 12 pounds
1 pint white wine
Granulated sugar

Select a good country ham and read the directions for preparing it. If it does not need boiling first, remove the skin with a sharp knife and place ham in a large roasting pan. Add the white wine, cover the pan and bake in a 350° oven for 2½ to 3 hours. If the ham must be soaked and boiled first, bake for only 1½ hours.

Take the ham from the oven and rub or sprinkle the fat well with granulated sugar. Raise the oven temperature to 450° and return the ham to the oven, uncovered, for 5 to 6 minutes, or until nicely glazed.

SAUCE À LA CRÈME

½ cup wine vinegar
6 to 8 whole shallots, finely chopped
2 tablespoons chopped fresh tarragon or 1½ teaspoons dried tarragon
½ cup broth or consommé
3 tablespoons ham broth
¾ cup heavy cream
3 egg yolks
2 tablespoons butter
½ teaspoon salt
½ teaspoon freshly ground black pepper
Chopped parsley

Put the vinegar, shallots, and tarragon in a pan and cook rapidly until reduced to one half volume. Transfer to a double boiler and add the broth, ham broth, and cream. Heat through over hot water. Beat the egg yolks and add a little of the hot liquid to them. Stir this mixture into the sauce and continue stirring and cooking over hot water until the sauce is thickened. Do not let it boil or it will curdle. Add the butter and seasonings and blend well. Fold in a little chopped parsley and serve with the baked ham.

SQUASH SOUFFLÉ
[NIKA HAZELTON]

 2 pounds winter squash, any type
 1 teaspoon salt
 ¼ teaspoon pepper
 ⅛ teaspoon ground thyme
 2 tablespoons butter, melted
 2 tablespoons heavy cream
 4 tablespoons grated Swiss cheese
 3 eggs, separated

Peel, seed, and cook the winter squash and mash or purée in a blender. Mix the squash with the salt, pepper, thyme, butter, cream, and cheese. Beat the egg yolks and blend them into the squash mixture. Beat the egg whites until stiff and fold them into the squash. Pour into a buttered 2-quart soufflé dish. Bake in a preheated 375° oven for about 20 to 30 minutes, or until the soufflé is set and golden on top.

BRAISED LEEKS
[JAMES A. BEARD]

For six servings, allow 12 to 18 leeks, according to size. Trim off the root end and all but an inch of the green tops and wash very well under running water, pulling the leaves apart to remove dirt and sand. Dry well on paper towels.

Heat 1 tablespoon butter and 3 tablespoons oil in a heavy skillet, add the leeks and brown lightly on all sides, sprinkle with salt and freshly ground black pepper to taste, and add ½ cup chicken stock and 2 table-spoons brandy. Cover, reduce heat, and simmer gently until just tender, but not soft and mushy. Add a squeeze of lemon juice and sprinkle with chopped parsley.

APPLE AND ORANGE TART
[MRS. JOHN SHERMAN COOPER]

  Butter
2 pounds cooking apples, peeled, cored, and sliced
2 oranges
2 to 3 tablespoons sugar
½ cup apricot glaze (see page 222)
  9″ pastry shell, prebaked in the flan ring (see page 424).

Butter a large casserole, add the apples, cover and cook over low heat without any liquid, stirring occasionally, until the apples are tender. Put through a sieve and return to the casserole with the grated rind of the oranges and 2 to 3 tablespoons sugar—taste first, since the amount of sugar needed depends on the tartness of the apples. Cook until thick and well blended. Cool. Pour into the pastry shell. Cut away all the white pith from the oranges and cut into thin crosswise slices. Arrange in an overlapping pattern on top of the apple purée. Brush the orange slices with warm apricot glaze.

Fall Dinner for Six

If you can get quail for this elegant party dinner, by all means do so, otherwise use the more easily obtainable squabs. The entrée and the quick-cooking vegetable are the only courses that take your last-minute attention. The celeriac remoulade should be made the day before, and the dessert is served cool (but not chilled).

  The delicacy of the little birds calls for a white wine—a fine Burgundy, Rhine or Moselle.

MENU

Celeriac Remoulade

Squab in Potato Nests

Braised Belgian Endive with Lemon Sauce

Poached Stuffed Pears, Sauce Anglaise

The Wine

A white Burgundy—Meursault or Montrachet;
a Steinberger or Scharzhofberger

CELERIAC REMOULADE
[ALEX D. HAWKES]

    2 small celeriac
    2 tablespoons lemon juice
    2 teaspoons salt
    4 tablespoons Dijon prepared mustard
    3 tablespoons boiling water
    ⅓ cup light olive oil
    2 to 3 tablespoons white wine vinegar
      Salt and freshly ground white pepper
    3 tablespoons minced fresh parsley
    2 teaspoons minced fresh chives

Peel celeriac and cut into tiny, even julienne strips about 2" long and ⅛" thick. Place in a bowl with lemon juice and salt, mix well, and allow to marinate at room temperature for 1 hour. To prepare dressing, place mustard in a large, warmed bowl, then add the boiling water a few drops at a time, whipping constantly with wire whisk or electric mixer set at medium speed. Continue to whip, adding the oil, a drop or two at a time. The dressing should be rather thick. Whip in the vinegar to taste, a drop or two at a time. Season to taste with salt and pepper. Gently mix in the marinated celeriac sticks, cover, and leave in refrigerator overnight. Turn into serving dish, sprinkle with the parsley and chives, and serve.

SQUAB IN POTATO NESTS
[JAMES A. BEARD]

    6 squab (quail may also be used)
  18 to 24 crushed juniper berries
    6 small sprigs thyme
    6 small sprigs parsley
     Salt, freshly ground black pepper
    6 slices prosciutto
    6 slices barding pork
  ½ cup armagnac
     Watercress or parsley
For the Nests:
    8 Idaho potatoes
  ¼ pound butter
    3 egg yolks
    1 teaspoon salt
    1 teaspoon freshly ground black pepper
  ¼ teaspoon nutmeg

Purchase the squab with their heads and legs intact. With the aid of small skewers or toothpicks and twine, secure the heads so that they will stay upright during the cooking process and for serving. Stuff each squab with 3 or 4 juniper berries, a sprig of thyme, a sprig of parsley, a pinch of salt and a few grains of freshly ground black pepper. Wrap each squab in prosciutto and then in barding pork and tie securely. Let them rest while you prepare the nests.

Peel and quarter the potatoes and cook in salted water until soft. Mash and combine with half the butter, the egg yolks, salt, pepper, and nutmeg. Whip well. Fill a pastry bag fitted with a large rosette tube and on a well-buttered baking sheet make 6 round nests about 5″ in diameter to hold the cooked squab. Brush well with the remainder of the butter, melted, and bake about 25 minutes in a preheated 375° oven until nicely browned.

Place squab on the bottom rack in the oven with the potato nests on the top rack. Roast for 15 to 20 minutes. Remove the nests and arrange on a preheated platter. Flame the squab with armagnac, and place them carefully on the nests so that the heads, tails, and feet extend. Spoon the pan juices over all and garnish with watercress.

NOTE: If using quail, sauté quickly on all sides in 6 tablespoons butter in a large skillet until nicely browned. Flame with armagnac before cooking in oven for 10 to 15 minutes.

BRAISED BELGIAN ENDIVE WITH LEMON SAUCE
[NIKA HAZELTON]

¼ cup butter
6 large heads Belgian endive, cut in half lengthwise
Salt, pepper to taste
Juice of 2 large lemons
1 cup hot chicken bouillon
2 eggs

Melt the butter in a large deep skillet. Arrange endive halves side by side in hot butter. Season with salt and pepper and add the juice of 1 lemon. Cook the endive over medium heat for 2 minutes on each side, or until lightly browned, turning halves carefully in order not to break them. Gradually add the hot chicken bouillon.

Reduce heat. Simmer endive, uncovered, for about 10 to 15 minutes, or until just tender. Beat the eggs with the remaining lemon juice and stir in the skillet juices. Pour this sauce over the endive. Serve immediately.

POACHED STUFFED PEARS, SAUCE ANGLAISE
[JAMES A. BEARD]

6 firm pears
½ cup finely chopped walnuts
½ cup chopped raisins
⅓ cup honey
2 cups sugar
1 cup water
Vanilla bean
A few chopped pistachio nuts
Candied violets

Core the pears from the bottom, leaving the stem in, and then peel. Make a paste of the walnuts, raisins, and honey, and stuff the pears with it. Seal stuffing in pear with small piece of foil.

126

Make a syrup in a large skillet with the sugar, water, and about 1 inch of vanilla bean, and poach the pears in it until just tender. Cool and serve with Sauce Anglaise flavored with Grand Marnier or cognac (see below). Decorate with the chopped pistachio nuts and candied violets.

SAUCE ANGLAISE

    1 cup milk
    1 cup heavy cream
    6 egg yolks
    ½ cup sugar
    ¼ cup Grand Marnier liqueur or cognac

Heat the milk and cream to the boiling point. Lightly beat the egg yolks and sugar together over hot water in the top of a double boiler. Gradually add the hot liquid, stirring vigorously. Stir constantly until the custard coats a wooden spoon or spatula. Do not allow the water to boil and do not overcook or the egg yolks will curdle. Meanwhile, heat the liqueur or cognac to boiling point in a small pan to volatilize the alcohol.

When the custard mixture just coats the spoon, stir in the Grand Marnier or cognac and cook gently a minute or two, then pour sauce into a bowl and stir until it cools.

Fall Regional Dinner for Six

This dinner of traditional American foods would be a good choice if you are entertaining visitors from overseas who are curious about American regional cooking, or for a small Thanksgiving dinner, if you crave a change from the usual turkey and cranberry sauce. Choose American champagne for this, or a domestic German-style white wine.

MENU

New England Baked Oyster Soup

Roast Loin of Pork Flambéed with Applejack,
with Horseradish Applesauce

Dried Corn Pudding

Salad of Young Spinach, Pennsylvania Dutch Dressing

Rich Pumpkin Pie with Cheddar Cheese or Whipped Cream

The Wine

New York State or California brut champagne
or Johannisberg Riesling

NEW ENGLAND BAKED OYSTER SOUP
[IRIS BROOKS]

> 6 cups half-and-half, or 3 cups milk and 3 cups light cream, com-
> bined
> 2 tablespoons butter
> 1 large rib celery, diced
> 12 salted soda crackers, lightly crushed
> Salt, cayenne pepper to taste
> Generous pinch curry powder (optional)
> 2½ to 3 dozen large oysters, shucked (reserve liquor)
> Sweet paprika

Preheat oven to 350°. Put the half-and-half in a large saucepan and heat it to just under boiling point. Reduce heat to a simmer and add the butter, celery, crushed crackers, and seasonings. Drop in the oysters, and add their liquor, strained through a triple fold of cheesecloth. When liquid is just under the boiling point, pour soup into an oven-proof tureen or large casserole. Put in oven and bake until top is brown, then stir under. Repeat the process 3 times, until the soup is golden brown. When stirring for the last time, add a light dusting of paprika. Serve directly from the tureen.

ROAST LOIN OF PORK FLAMBÉED WITH APPLEJACK
[JAMES A. BEARD]

> 1 loin of pòrk, loin or rib end, about 5 pounds, with chine bones
> cracked
> Salt, pepper, nutmeg
> ¼ cup applejack

Rub the loin well with salt, pepper, and nutmeg. Place on a rack in a roasting pan and roast in a 325° oven, allowing 25 minutes per pound, or until the internal temperature reaches 165° to 170° on a meat thermometer. Remove from the oven and flambé with the warmed applejack. Remove to a hot platter and allow to stand for 10 minutes before carving.

HORSERADISH APPLESAUCE
[JAMES A. BEARD]

To 1½ cups applesauce add 2 tablespoons freshly grated horseradish, or to taste, and a little grated nutmeg. Chill before serving.

DRIED CORN PUDDING
[JOSÉ WILSON]

> 1½ cups dried corn (available packaged)
> 3 cups boiling water
> 2 teaspoons sugar
> 1 teaspoon salt
> 4 tablespoons melted butter
> ½ cup light cream
> Buttered bread crumbs

Soak the dried corn in the water for 1 hour. Put in a saucepan and stir in the sugar, salt, and butter. Cook, uncovered, over very low heat, stirring now and then to prevent scorching, for about 30 minutes, or until corn has absorbed most of the liquid. Stir in the cream, pour into a baking dish, and cover the top with buttered crumbs (fine fresh bread crumbs mixed with melted butter) and bake at 350° until the crumbs are lightly browned, about 15 minutes.

SALAD OF YOUNG SPINACH, PENNSYLVANIA DUTCH DRESSING
[JOSÉ WILSON]

Either young and tender spinach leaves or the dandelion greens found in Italian markets at certain times of year can be used, as both have a sharp and bitter tang that contrasts well with the sweet-and-sour dressing.

> 6 slices lean bacon, cut into small pieces
> 3 tablespoons cider vinegar
> 2 tablespoons sour cream
> 1 egg yolk
> 1 tablespoon water
> 1 teaspoon flour
> 1 tablespoon sugar (or less, to taste)
>   Salt, freshly ground black pepper
>   Young spinach leaves or dandelion greens

Fry bacon until crisp. Remove and drain on paper towels. Pour off all but 2 tablespoons bacon fat. Mix in vinegar, sour cream. Combine egg yolk, water and flour, stirring until smooth, and add to pan. Cook over very low heat, stirring constantly, until thickened. Remove from heat and stir in sugar, salt and pepper to taste. Pour dressing over greens, scatter bacon on top and toss.

RICH PUMPKIN PIE
[JAMES A. BEARD]

> 1 recipe pâte sucrée (see page 425)
> 2 cups cooked puréed pumpkin or canned pumpkin
> 1 cup brown sugar
> 6 eggs, lightly beaten
> 2 cups cream
> ½ teaspoon salt
> 1 teaspoon cinnamon
> ½ teaspoon ground cloves
> ½ teaspoon mace
> ⅓ cup cognac
> 4 tablespoons finely chopped candied ginger

Line a 9″ pie tin with the pastry, place foil on the top, weight down with beans or rice, and bake in a 400° oven for 10 minutes. Remove beans or rice and foil.

Combine the pumpkin, sugar, eggs, cream, salt, spices and cognac and blend well. Pour into the pie shell and sprinkle with the candied ginger. Bake in a 375° oven for 30 to 35 minutes, or until set. Serve slightly warm with thin slices of Cheddar cheese or with whipped cream.

Seafood Dinner for Six

For those who love seafood, a dinner that breaks the rules by serving mussels as a first course, fish as the main course, is a pleasantly pardonable crime. Two white wines might be served, a young Loire white with the mussels, a fine white Burgundy with the rich sole.

MENU

Mussels au Gratin

Souffléed Filets with Potatoes Duchesse, Hollandaise Sauce

Steamed Cucumbers

Ginger Mousse

The Wines

A young Muscadet or Pouilly Fumé; a Meursault-Perrières

MUSSELS AU GRATIN
[JAMES A. BEARD]

    ½ pound butter
    4 cloves garlic, finely chopped
    6 shallots, finely chopped
    1 teaspoon basil
    6 tablespoons chopped parsley
      Salt, pepper
    48 mussels
    1 onion stuck with 2 cloves
      White wine (about 1 cup)
      Bread crumbs

Blend the butter and seasonings together and let stand 1 hour. Scrub and beard the mussels. Place them in a heavy skillet or pot with the onion and enough white wine to cover the bottom of the pot well. Cover and steam over a medium flame until the mussels open. When cool enough to handle, remove one half shell from each mussel. Spoon butter mixture on mussels and sprinkle with crumbs. Bake at 425°, just long enough to heat through. Serve on hot plates.

SOUFFLÉED FILETS WITH POTATOES DUCHESSE
[PHILIP S. BROWN]

    6 filets of sole or other white fish
    1 small onion or several shallots, finely chopped
    1 teaspoon salt
    1 tablespoon chopped parsley
    1½ cups or more dry white wine
    3 tablespoons butter
    3 tablespoons flour
    3 egg yolks
      Potatoes Duchesse (see recipe below)
    6 egg whites
    ½ cup freshly grated Parmesan cheese
      Hollandaise sauce (see page 420)

Place the filets, the onion or shallots, salt, and parsley in a shallow pan together with enough wine to barely cover. Poach very gently until just cooked through. Do not overcook. Transfer to a hot platter.

Reduce the poaching liquid to ¾ cup. In a saucepan blend the butter and flour over low heat, and simmer for 2 minutes. Stir in the hot liquid. Beat the egg yolks and add a little of the hot sauce to them. Then add to balance of sauce in pan and cook over low heat, stirring until the mixture thickens. Do not allow to boil. Correct the seasoning. Cool slightly.

Meanwhile make a border of the Potatoes Duchesse around a well-buttered oval baking dish, using a pastry bag and rosette tube. Lay the filets on the dish. Decorate with a few rosettes of potato if you like, and brush the filets with melted butter.

Beat the egg whites till stiff but not dry, and fold lightly into the sauce mixture. Heap over the filets and sprinkle with grated Parmesan cheese. Place in a 400° oven. Bake until puffy and brown. This should take about 20 minutes. Serve with Hollandaise sauce.

POTATOES DUCHESSE

    3 cups mashed potatoes
    4 tablespoons cream
    3 egg yolks
    1½ teaspoons salt
    ½ teaspoon freshly ground black pepper

The Potatoes Duchesse may be made ahead of time. Combine freshly mashed potatoes with the cream, egg yolks, and seasonings, and whip.

STEAMED CUCUMBERS

    6 firm cucumbers
    2 tablespoons melted butter
    1 tablespoon finely chopped parsley

Peel cucumbers and remove seeds. Cut into ½″ slices. Cook in a small amount of boiling salted water until just translucent and barely tender. Put in a strainer over hot water to drain and keep warm until ready to serve. Toss with melted butter and parsley.

GINGER MOUSSE
[ELISABETH ORTIZ]

> 4 eggs, separated
> 5 tablespoons sugar
> 1 envelope (1 tablespoon) unflavored gelatin
> 2 cups evaporated milk
> Pinch salt
> ½ cup light rum
> ½ cup preserved ginger, finely chopped

Beat the egg yolks with 4 tablespoons of the sugar. Soak the gelatin in ¼ cup water. Heat the milk almost to boiling point, stir in the softened gelatin until it is dissolved. Add the egg yolk–sugar mixture and stir over very low heat until the mixture coats the spoon. Remove from heat. Beat the egg whites with a pinch of salt and remaining tablespoon of sugar until they stand in peaks. Add the rum and preserved ginger to the cooled custard, mixing well. Fold in the egg whites, pour into a soufflé dish or mold, and refrigerate until set.

Hunter's Dinner for Six

Even if you don't have a hunting husband or family friend to keep your freezer stocked with game, the better meat markets can easily obtain venison for you, and it makes an interesting change from the usual roast beef. The gamey flavor of the venison and the richness of the Kentucky sauce merit a big red Burgundy, but if you don't want to rise to such heights, a full-bodied Rhône red of a good year would be perfectly acceptable.

MENU

Spinach Soup with Shrimp

Roast Saddle of Venison, Kentucky Sauce

Purée of Chestnuts

Brussels Sprouts

Watercress with Tart French Dressing

Prune Soufflé

The Wine

*Red Burgundy, such as Vosne-Romanée or Clos de Vougeot,
or Hermitage or Châteauneuf-du-Pape*

SPINACH SOUP WITH SHRIMP
[MRS. GEORGE Y. WHEELER II]

    2 tablespoons butter
    1 tablespoon grated onion
    3 tablespoons flour
    2 cups light cream
    3 cups cooked spinach
    1 cup condensed beef bouillon
      Salt, pepper
    ⅓ cup coarsely chopped cooked shrimps
    ½ cup sherry
    1½ cups chopped toasted almonds

Melt the butter in a heavy-bottomed, 2½-quart saucepan. Stir in the onion, then the flour. Cook slowly for 2 minutes without browning. Bring cream to a simmer in another pan. Remove onion mixture from heat and beat in the cream, blending thoroughly. Purée the spinach with the bouillon in an electric blender and add to the saucepan. Simmer slowly, stirring, for 10 minutes. Season to taste. Thin out, if necessary, with more cream or bouillon. Keep over simmering water, stirring occasionally, until 5 minutes before serving time. Then stir in the shrimps and sherry; simmer a moment or two, tasting, to evaporate the alcohol from the sherry. Serve in soup plates, and sprinkle the almonds on top.

ROAST SADDLE OF VENISON, KENTUCKY SAUCE
[VICE ADMIRAL WILLIAM J. MARSHALL]

> ½ cup Hoisin Sauce (available at Oriental food specialty shops)
> ½ cup honey
> ½ cup tomato purée
> ½ cup bourbon whiskey
> 1 small clove garlic, crushed
> ½ tablespoon minced fresh ginger root, or ¼ teaspoon powdered ginger
> 1 tablespoon soy sauce
> 6 to 8 pounds saddle of venison, preferably from a young buck
> Thin slices of salt pork
> Kentucky Sauce (see recipe below)

Mix together the first 7 ingredients. Pour over the venison and marinate for 48 hours, turning the meat occasionally. Remove the venison from the marinade and place it in a shallow roasting pan. Cover the top with salt pork, and insert a meat thermometer in a fleshy part of the meat, making sure it does not rest on a bone. Roast in a preheated 325° oven, basting frequently with the marinade, until the thermometer registers 125° for rare. (If the animal is older, adjust cooking time accordingly.) Discard the pork and serve with a sauceboat of Kentucky Sauce (see below) passed separately.

KENTUCKY SAUCE

> ½ cup dry red wine
> 1 tablespoon bourbon whiskey
> 1 teaspoon Worcestershire sauce
> ½ cup tart black-currant jelly
> ⅛ teaspoon salt
> 1 teaspoon flour
> ½ cup sour cream

Combine wine, whiskey, Worcestershire sauce, jelly and salt in a saucepan. Heat, stirring constantly, until the jelly melts. Blend flour with sour cream, add to the sauce and cook, stirring constantly, until thickened.

PURÉE OF CHESTNUTS
[MRS. ARCHIBALD B. ROOSEVELT, JR.]

   2 pounds fresh chestnuts, or 1 pound whole canned chestnuts
   2 stalks celery
   2 cups chicken stock
     Salt, freshly ground black pepper
  ⅛ teaspoon cinnamon
  ¼ teaspoon nutmeg
   1 teaspoon glace de viande (meat glaze)
   3 tablespoons sweet butter

Cut a ½" gash on the flat side of each chestnut, place in a hot oven or under the broiler for about 5 minutes, and peel off the shells and inner skins with a sharp knife.

Place chestnuts in a saucepan with the celery stalks and chicken stock, bring to a boil, cover, reduce the heat, and simmer gently for about 20 minutes, or until they are tender. Drain, reserving stock but discarding celery. Put through a ricer or sieve, and season with salt and pepper to taste, cinnamon, nutmeg, and glace de viande melted in a little hot water. Beat in the butter. If the purée is too thick, thin with a little of the reserved stock. If using canned, cooked chestnuts, heat in stock and then follow recipe.

BRUSSELS SPROUTS

For six servings, allow 3 packages frozen Brussels sprouts, or 1 quart fresh Brussels sprouts. If frozen, follow package directions.

For fresh Brussels sprouts, trim off stem end and remove any discolored outer leaves. Soak in salted water for 15 minutes, then cook uncovered in boiling salted water until just tender to the point of a knife, about 15 minutes, depending on size. Do not overcook. Nothing is worse than soft, mushy sprouts. Drain well and toss with butter.

PRUNE SOUFFLÉ
[STAR DUWYENIE]

    ½ pound pitted prunes
       Tea
    ½ cup sugar
       Lemon juice
    4 egg whites
       Whipped cream flavored with brandy

Stew the prunes in tea until soft. Add the sugar and mix well, and put through a coarse sieve. Add a little lemon juice. Beat the egg whites until stiff and fold into prune mixture. Turn into a buttered and sugared 1½-quart soufflé dish. Put dish in a pan of warm water and bake in a 350° oven for 25 minutes or 375° oven for 20 minutes. (Soufflé can be left in turned-off oven for several minutes without spoiling.) Serve with brandied whipped cream.

Italian Dinner for Six

The out-of-the-ordinary element here is the risotto—flavored and tinged with the ink of the squid and served Italian-style as the opening gambit for a light and appealing menu. As the main dish is cooked with white wine, you might serve an Italian white throughout the meal, a Soave, a Verdicchio, or a white wine from Tuscany.

MENU

Risotto Nero

Rolled Saltimbocca

Salad of Rugula and Shredded Cooked Beet, Oil and Vinegar Dressing

Peaches Galliano, Almond Macaroons

The Wine

Soave, Verdicchio

RISOTTO NERO
[GIORGIO CAVALLON]

    2 pounds squid
    5 tablespoons olive oil
    1 tablespoon butter
    2 cloves garlic, finely chopped
    3 shallots, finely chopped
    2 tablespoons chopped Italian parsley
      Salt and freshly ground black pepper
 1½ cups Italian short-grain rice
 2¾ cups chicken broth
  ½ cup clam juice
      Freshly grated Sardo cheese

Slit the squid lengthwise and clean, removing the eyes, the yellow sac behind the eyes, intestines, and the thin flat bone. Reserve the ink sacs that lie just behind the eyes. Rinse the squid and cut into strips about ¼″ thick. Heat the oil and butter in a heavy skillet and sauté the garlic, shallots, and parsley until tender but not browned. Add the squid and cook quickly, stirring, 2 minutes. Cover the pan and cook slowly about 10 minutes or until squid is just tender. Season to taste with salt and pepper. Remove squid from skillet, set half aside and chop remaining half fine. Return to the skillet. Add the rice. Heat the broth and clam juice together with the contents of the ink sacs, which turn the mixture black. Pour half of the hot broth into the skillet. Cover and cook slowly for 10 minutes or until liquid has been absorbed. Add remaining liquid and cook 10 minutes longer or until rice is barely tender; it should have a slight kernel in the middle. Add reserved squid, reheat and season to taste with salt and pepper. Serve with grated Sardo cheese.

ROLLED SALTIMBOCCA
[PHILIP S. BROWN]

    2 pounds veal escalopes, cut in 12 pieces
      Salt, pepper to taste
   12 thin slices prosciutto
      Fresh sage leaves
    4 tablespoons butter
  ½ cup white wine or Marsala

Season the escalopes with salt and pepper. Put a slice of prosciutto on each one and a leaf or two of sage. Roll up and fasten with toothpicks, then brown all over in butter. Add the wine, let it come to a boil, reduce heat, cover the pan and simmer the rolls for 10 minutes or until very tender. Serve with triangular croutons of fried bread.

VARIATION: Bocconcini are made in the same way, but a stick of Gruyère cheese, about 3″ long and ½″ square, is substituted for the sage. Cook the bocconcini rather quickly, so that the cheese doesn't melt and run out.

PEACHES GALLIANO
[LOU SEIBERT PAPPAS]

> 1 quart French vanilla ice cream
> 1 cup heavy cream
> ¼ cup Galliano liqueur or brandy
> 6 Babcock peaches (or other white variety or nectarines)
> Milk chocolate curls

Soften ice cream slightly. Whip heavy cream until stiff and fold in Galliano liqueur. Fold whipped cream into the ice cream, working quickly, and mixing just until blended. Return to the freezer until firm. Just before serving, peel, halve, and pit peaches. For each serving place 2 peach halves in a large wine glass or dessert bowl. Spoon Galliano over ice cream and garnish with chocolate curls. Serve with almond macaroons.

One-Pot Chicken Dinner for Six

The French poule-au-pot is a wonderful, flavorful party dish for a Sunday-night dinner or any time you don't feel like spending hours in the kitchen, for it practically cooks itself. The broth provides your first course and all you need to complete the menu is a simple fruit dessert. A white Burgundy goes beautifully with the delicately poached stuffed chicken.

MENU

Poule-au-Pot

Apples Bonne Femme with Cream

The Wine

Meursault or a French or American Pinot Chardonnay

POULE-AU-POT
[ELISABETH ORTIZ]

      3½- to 4-pound chicken
2½ cups stuffing (see recipe below)
 4 carrots, scraped and sliced
 1 medium onion, stuck with a clove
 2 stalks celery, cut in 2″ pieces
 3 sprigs parsley
 1 bay leaf
 ¼ teaspoon thyme
 1 clove garlic
 7 small leeks, well washed
    Salt, freshly ground pepper to taste
 3 quarts chicken stock, approximately
 3 medium white turnips, peeled and quartered
 3 parsnips, peeled and quartered

Stuff and truss the chicken. Place it in a large soup kettle, add 2 carrots, the onion, celery, parsley, bay leaf, thyme, garlic, 1 leek, salt and pepper, and enough stock to cover the chicken by at least 2 inches. Bring to a boil and skim. Reduce the heat so that the surface of the liquid barely moves, cover, and cook at this slow simmer until the chicken is almost tender. Remove chicken from the broth half an hour before it is done and keep warm. Strain the broth and discard the cooked vegetables. Skim off any excess fat, rinse the pot, return the chicken and broth to the pot with the turnips, parsnips, and remaining carrots and leeks and continue cooking until chicken and vegetables are done. Cooking time will be about 1½ to 2 hours in all for the chicken. To serve, carve the chicken and arrange on a large, heated platter surrounded by the stuffing and vegetables, moistened with a little broth. Serve the broth separately in soup bowls.

STUFFING FOR CHICKEN

> 2 tablespoons butter
> 1 medium onion, finely chopped
> 1 chicken liver
> ½ pound sausage meat
> 3 tablespoons chopped parsley
> ½ cup freshly made bread crumbs
> 1 egg
> 3 tablespoons dry white wine
>   Salt, freshly ground pepper to taste
> ¼ teaspoon thyme

Heat the butter in a frying pan and sauté the onion until tender but not browned. Remove the onion to a large bowl. Add the chicken liver to pan and sauté lightly in remaining butter. Remove liver, chop fine, and add to the onion. In the same pan sauté the sausage meat, breaking it up with a fork, until it begins to lose color. Drain off the excess fat. Add sausage meat and the remaining ingredients to the onion and mix well. Makes about 2½ cups.

APPLES BONNE FEMME WITH CREAM
[JAMES A. BEARD]

> 6 slices bread, cut in rounds
>   Butter
> 6 apples—greenings or Winesaps, cored
> 6 tablespoons sugar
>   Vanilla
>   Heavy cream

Sauté rounds of bread in butter until golden brown. Arrange in a buttered baking dish. Trim a small amount from the tops of the apples. Place on the rounds of toast. Fill each cavity with 1 tablespoon sugar, dot with butter and add a few drops vanilla. Bake in a 350° oven, basting with pan juices or adding more butter if needed. Serve warm with heavy cream.

Six Dinners for Two

There are often occasions when your entertaining is planned not for four, six or more, but just for two. It may be a tête-à-tête dinner with an old or new friend, a young couple's private celebration of a raise, or a quiet anniversary dinner for parents alone.

Because of its small scale, a dinner for two is the time to pamper yourself with luxuries which in larger quantities would wreak havoc with the budget—caviar, filet mignon, white truffles, a rack of hothouse baby lamb. Caution is needed when cutting down on amounts in standard recipes for four or six. It doesn't always work just to decrease the ingredients, so unless you are experienced at this kind of culinary legerdemain, stick with dishes that are easy to figure out and eschew complicated main dishes and desserts. A dinner for two should be easy on the cook, who is also a guest, so plan menus that can be done ahead, at least in part.

Celebration Dinner for Two

Much of this dinner can be prepared ahead of time, leaving only the main course and vegetables to be cooked. The chilled artichokes can be assembled just before serving time, the prepared crêpes left at room temperature to be filled, and then flambéed at the table. Drink champagne as an aperitif and with the artichokes, and a fine Burgundy or red Bordeaux with the beef.

MENU

Volga Artichokes
Tournedos, Sauce Diable
Mushroom Caps Filled with Tiny Green Peas
Fondant Potatoes
Strawberry Crêpes

The Wines

Blanc de blancs champagne; Vosne-Romanée or Château Lascombes

VOLGA ARTICHOKES
[ELAINE ROSS]

2 medium-size artichokes
¼ lemon
   1-ounce jar black caviar
¼ cup sour cream

Trim off the stem ends of the artichokes so that they stand upright. Slice off the top half, trim points from remaining leaves, and rub cut portions with the lemon. Cook, uncovered, in well-salted boiling water to cover for about 30 minutes, or until the bottom leaves pull out easily. Drain upside down until cool enough to handle. Scrape out the hairy center choke with a spoon. Chill until shortly before serving time. Then mix the caviar and sour cream and fill the center of each artichoke,

TOURNEDOS, SAUCE DIABLE
[PHILIP S. BROWN]

   Firm, slightly stale white bread
1 tablespoon clarified butter
3 tablespoons butter
1 tablespoon oil
2 tournedos (1″ to 1½″ thick)
2 thin slices baked ham

Dijon mustard
Julienne of baked ham
Watercress

Slice bread ¼″ thick, trim off the crusts, and cut into two rounds approximately the same size and shape as the tournedos. Heat clarified butter in a heavy skillet and sauté the rounds quickly on each side until crisp and delicately browned, adding more butter if necessary. Remove to a platter and keep warm.

Melt butter and oil in a heavy skillet, add tournedos and brown quickly on both sides over high heat. Then reduce the heat and continue cooking for 3 minutes on each side, which will give you rare meat.

Meanwhile cover the croutons with thin slices of baked ham and spread the ham sparingly with Dijon mustard. Put tournedos on croutons and pour over them Sauce Diable (see page 420) to which you have added fine julienne of baked ham. Garnish with watercress and serve immediately.

MUSHROOM CAPS WITH GREEN PEAS

6 large mushrooms
2 tablespoons butter
Salt, pepper
Lemon juice
1 package frozen petits pois

Remove the stems of the mushrooms and wipe the caps with damp paper towels. Sauté the mushroom caps in butter, sprinkling them with salt and pepper and adding a squeeze of lemon juice. Do not let them brown; they should be just cooked through, but still firm. Meanwhile, briefly cook petits pois and drain well. Spoon the peas into the sautéed mushroom caps.

FONDANT POTATOES

1 pound large boiling potatoes
3 tablespoons butter
2 tablespoons oil
Salt, pepper

Peel potatoes and scoop out balls with the larger end of a melon ball cutter. Heat butter and oil in a heavy skillet, add the potato balls in one layer, cover, and cook over medium heat for about 15 minutes, shaking the pan now and then, until golden brown on the outside and just tender to the point of a knife. Sprinkle with salt and pepper to taste before serving.

STRAWBERRY CRÊPES
[JAMES A. BEARD]

    6 small crêpes
    1 pint hulled strawberries
      Sugar
      Kirsch
      Whipped cream

Make crêpes, according to the recipe on page 425. Keep warm over hot water, wrapped in foil until ready to use. Slice strawberries, sprinkle lightly with sugar and marinate in kirsch to barely cover. Just before serving, drain the strawberries and roll them in the baked crêpes. Heat about ¼ cup kirsch, ignite and flambé the crêpes at table on a heat-proof dish or platter. If you like, serve with sweetened, kirsch-flavored whipped cream.

Anniversary Dinner for Two

While this is basically a very simple menu, and undemanding of the cook, the selection of oysters and quail puts it in the special-event category. You could, if you like, drink champagne with this dinner, or have a fine white Burgundy with the oysters and the quail, and a half bottle of red Bordeaux with the cheese.

MENU

Oysters Casino
Roast Quail with White Grapes
Green Salad—Brie Cheese
Frozen Mousse in Punch Cups
Danish Kisses

The Wines

Champagne or Chassagne-Montrachet; red Bordeaux,
such as a Château Léoville-Las-Cases

OYSTERS CASINO
[JAMES A. BEARD]

     1 dozen oysters on the half shell
     4 tablespoons butter
     ¼ cup finely chopped shallots
     ¼ cup finely chopped green pepper
       Tabasco sauce
     3 slices bacon
       Lemon juice

Arrange the oysters on the half shell on a pan of rock salt. Blend together the butter, shallots, and green pepper, and add a dash of Tabasco.

Broil the bacon until it is just about half cooked, but not crisp, and cut each slice in four pieces. Squeeze lemon juice on the oysters. Divide butter mixture equally between them, spooning it over the oysters. Top each one with a piece of bacon. (This part of the preparation may be done ahead.) When just about ready to serve, put the oysters under a very hot broiler and broil until the edges of the oysters curl, about 4 to 5 minutes. Serve very hot, with lemon wedges.

ROAST QUAIL WITH WHITE GRAPES
[MRS. WYATT COOPER]

       4 quail
       6 tablespoons butter
         Salt
         Freshly ground black pepper
         About 30 Thompson seedless grapes, peeled
       2 to 3 tablespoons cognac
      ¼ cup dry sherry, white wine, or vermouth
       1 cup chicken stock
    1½ teaspoons arrowroot
       1 teaspoon grated lemon zest
       1 to 2 teaspoons lemon juice

  Rub quail generously with butter, salt, and pepper. Put a lump of butter, salt, pepper, and 3 or 4 grapes in the cavity. Sprinkle with cognac. Place in a roasting pan and roast in a 450° oven for 12 to 15 minutes, basting thoroughly 2 or 3 times. While the quail are roasting, gently heat the remaining grapes in sherry and chicken stock in a small saucepan. Remove grapes with a slotted spoon, add to quail, and roast 5 more minutes. Remove quail to heated serving platter. Mix arrowroot into sherry and chicken stock and add to pan juices with grated lemon zest and lemon juice. Stir well, scraping up brown bits on bottom, and simmer until slightly thickened. Check seasoning. Pour sauce over quail and serve immediately. Serve two of these tiny birds per person.

FROZEN MOUSSE IN PUNCH CUPS
[ELAINE ROSS]

       2 tablespoons ground pecans
       1 teaspoon grated dark, sweet chocolate
       1 teaspoon minced candied fruit
       1 tablespoon crème de cacao liqueur
       1 teaspoon orange juice
       1 egg, separated
       2 tablespoons sugar

1 teaspoon grated orange rind
½ cup heavy cream, stiffly whipped
¼ teaspoon cocoa

Mix the pecans, grated chocolate, candied fruit, half the crème de cacao, and the orange juice. Beat the egg yolk and sugar until thick and light. Stir in the remaining crème de cacao and the orange rind. Fold in the stiffly whipped cream. Beat the egg white until stiff, but not dry, and fold into the cream mixture. Pour half the cream mixture into 2 punch cups, spoon some of the pecan mixture on top, and cover with the remaining cream mixture. Sift the cocoa over the mousse and freeze for 4 hours, or until firm.

NOTE: This mousse may be made as long as several weeks ahead and stored in a freezer.

DANISH KISSES
[ELAINE ROSS]

1 egg white
¼ cup sugar
1 teaspoon potato starch
⅛ teaspoon pulverized ammonium carbonate (available at drug-stores)

Beat the egg white until it forms moist peaks. Gradually add the sugar, beating all the while, until the sugar is dissolved and the mixture is thick and glossy. Sift the potato starch with the ammonium carbonate and fold into the meringue. Spoon the meringue into a pastry bag fitted with a plain round opening and pipe 16 to 20 mounds, spaced 1½″ apart, on a buttered cookie sheet. (Or drop the mounds from a tea-spoon.) Bake for 20 minutes in a preheated 200° oven, turn off the heat, and leave in the oven for 1 hour to dry.

Terrace Dinner for Two

This rather elegant menu might fit all kinds of occasions, besides show-ing you off as an accomplished cook. If the table for two can be set on a vine-covered terrace, or in front of a blazing fire, as the season dictates, so much the better. Candlelight sets the right romantic mood and the wine should do justice to this richly sensuous meal, so choose one of the rare and exquisite German Palatinate whites. A well-chilled Château d'Yquem would be sensational with the hazelnut roll.

MENU
[ELAINE ROSS]

Braised Sweetbreads Chanterelle

Cucumber and Peas   *Corn in Its Own Cream*

Hazelnut Roll

The Wines

German white—Diedesheimer, Forster or Annaberg; Château d'Yquem

---

BRAISED SWEETBREADS CHANTERELLE

    1 veal knucklebone
      4-ounce can Swiss chanterelle mushrooms
    2 large calves' sweetbreads (about ½ pound each, trimmed weight)
    1 tablespoon vinegar
    2 slices lean bacon, diced
    1 small onion, minced
    1 small carrot, minced
    1 stalk celery, minced
    2 tablespoons butter
    3 tablespoons Madeira wine
    ½ teaspoon salt, or more to taste
      Dash white pepper
    1½ tablespoons lemon juice
    1½ tablespoons minced parsley

Place the veal knucklebone in a saucepan. Drain the can of mushrooms, pour the juice over the bone, and add cold water to cover. Bring to a boil, reduce the heat, and simmer, covered, for 1½ hours. Uncover, reduce the stock to ¾ cup, and reserve.

Meanwhile, soak the sweetbreads in ice water for ½ hour. Drain and plunge them into boiling water to which the vinegar has been added. Reduce the heat, simmer for 5 minutes, drain sweetbreads, and plunge into ice water until they are cool. Carefully remove any fibrous matter or connective tissue from the sweetbreads with a small sharp knife. Cut them in half, lengthwise.

Sauté the bacon with the minced onion, carrot, and celery in the butter in a heavy saucepan until the onion is yellow. Heat the Madeira, ignite it, and pour over the vegetables. Add the sweetbreads and mushrooms and sauté over medium high heat until the sweetbreads have taken on color. Add the veal stock, salt, pepper, and lemon juice. Cook over high heat for 15 minutes, basting the sweetbreads constantly, until the juices are syrupy and the sweetbreads glazed. Sprinkle the parsley on top.

CUCUMBER AND PEAS

> 1 large cucumber, peeled, seeded, and cut into bite-size pieces
> 1 chicken bouillon cube, crushed
> ⅔ cup thawed, frozen peas

Put the cucumber and crushed chicken bouillon cube into a small saucepan. Cook, covered, over low heat for about 20 minutes, or until the cucumber is tender and translucent, stirring frequently. Add the peas and cook for 3 minutes, uncover and cook over high heat, stirring constantly, until peas are cooked and pan juices almost evaporated.

CORN IN ITS OWN CREAM

> 4 ears tender young corn
> 2 tablespoons butter
> Salt, pepper to taste

Cut the corn off the cobs, cutting through the top half of the kernels. Scrape off the remainder of the kernels and the milk with a spoon. Place in a small saucepan with the butter and cook, covered, over low heat for 5 minutes. Uncover, and continue to cook, stirring constantly, until mixture is creamy and the corn very tender. Season with salt and pepper.

NOTE: This may be made a short time ahead and reheated.

151

HAZELNUT ROLL

> 2 eggs, separated
> ¼ cup sugar
> 1 tablespoon plus 1 teaspoon flour, sifted
> ¼ cup apricot jam, softened
> ½ cup heavy cream
> ¼ cup finely chopped toasted hazelnuts
> Confectioners' sugar

Grease an 8″-square baking pan, line the bottom with waxed paper, and grease the paper thoroughly. Beat the egg whites until stiff, but not dry. Beat the yolks in a separate bowl with a generous half of the sugar until thick and light. Beat in the flour, fold in the beaten whites, and spread the batter in the prepared pan. Bake in a preheated 350° oven for about 13 minutes, or until the top springs back when pressed gently. Loosen the sides of the cake with a small, sharp knife, invert the cake on a piece of waxed paper, and peel off the top paper. Roll up the cake and cool.

When the cake is cool, unroll it and spread with the jam. Whip the cream until stiff with the remaining sugar, fold in the nuts, spread over the jam, and reroll the cake. Dust generously with confectioners' sugar.

Late Dinner à Deux After the Theater

If you are going to the theater during the week, it is often more relaxed to serve dinner late for once, rather than to try and rush it through. You might have cocktails and some fairly substantial appetizer, such as a quiche Lorraine or pâté en croûte, before you go. As you will be eating late, the menu should be light, something you can assemble and leave in the refrigerator to be quickly heated. With this dinner, have a gentle and refreshing white wine, cooled in the refrigerator while you are at the show.

MENU
[ELAINE ROSS]

Seafood Coquilles
Hearts of Palm Vinaigrette
Caraway Melbas
Pineapple in a Pineapple Shell

The Wine

Pouilly Fuissé or vinho verde

SEAFOOD COQUILLES

    1½ cups diced cooked lobster and shrimp
    1 shallot, minced
    2 tablespoons butter
    ½ lightly beaten egg
    ⅓ cup sour cream
    ¼ teaspoon anchovy paste
    1½ tablespoons capers, drained and chopped
    1 tablespoon freshly grated Parmesan cheese
    1 tablespoon fine dry bread crumbs
    2 teaspoons melted butter

Sauté the seafood and shallot gently in the 2 tablespoons butter, stirring constantly, for 3 to 4 minutes. Remove from the heat. Beat the egg into the sour cream, add the anchovy paste, capers and half the cheese. Mix with the seafood and shallot and heap into two coquilles or individual baking dishes. Sprinkle bread crumbs, remaining cheese and butter over the top. At this point, the coquilles may be refrigerated.

Bake in a preheated 425° oven for 15 minutes or until piping hot.

HEARTS OF PALM VINAIGRETTE

Drain a can of hearts of palm and toss, just before serving, with a sharp vinaigrette sauce. Serve sprinkled with chopped parsley.

CARAWAY MELBAS

    4 very thin slices seedless rye bread
    1 tablespoon soft sweet butter
    1½ teaspoons caraway seeds

Place the bread on a baking sheet, spread with the butter, and sprinkle with the caraway seeds. Bake in a preheated 325° oven for approximately 25 minutes, or until dry and crisp—the baking time will vary depending on the dryness of the bread and the thickness of the slices. These may be done ahead and popped in the oven with the coquilles for a couple of minutes to recrisp.

PINEAPPLE IN A PINEAPPLE SHELL

    1 ripe pineapple
    3 tablespoons sugar, or to taste
    1 tablespoon white crème de menthe
    Mint leaves (optional)

Cut the pineapple in half lengthwise, cutting straight through the fronds. Trim off any unsightly tips. Scoop out the flesh with a sharp knife, leaving a thin shell. Cut out the core and dice the flesh. Place half the pineapple in a small pan with 2 tablespoons of the sugar. Cook over low heat, stirring constantly, until the sugar dissolves. Cover and continue cooking until tender. Combine with the remaining uncooked fruit and sugar and stir in the crème de menthe. Chill until ready to serve, then spoon into the shells. Garnish with mint leaves, if desired.

Quick Dinner for Two

This is a good career-girl menu, because there is scarcely any last-minute preparation except for the dessert, which can be popped in the oven while you are dressing. A brut champagne, either imported or American, would give the meal a festive air, but if you don't want to go to that expense, white wine will do nicely.

MENU
[ELAINE ROSS]

Spiked Madrilène

Bay Scallops with Mustard Sauce

Curried Rice Salad

Blueberry Pudding Smitane

The Wine

Brut champagne or Pinot Chardonnay

SPIKED MADRILÈNE

1 can consommé madrilène
½ teaspoon lemon juice
¼ teaspoon Worcestershire sauce
Dash Tabasco sauce
¼ cup red wine

Combine the first four ingredients and bring to the boiling point. Put half the wine in each consommé cup and fill with the seasoned consommé.

BAY SCALLOPS WITH MUSTARD SAUCE

1½ tablespoons oil
1 pound bay scallops (or sea scallops cut in half)
2 teaspoons sugar
2 teaspoons prepared mustard
1 tablespoon wine vinegar
2 tablespoons sour cream
2 teaspoons minced parsley
1 head endive

Heat the oil in a heavy skillet. Add the scallops and cook over high heat, shaking the skillet constantly, until they begin to lose their translucence. Remove from the heat immediately, pour into a bowl, cool, and chill. Shortly before serving, drain the scallops of any juices that may have collected. Mix the sugar, mustard, vinegar, sour cream, and parsley. Pour over the scallops, toss well, and transfer to 2 individual plates. Garnish with endive leaves.

CURRIED RICE SALAD

> 2 teaspoons salad oil
> 1 teaspoon wine vinegar
> ½ teaspoon curry powder
> 1½ tablespoons chutney, minced
> 1 small tomato, peeled, seeded and chopped
> ½ small green pepper, cut into julienne strips
> 1 cup cold cooked rice
> Salt, pepper to taste

Mix the oil, vinegar, curry powder, and chutney. Combine with the tomato and green pepper and toss with the rice. Season with salt and pepper. Chill for several hours before serving (the salad could be molded in two custard cups, unmolded onto the plates with the scallops).

BLUEBERRY PUDDING SMITANE

> 2 cups blueberries
> 2 teaspoons cornstarch
> ½ teaspoon cinnamon
> 4 tablespoons sugar
> 1 teaspoon grated orange rind
> 1 egg, separated
> ⅓ cup sour cream

Mix the blueberries with the cornstarch, cinnamon, 2 tablespoons of sugar, and the orange rind. Pour into a small baking dish and bake in a preheated 375° oven for 10 minutes. Reduce the heat to 350° and bake about 25 minutes longer, or until the berries are cooked. Mix the egg yolk, sour cream, and remaining 2 tablespoons sugar. Beat the egg white until stiff, fold into the cream mixture, and spread over the berries. Bake about 20 minutes longer, or until flecked with gold. Serve warm or at room temperature.

Birthday Dinner for Two

The surprise here is the opening, spaghetti with a liberal measure of chopped truffles, served as a separate pasta course. As the accent in this meal is Italian, a white Italian wine would be in order with the first two courses.

MENU

Spaghetti with Anchovies and Truffles
Scaloppine with Mushrooms and White Wine
Broccoli Piemontese
Pears, Roman-Style

The Wine

Verdicchio

SPAGHETTI WITH ANCHOVIES AND TRUFFLES
[MYRA WALDO]

6 anchovies
¼ cup olive oil
2 cloves garlic, split
2 tablespoons tomato paste
¼ teaspoon freshly ground black pepper
2 white or black truffles, chopped
½ pound spaghetti

Wash and drain the anchovies to remove excess salt. Chop fairly fine. Heat the oil in a skillet and cook the garlic, add anchovies and mash into the oil with a wooden spoon. Mix the tomato paste with 1 cup water and add. Season with the pepper. Cook over low heat for 15 minutes. Taste for seasoning and stir in the truffles.

While the sauce is cooking, cook the spaghetti in plenty of rapidly boiling salted water. Drain well and put in deep soup plates. Pour the sauce over the spaghetti.

SCALOPPINE WITH MUSHROOMS AND WHITE WINE
[PHILIP S. BROWN]

    1 pound veal escalopes
      Salt, pepper, paprika, flour
    4 tablespoons butter
    2 finely chopped shallots
    2 ounces mushrooms, thinly sliced
    ½ cup white wine
    2 teaspoons chopped parsley
    ½ teaspoon chopped tarragon

Season the escalopes with salt, pepper and paprika and dust with flour. Sauté quickly in 3 tablespoons butter and transfer to a hot platter to keep warm. Add the shallots to the pan and cook for about 2 minutes, then add the mushrooms and cook, stirring, for 3 minutes longer. Add ¼ cup wine and cook until reduced by half, then add the herbs and remaining wine. Bring to a boil, swirl in the remaining tablespoon of butter and pour sauce over the veal.

BROCCOLI PIEMONTESE
[HELEN EVANS BROWN]

    1 bunch broccoli
    1 clove garlic, finely chopped
      Olive oil
      Salt, freshly ground pepper
    ½ cup white wine

Cook the broccoli in boiling, salted water until barely tender. Drain well. Sauté the garlic in enough oil to cover the bottom of a large skillet. When lightly browned, add the broccoli and spoon the hot oil and garlic over it. Add the wine and reduce quickly. Serve the broccoli with the pan juices poured over it.

PEARS, ROMAN-STYLE
[HELEN EVANS BROWN]

  2 medium pears, halved and cored
12 almonds, chopped
⅛ teaspoon almond extract
  1 tablespoon butter
½ cup sherry

Put the pears in a small baking dish. Mix the almonds, almond extract, and butter, and put a dab of the mixture in each cavity. Pour sherry over the pears and bake in a 350° oven for 30 minutes.

Supper Parties

The advantages of giving a late-evening supper are often overlooked. This is one of the pleasantest and least demanding ways to entertain, especially if you have been working all day and don't feel like cooking a big meal, or on a weekend night when you would like to enjoy the company of your friends in a relaxed and casual atmosphere.

Suppers are not only later than dinners, but also less structured and lengthy—usually just one dish and a dessert, perhaps bread and salad, with a simple American carafe wine, or one of the less expensive country wines of Europe. This is the time to serve uncomplicated food that is both satisfying and comforting to eat—a big platter of pasta, an all-in-one rice dish, a glorious peasant soup, or a regional stew or casserole. On the other hand, should you prefer something lighter and a touch more elegant, it can be something as easy as a pâté maison followed by oysters simmered in champagne in a chafing dish.

The chafing-dish supper is always a good idea, because it gives you a chance to be with your guests while you whip up something speedy and wonderful-smelling in front of them. (Any of the chafing-dish recipes in the breakfast party chapter work equally well for supper.)

The very informality of the supper party means that anything goes. You have great scope for versatility in the makeup of the menu. It can be a spur-of-the-moment meal, put together from pantry staples and what's in the refrigerator and freezer, or it can be based on a soup or some other dish that practically cooks itself, simmering away on the stove while you drink and talk with your guests. The soup and salad supper gives you the rare opportunity to concoct one of those hearty, delicious homemade soups that so frequently get eliminated from the other meals as far too heavy—chowders, borscht, bean and pea soups, for instance. As most of these soups are improved by reheating, they can be made ahead and refrigerated or frozen until needed. (This applies mainly to thick soups; those that contain cream should not be held, unless the cream can be added during the reheating.)

Should you be a foreign food addict and wish to experiment with something really unusual—a Caribbean casserole, a Mediterranean seafood dish, or one of those fascinating Middle East recipes based on chick peas or rice—there's no better time to try it out than at supper, when it can provide the *raison d'être* of the menu, for suppertime food is basically conversation food, to be lingered over, savored, and discussed. This is also the time to bring out your wonderful peasant pottery, huge antique tureens or platters, which in themselves are a superb and sufficient decoration for the supper table.

Soufflé Supper for Six

This is the kind of meal you can literally whip up at the last minute, after you have come back from an evening at the theater with friends, or on Saturday, after a busy day. The pastry shell can be made in the morning (or ahead of time, and frozen, unbaked), and then filled and popped into the oven with the soufflé. A blender makes short work of Hollandaise, but it really doesn't take long even if you make it by hand. Serve a light white wine with the soufflé.

MENU

[JAMES A. BEARD]

Shrimp and Clam Soufflé

Bibb and Mushroom Salad

Cherry Quiche

The Wine

Mâcon Blanc or Pinot Blanc

SHRIMP AND CLAM SOUFFLÉ

7-ounce can minced clams
½ pound raw shrimp, peeled and cleaned
1 teaspoon dill weed, or 1 tablespoon fresh dill
1 teaspoon salt
½ teaspoon freshly ground black pepper
5 egg yolks
6 egg whites

Put all ingredients except the egg whites in the blender and blend for 30 seconds.

Beat the egg whites until stiff but not dry. Remove the mixture from the blender and fold in ⅓ of the egg whites rather thoroughly. Fold in the remaining egg whites very lightly. Pour the mixture into 6 buttered individual soufflé dishes, or 1 large soufflé dish, no more than ⅔ full.

Place individual dishes in a pan of hot water and bake at 375° for 15 to 17 minutes. If you use one large dish, bake at 375° for 30 minutes. Serve with Hollandaise sauce (see page 420).

BIBB AND MUSHROOM SALAD

6 heads Bibb lettuce, cut in quarters
½ pound firm white mushrooms, stemmed and thinly sliced
2 tablespoons chopped parsley
Vinaigrette sauce flavored with basil

Since the Bibb lettuce is being served in quarters, it will take extra care in washing to see that all the dirt is removed from the tightly packed leaves. Place the Bibb and mushrooms in the salad bowl, sprinkle with the parsley, and toss with the vinaigrette sauce.

CHERRY QUICHE

Prebaked 9″ sweetened rich pastry shell (see page 424)
1-pound can Bing cherries, drained
2 tablespoons kirsch liqueur
4 eggs
1 cup cream
¾ cup sugar

Mix the cherries with the kirsch and arrange in the pastry shell. Beat the eggs lightly and combine with the cream and sugar. Pour over the cherries. Bake in a 375° oven for 25 to 30 minutes or until set. Remove to a rack to cool.

Light, Late Supper for Six

A good menu to serve late in the evening, when you don't feel like eating very much. Champagne would be perfect with this simple but elegant meal. If you feel the need of something sweet to end with, why not Irish coffee?

MENU

Terrine of Chicken Livers with Ham
Toast and Sweet Butter
Champagne Oysters
Irish Coffee

The Wine

Champagne—Brut or Nature

TERRINE OF CHICKEN LIVERS WITH HAM
[JAMES A. BEARD]

    1 pound chicken livers, trimmed
    ¾ cup port or Madeira
    1 tablespoon salt
    2 tablespoons chopped parsley
    1 bay leaf
    ¼ teaspoon Spice Parisienne or quatre épices
    1 pound chicken hearts, chopped
    ½ pound cooked ham, chopped
    1 pound good sausage meat
    ½ cup soft bread crumbs
    1 egg, slightly beaten
      Thin slices of barding pork
      Flour and water paste

Marinate the chicken livers in the port or Madeira and the seasonings. Combine the chicken hearts, ham, sausage meat, and the bread crumbs. Blend with the egg. Remove the chicken livers and bay leaf from the marinade and add the marinade to the forcemeat mixture. Mix well. Line a 2-quart terrine with the thin slices of barding pork. Alternate layers of the forcemeat mixture and the chicken livers, ending with forcemeat. Top with a piece of barding pork and the bay leaf from the marinade. Cover and seal the terrine with flour and water paste. Bake in a 375° oven for 1½ to 2 hours. Cool. Serve from the terrine with toast and butter.

CHAMPAGNE OYSTERS
[RUTH CONRAD BATEMAN]

    1½ pints oysters
     6 French rolls
       Butter
       Salt, freshly ground pepper
       Minced parsley
    ⅓ cup champagne (or dry white wine)

Drain oysters very well in strainer or colander. Cut tops off French rolls; hollow slightly and spread inside with butter. (Butter soft side of tops also, for mopping up the oyster juices.) Heat rolls briefly in 400° oven, or toast lightly under the broiler. Heat ¼ cup butter in blazer pan of chafing dish over direct heat, or in a heavy skillet. Add oysters and baste well with butter. Season with salt and a few grindings of pepper. Add parsley and champagne. Cover and heat until oysters become plump and edges curl, just a few minutes. Pile hot into French rolls; spoon pan juices on top. Serve at once, with champagne, of course.

IRISH COFFEE

For each serving, put 1½ ounces Irish whiskey into a warmed stemmed glass, add sugar to taste, and fill to within an inch of the top with hot, strong coffee. Stir until the sugar dissolves. Pour heavy cream, very lightly whipped until it has just enough body to stay on top of the coffee, over the back of a spoon onto the surface of the coffee. Sip the hot, sweet spirituous coffee through the cold cream.

Summer Supper for Eight

A delicate party supper for a hot evening, all of which can be prepared ahead—and served buffet-style if you wish, or on individual trays in the garden. With this have plenty of chilled white wine.

MENU

Mussels en Coquille
Rolled Chicken Pâté with Thin Toast
Salad of Julienne Endive and Sliced Mushrooms, French Dressing
Fresh Peaches in Champagne

The Wine

Castel Byria or Pinot Chardonnay

165

MUSSELS EN COQUILLE
[ELAINE ROSS]

    3 quarts mussels
    1 cup dry white wine
    1 bay leaf
    4 sprigs parsley
    2 scallions, minced
    1 cup mayonnaise
    2 teaspoons Dijon mustard
    1 tablespoon drained capers, chopped
    ⅓ cup minced parsley

Scrub the mussels under cold running water and scrape off as much of the beard as possible with a small sharp knife. Bring the wine to a boil in a large pot, add the bay leaf, parsley sprigs, and scallions, and cook for 2 minutes. Add the mussels, cover the pot tightly and cook over high heat, shaking the pot frequently, for 5 minutes. Remove the mussels from their shells, discarding any whose shells have not opened. Cool and chill the mussels.

Combine the mayonnaise, mustard, capers, and 3 tablespoons of the minced parsley. Mix with the chilled mussels, divide among 8 coquilles, sprinkle with remaining parsley, and chill until serving time.

ROLLED CHICKEN PÂTÉ
[JAMES A. BEARD]

This is an Italian recipe, thoroughly delicious, easy to do, and a delight for summer menus when a pork and liver pâté might be too heavy.

    8 tablespoons butter
    1 medium onion, thinly sliced
    1 stalk celery, cut in julienne strips
    1 carrot, cut in julienne strips
    1 tablespoon salt
    ¼ teaspoon Spice Parisienne or quatre épices
    2 large chicken breasts
    1 pork chop, about 6 to 7 ounces

¾ pound sweet butter, softened
⅓ cup cognac
2 tablespoons shelled pistachio nuts
1 pound prosciutto, sliced

Combine the 8 tablespoons butter, onion, celery, carrot, salt, and spice in a heavy saucepan. Add the chicken and pork chop. Cook, uncovered, over medium heat until tender. Do not overcook. Remove the chicken and pork from the saucepan and cool. Trim away skin, fat, and bone. Grind the meats using the finest blade. Beat into the softened sweet butter, adding the cognac and pistachio nuts as you beat. It is a good idea to use an electric mixer with a paddle attachment, if you have one.

Taste the pâté for seasoning. Turn out on a piece of waxed paper.

On two other pieces of waxed paper or plastic wrap arrange overlapping slices of prosciutto, forming two 10″ squares. Divide the chicken-pork mixture and form into two rolls. Place one roll on each of the prosciutto squares. Roll tightly, without squeezing, so the pâté is completely enveloped by the prosciutto. Place in polyethylene bags and refrigerate for 24 hours before serving. Cut in slices about ½″ thick and serve with toast.

FRESH PEACHES IN CHAMPAGNE

Peel eight large ripe peaches and prick the flesh in a few places with a fork. Put each one in a large balloon-shaped wine glass or goblet and pour over it enough chilled champagne to cover. Serve at once. The guests first drink the wine and then eat the wine-soaked fruit with a spoon.

Shore Supper for Eight

If you spend the summer at a spot where you can get fresh seafood, there's nothing more delightful for a casual, come-as-you-are weekend supper on the terrace than a huge seafood stew. All you need with this is bread and wine, followed by a platter of cheese and fresh fruit. Provide plenty of napkins or, preferably, terry fingertip towels that can be tossed in the washing machine next day.

MENU

Portuguese Seafood Stew
Hot French Bread
Cheese Board
Fresh Fruits of the Season

The Wine

Vinho verde

PORTUGUESE SEAFOOD STEW
[MRS. DAVID EVINS]

> 4 dozen mussels
> 4 dozen clams
> 3 medium onions
> ¼ cup olive oil
> 2 cloves garlic
> 1 medium bunch parsley, very finely chopped
> 1 large can tomatoes packed in tomato purée
> Salt, freshly ground pepper
> 2 dozen large shrimp
> Several parsley sprigs
> ½ 10-ounce box frozen tiny white onions
> 2 pounds halibut
> 1 pound bay scallops
> 3 medium lobsters, boiled

Wash and scrub shells of mussels and clams very well. Soak for several hours in cold water.

Mince two of the onions. Cook them in olive oil over very low heat for about 10 minutes, until soft but not browned. Add garlic, parsley, and tomatoes. Cover and simmer ½ hour, stirring to make sure it does not burn.

Separately steam mussels and clams—just covered with water and seasoned with salt and pepper—until shells open (discard any that do not open). Remove mussels and clams from their shells, reserving 6 of each in the shell for garnish. Add enough steaming liquid to the tomato mixture to give the flavor; set aside remaining liquid. Gently boil the shrimp in a court bouillon of water to cover, the remaining onion, a few sprigs of parsley, and salt and pepper until cooked, about 7 minutes. When cooked, cool shrimp in liquid. Strain this liquid into the tomato mixture. Add the frozen onions to the tomato mixture and cook for 10 minutes.

Rinse the halibut and scallops. Cut halibut into chunks. Add halibut and scallops to tomato mixture and cook very slowly, covered, until firm but tender, about 10 minutes. Season.

Add shrimp, mussels, and clams to the stew. Remove lobster meat from all the shells but the claws. Add to stew 5 minutes before serving and heat through. If necessary, add more of the mussel-clam liquid. Stew should be liquid and souplike.

Serve the stew in a tureen. Garnish with lobster claws and reserved mussels and clams.

Caribbean Supper for Six

An unusual menu that you might serve as a bon voyage supper for friends who are off to the islands for vacation, as a pretaste of delights in store. The escovitch fish (the name derives from the Spanish *escabeche*, or pickled) hails from Jamaica, the chicken and rice casserole, with its exotic blend of flavors, from Dominica. The light, refreshing citrus sherbet at the end of the meal acts as a palate cleanser and digestif. A light Spanish or Portuguese white wine would be best with the flavors of the casserole.

MENU

Escovitch Fish

Chicken Calypso

Citrus Sherbet

The Wine

Spanish white Rioja or Portuguese vinho verde

ESCOVITCH FISH
[ELISABETH ORTIZ]

> 4 green peppers, hot or mild, sliced lengthwise into thin strips
> 2 onions, thinly sliced
> 4 carrots, thinly sliced
> 2 bay leaves, crumbled
> 6 tablespoons olive oil
> ½ cup vinegar
>   Salt, freshly ground pepper to taste
> 2 pounds snapper or other white fish filets

Put the sliced peppers, onion, carrots, bay leaves, 2 tablespoons olive oil, vinegar, 2 cups water, salt, and pepper into a saucepan. Cover and simmer for about 20 minutes. Meanwhile heat the remaining 4 tablespoons olive oil in a skillet and sauté the fish filets until they are golden brown. Drain and put into a serving dish. Pour the hot sauce over the fish. Serve hot or cold.

CHICKEN CALYPSO
[ELISABETH ORTIZ]

> 5 tablespoons olive oil
>   3½- to 4-pound fryer, cut into serving pieces
> 2 cups rice
> 1 medium onion, finely chopped
> 1 clove garlic, chopped
> 1 bell pepper, seeded and chopped
> 1 small hot green pepper, seeded and chopped
> ½ pound mushrooms, sliced
> ½ teaspoon saffron
>   2"- to 3"-piece of lime peel
> 1 tablespoon lime juice
> ¼ teaspoon Angostura bitters
> 4 cups chicken stock
>   Salt, freshly ground pepper to taste
> ¼ cup light rum

Heat 3 tablespoons of the olive oil in a skillet and sauté the chicken pieces until brown all over. Remove to a casserole. Add the rice, onion, garlic, bell pepper, and hot pepper to the oil remaining in the skillet, and sauté, stirring, until the oil is absorbed, being careful not to let the rice scorch. Add to the chicken in the casserole. Add the remaining 2 tablespoons of oil to the skillet and sauté the mushrooms over fairly high heat for 5 minutes. Add to the casserole with the saffron, lime peel, lime juice, bitters, chicken stock, salt and pepper. Cover and simmer gently until rice and chicken are tender and the liquid is absorbed, about ½ hour. Add the rum and cook, uncovered, for 5 minutes longer.

CITRUS SHERBET
[ALEX D. HAWKES]

> ½ teaspoon unflavored gelatin
> 1 tablespoon cold water
> 2 cups boiling water
> ¾ cup sugar
> ½ teaspoon shredded fresh mint (optional)
> ¼ cup fresh citrus juice, ideally a mixture of more than 1 type of fruit juice (try a mixture of sweet and tart juices)
> ⅛ teaspoon salt
> 1 egg white, beaten stiff

Add gelatin to cold water, stirring until softened. In saucepan mix the boiling water, sugar, and, if desired, shredded mint. Bring to a boil, and boil for 5 minutes. Cool slightly and add citrus juice, salt, and softened gelatin mixture, stirring well. Turn into a freezer tray, and freeze until mixture becomes almost firm. Remove to a bowl and beat thoroughly with rotary beater. Fold in beaten egg white and return to freezer until firmly frozen. Garnish as desired.

Soup and Salad Supper for Six

A quick and easy supper menu, which can be adjusted according to the season, as you can serve the borscht hot or icy cold. A loaf of good pumpernickel is the natural accompaniment for this Russian food. You could, if you like, follow with fresh pears and cheese.

171

MENU
[IRIS BROOKS]

Quick Borscht

Veal Salad Russe

Pumpernickel

Pears and Cheese

QUICK BORSCHT

    1-pound can whole baby beets
    10½-ounce can beef consommé
2 teaspoons meat extract
    Sugar
1 large bay leaf
    Juice of 1 large lemon, strained
    Salt, black pepper to taste
2 eggs

Drain the liquid from the beets and combine it with the consommé in a large saucepan. Add the meat extract and ½ soup-can of water, 1 tablespoon sugar, and bay leaf, and bring to a boil. Halve and slice ⅓ of the beets and shred the rest on a hand grater. Add the beets to the soup and simmer 5 minutes. Add the lemon juice to the soup, tasting as you add. There's no way to measure just how much more lemon juice or sugar you may need. Keep sampling and adding lemon juice and sugar until the soup is briskly but pleasantly sweet-and-sour. Season with salt and pepper. Remove the bay leaf.

Beat the eggs briskly with 2 tablespoons water. Bring the soup to a rolling boil and pour the eggs in gradually, stirring constantly, so that eggs form a curd. If you like, you can pour the hot soup over a whole potato in each bowl or, to serve it icy cold, omit the eggs and put about 4 tablespoons sour cream into each plate before adding the soup.

VEAL SALAD RUSSE

> 3½ cups diced veal, cooked and cooled
> 1½ cups each: boiled potato, peeled and cooled; cucumber, peeled and seeded; and tart red apple, unpared and seeded; all diced
> ⅔ cup diced kosher dill pickle, drained
> 1½ cups Russian Mayonnaise (see recipe below)
> Minced chives
> Watercress

Toss all ingredients except the chives and watercress together thoroughly. Chill well. Serve sprinkled with chives and garnished with watercress.

RUSSIAN MAYONNAISE

> 2 hard-cooked egg yolks, sieved
> 1 teaspoon each: salt, dry mustard, and sugar
> ½ teaspoon freshly ground white pepper
> Dash of beefsteak sauce
> 1½ cups sour cream
> 3 tablespoons peanut oil
> 1 tablespoon vinegar
> 1 teaspoon lemon juice, strained
> 1 teaspoon each: minced fresh tarragon, flat (Italian) parsley, and chervil

Rub the yolks to a smooth paste with the salt, mustard, sugar, pepper, and beefsteak sauce. Blend in the cream, a little at a time, working to a smooth thick sauce. Stir in the oil briskly. Add the vinegar and lemon juice, stirring well to combine thoroughly. Add the fresh herbs and chill before serving. Makes about 2 cups.

Festive Supper for Six to Eight

For a group of friends who love investigating exotic foods, *chello,* or Persian rice, cooked in a special way until it is crisp and golden brown on the bottom, makes an interesting departure from the more familiar

173

pilafs. You don't really need a salad with this, but if you'd like the contrast, a salad of oranges and red onions would be delicious. A rather flowery white wine would go well with this.

MENU

Persian Rice with Lentils and Chicken
Orange and Onion Salad
Lemon Ice Box Tart

The Wine

California Johannisberg Riesling

PERSIAN RICE WITH LENTILS AND CHICKEN
[PAULA PECK]

- ¼ cup dried apricots, coarsely chopped
- 3 tablespoons salt
- ¾ cup lentils
- ½ cup blanched, sliced almonds (or coarsely chopped salted pecans)
- 1½ cups (approximately) sweet butter
- 1 medium onion, chopped
- 1¼ cups long-grain rice
- 1 teaspoon pepper
- 3 whole chicken breasts, boned, skinned, halved, and cut into ½" cubes
- 3 teaspoons fresh chopped dill

Cover chopped apricots with warm water and allow them to soak for half an hour before cooking time unless they are very soft, in which case soak them only when you begin to cook.

Bring 3 cups water to a boil in a large pot, seasoning it well with 1 tablespoon salt. Add lentils and cook until they are slightly more than half done. (It is difficult to give timing for this because lentils often vary.) When cooked, keep warm in a colander under warm running water.

Sauté nuts in ¼ cup butter until golden. Remove from pan, leaving any remaining butter in pan. Sauté onion in this butter, adding a little more butter if necessary, until they are soft and just beginning to brown lightly. Remove from heat and set aside with the almonds. Meanwhile, bring 6 cups water to a boil and season well with 2 tablespoons salt. Sprinkle in the rice. Stir with a wooden spoon, so that the rice doesn't stick to the bottom of the pot, until water begins to boil again. Then boil without stirring for 7 to 8 minutes, or until it is just about half cooked. Pour into a colander and rinse with very hot water.

Drain both rice and lentils well, combine, sprinkle with pepper, and toss lightly with 2 forks so that the lentils are mixed through the rice.

Melt remaining cup butter. Pour ¼ cup of the butter into a heavy 4-quart pot. Sprinkle in the rice-lentil mixture very lightly, forming a sort of pyramid on top of the butter.

Pour remaining melted butter over mixture. Cover pot with a clean, folded cloth, and a tight-fitting lid. Place over very low heat for about 1 hour. Remove lid and allow rice-lentil mixture to dry out for about 5 minutes. Taste for salt and sprinkle more on if necessary.

In the meantime, drain apricots, squeezing out water with your hand. Have raw chicken cubes at room temperature. Add chicken to rice mixture and toss in gently with a fork. The heat of the rice will cook the chicken sufficiently.

As soon as chicken is mixed into the rice, add the nuts, sautéed onion, apricots, and dill. Toss in gently without disturbing the crisp bottom layer of rice and lentils.

Serve at once, scooping up a little of the crisp bottom layer to top each serving.

ORANGE AND ONION SALAD
[JAMES A. BEARD]

    4 large oranges
    2 large red onions
   ½ teaspoon crushed rosemary (or fresh rosemary leaves)
   ½ cup olive oil
    3 tablespoons orange juice
    1 tablespoon lemon juice
    1 teaspoon salt
   ½ teaspoon freshly ground black pepper
    1 head curly chicory

Peel oranges with a sharp knife, removing all white pith. Section by cutting in between the thin membranes. Slice onions very thinly and separate into rings. Combine orange sections and onion slices and sprinkle with rosemary.

Combine olive oil, orange juice, lemon juice, salt and freshly ground black pepper.

Pour this dressing over the salad, add 1 head curly chicory, washed and chilled until crisp, and toss well.

LEMON ICE BOX TART
[ELAINE ROSS]

    4 egg whites
  ¼ teaspoon cream of tartar
 1¾ cups sugar
   5 egg yolks
    Grated rind of 1 lemon
  ½ cup lemon juice
 1½ cups heavy cream

Beat the egg whites until foamy, add the cream of tartar, and beat until the whites hold soft peaks. Gradually add 1 cup of the sugar, beating constantly until the meringue is thick and shiny. Spread the meringue over the bottom and sides of a well-buttered 9½″ pie plate. Bake in a preheated 250° oven for 1 hour. Cool.

Combine the egg yolks, ½ cup sugar, lemon rind and juice in the top of a double boiler. Cook, stirring frequently, until thick. Cool. Whip the cream until stiff with the remaining ¼ cup sugar. Spread half the cream over the cooled meringue. Cover with the cooled lemon mixture and top with the remaining cream. Refrigerate 24 hours.

Pasta Supper for Eight

Small turkeys, weighing five to six pounds, may be used for the main dish, or frozen turkey parts. With this hearty supper, all you need is a green salad, and a granita to follow—you might make both a lemon and orange granita and serve the lemon in orange shells, the orange in lemon shells, for a pretty touch. Drink a light Italian red wine with the pasta.

MENU

Tuscan Turkey and Pasta

Green Salad Tossed with Garlic Croutons and Anchovies,
French Dressing

Orange Granita   Lemon Granita

The Wine

Valpolicella or Chianti

TUSCAN TURKEY AND PASTA
[JAMES A. BEARD]

    5- to 6-pound turkey, cut in quarters
1 onion, stuck with 3 cloves
2 stalks celery
2 to 3 sprigs parsley
2 small dried hot peppers
2 large onions, coarsely chopped
3 tablespoons butter
3 tablespoons olive oil
6 large ripe tomatoes, peeled, seeded, and chopped
½ cup fresh chopped basil leaves or 2 to 3 teaspoons dried basil
    Salt, freshly ground black pepper to taste
2 to 3 pounds spaghettini
    Grated Romano and Parmesan cheeses

Cover the turkey pieces with water and add the onion stuck with cloves, celery, parsley, and hot peppers. Bring to a boil. Reduce the heat, skim off any scum on the surface, cover and simmer until the turkey is tender, but not falling from the bones. Remove turkey and cool until the pieces can be handled, then remove the meat from the bones in small pieces. Strain the broth and reduce by rapid boiling to 4 cups.

Sauté the chopped onions in the butter and oil until wilted, add the tomatoes and simmer until the tomatoes are melted into the onions. Add the basil, salt and freshly ground pepper to taste. Combine with the 4 cups broth and cook down for 20 minutes. Add the diced turkey and heat through.

177

Meanwhile, cook the spaghettini in rapidly boiling salted water until *al dente*. Drain well, toss with a little olive oil and put on a large hot platter. Spoon some of the turkey mixture over the top and serve the remainder in a bowl. Serve the grated cheeses separately, in bowls, to sprinkle on the top.

LEMON GRANITA
[LOU SEIBERT PAPPAS]

> 1¼ cups sugar
> 2 cups water
> 1 cup lemon juice
> 1 teaspoon grated lemon zest

Combine sugar and water in a saucepan, bring to a boil, and boil 2 minutes. Remove from heat and stir in lemon juice and zest. Freeze in an ice cream freezer according to manufacturer's directions, or pour into ice cube trays and freeze until solid.

Remove from freezer, chop coarsely, and turn into a mixing bowl. Beat with an electric mixer, until smooth and slushy. Turn into a plastic container, cover, and freeze until firm. If desired, serve in scooped-out lemon shells and place on citrus leaves. This will make about 3 cups of granita.

ORANGE GRANITA
[LOU SEIBERT PAPPAS]

> ¾ cup sugar
> 1 cup water
> 2 cups orange juice
> 2 tablespoons lemon juice
> 1 teaspoon grated orange zest

Combine sugar and water in a saucepan, bring to a boil, and boil 2 minutes. Remove from heat and stir in orange juice, lemon juice, and orange zest. Freeze in an ice cream freezer according to manufacturer's directions or pour into ice cube trays and freeze until solid. Remove from freezer, chop coarsely, and turn into a mixing bowl. Beat with an electric mixer, starting at low and gradually increasing to high speed, until it becomes smooth and slushy. Turn into a plastic container, cover, and freeze until firm. This will make about 3 cups of granita.

Sunday Night Supper for Eight

The pork casserole is a great party dish, because it needs nothing as accompaniment but a tossed green salad and a couple of loaves of crusty French bread. The preparation for the main dish and the dessert can both be done ahead of time. Carafes of a simple white wine or a pleasantly fruity rosé are best with this.

MENU

Pork with Fruited Lentils
Tossed Salad of Mixed Greens
Hot French Loaves
German Cheesecake

The Wine

Carafes of chilled California Chablis or Grenache Rosé

PORK WITH FRUITED LENTILS
[LELIA CARSON COX]

1¾ pounds lean pork, cubed
1 tablespoon butter
1 large onion, chopped
2 cloves garlic, minced
4 medium tomatoes, peeled and chopped
1½ cup lentils
4 cups water
3 teaspoons salt
¼ teaspoon ground pepper
1 teaspoon ground coriander
2 barely ripe bananas, cut in 1″ slices
1½ cups drained pineapple chunks

Trim all fat off pork. In deep, wide skillet or Dutch oven, spread pork out and barely cover with water. Simmer until liquid evaporates. This usually takes about an hour; if by this time liquid still remains, pour it off, add butter and brown the pork on all sides. Add onion and garlic and sauté until golden. Add tomatoes and simmer very slowly. Meanwhile cook the lentils slowly in 4 cups water until barely tender— about 40 minutes. Do not drain. Pour lentils into pork mixture and mix well. Add seasonings. Simmer 30 minutes or longer, stirring occasionally. A few minutes before serving, only long enough for the fruit to become barely warm, add bananas and well-drained pineapple (fresh or canned).

GERMAN CHEESECAKE

      18 pieces zwieback
      ¼ cup melted butter
       2 tablespoons sugar
       2 eggs, separated
      ½ cup sugar
       1 tablespoon lemon juice
           Zest of ½ lemon
       1 teaspoon vanilla extract
       1 pound cream cheese, cubed
       1 cup sour cream
       1 tablespoon sugar

Preheat oven to 300°. Place 6 pieces zwieback in blender container, cover, and run on a low speed until crumbled. Empty into a bowl and repeat with remaining zwieback. Mix in melted butter and 2 tablespoons sugar and press into the bottom of a 9″ spring-form pan. Bake 5 minutes. Cool. Put egg yolks, ½ cup sugar, lemon juice, lemon zest, half the vanilla extract, and half the cheese into blender container, cover, and run on medium speed until smooth. Add remaining cheese and continue to blend until very smooth. Beat egg whites with a whisk or rotary beater until stiff. Fold cheese mixture into egg whites, pour into pan with crust, and bake 45 minutes. Put sour cream, 1 tablespoon sugar, and remaining vanilla into blender container, cover, and process on a low speed until smooth. Spread evenly over top of cake and return to oven for 10 minutes. Cool cake, remove rim of pan before serving.

Winter One-Dish Supper for Eight to Ten

The simplest of all suppers for a Sunday night is a huge kettle of hearty, steaming soup with masses of hot French bread, carafes of red wine, and a lusciously sweet tart to follow.

MENU

Beef, Vegetable, and Barley Soup
Hot French Bread
Meringued Applesauce Tart

The Wine

Carafes of California Mountain Red Burgundy or Zinfandel

BEEF, VEGETABLE, AND BARLEY SOUP
[NIKA HAZELTON]

    1 pound lean beef—round, chuck, or soup meat
    2 cloves garlic
    2 bay leaves
    1 cup medium barley
    2 medium carrots, sliced
    2 medium stalks celery, sliced
    4 leeks, white and green parts, sliced
    4 tomatoes, peeled, seeded, and chopped
    2 teaspoons salt
  ½ teaspoon pepper
  ½ teaspoon thyme or marjoram
1½ pounds cabbage, coarsely chopped
    3 tablespoons butter
    1 medium onion, thinly sliced
    1 tablespoon flour
    4 medium potatoes, peeled and sliced or diced
  ½ cup minced parsley, or minced dill weed
     Sour cream

181

Put the meat in a deep kettle, add 12 cups water and bring to a quick boil. Skim thoroughly. Lower heat and add the garlic, bay leaves, barley, carrots, celery, leeks, tomatoes, salt, pepper, and thyme. Simmer, covered, over low heat for 1 hour. Meanwhile, put the cabbage into a deep bowl and add boiling water to cover. Let stand 5 minutes; drain. Heat the butter in a heavy saucepan until it turns brown. Add the onion and flour and cook, stirring constantly, until browned. Add the cabbage and blend. Simmer, covered, over low heat for 20 minutes, or until cabbage turns pinkish (see NOTE). Add a few tablespoons of kettle liquid to prevent scorching. Stir occasionally.

Add the cabbage with the potatoes to the soup. Simmer about 20 minutes more, or until potatoes are tender, stirring occasionally. If soup appears too thick, add a little more water. At serving time, remove meat from soup, dice, and return to the soup. Sprinkle with parsley or dill. Serve scalding hot, with sour cream.

NOTE: Braising the cabbage separately this way gives the soup a far better flavor.

MERINGUED APPLESAUCE TART
[ELAINE ROSS]

> ¼ pound sweet butter, softened
> 1 cup sugar
> 2 egg yolks
> ½ teaspoon almond extract
> ½ teaspoon vanilla
> 1¼ cups flour
> 2 cups thick applesauce
> 4 egg whites

Place the butter, ½ cup sugar, egg yolks, almond extract, vanilla, and flour in a bowl. Mix the ingredients with your hands until they form a smooth dough. Press the dough evenly over the bottom and ¾" up the sides of a 9" spring-form pan or 10" pie plate. Bake in a preheated 350° oven for 35 minutes, or until the crust is golden. Remove from the oven and reduce the heat to 325°.

Spread the applesauce on the crust. Beat the egg whites until stiff. Add the remaining ½ cup sugar gradually, continuing to beat until the meringue is thick and glossy. Spread over the applesauce, making sure to seal the meringue to the pan to prevent its shrinking during baking. Bake the tart for 15 to 20 minutes, or until the meringue topping is flecked with brown.

Buffet Parties

While a buffet is indisputably the easiest way to entertain a large number of guests, unhappy memories of soggy salads, overcooked turkeys, stringy hams, and anonymous casseroles cause many people to shy away at the very mention of the word. Such dispirited forms of entertaining bear no relation to the civilized and companionable meal a buffet can be, given a little care and forethought.

One of the reasons why the ham and turkey duo became such standard fare is that these are foods that feed a lot of people and don't suffer unduly from waiting. If you stop to think about it, there are many other dishes with the same virtues—curries and ragoûts, pâtés and terrines, cold roast meats with sauces (such as vitello tonnato), and almost anything cooked in pastry or encased in aspic. The thing to bear in mind is that the food should always be in prime condition when it is eaten, neither lukewarm nor dried up, but that's no real problem if you take full advantage of today's crop of highly efficient heating and chilling devices. The only exception is the green salad, which inevitably becomes limp and unappetizing if held too long. The answer is to use the crispest, hardiest greens available, such as romaine or endive, which can stand up to a long wait, toss them with the smallest amount of dressing, and put them on the table at the very last minute. For a really large party, it's a good idea to have a second bowl of greens chilling in the refrigerator, ready to replace the first when it shows signs of wilting. Other types of salad, other than the leafy green kind, are excellent for buffets. Rice salads, with diced vegetables mixed in, are excellent with meats, fish or poultry, and pretty impervious to time. So are platters of vegetables crisply cooked and dressed with a vinaigrette sauce, or tomato shells or cucumber cups stuffed with diced vegetables bound with mayonnaise.

One of the main advantages of buffet entertaining is that you aren't restricted to just a couple of dishes. If you wish, you can have a choice of two entrées, two salads, or a vegetable and a salad, and two desserts. As some people like a taste of everything, make sure that all the foods have an affinity and that there are no clashing conflicts of taste, and do provide plenty of plates, so your guests can take a separate one for salad (nothing is drearier than once-crisp greens awash in sauce), or sample two different dishes without having to put the whole thing on one plate.

Buffet food doesn't have to be strictly fork food, but it should be easy to eat (the less bone the better) and served in small manageable portions. No matter how good the food tastes or how hungry they are, people are apt to give up without finishing if they have to pick, poke, and struggle. Anything that is just too hard to cope with should be ruled out. And if you cherish your guests and want them to remember you fondly, you'll provide sit-down space for everyone, even if it is no more than a card table or a tray table, and put pepper mills and salt shakers out so they can season their food to taste.

A buffet can be as simple or as elaborate as your fancy and the guest list dictates. For a big holiday party, you'll obviously be more ambitious than you would if you were just having a small group for a summer meal on the terrace. A few well-prepared dishes suited to the occasion and the time of day are all that is required, and if you want to enjoy your own party, you'll keep away from things that need last-minute attention in favor of foods that can be wholly or partly cooked ahead.

Italian Buffet for Eight

This is a pleasant menu for a summer buffet, and relatively simple, as the whole thing can be done in the morning. As an alternate dessert for calorie-counters, have a big bowl of ripe strawberries, lightly sugared and bathed in a light red wine (about 1½ cups to 3 pints strawberries). Drink a white Italian wine with the veal.

MENU

Artichokes à l'Italienne
Cold Roast Filet of Veal, Italian Sauce
Rice Salad with Peas and Pimientos
Caprese Chocolate and Almond Cake
Strawberries in Red Wine

The Wine

Verdicchio or Chiaretto del Garda

ARTICHOKES À L'ITALIENNE
[ELAINE ROSS]

- 4 packages frozen artichoke hearts
- 12 tablespoons olive oil
- 4 tablespoons lemon juice
- ½ teaspoon freshly ground black pepper
- 2 small garlic cloves, mashed
- 4 tablespoons crumbled Gorgonzola cheese
- Salt to taste

Cook artichoke hearts according to package directions. Drain well. Combine the remaining ingredients to make a dressing. Pour over the hot artichoke hearts and cool.

COLD ROAST FILET OF VEAL
[ELAINE ROSS]

Rub the filet well with salt and pepper, then wrap with bacon slices and tie securely. Place on a rack in a shallow roasting pan. Roast in a 325° oven, basting from time to time with the pan juices mixed with 1 cup white wine, until the veal reaches an internal temperature of 165°. Remove the bacon for the last 15 minutes. Cool. Slice and serve with the thick Italian Sauce (see below).

185

ITALIAN SAUCE

  1 medium eggplant, sliced ½" thick
  1 teaspoon salt
  ⅓ cup olive oil
  1 medium onion, peeled and chopped
  1 green pepper, seeded and coarsely chopped
  1 tomato, peeled, seeded, and coarsely chopped
  2 tablespoons tomato paste
  1 clove garlic, very finely minced
  ¼ teaspoon coarse black pepper
  ½ teaspoon sugar
  1 cup chicken, meat, or vegetable stock
  3 tablespoons freshly grated Romano cheese
  ⅓ cup mayonnaise

Sprinkle the eggplant with salt and let stand for half an hour. Wipe the slices dry and sauté them in ¼ cup of the oil until slightly brown on both sides. Remove the eggplant, cut into cubes and reserve. Sauté the onion and pepper in a large, heavy skillet in the remaining oil over medium heat, until the onion is golden. Add the cubed eggplant, tomato, tomato paste, garlic, pepper, sugar, and stock and simmer, covered, for ½ hour, or until the vegetables are very tender. (Add more liquid if necessary during cooking.) Stir in the cheese, remove from the heat, adjust seasonings and cool. Blend in the mayonnaise and chill. Makes 4 cups.

RICE SALAD WITH PEAS AND PIMIENTO
[ELAINE ROSS]

  1½ cups long-grain rice
  ¾ cup French dressing
  1 package frozen peas, cooked
  2-ounce can pimiento

Pour 2 quarts of water into a saucepan and bring to a rolling boil. Add the rice slowly and cook for 14 minutes, or until tender, but still firm. Drain thoroughly, add the salad dressing and peas. Drain the pimiento and cut into julienne strips, saving all the scraps. Mince the scraps, fold them into the rice, pack the rice in a bowl, and chill. At serving time, unmold onto a platter and arrange the pimiento strips in a decorative pattern over the dome of rice.

CAPRESE CHOCOLATE AND ALMOND CAKE
[COUNTESS MARGARET WILLAUMEZ]

> 1 cup butter
> 1 cup plus 2 teaspoons sugar
> 4 eggs, separated
> 7 ounces unsweetened chocolate
> 1⅔ cups blanched almonds
>   Confectioners' sugar

Cream butter and sugar together. Beat in egg yolks. Put chocolate and almonds through a grinder until they come out seed-pearl size. Add chocolate and almonds to butter-sugar mixture. Beat egg whites until stiff and carefully fold into chocolate mixture. Pour into foil-lined buttered 8″ spring-form pan. Bake in a 300° oven for 40 minutes. Cake will be fudgy, about 1½ inches high. Carefully remove from pan and peel off foil. Sprinkle confectioners' sugar on top and draw trellis design in sugar with a knife.

German Buffet for Ten

Berner Platte, a close cousin of the Alsatian choucroute garnie, is a good buffet party dish for robust eaters. All the ingredients can be cooked beforehand and assembled at serving time. With this, have a German Rhine wine.

MENU
[NIKA HAZELTON]

Smoked Fish with Horseradish Cream, Mustard Mayonnaise,
and Lemon Quarters
Thin Brown Bread and Butter Sandwiches
Berner Platte

Hazelnut Torte

The Wine

Johannisberg Riesling

SMOKED FISH

Arrange on a platter or board a selection of sliced smoked white fish, trout, salmon, sturgeon and eel. Provide capers, oil, a pepper mill and lemon wedges for the smoked salmon, a mustard mayonnaise with chopped dill for the whitefish, and sour cream with freshly grated horseradish for the trout. With this have thin sandwiches of buttered rye or pumpernickel bread.

BERNER PLATTE

First pot:
 2 tablespoons bacon fat or other shortening
 1 onion, chopped
 2 cups sauerkraut
 4 juniper berries, crushed
 1 cup dry white wine
 6 smoked pork chops (about 3 pounds)
 ½ pound bacon, in one piece
  12″ Polish sausage or mild Italian sausage

Second pot:
 3 pigs' hocks
 6 pigs' ears and 2 pigs' tongues or 1 small beef tongue, fresh or smoked, ready to cook

    2 quarts water
    2 teaspoons salt
    ⅓ cup sliced celery
    1 leek or 1 medium onion, chopped
    1 carrot, sliced

Third pot:
    6 medium potatoes, peeled and quartered

Fourth pot:
    1 pound string beans
    2 tablespoons butter
    Salt, pepper

To prepare first pot, melt fat or shortening in Dutch kettle, and brown onion. Add sauerkraut, juniper berries, and white wine. Place pork chops and bacon on sauerkraut. Simmer covered over low heat for 1 hour. Add Polish or Italian sausage. Simmer covered for 1 more hour.

To prepare second pot, place hocks, ears and tongues in Dutch kettle. Add water, salt, celery, leek (or onion) and carrot. Simmer covered over low heat about 1 hour, or until meat is tender.

To prepare third pot, cook potatoes in boiling salted water until tender. Drain. Shake in pan in which they were cooked over lowest possible heat to dry. Cover with clean kitchen towel, keep warm.

To prepare fourth pot, cook string beans in boiling salted water in the usual manner. Season with butter, salt and pepper to taste. Keep warm.

To assemble Berner Platte, slice all meats. Heat 2 large serving platters. Place sauerkraut on first platter. Arrange pork chops, sliced bacon, and sliced sausage on top in rows. Place string beans on second platter. Arrange pigs' hocks, ears, and sliced tongue on top in rows. Serve steamed potatoes separately. Have a choice of several kinds of mild and hot mustards on the table.

HAZELNUT TORTE

¼ cup butter
½ cup sugar
8 eggs, separated
4 ounces semi-sweet chocolate
2 teaspoons grated lemon rind
½ cup fine dry bread crumbs
1 cup toasted hazelnuts, ground
2 cups heavy cream, whipped, sweetened to taste

Cream the butter until soft. Add the sugar and beat well. Beat in the egg yolks, one at a time, beating well after each addition, until the mixture is thick and lemon-colored (it is best to use an electric beater). Melt the chocolate over hot water. Stir the chocolate into the egg mixture. Beat in the lemon rind, bread crumbs and ½ cup of the hazelnuts. Beat the egg whites until very stiff and fold into the batter. Grease three 8″ layer-cake pans and line the bottoms with wax paper. Spread batter evenly in the pans. Bake in a preheated 325° oven about 30 minutes, or until a light touch with the finger leaves no depression in the cake. Turn out on a wire rack and cool. Do not remove wax paper until ready to frost. Fill and frost with the whipped cream. Sprinkle with the remaining hazelnuts.

No-Trouble Buffet for Eight to Twelve

If you're having friends in for bridge, this is a surefire menu on all counts. You can prepare the casserole in advance and pop it in the oven an hour before the game ends. All it requires is a place to balance a plate, for the main dish is designed to be eaten with a fork. If you want to serve something first, you might make up an appetizer that can be brought out of the refrigerator and handed around with cocktails. Have a young white wine with the chicken.

MENU

Swedish Smoked Salmon Balls
Chicken à la King Casserole
Salad of Endive Spears with French Dressing, Chopped Parsley
Fresh Pineapple with Framboise

The Wine

Alsatian Riesling or Muscadet

SWEDISH SMOKED SALMON BALLS
[PHILIP S. BROWN]

> 1 pound smoked salmon
> ½ pound cream cheese
> 1 teaspoon lemon juice
> 1 tablespoon light cream
> Salt, pepper to taste
> Dill weed or finely chopped fresh dill

Grind the salmon, using the fine blade of the food chopper. Combine with the cream cheese, lemon juice, cream, salt and pepper. Roll into marble-size balls. Roll in dill weed or fresh dill. Chill and serve on picks. Makes 40 to 50 balls. This is an easy appetizer that can be made ahead and kept in the refrigerator until cocktail time.

CHICKEN À LA KING CASSEROLE
[NIKA HAZELTON]

- 1½ cups chicken broth
- 1½ cups light cream or milk
- 1 medium onion, stuck with 3 cloves
- Butter (about 1 cup)
- 6 tablespoons flour
- 2 cups sliced mushrooms
- ½ cup minced green pepper
- ½ cup diced pimiento, cut into ¼" dice
- 4 cups diced cooked chicken
- 2 teaspoons salt, or to taste
- ½ teaspoon pepper, or to taste
- 2⅔ cups long-grain rice
- 1 cup grated Parmesan or Swiss cheese
- 3 egg yolks, beaten

Combine the chicken broth, cream, and onion and simmer for 5 minutes. Remove the onion and keep liquid hot. Melt 6 tablespoons of the butter and stir in the flour. Cook, stirring constantly, for 2 minutes. Do not let brown. Add the hot liquid all at once (discard onion) and cook over low heat, stirring constantly, until the sauce is smooth and thickened. Remove from heat. Heat 4 tablespoons butter in another saucepan and cook the mushrooms and green pepper 5 to 7 minutes, stirring frequently. Stir into the sauce. Add the pimiento, chicken, salt and pepper. Remove from heat.

Meanwhile cook the rice in plenty of boiling salted water until barely tender. Drain thoroughly. Melt ⅓ cup butter and combine with the rice, ½ cup of the cheese, and beaten egg yolks. Mix well. Put ⅔ of the rice mixture into a greased 3-quart casserole. Press the rice against the bottom and sides, leaving a well in the middle. Put the chicken filling into the well. Spoon the remaining rice over the filling, taking care that it is completely covered. Sprinkle remaining ½ cup cheese over top. Bake in a preheated 350° oven for about 1 hour, or until top is golden.

NOTE: Two tablespoons brandy or sherry may be added to the cooked filling, if you wish.

Kitchen Buffet for Ten to Twelve

For an informal party, take advantage of the fact that guests naturally gravitate to the spot where things are cooking by making the kitchen, rather than the dining room, your buffet headquarters. Set plates, flatware, and napkins on the countertop, let everyone help themselves to soup from a big iron kettle on the stove, then come back for the main course and later, the dessert, each time returning their dishes and picking up fresh plates and flatware, which makes it infinitely easier for you to cope with the party debris.

MENU

Russian Barley and Mushroom Soup
Stuffed Cabbage
Steamed Potatoes   *Hot French Bread*
Quiche Cassonade

The Wine

Lightly chilled Beaujolais de l'année

RUSSIAN BARLEY AND MUSHROOM SOUP
[KAY SHAW NELSON]

  3 ounces dried mushrooms
  ½ cup chopped onion
  1 leek, chopped
  3 tablespoons butter
  1 cup diced carrots
  ⅓ cup pearl barley
  1 teaspoon salt
  4 peppercorns
  2 cups diced potatoes
  2 bay leaves
  1 cup sour cream
  Chopped fresh dill

Soak the mushrooms in lukewarm water to cover for 20 minutes. Drain, pressing to extract water. Slice mushrooms. Sauté the onion and leek in the butter in a large saucepan until tender. Add the carrots, barley, salt, peppercorns, and 2 quarts water. Bring to a boil. Lower the heat and simmer, covered, for 1 hour. Add the potatoes, bay leaves, and mushrooms. Continue to simmer until the vegetables are tender, about 45 minutes. Mix in the sour cream just before serving. Garnish with chopped dill.

STUFFED CABBAGE
[HELEN EVANS BROWN]

> 1 large savoy cabbage, outer leaves left on
> 3 pounds ground lean beef
> 1 pound ground veal
> 1 cup finely chopped yellow onion
> 2 teaspoons finely chopped garlic
> 3 tablespoons finely chopped parsley
> 1 teaspoon each: dried thyme, ground nutmeg, paprika, ground black pepper
> 2 teaspoons salt
> 3 whole eggs
> ½ pound bacon
> 1 each: white onion, carrot, stalk of celery, all sliced
> 2 small bay leaves
> 2½ cups chicken stock

Cut a thin slice from the stalk of the cabbage so it will stand. Remove any damaged outer leaves carefully, without spoiling the shape of the cabbage. Stand it on a rack over a pan (or in a sink) and slowly pour boiling water on it to loosen the leaves. Gently push leaves back with two wooden spoons until you get to the heart.

Mix the ground meats, chopped onion, garlic and parsley, herbs (except bay leaves), seasoning and eggs in a large bowl. Work together with the hand until thoroughly blended. Stuff and reshape the cabbage, starting at the heart. Hold leaves together with toothpicks and tie securely with crisscross pieces of string.

Line the inside of a deep heavy Dutch oven with slices of bacon, scatter over them the sliced onion, carrot, and celery. Stand the stuffed cabbage on top, sprinkle with a little salt and pepper, add the bay leaves and stock. Cover pan with lid and seal it with a thick flour-and-water paste. Cook in a 275° oven for about 3 hours. Remove and allow to stand for 5 minutes before carefully removing the cover. To serve, place the cabbage on a shallow round earthenware platter, strain juices over it and cut into wedge-shaped pieces, like a cake.

QUICHE CASSONADE
[JAMES A. BEARD]

> 1 yeast cake or 1 package granular yeast
> ¼ cup hot water (110° to 115°)
> 1 tablespoon sugar
> 1 teaspoon salt
> 6 tablespoons softened butter
> 2½ to 3 cups flour
> 2 eggs, lightly beaten
> 2 cups dark-brown sugar
> 8 eggs
> 2 to 2½ cups heavy cream

Dissolve the yeast in hot water with the sugar, salt, and butter. Work this mixture with the flour and beaten eggs to make a rather firm, smooth paste. Beat well with your hand or beat for about 5 minutes in an electric mixer equipped with a dough hook. If an electric mixer is not used, knead lightly on a floured board for 5 minutes, adding enough flour to make a firm but somewhat soft dough. Place in a buttered bowl and cover. Let rise in a warm spot until double in bulk—about 1 hour. Punch down and knead lightly. Roll on a floured board about ¼″ thick. Divide into two portions and line two 8″ flan rings, tart pans, or pie tins with the dough. Do not prebake.

Sprinkle the shells well with the dark-brown sugar. Mix the 8 eggs and cream thoroughly together, and pour over the sugar. Bake in a 375° oven until the custard is just set. Serve warm.

Teen-Age Birthday Buffet for a Crowd

If you want your teen-ager's birthday party to be a roaring success, all you need to do is provide the kind of food that gets the youth vote today, then gracefully retire. You might set up a portable oven, in the family room or on the terrace, with trays of the unbaked tiny pizzas to be topped with whatever way-out combinations the guests dream up. If you don't want to make tortillas for the tacos, you can buy them frozen or canned. Should you wish to, there's a recipe on page 300, also one for frijoles refritos. The guacamole recipe is on page 369. Canned chiles and taco sauces can be bought at most specialty food shops, Latin American markets, and some supermarkets, depending on what part of the country you live in.

For dessert, have an ice cream sundae bar. Provide quarts of ice cream of different flavors and all the other fixings—frozen raspberries and strawberries in syrup, thawed; jams and preserves; chocolate syrup; bananas; chopped nuts; whipped cream and candied or maraschino cherries. This, with your offspring's favorite birthday cake, should be sufficient to assuage the healthiest of appetites.

MENU

Tiny Pizzas   Tacos with a Choice of Fillings
Ice Cream Sundaes   Birthday Cake
Soft Drinks, Pink Lemonade, Pitchers of Orange Juice

TINY PIZZAS
[JAMES A. BEARD]

These may be prepared with a pizza dough or with refrigerated biscuits. If you use the latter, roll them or pat them out very thin and brush the surface with a little olive oil before spooning on the filling.

> 1 cake or package yeast
> 1 cup warm water (110° to 115°)
> 1 tablespoon salt
> 1 teaspoon sugar
> Olive oil
> Approximately 4 cups flour
> Onion Purée or Tomato Sauce (see recipes below)
> Thin slices of Mozzarella or Switzerland Gruyère cheese, or grated Gruyère cheese
> Thin slices of salami, pepperoni, or any good cured sausage

Anchovy filets
Soft Italian olives
Tuna filets
Grated Parmesan or Romano cheese
Hot peppers
Dried or fresh thyme or basil

Dissolve the yeast in the warm water with the salt and sugar. Combine with 2 to 3 tablespoons olive oil and about 2 cups of flour. Roll out on a floured board and knead in enough flour to make a stiffish dough. Continue kneading until the dough is smooth and elastic. Place in a warm, draft-free spot and let rise until double in bulk. Punch down. Divide the dough in half, roll out, and cut into rounds varying from 2½" to 4" in diameter. Arrange on buttered cookie sheets and brush with olive oil. Spoon Onion Purée or Tomato Sauce on the pizzas and top with your choice of any of the remaining ingredients. You can, of course, add anything to your pizzas that imagination and taste suggest. A sprinkling of oregano is the traditional seasoning, but try thyme or basil instead. The flavor is much subtler. If fresh basil is in season, use it lavishly. Brush the prepared pizzas lightly with oil and bake in a 400° oven until crisp. Serve at once. Make plenty of these little goodies.

ONION PURÉE

3 large onions, finely chopped
4 to 5 tablespoons butter
1 teaspoon salt

Sauté the onions gently in the butter until they begin to turn golden. Season with salt. Cover and steam for about 10 minutes, or until quite soft, then cook down until most of the liquid has evaporated—they should be almost a paste. Anchovies and soft black olives make an excellent topping.

TOMATO SAUCE

12 to 14 ripe tomatoes, peeled, seeded, and chopped (or two 29-ounce cans Italian plum tomatoes)
3 tablespoons butter
3 tablespoons olive oil
1 teaspoon salt
2 teaspoons sugar
1 clove garlic, crushed
1 medium onion, sliced
1 6-ounce can Italian tomato paste
1 tablespoon chopped fresh basil or 1 teaspoon dried
Freshly ground black pepper to taste

Unless the tomatoes are very ripe and flavorful, it is better to use the canned Italian plum tomatoes. Cook fresh tomatoes in a heavy skillet with the butter and oil until heated through. Add salt, sugar, garlic, and onion. Cook down well, stirring from time to time. Add tomato paste and seasonings and cook for about 15 to 20 minutes over medium heat. Strain through a fairly coarse sieve. Correct seasoning. Makes about 3 cups.

TACOS
[ELISABETH ORTIZ]

Tacos are small (4″) tortillas stuffed with various mixtures, rolled, fastened with a toothpick, fried in lard and served with various sauces and chiles on the side, or served unfried so that they can be partly unrolled and filled with extras to individual taste. In the United States the taco is not rolled, but simply folded in half. In Mexico they are always rolled.

For a taco party set out bowls of various sauces, canned chiles, chopped lettuce, fried chopped chorizo (hot Spanish sausage), shredded chicken and pork, guacamole, frijoles refritos or either of the following taco fillings. Serve with hot tortillas to be filled and eaten unfried.

TACO FILLINGS

Tacos de Jamon: Mix together 1 cup chopped boiled ham, 1 table-spoon finely chopped onion, 3½-ounce package mashed cream cheese, 2 medium, peeled, seeded, and chopped tomatoes, and chopped canned serrano or jalapeño chile to taste. Makes enough to stuff 12 small tortillas. Serve with guacamole.

Tacos de Frijol: Stuff tacos with frijoles refritos, strips of jalapeño chile, Monterey Jack or similar cheese, and serve with guacamole.

Curry Buffet for Twenty to Twenty-Four

As long, slow cooking is the secret of Indian curry dishes, it really isn't difficult to prepare enough of them for a big buffet dinner because nothing really needs last-minute watching. The traditional way of serving an Indian meal is to have a small helping of a number of different dishes—curried meat, chicken, fish, vegetables, plain rice, dal (lentils), a couple of pickles or chutneys, a yoghurt-based raita, and some form of Indian bread. These are served individually on a metal tray, or *thali*, with the rice or bread in the center and the other foods in small bowls around it. You can easily adapt this idea to buffet service by having large dinner plates or inexpensive round lacquer Japanese trays on which a portion of each dish can be accommodated. Indians eat with the fingers of their right hand, but Westerners will expect forks. A recipe for a typical Indian bread, chapati, is given, but you may prefer instead to use pappadums, which come canned and need only to be fried in hot oil.

Indian desserts tend to be intensely sweet and not very pleasing to Western tastes. A better choice would be fresh tropical fruits or ice cream or sherbet with fresh fruit. Alcoholic beverages are not served with meals in India, but here it is customary to have cold beer which offsets the spiciness of the curries.

MENU
[ELISABETH ORTIZ]

Madras Chicken Curry   *Kofta Curry*   *Mughlai Biryani*
Vegetable Bhaji   *Dal*   *Boiled Rice*
Fresh Mint Chutney   *Cucumber Raita*   *Lemon or Lime Pickle*
Pappadums   *Chapatis*
Platter of Fresh Tropical Fruits (Mangoes, Pineapple, Bananas, Papaya)

The Drink

Chilled beer

MADRAS CHICKEN CURRY

    4 tablespoons ghee or unsalted butter
3½- to 4-pound chicken, cut into serving pieces
    2 medium onions, finely chopped
    2 cloves garlic, chopped
    2 tart, green apples, peeled, cored, and coarsely chopped
    2 medium bananas, sliced
    2 tablespoons pungent curry powder
    ¼ cup raisins
    2 tablespoons mango chutney, coarsely chopped
    1 teaspoon ground ginger
    1 teaspoon Spanish (hot) paprika or cayenne pepper
    ½ teaspoon freshly ground black pepper
    Salt
    2 cups chicken stock (approximately)
    Juice of ½ lemon

Heat the ghee in a large, heavy frying pan and sauté the chicken pieces until golden. Transfer them to a heavy casserole. Sauté the onions, garlic, apples, and bananas in the remaining ghee until the onion is tender. Remove to the casserole with a slotted spoon. Stir the curry powder into the fat remaining in the pan, adding a little more if necessary, and cook for 5 minutes, stirring from time to time, being careful not to let it burn. Add this to the casserole with the raisins, mango chutney, ginger, Spanish paprika, black pepper, salt to taste, and chicken stock to cover (about 2 cups). Cook, covered, for ½ hour, then continue cooking uncovered until the chicken is tender and gravy is thick. Before serving, stir in lemon juice. Serve with plain boiled white rice.

KOFTA CURRY (MEATBALL CURRY)

　　1 pound round steak, ground twice
　　1 medium onion, finely chopped
　　2 cloves garlic, chopped
　　1 tablespoon mint leaves, chopped
　¼ teaspoon ground ginger
　¼ teaspoon cayenne pepper
　¼ teaspoon ground cloves
　　　Salt, freshly ground black pepper to taste

Mix all the ingredients together very thoroughly and shape into balls the size of walnuts. Set aside while making the sauce (see below).

SAUCE

　　4 tablespoons salad oil
　　1 medium onion, chopped
　　2 cloves garlic, chopped
　　1 tablespoon fresh ginger root, chopped
　1½ teaspoons ground coriander seeds
　　1 medium tomato, peeled and coarsely chopped
　　2 8-ounce containers plain yoghurt
　　　Salt, freshly ground black pepper
　½ cup water

Heat the oil in a frying pan and sauté the onion, garlic, and ginger until the onion is tender but not browned. Add the coriander and tomato and cook for 3 or 4 minutes longer. Add the yoghurt, salt, and pepper to taste and simmer for 5 minutes to blend.

Add the water and the meatballs and simmer for 15 minutes or until the meatballs are cooked through. Makes about 24 meatballs.

MUGHLAI BIRYANI (LAMB CURRY)

    2 cups rice
    3 large onions, thinly sliced
    1 pound unsalted butter
    1 cup blanched almonds, ground
    1 tablespoon fresh ginger root, chopped
    6 cloves garlic, chopped
    ½ teaspoon cayenne pepper
    3 pounds lean, boneless lamb, cut into 1″ pieces, or 3 pounds
      chicken similarly cut
      Beef or chicken stock or water
    2 8-ounce containers of yoghurt
    ½ teaspoon ground cloves
    ¼ teaspoon ground cardamom
    ½ teaspoon ground cinnamon
    1 teaspoon ground cumin
    2 tablespoons fresh hot green peppers, seeded and chopped
    3 tablespoons chopped coriander leaves
    1 tablespoon chopped mint
      Juice of 2 lemons (approximately ½ cup)
      Salt and freshly ground black pepper
    1 cup milk
    ¼ teaspoon ground saffron

Cook the rice in a large quantity of boiling salted water for 15 minutes, drain, and set aside.

Sauté the onions in 4 tablespoons of the butter until golden brown. Set aside.

In 2 tablespoons of butter lightly sauté the almonds, ginger, garlic, and cayenne pepper, and mix thoroughly with the lamb or chicken. Put the meat in a large, heavy casserole, cover with stock or water, and simmer gently, partially covered, about 1½ hours for the lamb and ¾ hour for the chicken. There should be only about 1 cup of liquid left. If necessary, remove the meat and reduce the gravy over brisk heat.

Drain the yoghurt through cheesecloth and mix thoroughly with the cloves, cardamom, cinnamon, cumin, fresh hot peppers, coriander, mint, lemon juice, salt and freshly ground black pepper to taste. Add yoghurt mixture and half the fried onions to the meat in the casserole, mixing well.

Spoon half the rice over the meat to cover it, then a layer of the remaining onions and rice. Melt the remaining butter and pour over the rice. Mix the saffron and milk together and pour on top. Cover and cook in a 300° oven for 1 hour.

To serve, either garnish the casserole with sliced hard-cooked eggs, fried slivered almonds, and fried golden raisins, or remove the rice, heap the meat on a large platter, cover with the rice, and garnish with the eggs, almonds, and raisins.

VEGETABLE BHAJI (FRIED VEGETABLE CURRY)

   4 tablespoons ghee or unsalted butter
   2 medium onions, finely chopped
   2 teaspoons mild curry powder
   ⅛ teaspoon cayenne pepper
   ¼ teaspoon powdered ginger
  12 new potatoes, scraped and cubed
   2 medium tomatoes, peeled, seeded, and chopped
   2 cups peas
     Salt
   1 tablespoon lemon juice
   1 tablespoon chopped fresh coriander

Heat the ghee in a large heavy frying pan that has a cover. Sauté the onions until they are golden brown. Add the curry powder, cayenne pepper, and ginger, and cook, stirring, for 1 or 2 minutes. Add the potatoes and tomatoes and cook, stirring frequently for about 10 minutes. Add the peas and cook for 2 or 3 minutes longer. Add salt to taste. Pour in 1 cup of hot water, adding more if necessary during the cooking process. Bring to a boil, cover, and cook over very low heat until the potatoes are tender, about 15 minutes, and the bhaji is dry. Just before serving add the lemon juice and coriander. Serves 6. Double the recipe, if you wish.

NOTE: Carrots, green beans, artichokes, cauliflower, and eggplant, cut into small pieces, can be variously combined and cooked in this way. Yoghurt may be used instead of water to cook the vegetables, in which case omit the lemon juice.

DAL

Lentils are served as a side dish with all types of Indian curries

1 pound lentils
Salt
4 tablespoons unsalted butter
2 medium onions, finely chopped
2 medium tomatoes, peeled, seeded, and chopped (optional)
¼ teaspoon ground turmeric
¼ teaspoon ground cumin
¼ teaspoon cayenne pepper
1 tablespoon fresh coriander leaves, chopped (optional)

Put the lentils, water to cover, and salt to taste in a saucepan, cover, and cook until almost done. The quick-cooking variety takes only about 20 minutes. Meanwhile heat the butter in a frying pan and sauté the onions, with tomatoes if desired, until golden brown. Add the turmeric, cumin, and cayenne pepper and mix thoroughly, off the heat. Stir the onion mixture into the lentils and continue cooking until the lentils are done, about 5 minutes. Just before serving, garnish with the coriander. Serves 6. Double or triple the recipe, if you wish.

NOTE: Cubed potatoes, eggplant, or peas may all be added to the lentils when cooking.

CUCUMBER RAITA

Raitas are cold dishes made with yoghurt, vegetables, occasionally fruits, and seasonings. The vegetable raitas are served with curries. Their cool, rather tart flavor makes a pleasant contrast to a hot or pungent curry. The fruit raitas are served as dessert.

2 8-ounce containers plain yoghurt
Salt, freshly ground black pepper
1 teaspoon caraway seeds
1 fresh hot green pepper, seeded and chopped
1 tablespoon coriander leaves, chopped
1 cucumber, peeled and grated

Beat the yoghurt until it is smooth, add salt and pepper to taste and the remaining ingredients. Mix well and refrigerate for a short time before serving. Serves 6. Makes about 2½ cups. Triple the recipe for buffet service, or use a raita variation.

VARIATIONS: Tomato Raita—omit the cucumber and add sliced tomatoes; Potato Raita—add diced boiled potatoes instead of cucumber; Mint and Onion Raita—instead of the cucumber add 2 finely sliced onions and 3 tablespoons chopped mint leaves. (Other cooked and well-drained vegetables such as zucchini and eggplant can also be used.)

FRESH MINT CHUTNEY

      2 ounces mint leaves
      1 small white onion
      2 fresh hot green chili peppers
      1 teaspoon fresh ginger root, chopped
      ½ teaspoon sugar
      1 teaspoon salt
        Juice of ½ lemon

Wash the mint, drain, and grind to a paste with the onion, peppers, ginger, sugar, and salt. Add the lemon juice, mixing well. Refrigerate until ready to use. Fresh coriander leaves may be used instead of mint. Yields about 1 cup.

LEMON OR LIME PICKLE

      4 large lemons or limes (about 1 pound)
      2 tablespoons salt
      4 large cloves of garlic, peeled
      ½ pound raisins
      1 teaspoon Spanish (hot) paprika or cayenne pepper
      2 teaspoons ground ginger
      2 cups white vinegar
     12 ounces granulated sugar

Slice the lemons or limes lengthwise into quarters but do not sever them. Remove the seeds. Sprinkle with the salt, and put them in a bowl in a cool place for 4 days, turning them quite often. On the third day put the garlic, raisins, paprika, and ginger into a bowl with the vinegar and allow to stand for 24 hours. Mince the lemons and the raisins and mix together with all the liquid in a heavy saucepan. Add the sugar, bring to a boil, reduce the heat, and simmer, stirring occasionally until the liquid has reduced and thickened. Allow to cool, bottle, and refrigerate. Makes about 4 cups.

CHAPATI

    3 cups whole-meal flour
    1 cup all-purpose flour
    1 teaspoon salt
      Water
      Butter

Sieve both flours together with the salt into a large bowl. Add enough water to make a fairly stiff dough. Knead thoroughly until the dough is smooth and elastic. Cover with a damp cloth and leave for 2 or 3 hours. Knead again thoroughly. Cut pieces the size of a small egg and form into round balls. Roll out as thin as possible into circles. Heat an ungreased griddle and cook the chapatis, one by one, for about 20 seconds, then turn and cook until light spots appear on the top side, turn again and cook until the chapati puffs up and browns. Butter and keep warm. Serve as soon as possible after cooking. Serves 6. Increase this recipe for buffet service according to how many chapatis are needed.

Cold Buffet for Twenty

This is a delightful summer party menu, but be sure, if the day is hot, that you keep the salmon and filet chilled until the last minute and don't let them sit unprotected on the table too long, or the aspic will melt. This kind of buffet is better served indoors than out. The frozen desserts, too, should not be brought out until the guests are ready to eat them. Serve chilled white and red wines with this.

MENU

Terrine of Duck with Orange

Salmon in Aspic   Filet of Beef in Aspic

Wilted Cucumber with Dill

Tomatoes Stuffed with Salade Russe

Potato and Hearts of Palm Salad

Endive Salad

Rolls   French Bread

Frozen Daiquiri Soufflé   Tortoni Alexis

The Wines

Pouilly Fuissé and lightly chilled Fleurie

TERRINE OF DUCK WITH ORANGE
[JAMES A. BEARD]

    6-pound duck
¼ pound baked ham
¼ pound pork fat
    Salt
¼ teaspoon Spice Parisienne or quatre épices
⅔ cup Grand Marnier liqueur
½ pound lean pork
½ pound veal
½ pound fresh pork siding or fat pork
 2 cloves garlic
 2 teaspoons tarragon
 1 bay leaf, crushed
½ teaspoon Tabasco sauce
 2 eggs
    Salt pork strips
 2 cups aspic (see recipe below)
    Juice of 1 orange
 1 orange, thinly sliced

207

Bone the duck completely, remove the breast meat, and save the skin. Cut the breast, the ham, and the pork fat into ½″ cubes. Add 2 teaspoons salt, the spice, and ⅓ cup of the Grand Marnier. Marinate for 2 hours.

Grind the lean pork, veal, fat pork, and the rest of the duck meat with the garlic, 1 tablespoon salt, tarragon, bay leaf, and Tabasco. Beat the eggs lightly and add to the mixture. Combine with the cubed meats and the marinade, and mix thoroughly. Line a terrine with a few strips of salt pork, add the meat mixture, and cover with the duck skin. Bake in a 350° oven for 1½ to 2 hours, or until the liquid and fat are completely clear. Cool 15 minutes. Weight the terrine and let it cool until the next day.

To serve: remove the weight and unmold the terrine. Carefully remove all the fat from the terrine and the pâté. Save the natural jelly. Replace the pâté in the terrine. Add the jelly to the aspic with the orange juice and remaining ⅓ cup Grand Marnier. Cover the pâté with orange slices, and then spoon the aspic over it. Chill thoroughly. Serve from the terrine or on a platter decorated with orange slices which have been dipped in aspic and chilled.

ASPIC

> 3 envelopes unflavored gelatin
> 1½ pints clarified veal, beef, or chicken stock
> ¼ cup white wine

Soften gelatin in ¾ cup cold water. Heat broth and wine to the boiling point and combine with the gelatin. Stir until thoroughly melted. Chill. If aspic is to be used for chopping, add another envelope of gelatin and pour it into a large platter or flat pan to chill.

SALMON IN ASPIC
[PHILIP S. BROWN]

> 8- to 10-pound whole salmon
> Court bouillon
> 1 egg white, slightly beaten, and egg shell
> 2 envelopes unflavored gelatin
> 2 hard-cooked eggs, sliced
> Stuffed green olives, sliced

Fresh tarragon leaves (if available)
½ pound cooked shrimp, cleaned
Parsley

Poach the fish in court bouillon until done; skin and chill. Reheat the court bouillon, add the egg white and egg shell, let come to a boil, then remove from heat. Let it stand for a few minutes to settle, then strain through a linen cloth wrung out in cold water. There should now be 4 cups of very clear liquid. Dissolve the gelatin in ½ cup cold water, add to the hot clarified bouillon, and allow to cool. When the aspic starts to congeal, brush the salmon with a thin coating, then decorate with hard-cooked egg slices, stuffed olive slices, and tarragon leaves, and chill again until they stay firmly in place.

Now pour the rest of the aspic evenly over the fish, covering it completely with a shimmering transparent coat. Garnish prettily with the cooked shrimp, put a wreath of parsley around the edge of the platter, and serve with pride. For a finishing touch, make more aspic, pour it into a shallow pan to set, then dice small and strew around the fish.

FILET OF BEEF IN ASPIC
[PHILIP S. BROWN]

5- to 6-pound tenderloin
Lardoons (strips of pork fat)
Truffles, halved or quartered
3 to 4 tablespoons butter
Madeira or port
2 cups beef aspic
Balls of pâté de foie gras rolled in finely chopped truffles for garnish

Trim the ends from the whole tenderloin (save them for Stroganoff) and bard it well with strips of pork fat. With a clean knife-sharpening steel, make a hole through the meat lengthwise, and fill it with halved or quartered truffles, pushing them in from both ends. Brown the meat well on all sides in the butter in a heavy skillet, then lower the heat and cook for half an hour, turning occasionally and basting now and again with a little Madeira or port. When done, cool the meat, then chill in the refrigerator.

Have ready a strong beef aspic flavored with a little Madeira or port.

209

If aspic is set, heat very slightly until just softened but still syrupy. Divest meat of its barding fat and put it on a cake rack. Spoon a thick layer of the aspic over it. Put it in the refrigerator until set, then spoon on more aspic if necessary. Pour any remaining aspic into a shallow pan and refrigerate until set. Put the aspic-covered filet on an oval platter and rake the surface with a fork. Chop the remaining set aspic and arrange it around the meat. Garnish the dish with pâté de foie gras balls. When the filet is sliced, each thin slice of pink meat will have a black piece of truffle in its center, a shimmering layer of aspic around its rim.

WILTED CUCUMBERS WITH DILL
[HELEN EVANS BROWN]

> 8 slender cucumbers, peeled and thinly sliced
> 8 green onions, minced
>   Minced fresh dill to taste
>   Salt to taste
>   Mayonnaise

Arrange a layer of cucumbers in a shallow bowl, sprinkle with some of the onion, dill and a little salt. Spread with a ¼"-thick layer of mayonnaise. Repeat until all ingredients are used, cover and chill. Before serving, mix gently. The cucumbers will be wilted and the juices mingled with the mayonnaise to make a creamy sauce.

TOMATOES STUFFED WITH SALADE RUSSE

Allow half a large tomato per person, scoop out flesh and seeds, leaving a firm shell, and fill with salade Russe, which is made by blending cooked diced carrots, tiny peas, finely cut green beans and diced cooked potatoes with a homemade mayonnaise. Canned vegetables may be substituted for fresh, but they won't be as good, for the texture of the various vegetables should be crisply tender.

POTATO AND HEARTS OF PALM SALAD (see page 118)

ENDIVE SALAD

Cut Belgian endive into julienne strips, sprinkle with finely chopped parsley, and toss with a mustard-flavored vinaigrette sauce. This is an excellent salad for buffet service, as it does not wilt quickly like the usual green salad.

FROZEN DAIQUIRI SOUFFLÉ
[JULIE DANNENBAUM]

- 10 eggs, separated
- 2 cups sugar
- ½ cup lime juice
- ½ cup lemon juice
  Grated zest of 2 lemons and 2 limes
  Salt
- 2 tablespoons plain gelatin
- ½ cup rum
  Oil
- 3 cups heavy cream
  Crystallized violets
  Lime slice
  Crushed pistachio nuts

Beat egg yolks until light and fluffy. Add 1 cup sugar gradually and beat until smooth and light in color. Add lime and lemon juice, grated zest, and a pinch of salt. Mix until well blended. Stir over low heat until it thickens. Soak gelatin in rum and stir into hot custard until it is dissolved. Cool. Oil a 6-cup soufflé dish and wrap an oiled paper collar around top. Beat egg whites until stiff. Whip 2 cups of the cream over ice until stiff, adding remaining sugar. Fold egg whites into the custard, then whipped cream. Pour into the soufflé dish and chill. Whip remaining cream. Remove paper collar and, using a pastry bag, decorate top with whipped-cream rosettes. Put crystallized violets on rosettes around edge of soufflé, and a lime slice twisted, on a center rosette. Holding crushed pistachio nuts in palm of hand, spread gently onto sides. Soufflé improves in flavor if made a day in advance and kept in refrigerator; it can also be made ahead and frozen.

TORTONI ALEXIS
[LOU SEIBERT PAPPAS]

> 1½ cups crumbled almond macaroons
> 2 tablespoons kirsch liqueur
> 1 cup heavy cream
> 3 tablespoons framboise liqueur
> 1 quart vanilla ice cream, softened
> ¾ cup toasted chopped blanched almonds
> ½ cup shredded semi-sweet chocolate

Sprinkle macaroon crumbs with kirsch. Whip cream until stiff and beat in framboise. Using a chilled bowl, beat ice cream until light and mounding and quickly fold in whipped cream, almonds, chocolate, and saturated macaroon crumbs. Turn into a 2-quart ice cream mold. Cover and freeze until firm. To serve, dip mold in hot water for a few seconds and invert onto serving dish.

Champagne and Charcuterie Buffet for Twenty or More

This is a very festive and elegant menu for a special occasion, perhaps at midnight after a dance, or in honor of an out-of-town guest you want your friends to meet, in a more civilized way than at a cocktail party. The size of your guest list will dictate the amount of food to be served, and also the number of champagnes, but count on at least one ham and a couple of pâtés.

MENU

Terrine aux Aromates   *Veal and Ham Terrine*
Pâté Maison
Freshly Made Toast   *Homemade Melba Toast*
Smithfield Ham   *Country Ham*
Tiny Hot Biscuits
Buttered Light Pumpernickel
Strawberries "75"

The Wines

*A choice of special cuvées, such as
Moët et Chandon Dom Pérignon Brut,
Charles Heidsieck Cuvée Royale Brut,
Laurent Perrier Grand Siècle,
Bollinger Brut Special Cuvée
Taittinger Comtes de Champagne Blanc de Blancs*

TERRINE AUX AROMATES
[JAMES A. BEARD]

> 1 pound bacon
> 3 pounds spinach, or 2 packages frozen chopped spinach
> 3 tablespoons chopped parsley
> 1 medium onion, finely chopped
> 2 large or 3 small cloves garlic, finely chopped
> 1 tablespoon finely chopped fresh basil or 1 teaspoon dried basil
> 1 cup small Italian or French black and green olives (pit before measuring)
> 1½ pounds coarsely ground pork, ¾ of it lean, ¼ fat
> Salt, freshly ground pepper to taste
> 2 eggs
> ½ teaspoon each thyme and rosemary
> Dash of nutmeg
> Dash of Tabasco sauce
> ⅓ cup cognac
> ½ pound uncooked ham, sliced
> 2 large bay leaves
> Flour-and-water paste

Line the bottom and sides of a large terrine with strips of the bacon. Cook the spinach just until wilted. (If frozen spinach is used, merely thaw and press water through a sieve. Do not cook.) Chop spinach very fine and combine with half the chopped parsley, onion, garlic, and basil, and half the pitted olives.

Combine ground pork with salt, freshly ground pepper, eggs, the remaining herbs and seasonings (except the bay leaves), and the cognac. Place half the pork mixture on the bottom of the terrine, cover with thin slices of ham, then with half the spinach mixture. Next add a layer of pork, about half the remaining amount, then ham, spinach, and finally the rest of the chopped pork. Press down well and place the two bay leaves on top.

Cover with foil, place the lid on top and seal with flour-and-water paste. Place the terrine in a pan of boiling water and bake in a 350° oven for 1½ hours.

Remove and cool. Then put a board or plate and weights on top of the terrine and chill until firm. Unmold onto a platter or serve from the terrine.

NOTE: To taste for seasoning, put a little of the pork mixture in a skillet and fry until thoroughly cooked, then add whatever seasoning is lacking to rest of mixture.

VEAL AND HAM TERRINE
[JAMES A. BEARD]

Salt pork or bacon slices
2 pounds veal scaloppine, pounded very thin
2 to 2½ pounds thinly sliced ham or Canadian bacon
1 tablespoon (approximately) salt
½ teaspoon freshly ground black pepper
⅓ cup chopped parsley
6 shallots, finely chopped
1 teaspoon thyme
1 bay leaf
½ cup (approximately) white wine

Line a 9″-long loaf-shaped terrine or casserole with thin slices of salt pork or bacon. Beginning and ending with veal, alternate layers of veal scaloppine and ham or Canadian bacon. (Taste the bacon or ham before cooking to gauge the salt content as this will affect the seasoning.) Sprinkle each layer with salt, pepper, parsley, shallots, and thyme. Place bay leaf on top and pour white wine over all. Cover the terrine or casserole and bake in a 325° oven for 2 to 2½ hours, or until the juice in the terrine runs clear.

Weight the terrine well as it cools. Unmold before serving and cut in medium slices.

VARIATION: Alternate layers of veal, ham, or Canadian bacon with thinly sliced calves' liver, which gives a very rich flavor and produces a most interesting change in the terrine. Substitute Madeira for the white wine.

PÂTÉ MAISON
[DIONE LUCAS]

    1 pound bacon
    ½ cup brandy
    5 chicken livers
  1½ pounds pork liver
    1 pound beef liver
    ½ pound calves' liver
    1 egg, beaten
    ¼ cup sour cream
    1 clove garlic, finely minced
    2 teaspoons salt
    1 teaspoon freshly ground black pepper

Line a pâté mold or terrine 11" long by 5" wide by 4" deep with slices of bacon, draping them over the bottom and up the sides until the interior of the mold is completely covered with overlapping slices of bacon. Sprinkle the bacon with a little of the brandy. Soak livers in the remaining brandy.

Finely grind the pork, beef, and calves' liver and mix in the beaten egg, sour cream, and the brandy drained from the chicken livers. Add the garlic, salt, and pepper and mix thoroughly with a wooden spoon.

Half fill lined mold with this mixture, then arrange the chicken livers in a row down the center. Cover with the remaining liver mixture, fold overhanging ends of bacon over it, and place more bacon slices on top until it is completely covered. Cover top of the mold with heavy-duty aluminum foil, pressing it firmly around the rim. Place the mold in a roasting pan of hot water and bake in a 300° oven for 2½ hours. Remove from oven and allow to cool in water. Remove mold from water. Place a foil-covered brick or similar rectangular weight on top of the foil to press the pâté down firmly and chill for 24 hours before serving. Turn out of mold onto a serving platter and surround with chopped set aspic.

STRAWBERRIES "75"
[JOSÉ WILSON]

For every cup of hulled strawberries, allow about 1 tablespoon sugar and 1 to 2 tablespoons gin, or to taste. Heap strawberries in a glass bowl and sprinkle with sugar and gin, add a squeeze of lemon juice, and leave to marinate for 2 hours. At serving time, pour chilled champagne to barely cover the strawberries. Serve with champagne biscuits.

Expandable Buffet for Twenty or Thirty

The informality of summer weekend entertaining fosters parties that grow like a beanstalk, swelled by last-minute invitations, your neighbor's house guests, and your children's friends. This menu, while planned for a guest list of twenty, can easily stretch to feed another ten or twelve. Just have plenty of reserves of canned and bottled foods and sausages for the hors d'oeuvre table, and canned beans, sausages, and cooked ham for the main dish, an easily expandable casserole.

Don't worry about leftovers. The fresh foods will keep for several days in the refrigerator.

For a party of this size, you will certainly need help in the kitchen to attend to the last-minute preparation and serving, and the washing up. With the food, have a choice of chilled beer, and red and white wines en carafe.

MENU
[JAMES A. BEARD]

Hors d'oeuvre Table
Potée Berrichonne
Infinite Variety Salad
Refrigerator Biscuits and Crescent Rolls
Fruit Flans

The Drinks

Chilled beer, carafes of California white and red jug wines

HORS D'OEUVRE TABLE

This can be set up on the terrace, in the garden under a parasol, or where you will. Provide cutting boards for the sausages and raviers for the anchovies, olives, onions, pickled peppers, and other vegetables.

SARDINES

Arrange a selection of French or Portuguese sardines on a platter. Garnish with lemon wedges.

SHRIMP OR CRAB

Fill a bowl with shrimp, and accompany with a good homemade mayonnaise; or use crabmeat with an herbed vinaigrette sauce.

ITALIAN PICKLED PEPPERS AND PIMIENTOS

Drain and arrange on a dish.

ANCHOVIES

Arrange alternate layers of anchovy filets, finely cut scallions, and chopped parsley, adding oil from anchovies. Top with chopped parsley.

BRAUNSCHWEIGER

Try to get the variety called "goose liverwurst." Buy 2, slice 1, and keep the other in reserve in the refrigerator.

SALAMI

Buy 1 or 2 whole salamis, either Italian or Hungarian. Thinly slice as needed.

SUMMER SAUSAGE OR CERVELAT

Buy 1 or 2 of each and thinly slice as needed.

SPICED OLIVES

Choose several different types of olives, both green and black—Greek, Italian, small Spanish, soft black, American ripe olives. Stuffed olives are not suitable. You will need at least 2 to 3 pints, possibly 4 to 6 pints. Place in a gallon jar or crock and add 1 tablespoon freshly ground black pepper, 10 to 12 garlic cloves, crushed, 10 to 15 hot peppers, 2 lemons (sliced paper-thin), and 3 or 4 sprigs fresh dill. Add olive oil; the mixture should be almost covered.

These proportions may be changed to taste. Mix olives and seasoning well and allow to stand for several days or a week—the longer the better. Leftover olives will keep for at least another week.

TOMATO SALAD

Slice ripe tomatoes and dress with a vinaigrette sauce and a little chopped fresh basil.

RADISHES

Clean radishes and put in iced water to crisp before serving.

ONIONS MARSEILLAISE

> 5 pounds small white onions
> 1½ cups olive or peanut oil
> 1½ cups white wine
> 2 teaspoons salt
> 1 teaspoon freshly ground black pepper
> 1 teaspoon thyme
> 1 or 2 cloves garlic
> 1 bay leaf
> Hearty pinch saffron
> 2 tablespoons tomato paste
> 1 cup sultana raisins

Pour boiling water over the onions and leave for 5 minutes to loosen skins. Peel. Arrange the peeled onions in 1 large skillet or 2 smaller ones and add the oil, wine, 1 cup water, salt, pepper, thyme, garlic, and bay leaf. Poach the onions gently until tender, but still crisp. Add just enough saffron to give color and flavor, and stir in the tomato paste and the raisins. Cook for 12 minutes or so until the raisins are puffy. Transfer the onions to a serving dish. Reduce the sauce a bit and pour over the onions. Cool and chill.

POTÉE BERRICHONNE

For this dish, it is best to cook a whole ham according to the accompanying directions and slice as needed. Any surplus can be used for sandwiches, in salad, or ground for a mousse. Also have on hand extra sausages and 6 to 8 cans kidney beans.

    4 pounds red kidney beans
    2 whole onions, each stuck with 2 cloves
    2 cloves garlic
    1 bay leaf
  1½ teaspoons thyme or more, to taste
      Salt, pepper
    5 large onions, peeled and diced
    ¼ pound butter
    4 to 5 pounds cooked ham, thickly sliced
    3 to 4 pounds sausage: kielbasy, Italian sausages, or Italian cotechino
      Red wine
      Bread crumbs
      Bacon strips
      Chopped parsley

Cover beans with water and bring to a boil. Boil for 10 minutes and then let stand for an hour. Add whole onions, garlic, bay leaf, thyme, and about 2 to 3 tablespoons salt. Bring to a boil again, and simmer until tender. Cool. (This quantity of beans may seem excessive, but it will be just enough for 20 people.)

Sauté diced onions in butter, adding more butter if needed. Salt and pepper to taste. Cook until soft, but not brown. Dice the ham slices and slice the sausage.

Arrange layers of beans, onions, ham, and sausage in baking dishes or casseroles. Taste beans for seasoning and add salt, pepper, and more thyme, if needed. Add just enough red wine to cover the beans. Bake in a 350° oven for 1 hour. Sprinkle with bread crumbs and top with strips of bacon. Return to the oven and bake at 300° for another 45 minutes. If the wine has cooked away, add more. Just before serving, sprinkle with chopped parsley.

NOTE: If you must draw on your reserves to feed more guests, drain the canned beans and combine with ham, sausage, extra sautéed onions, and wine. Add 2 cloves garlic, finely chopped, and a bay leaf and bake as above.

INFINITE VARIETY SALAD

Make your salad from any preferred combination of Bibb lettuce, Boston lettuce, romaine, watercress, radishes (sliced), cucumbers (seeded and sliced), cherry tomatoes, spinach leaves, young zucchini (sliced), celery (sliced), gratted raw carrots, grated raw beets, scallions, sliced sweet onions, parsley. Wash, trim, and prepare your ingredients, combine, and store in large plastic bags until ready to use.

Toss with a vinaigrette sauce made with 3 parts olive oil to 1 part vinegar. For a basic quantity; mix 1½ cups oil, ½ cup vinegar, 1 tablespoon salt, 1 teaspoon freshly ground black pepper, and chopped tarragon or basil to taste. If you like the flavor of garlic, rub 2 or 3 cloves into the salt before adding it to the dressing, or rub the ends of stale loaves of French bread with garlic and toss with the salad. Be sure all ingredients are crisp and dry before you toss the salad, or the vinaigrette sauce will become too diluted.

REFRIGERATOR BISCUITS AND CRESCENT ROLLS

Biscuits and crescent rolls from the refrigerated cases in the supermarket are perfect for this kind of menu, because they can be kept on hand and baked as needed. Before baking, dip biscuits in butter. Butter crescent rolls prior to rolling. Bake according to package directions.

FRUIT FLANS

Prepare your favorite pastry recipe and bake pie shells in flan rings or pie tins. You will need 5 shells for 20 people, but make 2 more to keep in reserve. You can bake the shells well ahead of the party and store them in the refrigerator. If you prefer, buy ready-baked pie shells. When ready to serve, fill shells with fresh or poached peaches, or fresh strawberries or raspberries. Brush with Apricot Glaze (see below). Serve with sweetened whipped cream flavored with kirsch or cognac.

221

APRICOT GLAZE

    2 pints apricot preserves
    2 tablespoons kirsch or cognac

Heat the preserves to the boiling point and let bubble for 3 minutes. Add the kirsch or cognac and remove from the heat. Strain through a fine sieve. Cool slightly before glazing the fruit. This makes enough glaze for 3 to 4 flans.

Big Party Fondue Buffet

Fondues make a lot of sense for a big buffet party. They are enduringly popular, promote participation and mingling and, once you have made the initial preparation of the food, the guests do the cooking and serving themselves.

Since the early days, when fondue meant cheese melted with wine and kirsch, the number of dishes dubbed "fondue" has proliferated. Nowadays you can have a fondue Bourguignonne (with beef and sauces, cooked in oil and butter), a fish version of this, a fondue Orientale, cooked in bouillon, and, newest of all, dessert fondues. As "fondue" can be loosely translated as "melted," there's really no end to the number of fondues that your ingenuity might devise. So pick your favorites. If you have the space and the tables (card tables with round fitted tops, draped with a cloth, are good for this type of buffet), you might set up each fondue separately and let guests wander from one to another in their own sweet time. White wine goes with the cheese and fish fondues, red with the beef.

MENU

La Vraie Fondue

Fondue Bourguignonne   *Fish Fondue Bourguignonne*

Fondue Orientale

Fondue au Chocolat   *Fruit Fondue au Rhum*

The Wines

With the cheese and fish: Swiss Neuchâtel and Fendant

With the beef: Swiss Dôle du Mont

LA VRAIE FONDUE
[NIKA HAZELTON]

In Switzerland, this most glorious of all dunks is made on the kitchen stove in a "caquelon," a heavy earthenware or cast-iron casserole that holds the heat. It is then placed on a warmer (for the fondue must be kept hot) in the middle of the table for serving. A heavy chafing dish is good for making fondue, which must be cooked over very low heat or the cheese will become stringy.

   1 pound natural Switzerland cheese (Emmenthal, Gruyère, or a mixture of both)
   2 tablespoons flour
   1 clove fresh garlic, cut
   2 cups dry white wine
   3 tablespoons kirsch or 4 tablespoons cognac
    Nutmeg, pepper and salt to taste
   2 loaves crusty Italian or French bread, cut into bite-size pieces, each with some crust

Shred cheese or cut into small, transparent slices. Dredge cheese with flour. Rub the cooking utensil with the cut sides of the garlic. Pour in the wine, set over low heat. When wine is heated to the point that air bubbles rise to the surface, add cheese gradually, stirring constantly with a wooden spoon. Stir until cheese is melted. Stir in kirsch, and a pinch of nutmeg, pepper and salt. Keep fondue hot, but below the simmering point. If the mixture becomes too thick, thin with a little wine, a tablespoon at a time. Serve with the bite-size pieces of bread, which are speared on special two-pronged forks (or ordinary forks) and dipped into the fondue.

FONDUE BOURGUIGNONNE
[NIKA HAZELTON]

This consists of cubed meat, cooked in hot fat, dipped in various sauces and accompaniments. Each guest cooks his own at the table, in a special set that can be bought at fine housewares stores, or in a small, deep saucepan set over a spirit or electrical warmer, in a chafing dish or in an electric skillet.

To set the table for fondue Bourguignonne, place the heating unit in the middle of the table, within easy reach of the guests. Place salt and paprika shakers, pepper mills, sauces, and other fondue accompaniments around it. For each guest, allow two forks, a plate with the prepared meat, a salad plate, and napkins.

To prepare the fondue Bourguignonne, allow about ½ pound of lean sirloin, tenderloin, or other tender beef for each serving. Cut meat into ¾" to 1" cubes, and place on small wooden or china plates decorated with greens. In the kitchen, half fill the fondue saucepan with oil or clarified butter. (Some prefer oil, others butter—but the butter must be clarified.) Heat to boiling point and set on heating unit. Put in a small piece of bread to prevent sputtering.

To cook and eat the fondue Bourguignonne, each guest first helps himself to sauces and other accompaniments, which he puts on his salad plate. He then spears a piece of meat with the first fork and dips it into the boiling fat, cooking it to his liking. Since the fork will be very hot by this time, the guest transfers his meat to the second fork and dips it into the sauce of his choice. While he is eating, the first fork will have cooled, and he will use it to cook the next piece of meat.

The charm of a fondue Bourguignonne, which has nothing to do with the real fondue save similar equipment, lies in the number of sauces and side dishes, which can be as fanciful as the hostess wishes. Make your choice from any of the following:

> Béarnaise or Hollandaise Sauce (a must)
> Mustard Sauce
> Horseradish Cream (cold or hot)
> Sauce Diable
> Hot and mild mustards

Mixed pickles
Chutney
Tomato Catsup
Mushroom Catsup
Pickled onions
Olives
Fresh grated horseradish or bottled horseradish
Pickled mushrooms

FISH FONDUE BOURGUIGNONNE
[RUTH CONRAD BATEMAN]

Shrimp and cubed swordfish with appropriate sauces makes an interesting switch from the beef used in the original recipe.

1 pound medium shrimp, peeled and deveined
1 pound swordfish steaks, cut into 1″ cubes
Salad oil, butter
Sauce Remoulade, Sashimi Sauce, Dill Sauce (see recipes below)

Put the prepared shrimp and swordfish on a large serving platter with sprays of watercress and parsley to garnish. When you are ready to cook, arrange on the buffet table a heatproof tray holding the fondue Bourguignonne set or chafing dish, the fish platter, and another tray with the sauces and fondue forks. Measure out enough oil and clarified butter, in equal proportions, to fill the fondue pan to 1½″ depth. Heat oil and butter in a saucepan over gas or electric burner until sizzling hot. Pour mixture into fondue pan and set over alcohol burner. Each guest spears a shrimp or cube of swordfish with a long fondue fork or metal skewer and cooks it in the hot fat until done. This only takes a minute or so. The cooked food is then transferred from the hot fondue fork to a plate, speared with an ordinary fork, dipped into the desired sauce, and eaten.

During the cooking, the heat under the fondue pan should be kept high. If the oil cools down, reheat it briefly on the kitchen range.

SAUCE REMOULADE

Mix together 1 cup mayonnaise, 1 chopped hard-cooked egg, 2 tablespoons hot prepared mustard or 1 teaspoon dry mustard, 1 minced clove garlic, 1 teaspoon dried tarragon, 1 teaspoon anchovy paste, and 1 teaspoon capers.

SASHIMI SAUCE

Mix together 1 cup Japanese soy sauce, ½ teaspoon dry mustard blended with 1 tablespoon salad oil, and 1 tablespoon grated, peeled fresh ginger root.

DILL SAUCE

Blend together 1 cup sour cream, 1 tablespoon minced parsley, 1 tablespoon lemon juice, and 1 teaspoon chopped chives, 1 teaspoon grated onion, and chopped fresh or dried dill to taste.

FONDUE ORIENTALE
[NIKA HAZELTON]

The most recent of Swiss table procedures, this resembles the fondue Bourguignonne, except for the fact that the meat is cooked in boiling hot bouillon rather than fat.

For Fondue Orientale, substitute beef or chicken bouillon for the hot fat. The bouillon must continue to boil throughout the meal.

The meats can be varied, and include lean veal and pork besides the beef. Lamb or veal kidneys may also be used. These should be soaked in cold water for ½ hour before using (change the water 3 times, drain and dry) and all the hard cores removed.

Have the butcher slice the meats into wafer-thin, bite-size pieces. Or slice the meats at home, freezing them slightly to make the job easier.

Beef, veal, and kidneys should be lightly cooked in boiling bouillon, but pork must be well cooked.

Serve the fondue Orientale with the same sauces and accompaniments listed for the fondue Bourguignonne.

FONDUE AU CHOCOLAT

6 3-ounce bars Toblerone chocolate, broken into triangular pieces
1 cup heavy cream
4 tablespoons Cointreau or Grand Marnier liqueur
For dunking: long fingers of sponge or angel-food cake: lady fingers; tiny profiteroles or cubes of French bread; orange sections.

Combine the chocolate, cream, and liqueur in a saucepan and stir over very low heat until chocolate is melted and mixture smooth. Keep warm over a candle warmer or low flame.

FRUIT FONDUE AU RHUM
[ELAINE ROSS]

> 3 cups light-brown sugar
> 6 tablespoons sweet butter
> 1 cup light cream
> 4 tablespoons dark rum
> Assorted fruits for dunking: fresh pears, peaches, apples, bananas, fresh or canned pineapple, cut into bite-size pieces, strawberries, pitted dark sweet cherries

Mix sugar, butter and cream in a saucepan and bring to a boil over medium heat, stirring constantly. Boil briskly for 3 minutes or until sauce thickens. Remove from heat, set aside for 3 minutes, then stir in rum. Serve warm or cold.

Select an assortment of fruits and arrange them on a platter so guests can help themselves. Fresh fruit should be peeled, canned fruit thoroughly drained and patted dry. Place a small ramekin or custard cup of rum sauce on each dessert plate, or keep sauce hot in a pan over low heat.

Low-Calorie Meals

There comes a time in the life of everyone who loves good food and wine when cutting calories for a week, or two, or even longer becomes absolutely essential. The prospect needn't be depressing if you approach it sensibly and logically. Dieting is not necessarily synonymous with self-denial, and you don't have to give up all the pleasures of the table in order to lose ten pounds. Many of the foods that sound most self-indulgent are, paradoxically, the best for you. Oysters and caviar, smoked salmon and sturgeon. Mussels steamed in white wine, bouillabaisse, bollito misto, tiny roast squab or game birds, shish kebab, chicken teriyaki, Chinese food.

First, give some thought to the foods you usually eat and re-educate your taste, so that you learn to prefer foods that are lower in calories, like seafood and raw fruit, salads and fresh vegetables. Second, heed the advice of Ovid, "Stop short of appetite; eat less than you are able." We all tend to eat more than we need—and often, more than we really want. If you taper off your usual daily quota of food, you'll lose weight gradually and still be able to eat well and deliciously.

Many foods really taste so much better when they are divorced from their traditional high-calorie accompaniments. Have you ever appreciated the sea-fresh flavor of cracked crab or lobster, with just a touch of lemon juice to heighten its sweetly salty savor, rather than tasting it through a blanket of rich mayonnaise? Or the splendid earthiness of a boiled or baked potato (a mere 100 calories, au naturel) seasoned with a little coarse salt and a grind of black pepper, freed from the usual lavishments of sour cream or butter? Poach your chicken instead of frying or sautéing it and you'll find the taste purer, infinitely more delicate.

If you do have a hankering for dessert, don't agonize. Just choose something sweet and low—a handful of ripe cherries, a fresh pear, a dozen strawberries, or a soufflé made with fruit purée and egg whites.

There's absolutely no reason not to cook as well as you would normally. Look on it as a challenge to your ingenuity and culinary skill, whether you're making a meal for the family or dinner for friends. After all, if the chefs of the top hotels in Vichy, where the French go to recover from the ravages of haute cuisine, can do it, so can you.

Think *maigre*, rather than *gras*. Trim fat from meat and, if you're browning it for a ragoût, sear it under the broiler instead of in butter. Substitute potato starch for flour in a sauce (1 teaspoon of the former has all the thickening power of 1 tablespoon of the latter). Cool stocks and skim off every last little pearl of fat before using them in soups and sauces. Stir yoghurt, rather than cream, into a soup—it's tarter, fresher, subtler, a new flavor high. Use wine in cooking with a free hand—the calorie-high alcohol burns off, only the taste remains. Dust plainly cooked vegetables with a flurry of chopped fresh herbs—tarragon, chervil, parsley, what have you.

Presentation of food is half the battle when you are cutting down on portions. As the Japanese know, a small helping of any dish, imaginatively and attractively presented, seems like more, for you enjoy it first with your eyes, then slowly savor it with your taste buds.

A Week of Low-Calorie Meals

The menus in this section will serve four on weekdays, six at weekends, to allow for guests, but they may, of course, be adjusted. The main thing is that the meals are interesting and varied, unlike the usual dieter's fare, and a family could stay on them without anyone getting bored or going hungry—or being aware that calories were being cut. The meals are not intended for the stringent dieter who is trying to lose a lot of weight in a short time, but rather for those who want to follow a reasonable and rational routine by eliminating rich foods, cutting down on fat and starch intake, and reducing the calories of certain main dishes and desserts by the use of skimmed milk, yoghurt, and sugar substitutes. The menus can be decalorized even further by eliminating desserts and eating only a salad or cottage cheese for lunch instead of a regular meal. Remember, however, that a balanced diet should supply a certain amount of fats and carbohydrates in addition to protein. Breakfast, too, should include protein in the form of eggs, meat or fish, fruit or fruit juice, and a slice of toast with a small pat of butter.

While wines are not specified in the menus, a glass of white or red wine with dinner doesn't add much to the day's calorie count, provided you don't have cocktails, too. And for those who just have to nibble something before dinner, even if they are only sipping a diet drink or Perrier water, here are some suggestions for appetizers.

COUNT-NO-CALORIES APPETIZERS
[RUTH ELLEN CHURCH]

Any of these, crisped in ice water: carrot sticks or curls, celery fans, turnip slices or sticks, fennel slices, radish roses, cucumber strips, zucchini strips. A sprinkling of seasoning salt helps to make them interesting.

Raw mushrooms with lemon juice and salt, raw asparagus, strips of dill pickle, green pepper squares, pickled onions, cauliflower and cherry tomatoes. All have a negligible calorie content.

12- TO 25-CALORIE APPETIZERS
[RUTH ELLEN CHURCH]

Melon cuts wrapped with a paper-thin piece of prosciutto, or a cucumber strip with a thin slice of smoked salmon.

Raw crisp vegetables with Cottage Cheese and Red Caviar Dip or Tomato-Sour Cream Dip (see below).

COTTAGE CHEESE AND RED CAVIAR DIP

1 cup low-calorie cottage cheese
1 jar (2 ounces) red caviar

Whirl the cottage cheese smooth in a blender, add caviar, and serve as a dip for crisp vegetables. Calories per tablespoon: about 20.

TOMATO-SOUR CREAM DIP

> ½ cup tomato sauce
> ½ cup low-calorie sour cream or yoghurt
> ½ teaspoon salt
>   Black pepper
> 1 slice onion
> ¼ cup prepared horseradish

Blend all ingredients until smooth in electric blender. A few sprigs of parsley may be added. Use as a dip for crisp vegetables. Calories per tablespoon: about 12.

50-CALORIE APPETIZERS
[RUTH ELLEN CHURCH]

> 4½ medium-size shrimp (9 halves of split shrimp) sprinkled with lemon juice and pepper, or pickled without oil
> ½ stuffed egg on leaf lettuce with bit of anchovy, truffle, sardine or caviar on top (yolk whipped with hot or prepared mustard and skim milk—no mayonnaise)
> 3 raw clams served in small cup with mustard-flavored soy sauce
> 2 or 3 chicken hearts or 3 halves chicken liver marinated in ginger and soy sauce and broiled on skewer
>   Crisp cucumber cup filled with crabmeat
>   Lobster-claw meat from boiled lobster, small portion

COTTAGE CHEESE DIP
[BETTY WASON]

> 1 cup creamed cottage cheese
> ½ cup yoghurt
>   4-ounce wedge of blue cheese (optional)
> 2 tablespoons oil
>   Salt, pepper to taste

Combine all ingredients in a blender and whirl until smooth. Serve with raw vegetables. It may also be used as diet dressing for salad greens.

CUCUMBER CUPS WITH COTTAGE CHEESE
[HELEN EVANS BROWN]

      1 cucumber, about 7" long
    ¼ cup cottage cheese
      1 tablespoon chopped green onion
    ¼ teaspoon dried dill, oregano, or tarragon
      2 tablespoons finely chopped celery
        Salt, pepper, paprika

Peel cucumber and cut into 1" sections. Scoop out insides to form tiny cups. Combine cottage cheese, green onion, dried herb, celery, and salt and pepper to taste. Fill cucumber cups with mixture and sprinkle tops with paprika.

MUSHROOMS STUFFED WITH COTTAGE CHEESE
[BETTY WASON]

Marinate large raw mushroom caps in water to which lemon juice and salt have been added. Remove, drain, and fill mushroom caps with mixture of cottage cheese, grated onion, salt to taste, a little curry powder, or a dash of powdered ginger or mustard. Sprinkle paprika over top.

CELERY-STUFFED CELERY
[ELAINE ROSS]

      8 wide pieces celery, 3" to 3½" long
    ½ cup small-curd cottage cheese
    ¼ cup very finely minced celery
      1 tablespoon minced parsley
        Seasoned salt

Fringe ends of celery with a knife, and put in ice water for an hour. Drain and dry. Mix the cottage cheese, minced celery, and parsley, and put a mound of the mixture on the center of each piece of celery. Sprinkle generously with seasoned salt. Keep refrigerated until serving time. (Do not assemble more than an hour ahead.)

CRABMEAT CANAPÉS
[BETTY WASON]

> 1 cup crabmeat, flaked
> 2 tablespoons olive oil
> ½ teaspoon cumin
> 1 teaspoon grated onion
> 2 tablespoons minced parsley
> Few drops lemon juice
> 3 or 4 green peppers, cut into 1″ squares

Place all ingredients except the green pepper in a blender. Blend to a paste. Spread paste on the green pepper squares.

TUNA SALAD CANAPÉS
[BETTY WASON]

> 7-ounce can tuna, well-drained
> 1 teaspoon grated onion
> Few drops lemon juice
> ½ cup minced celery
> ¼ cup diced pimiento
> ½ teaspoon curry powder
> 2 tablespoons commercial sour cream
> Cucumber slices or 2″ pieces celery

Combine all the ingredients except the cucumber slices or celery pieces, toss lightly to blend well. Spread on cucumber slices, or use as a stuffing for celery.

SMOKED OYSTERS IN CHERRY TOMATOES
[BETTY WASON]

Cut a slit in the top of each cherry tomato and insert a smoked oyster.

GORGONZOLA IN CELERY
[BETTY WASON]

Cut celery stalks in 1½″ pieces and place a dab of Gorgonzola cheese in each.

SHRIMP IN BEER
[BETTY WASON]

Heat 1 cup beer with ½ teaspoon salt and ¼ teaspoon oregano. When boiling, add 1 pound shelled small shrimp, lower heat, cover, cook 2 minutes only. Turn off heat, leave shrimp in liquid for 10 minutes. Drain and serve cold, but not chilled.

BROILED CHICKEN LIVERS
[BETTY WASON]

Marinate 1 pound chicken livers (each one halved) in a mixture of ¼ cup oil, ¼ cup sherry, ½ teaspoon salt, pinch of curry powder. Remove livers from marinade and spread out on foil-lined broiler pan. Broil 4″ from heat just until lightly browned, turn over, broil on the other side until firm but not browned. Serve hot from broiler, on toothpicks.

PICKLE IN TONGUE
[BETTY WASON]

Slice smoked tongue very, very thin. Wrap each slice around a chunk of dill pickle.

SASHIMI
[BETTY WASON]

Serve fresh raw tuna, cut into small squares, with a green mustard sauce as the Japanese do—it makes a wonderful hors d'oeuvre. The fish, of course, must be absolutely fresh for this purpose. The green mustard sauce may be purchased in Oriental grocery stores.

FRANKFURTERS IN SHERRY
[BETTY WASON]

Heat cocktail frankfurters in sherry in a chafing dish, using just enough wine to cover bottom.

Monday Luncheon for Four

MENU

Crab-Stuffed Zucchini

*Salad of Raw Mushrooms and Spinach with
Lemon Juice and Cracked Pepper*

Coffee Jelly

CRAB-STUFFED ZUCCHINI
[BETTY WASON]

    4 zucchini (about 5″ long)
    2 minced shallots or 1 tablespoon minced onion
    1 tablespoon butter or oil
    ½ green pepper, chopped
    1 medium tomato, peeled and chopped
    ½ teaspoon basil
    ½ teaspoon salt
    ¼ teaspoon freshly ground pepper
    1 tablespoon cornstarch
    ¾ cup dry white wine
    1 teaspoon soy sauce
    2 cups crabmeat (canned, frozen, or fresh), flaked
      Few drops lemon juice
      Grated rind of ½ lemon

Cut the zucchini in half lengthwise. Scoop out seedy interior, leaving ½″ shell. Place in a saucepan and add boiling salted water to cover. Cook 2 minutes, then turn off heat and let zucchini stand in water 5 minutes. Drain.

Cook the shallots or onion in the butter until soft. Add the green pepper, tomato, and seasonings and simmer 5 minutes. Stir in the cornstarch, then the wine and soy sauce. Add the crabmeat and heat through. Add the lemon juice and rind. Fill zucchini with this mixture. Serve at once, or reheat in broiler, 5″ to 6″ from heat, until sauce is lightly glazed.

COFFEE JELLY
[JAMES A. BEARD]

> 1 envelope unflavored gelatin
> 3 cups freshly made, boiling coffee (espresso, instant, or regular)
>   Sugar substitute to taste, if desired
>   Grand Marnier liqueur

Soften the gelatin in ¼ cup water, add the boiling coffee, and stir until gelatin is dissolved thoroughly. Add sugar substitute if desired. Pour into 4 individual molds or into a 1½-quart mold and chill. Unmold. Serve each portion with a little Grand Marnier, about 1 teaspoon.

Monday Dinner for Four

MENU

Consommé

Braised Veal Chops

Stir-Fry Asparagus

Poached Pears

BRAISED VEAL CHOPS
[ELAINE ROSS]

 4 veal chops, 1″ thick
 2 large chicken livers
 1 teaspoon butter
 1 tablespoon bottled Sauce Robert
 1 tablespoon minced parsley
 1 tablespoon fine bread crumbs
 2 tablespoons minced celery
 1 tablespoon oil
 3 tablespoons dry vermouth
 ¾ cup chicken stock
   Flour
   Skimmed milk
   Salt, pepper to taste

Have the butcher cut a large pocket in each of the chops. Sear the chicken livers in the butter, chop them coarsely, and add the Sauce Robert, parsley, bread crumbs, and celery. Divide the filling among the chops and secure the openings with toothpicks. Heat the oil in a heavy skillet, brown the chops on both sides, add the vermouth and chicken stock and bring to a boil. Reduce the heat, cover the skillet, and simmer until the chops are tender. Remove the chops to a serving platter and keep warm. Measure the pan juices. You will need about 1 cup. Blend 1 tablespoon flour with 1 tablespoon skimmed milk, add this to the measured pan juices, pour back into the skillet and cook, stirring constantly, until thickened. Season with salt and pepper. Pour sauce over the chops and serve immediately.

STIR-FRY ASPARAGUS
[ELAINE ROSS]

 1½ pounds asparagus, trimmed, or 2 packages frozen asparagus
    spears
  2 tablespoons vegetable oil
  1 teaspoon soy sauce
  1 teaspoon lemon juice

Peel the trimmed asparagus with a vegetable peeler and cut into ¼"-thick diagonal slices. If you are using frozen asparagus, slice the same way with a very sharp knife.

Heat a wok or heavy skillet, add the oil and sauté the asparagus, stirring constantly, until the pieces start to brown. Cover and cook for 2 or 3 minutes, or until crisply tender. Stir in the soy sauce and lemon juice and serve immediately.

POACHED PEARS
[JAMES A. BEARD]

>   Sugar substitute
>   4 firm pears, peeled and cored, but left whole
>   Eau de vie de poire (pear brandy)

Prepare a syrup with enough water to cover the pears and sugar substitute to taste. Boil this for 5 minutes, then add the pears and poach them until tender, but not mushy. Cool in the syrup.

Serve the chilled pears with a little eau de vie de poire poured over them at the last minute.

Tuesday Luncheon for Four

MENU
[BETTY WASON]

Baked Stuffed Tomatoes

Spinach with Caraway

Honeydew or Cantaloupe Wedges

BAKED STUFFED TOMATOES

>   4 extra-large tomatoes
>   ¼ cup cottage cheese
>   1 tablespoon grated onion

1 tablespoon minced parsley
1 cup chopped cooked or canned shrimp, crabmeat, or well-drained tuna
  Salt to taste
2 eggs, beaten
4 tablespoons fine dry bread crumbs
2 tablespoons melted butter or margarine
1 tablespoon (approximately) olive oil

Scoop out the centers of the tomatoes, leaving a ¼″ shell. Force tomato pulp through a sieve, discarding seeds. Combine the cottage cheese, onion, parsley, desired seafood, salt to taste, tomato pulp, and eggs. Stuff tomatoes with this mixture, sprinkle with crumbs and dot with butter. Brush outside of tomatoes lightly with olive oil. Bake in a 375° oven for 45 minutes, or until skin of tomatoes is lightly wrinkled.

SPINACH WITH CARAWAY

1½ pounds spinach or 1 package frozen spinach
½ teaspoon caraway seeds
1 tablespoon butter
  Few drops lemon juice

Cook spinach until just wilted (if using frozen spinach, cook according to package directions). Drain thoroughly. Crush caraway seeds in a mortar and work in the butter and lemon juice. Place on hot spinach and allow to melt.

Tuesday Dinner for Four

MENU

Broiled Anchovy Shrimp
Dieter's Shish Kebab
Apple and Banana Chiffon

BROILED ANCHOVY SHRIMP
[CRAIG CLAIBORNE]

  1½ pounds raw shrimp
   ¼ cup olive oil
   2 cloves garlic, finely minced
   1 tablespoon anchovy paste
    Juice of 1 lemon
   1 tablespoon finely chopped shallot or green onion
   ¼ cup finely chopped parsley
   1 teaspoon dry mustard
   ½ teaspoon salt
    Freshly ground black pepper to taste

Cut through the arched shell of each shrimp with a pair of kitchen shears, cutting down to, but not through, the last tail segment. Remove the shell, but leave the tail on each shrimp. Rinse the shrimp to remove intestinal vein, then pat dry with paper towels. Place the shrimp in a mixing bowl.

Combine the remaining ingredients and beat with a fork until blended. Pour the marinade over the shrimp and let stand at room temperature about 1 hour.

Broil the shrimp, turning once, until cooked through.

DIETER'S SHISH KEBAB
[BETTY WASON]

  1½ pounds lean lamb from leg, cut into cubes
   1 cup buttermilk or skim-milk yoghurt
   ¼ teaspoon freshly ground black pepper
    Pinch of thyme
   8 to 12 large mushroom caps, or 2 yellow squash or zucchini squash, thickly sliced
   2 tablespoons oil blended with ¼ teaspoon salt
   2 green peppers, cut into squares
   8 to 12 cherry tomatoes
   8 canned whole onions

Place the meat in a large bowl and add the buttermilk, pepper, and thyme. Marinate for at least 1 hour, turning once. Meantime marinate the mushrooms or squash slices in the seasoned oil, turning so that surfaces are well covered with the oil. Drain the meat and arrange on skewers alternately with the vegetables. Broil under broiler 2" to 3" from heat, until meat is nicely browned and sizzling.

APPLE AND BANANA CHIFFON
[ELAINE ROSS]

> 1 tablespoon (1 envelope) gelatin
> 2 eggs
> 3 tablespoons sugar
> 2 medium-size very ripe bananas
>   Thick applesauce
> ½ teaspoon vanilla
> 1 tablespoon sour cream
>   Nutmeg

Soak the gelatin in a small saucepan in 3 tablespoons cold water, dissolve over low heat, and cool. Beat the eggs and sugar in an electric mixer at high speed for 10 minutes, or until thick and light. Meanwhile, mash the bananas and add enough applesauce to make 1½ cups altogether. Stir in vanilla, sour cream, and gelatin. Fold in egg-sugar mixture. Pour into 4 bowls. Sprinkle with nutmeg. Chill until set.

Wednesday Luncheon for Four

MENU

Watercress Soup
Baked Striped Bass
Sauté of Squash, Spoleto-Style
Fresh Pears

WATERCRESS SOUP
[RUTH ELLEN CHURCH]

1 bunch watercress
3 to 4 cups chicken broth, fat-free
4 tablespoons dry white wine

Put watercress and part of the chicken broth in an electric blender (discard stems first) and blend until fine. Add to the rest of broth and simmer 5 minutes. Add wine.

BAKED STRIPED BASS
[ELAINE ROSS]

2½- to 3-pound striped bass, fileted
½ teaspoon salt
Grinding of coarse pepper
1 medium onion, minced
1 tablespoon butter, melted
1 cup minced or thinly sliced mushrooms
1 cup Italian canned plum tomatoes, coarsely chopped
¼ cup milk
1 teaspoon Worcestershire sauce
2 tablespoons bread crumbs

Place the filets, side by side and skin side down, in a lightly greased, shallow, oven-to-table baking dish. Sprinkle the fish with half the salt and pepper, and bake uncovered in a preheated 375° oven for ½ hour.

Meanwhile, prepare the sauce: Sauté the onion in half the butter until golden, add the mushrooms, and sauté one minute longer. Add the remaining ingredients, except the bread crumbs, and spoon over the partially baked fish. Mix the bread crumbs with the remaining melted butter, sprinkle over the fish and bake an additional 20 to 30 minutes, or until the fish flakes easily.

SAUTÉ OF SQUASH, SPOLETO-STYLE
[ELAINE ROSS]

¾ pound tender young zucchini
¾ pound yellow summer squash
2 teaspoons oil
1 small clove garlic, crushed
⅓ teaspoon Italian herb seasoning
½ teaspoon salt
Dash white pepper

Trim off the ends of the zucchini and squash, and cut them into bite-size pieces. Heat a heavy skillet over high heat, add the oil, and when it is hot, add the vegetables. Cook, stirring and turning the vegetables constantly, until they are golden. Add the seasonings, lower the heat a little and cook, stirring frequently, for 10 minutes, or until the vegetables are tender.

Wednesday Dinner for Four

MENU

Tomato Bisque
Breast of Chicken with Wild Rice and Orange Sauce
Granita di Caffé

TOMATO BISQUE
[ELAINE ROSS]

2 cups tomato juice
2 cups buttermilk
6 drops Tabasco sauce
2 teaspoons lemon juice
1 teaspoon Worcestershire sauce
Salt, pepper to taste

Combine all the ingredients and add seasonings, if needed. (It is impossible to specify exact amounts of seasonings since they depend on the seasonings already in the tomato juice.) Serve well chilled, in soup cups, goblets or Old Fashioned glasses.

BREAST OF CHICKEN WITH WILD RICE AND ORANGE SAUCE
[RUTH ELLEN CHURCH]

      4 8-ounce chicken breasts, boned
    2½ cups chicken stock
      1 onion, sliced
      1 tablespoon melted butter
         Zest of 1 orange, cut in strips
     ½ green pepper, cut in fine strips
    1½ tablespoons cornstarch
     ½ cup dry white wine
      2 cups cooked wild rice

Simmer chicken breasts until tender in 1 cup stock with onion. Pat dry, using paper towels; brush with butter and brown under the broiler. Meanwhile simmer orange zest and green pepper in remaining stock 5 minutes, add cornstarch mixed with wine, and cook until thickened. Serve chicken breasts on wild rice, with hot sauce.

GRANITA DI CAFFÉ
[JAMES A. BEARD]

      8 tablespoons Italian-roast coffee, ground for espresso
         Sugar substitute to taste
      4 cups boiling water

Combine the coffee, sugar substitute, and boiling water in a glass or pottery coffeemaker. Steep for 30 to 40 minutes. Let cool and strain through a filter paper. Freeze in ice trays or other container, stirring several times during the freezing process. Serve in sherbet glasses.

Thursday Luncheon for Four

MENU

Carrot Soup
Endive with Ham
Strawberries with Kirsch

CARROT SOUP
[RUTH ELLEN CHURCH]

    4 crisp young carrots, pared and sliced very thin
    4 sprigs parsley tied with 1 celery top, 1 slice onion
    4 cups beef, veal or chicken broth, fat-free

Cook carrots and flavoring vegetables in the broth until carrots are barely tender. Remove parsley, celery, and onion before serving.

ENDIVE WITH HAM
[ELAINE ROSS]

For each serving:
    2 thick heads endive
      Dash nutmeg
    2 strips Canadian bacon or ham approximately ⅓″ by ⅓″ by 3″
    ½ cup well-seasoned chicken stock
    ¼ hard-cooked egg, finely chopped

Cut out the root ends of the endive and cut each head lengthwise almost in half. Dust lightly with nutmeg, place a strip of Canadian bacon or ham down the slit center of each head, and place the endive side by side in a small shallow baking dish. Pour in the chicken stock, cover the pan completely with foil, and bake in a preheated 375° oven for 40 minutes, or until tender. Remove the foil, raise the heat to 425° and bake, basting frequently, until the liquid has almost evaporated.

Remove pan from oven, transfer endive to a hot plate. Sprinkle the endive with chopped egg and serve immediately.

Thursday Dinner for Four

MENU

Smoked Salmon with Lemon and Capers
Taj of India Chicken Korma
Fresh Pineapple with Kirsch

TAJ OF INDIA CHICKEN KORMA
[HELEN EVANS BROWN]

   2-pound broiler-fryer, cut into serving pieces
1 cup yoghurt
  Salt
1 medium onion, chopped
½ green pepper, chopped
2 teaspoons butter
1 tablespoon fresh chopped cilantro
½ teaspoon grated fresh ginger
1 teaspoon turmeric
1 clove garlic, pressed
2 small tomatoes, peeled and chopped
1 tablespoon grated coconut

Yoghurt Sauce:
  1 cup yoghurt
  4 green onions, chopped
  ⅓ cucumber, peeled, seeded and grated
    Salt, pepper, cayenne pepper

Marinate chicken for a few hours or overnight in 1 cup yoghurt seasoned with ¾ teaspoon salt. Simmer in yoghurt until chicken is tender and most of the liquid has disappeared. Meanwhile, sauté onion and green pepper in butter. Add cilantro, ginger, turmeric, garlic, and ¾ teaspoon salt. Cook, stirring, until onion is lightly colored, then add tomatoes. Cook until well blended, add chicken, and reheat. Serve sprinkled with coconut and accompanied by yoghurt sauce made by combining the yoghurt, green onions, cucumber, salt and pepper to taste, and a dash of cayenne pepper.

Friday Luncheon for Four

MENU

Cucumber Soup
Broiled Halibut with Peaches
Beans and Bean Sprouts
Low-Calorie Gelatin Dessert

CUCUMBER SOUP
[ELAINE ROSS]

> 1 bunch scallions, roots trimmed
> 1 tablespoon oil
> 2 medium cucumbers, peeled, seeded, and cubed
> 2½ cups chicken consommé
> 1 teaspoon fresh thyme leaves or ½ teaspoon dried thyme
> 1½ tablespoons lemon juice
> 1 teaspoon sugar
> ⅔ cup skimmed milk
> Salt, pepper to taste

Slice the scallions, including about 4″ of the green leaves, and sauté them in the oil for 5 minutes over medium heat. Add the cucumbers and cook 5 minutes longer. Add the consommé, thyme, lemon juice, and sugar, and bring to a boil. Reduce the heat to medium, cover, and cook for 20 minutes, or until the vegetables are very tender. Cool for a few minutes, then purée a portion at a time in an electric blender. Add the milk and season with salt and pepper. To serve hot, heat just to boiling point, or chill and serve cold.

BROILED HALIBUT WITH PEACHES
[BETTY WASON]

    2 tablespoons olive oil
    ½ teaspoon salt
    ½ teaspoon paprika
      Freshly ground black pepper to taste
    2 shallots, minced
    1 teaspoon fresh or ¼ teaspoon dried thyme
    4 halibut steaks, 1″ thick (about 2 pounds fish altogether)
    2 fresh peaches, peeled, stoned, and halved
    ¼ cup rosé wine

Blend the oil, salt, paprika, pepper, shallots, and thyme. Brush the fish with this seasoned oil and let stand about 15 minutes. Arrange fish on a foil-lined broiler pan and peach halves on either side of the fish. Broil fish 4″ from heat until it is lightly browned and flakes easily, basting both fish and peaches with wine as they cook.

BEANS AND BEAN SPROUTS
[ELAINE ROSS]

    1 package frozen French-style green beans
    1 medium onion, finely minced
    2 teaspoons oil
    2 teaspoons soy sauce
      1-pound can bean sprouts

Cook the frozen beans according to package directions, drain, and set aside. Sauté the onion in the oil over low heat until it is tender and golden. Stir in the soy sauce, add the bean sprouts and beans, and heat all together, stirring constantly, until hot.

Friday Dinner for Four

MENU

Celery and Radishes
Costa Brava Casserole
Peaches with Red Wine

COSTA BRAVA CASSEROLE
[BETTY WASON]

> 4 small lobster tails (3 to 4 ounces each)
> 2 whole chicken breasts, boned and cut into 2″ cubes
>   Salt, pepper to taste
> 2 tablespoons butter
> 1 tablespoon olive oil
> ½ pound lean pork or ham, cubed
> 3 shallots, minced, or 1 small white onion, minced
> 1 tomato, peeled and chopped
> ¾ cup dry white wine
> ½ cup canned beef gravy
> 1 tablespoon brandy
> 2 tablespoons minced parsley

Trim the lobster tails by removing the undershell. Place each on a cutting board and cut down center of back with a sharp knife. Hold under the hot water and gently pull the flesh partially away from the shell. Set aside.

Dust the chicken with salt and pepper, then brown on all sides in the butter and oil in a flameproof casserole. Remove. Add the pork or ham to the butter and oil and sauté until brown and crisp. Remove pork. Add the shallots or onion and the tomato to the same pan and cook until soft. Add the wine, the sautéed chicken and pork, and the lobster. Cover and cook over low heat for 15 minutes. Add the beef gravy, brandy, and parsley, stir to blend, and simmer uncovered 5 minutes longer. Serve with or without rice—dieters may have ½ cup.

Dieter's tip on cooking rice: If the raw rice is washed with 5 or 6 changes of water, much of the starch will be removed and each rice grain will be separate. Put rice in a saucepan and add water to cover completely; stir to loosen the starch. Drain thoroughly through a sieve, then repeat process until the water is quite clear.

PEACHES WITH RED WINE

    4 large ripe peaches
      Sugar substitute to taste
      Dry red wine, such as Pinot Noir

Scald and peel the peaches. Remove stones and cut into thin slices. Place in a deep glass serving dish and sprinkle to taste with sugar substitute. Cover with red wine and chill thoroughly before serving.

Saturday Luncheon for Six

MENU

Roast Rock Cornish Game Hen with Tarragon and Olives
Mushroom Plaki
Fresh Raspberries with Framboise

ROAST ROCK CORNISH GAME HEN WITH TARRAGON AND OLIVES
[JAMES A. BEARD]

    For each serving:
      1 teaspoon tarragon
      6 small green olives
      1 small onion
      2 rashers bacon
      1 game hen
      Salt, pepper

Combine the tarragon, olives, onion, and 1 rasher of bacon, cut into pieces; stuff the hen. Place second rasher across breast of hen. Sprinkle with salt and pepper. Roast on a rack in a shallow pan in a 350° oven for approximately 45 minutes—15 minutes on each side and 15 minutes breast up.

MUSHROOM PLAKI
[HELEN EVANS BROWN]

> 1 pound onions, sliced
> 1 clove garlic, pressed
> ¼ cup minced parsley
> 1 tablespoon olive oil
>   Salt, pepper to taste
> 1 pound mushrooms, sliced
> ¼ cup bouillon
> 1 cup yoghurt

Sauté onions, garlic and parsley in oil until tender. Season with salt and pepper. Cook mushrooms in bouillon for 5 minutes. Put half the onion mixture in a casserole, cover with mushrooms, and top with remaining onion. Bake in a 350° oven for 25 minutes. Serve with yoghurt.

FRESH RASPBERRIES WITH FRAMBOISE (see page 291)

Saturday Dinner for Six

MENU

Brains Chiffonade
Roast Loin of Veal
Vegetable Mélange
Peach Soufflé

BRAINS CHIFFONADE
[HELEN EVANS BROWN]

> 3 calves' brains
> 1 tablespoon lemon juice
> Salt
> 1 small onion, finely minced
> 1 hard-cooked egg, minced
> 2 tablespoons tarragon vinegar
> 1 pimiento, minced
> 2 tablespoons minced parsley
> 2 tablespoons white wine
> Dash of Tabasco sauce

Cook the brains in water to cover with the lemon juice and 2 teaspoons salt for 15 minutes. Drain and plunge into cold water. Clean and slice brains. Cover with a chiffonade dressing made by combining the onion, egg, vinegar, pimiento, parsley, wine, Tabasco, and salt to taste. Serve chilled.

ROAST LOIN OF VEAL
[JAMES A. BEARD]

> Loin or rack of veal, 4 to 5 pounds
> 1 clove garlic
> 2 teaspoons tarragon
> Salt, freshly ground black pepper
> Bacon strips
> White wine

Rub the veal well with garlic, tarragon, salt and pepper, and place on a rack in a shallow roasting pan. Place strips of bacon over it and roast in a 325° oven for approximately 22 minutes per pound, or until the meat thermometer registers 165°. Baste occasionally with a little white wine blended with the pan juices. Remove the bacon for the last half hour.

VEGETABLE MÉLANGE
[JAMES A. BEARD]

2 tablespoons olive oil
2 medium onions, peeled and thinly sliced
2 green peppers, seeded and cut in strips
4 medium tomatoes, peeled, seeded, and sliced
1 clove garlic, minced
1 tablespoon chopped fresh dill
  Salt, freshly ground black pepper
2 or 3 small strips of lemon rind

Heat the oil in a large frying pan that has a tight-fitting cover. Add the onions and peppers, the onions at one side of the pan and the peppers at the other. Cover the pan, reduce the heat, and let the vegetables steam for about 10 minutes. Remove cover and add tomatoes, garlic, dill, salt and pepper to taste, and lemon rind. Cover and cook another 5 or 6 minutes; the vegetables should still retain some of their crispness and texture.

PEACH SOUFFLÉ
[RUTH ELLEN CHURCH]

8 egg whites (1 cup)
¼ teaspoon salt
¼ teaspoon cream of tartar
3 tablespoons sugar
1 cup puréed dietetic-pack peaches
2 tablespoons Cointreau liqueur

Whip egg whites with salt and cream of tartar until they hold a peak. Gradually beat in sugar. Combine puréed peaches and Cointreau and carefully fold into the egg whites. Pour into a 1½-quart soufflé dish with a foil collar tied around it to give an extra 2″ depth. Bake at 400° for 20 to 25 minutes. Carefully remove collar and serve soufflé at once.

Sunday Luncheon for Six

MENU

Sole à la Normande
Pimiento Egyptienne
Boston Lettuce with Roquefort Dressing
Lemon Sherbet

SOLE À LA NORMANDE
[RUTH ELLEN CHURCH]

6 filets of sole or other white fish
3 medium onions, chopped fine
1 cup water
1 cup dry white wine
2 tablespoons butter
2 tablespoons flour
3 tablespoons finely chopped parsley
Salt, pepper to taste
Finely chopped green onions

Place filets in baking dish. Tie onions in a cheesecloth bag. Add to fish with water and wine. Cover and bake at 350° for 15 minutes, or until fish flakes when tested with a fork. Drain off cooking stock. Make sauce by blending butter and flour, adding 1 cup stock, parsley and seasonings, and cooking until smooth and thickened. Pour the sauce over the filets and sprinkle chopped green onions on top.

PIMIENTO EGYPTIENNE
[HELEN EVANS BROWN]

> 6 whole canned pimientos
> ¾ cup broiled chopped mushrooms
> 2 tablespoons chopped red onion
> Mixed herbs
> Salt to taste

Stuff each pimiento with 2 tablespoons mushrooms mixed with 1 teaspoon onion, a pinch of herbs, and salt to taste.

ROQUEFORT DRESSING
[HELEN EVANS BROWN]

> 1 ounce Roquefort cheese, crumbled
> 1 tablespoon cognac
> ½ small clove garlic
> 1 tablespoon white wine vinegar
> ½ teaspoon salt
> Dash of pepper
> 1 cup yoghurt

Combine all ingredients in a blender and whirl until smooth. Makes 1¼ cups.

Sunday Dinner for Six

MENU

Danish Pickled Oysters
Beef Brisket with Horseradish Sauce
Celery Provençal
Cherries Flambé

DANISH PICKLED OYSTERS
[HELEN EVANS BROWN]

  1 quart medium-size oysters with liquor
  1 onion, sliced thin
  1 lemon, sliced thin
  1 cup white wine vinegar
  2 teaspoons pickling spices
     Salt, freshly ground white pepper to taste
  2 tablespoons minced parsley

Cook oysters in their liquor until the edges curl, then drain (saving liquor) and plunge into ice water. Drain again, and arrange on a flat serving dish. Cover with onion and lemon slices. Add vinegar and pickling spices to oyster liquor and simmer 10 minutes. Strain over oysters, sprinkle with salt, pepper and parsley. Chill before serving.

BEEF BRISKET WITH HORSERADISH SAUCE
[RUTH ELLEN CHURCH]

Trim fat from beef before you cook it. Stock can be strained, chilled, skimmed of fat and served as soup.

  3 to 4 pounds fresh boneless beef brisket
  1 onion
     Cluster of celery tops
     Salt, whole peppercorns
  ½ cup prepared horseradish
  1 tablespoon lemon juice
  1 tablespoon chopped pimiento
  1 cup thin white sauce made with skimmed milk
     Freshly ground coarse pepper

Put beef in a saucepan with water to cover; add onion, celery tops, a tablespoon of salt, and a few peppercorns. Simmer 3 to 4 hours, or until tender. Add horseradish, lemon juice and pimiento to white sauce. Slice cooked beef, sprinkle with pepper and serve with the horseradish sauce.

CELERY PROVENÇAL
[HELEN EVANS BROWN]

> 6 celery hearts (about 3½ ounces each)
> 1 cup consommé
> 1 tablespoon olive oil
> 2 cloves garlic, finely minced
> 3 small tomatoes, peeled, seeded and diced
> Salt to taste
> Pinch of powdered saffron

Split celery hearts and cook, covered, in consommé until tender (add water if necessary). Heat oil in a skillet and sauté garlic until soft. Add tomatoes, salt, and saffron, and cook down a little. To serve, arrange celery on a dish, cut side up, reduce remaining consommé to ¼ cup, and pour over celery. Divide tomato mixture between celery and spoon some on top of each serving.

CHERRIES FLAMBÉ
[HELEN EVANS BROWN]

> 4 cups pitted Bing cherries
> 2 cups red Bordeaux or Cabernet Sauvignon wine
> 1 cinnamon stick
> 1 clove
> Sugar substitute (optional)
> 1 tablespoon cornstarch mixed with a little water
> ¼ cup rum

Cook cherries in wine with cinnamon stick and clove until partially tender. Drain and reserve cherries. Reduce sauce to one half and sweeten, if desired, with sugar substitute. Thicken sauce with cornstarch mixture. Return cherries to sauce and reheat. Heat rum, flame, pour over cherries. Serve when flames die down.

Outdoor Parties

There has always been an American tradition of cooking and eating outdoors. The clambake and the luau, although thousands of miles apart geographically, are proof enough. Today's alfresco feasts, while updated, are part of the same tradition, whether they be spiffy Saturday night dinners on a candlelit terrace, come-as-you-are buffets around the pool, gregarious tail-gate or beach picnics with everyone from the kids' friends to the family dog, or select little sailing parties where the food is less important than the sport.

One of the greatest virtues of eating outdoors is that almost any kind of food goes, provided it is satisfying enough for appetites sharpened by fresh air. In the relaxed atmosphere of the patio or terrace, the pool or the beach, you can allow yourself a lot more latitude in the type and range of food you serve. People, it seems, have more adventurous palates outside the house than inside. So why not give them a Mexican, Middle East, or Mediterranean menu, rather than the old outworn outdoor cliché of the grilled steak and tossed salad? Outdoor parties are more fun for everyone, the hostess included, if now and then you serve something completely unexpected, like a huge bowl of tiny juicy crawfish to be eaten with the fingers, a luncheon of nothing but hors d'oeuvre, or a marvelous aromatic pot of seafood stew.

258

Obviously your outdoor menus can be as varied, as simple, or as elaborate as you please, but you'll save yourself a lot of unnecessary effort if you plan at least one or two dishes that can be made ahead and refrigerated, or reheated at the last minute, with only the main course cooked on the spot. As most men like to unleash their creative cooking talents over the barbecue grill, you can hand this chore over to your husband while you concentrate on getting the rest of the meal to table.

On the other hand, if you are doing most of the cooking outdoors, it's a good idea to have two grills going, one to cook the main course of meat, poultry, or fish, the other to keep the accompanying dishes warm until serving time. And if you are barbecuing meat, be sure to set the table to windward of the grill so it isn't blanketed in a cloud of odoriferous smoke.

As most, though not all, outdoors meals are summertime pleasures, take advantage of the fresh produce that is at its peak then, fruits for your desserts, and as many fresh vegetables as possible—in salads, grilled, or cooked and sauced as simply as possible. As the bulk of summer entertaining is done at weekends, usually at the shore or in the country, you'll have to forget about your normal routine and be ready to cope with any eventuality, from guests who get held up in traffic on Friday night to drop-in additions to your Saturday-night barbecue or Sunday lunch. Weekend entertaining will be more carefree if you work out an advance plan for meals, spend the week making a few desserts or soup bases you can keep in the freezer, and generally try to keep to dishes that are not unduly complicated—simple foods are the most welcome in the hot summer months, anyway. Plan your menus around fresh local produce and eliminate recipes that require exotic ingredients you don't stand a chance of running to earth in the local supermarket. Bring with you, or have sent from the city, anything you just can't cook without, such as fresh ginger root, imported Parmesan cheese, canned chiles, shallots, hard-to-get spices and seasonings like green peppercorns or turmeric. Think ahead. Cook more beef or chicken or vegetables than you need. The meats can go into a salad, or be served cold on a buffet, the vegetables marinated in a vinaigrette sauce and used as a first course or salad.

Remember that in summertime the living should be easy—and that includes cooking and entertaining.

Elegant Outdoor Dinner for Six

Eating outdoors doesn't necessarily mean being casual. You can serve just as superb and interesting a dinner as you would inside the house, and there's really no summer pleasure to equal that of dining on the terrace by the light of candles in tall hurricanes, with the women guests in long dresses and the men in white dinner jackets. While there is nothing complicated about this dinner, it does consist of foods that deserve your best wines—a white Burgundy with the oysters and a red château-bottled Bordeaux of a good year with the steak and the cheese and fruit course. A Madeira would make a fine ending for this memorable meal, with a dish of nuts in the shell, provided you can find a really good, aged, dry Sercial or the sweeter Bual.

MENU
[PHILIP S. BROWN]

Oysters on the Half Shell

Steak Marchand de Vin

Hashed Brown Potatoes   *Asparagus with Melted Butter*

Ripe Pears   *Assorted Cheeses*

Nuts

The Wines

Chassagne-Montrachet or Chablis; a fine red Bordeaux—
Château Petrus or Château Margaux; Madeira

OYSTERS ON THE HALF SHELL

Allow 6 oysters per person. Serve on the half shell on a bed of ice. Lemon is the ideal accompaniment—don't mask the delicate flavor with cocktail sauce, horseradish, or overpowering condiments. If you wish, make thin sandwiches of brown bread and sweet butter, trim off the crusts, and cut in fingers, to serve with the oysters.

STEAK MARCHAND DE VIN

6 green onions or shallots, chopped
Butter
¾ cup good red Bordeaux wine
1 cup brown sauce (see page 419) *or* 1 can (10¾-ounce) beef gravy
3-pound top sirloin or prime-grade rump steak, 1½″ to 2″ thick
2 tablespoons lemon juice

Prepare the sauce marchand de vin: Sauté the chopped onion in ¼ cup butter until wilted. Add the wine and cook until reduced to ⅓ cup. Add the brown sauce or gravy and heat.

Grill the steak as usual over a medium fire. (If you are lucky enough to have some dried grapevine trimmings, pile them on the coals and let them burn down before grilling; they add a marvelous flavor.) When cooked to perfection, remove the meat to a hot platter and top with a lump of butter. Add 2 tablespoons of butter and the lemon juice to the sauce, and serve with the steak.

HASHED BROWN POTATOES

Allow one good-sized boiled or baked potato for each serving. Cut in small dice. For each potato, melt 2 tablespoons butter in a heavy skillet and add the diced potatoes, stirring until they are well coated with butter. Cook over a very low flame until a brown crust forms on the bottom (add more butter if necessary). When beautifully browned, fold over like an omelette and turn out on a hot platter.

ASPARAGUS WITH MELTED BUTTER

Allow ½ pound asparagus per serving. Clean and remove tough ends. Place asparagus in a large skillet of boiling salted water, bring the water back to a boil, and boil only until tender-crisp, about 8 to 12 minutes, depending on the size of the stalks. Do not overcook. Drain and heap on a linen napkin on a platter. Serve with melted butter (the clear part only), to be poured over the asparagus at table. Serve in the French manner—i.e., as a separate course, as asparagus is considered an enemy of wine.

Friday Night Dinner for Six

Simple food, beautifully prepared, and some intriguing flavor combinations—that's the secret of this Friday night dinner. It's a cinch to do if you are expecting guests for the weekend and are not sure what time they'll arrive, because everything can be cooked very speedily, and the sardine pâté made in the morning. With the kidneys, have a light red wine, such as a Beaujolais, and use the same wine in the sauce.

MENU

Sardine Pâté in Lemon Shells

Veal Kidneys en Brochette, Mushroom Sauce

Purée of Spinach and Watercress

Noodles with Poppy Seeds

Endive Salad, French Dressing

Strawberries Carcassonne

The Wine

Beaujolais—a Brouilly or Fleurie

SARDINE PÂTÉ IN LEMON SHELLS
[ELISABETH ORTIZ]

    2 tablespoons lemon juice
    1 thin slice onion
    4 sprigs parsley
       8-ounce package cream cheese, cubed
    2 4-ounce cans sardines in oil, drained
       Tabasco sauce
    6 medium lemons
       Chopped parsley for garnish

Put the lemon juice, onion, parsley, cream cheese, sardines, and Tabasco to taste in the blender container in the order listed. Cover and run on high speed until smooth, but do not overblend, if necessary stopping and scraping down sides with a rubber spatula. Makes about 1 cup.

Cut a slice off the stalk end of the lemons and scoop out all the pulp. Cut a thin slice off the other end so the lemon shells stand upright. Fill shells with sardine pâté, and sprinkle with chopped parsley. Serve with hot toast.

VEAL KIDNEYS EN BROCHETTE, MUSHROOM SAUCE
[PHILIP S. BROWN]

   3 veal kidneys, with fat (if possible), about 1 pound each
     Salt, pepper
   1 clove garlic, chopped
   3 shallots, chopped
  ¼ cup butter
  ½ pound mushrooms, cleaned and sliced
  ¼ teaspoon dry mustard
   1 cup red wine
  ¾ cup brown sauce (see page 419) or brown gravy
     Beurre manié (butter and flour mixture)
     Parsley

Trim the fat off the veal kidneys with a sharp knife so that ¼" to ½" is left as a covering. Sprinkle them well with salt and pepper, string on the spit whole, running the spit through them lengthwise, and fasten firmly with the holding forks so that the center ones won't spin on the spit. (If you have more than your spit will accommodate this way, spit them through the middle, then fasten the ends together with long skewers.) Roast over a medium fire until the fat has pretty well melted away. If there is no fat on them, wrap in barding pork. They should not be overcooked—about 30 to 45 minutes is right for average-size veal kidneys.

Meanwhile, prepare the mushroom sauce: Sauté the garlic and shallots in the butter until wilted and just beginning to color. Add the mushrooms, stirring until they begin to soften. Then add salt and pepper to taste, the mustard and red wine. Simmer, covered, for 20 minutes, stir in the brown sauce or gravy, cover, and simmer for another 10 to 15 minutes. Thicken with beurre manié as needed. Should the sauce get too thick, add a little more red wine. Taste for seasoning.

Remove kidneys from spit onto a carving board and carve into ½″ slices. Garnish with parsley and serve with mushroom sauce. Each of these veal kidneys will serve 2.

PURÉE OF SPINACH AND WATERCRESS
[PHILIP S. BROWN]

    3 bunches spinach
    2 bunches watercress
    1 garlic clove
    ¼ pound butter
      Salt, pepper to taste
      Nutmeg
      Thin slices lemon

Wash and pick over the greens carefully, keeping them separate. Cook them in two pots in the water which clings to the leaves. As they wilt, turn with tongs to get the top leaves to the bottom. When thoroughly wilted, tender, and still bright green, drain thoroughly, and either chop together very fine or put through a food mill. Crush the garlic a little with the side of a knife, or make small cuts all over it with a sharp knife. Add the garlic to the hot greens and mix in the butter, salt, pepper and a grating or two of nutmeg. Remove the garlic and discard. Arrange in a serving dish and reheat in the oven if necessary. Garnish with slices of lemon.

NOODLES WITH POPPY SEEDS
[PHILIP S. BROWN]

    ¾ pound narrow noodles
    ⅓ cup butter
      Salt, pepper
    2 tablespoons poppy seeds

Cook the noodles in boiling salted water until just tender, but not mushy. Drain well, lifting with a fork to let the steam escape. Put into a heated serving dish, mix with the butter, salt, pepper, and most of the poppy seeds. When well mixed and ready to serve, sprinkle the top with the remaining poppy seeds.

ENDIVE SALAD
[PHILIP S. BROWN]

The salad should be very plain and simple. For each 2 persons, separate 1 head of endive and arrange the leaves on individual plates. Dress with a simple French dressing, sprinkle with minced parsley, and serve cold.

STRAWBERRIES CARCASSONNE
[JAMES A. BEARD]

Choose ripe, flavorful strawberries, and allow about 8 per serving. Sugar lightly to taste. Squeeze lemon juice over them and give them a generous sprinkling of freshly ground black pepper. Toss well. Just before serving, add about 2 tablespoons Armagnac per serving and toss again. This makes an unusual and extraordinarily good blend of flavors.

Sunday Night Dinner for Six

An absolutely delightful selection of foods for a summer evening with some unusual elements—a cold split pea soup, boned and grilled legs of lamb, an English summer pudding—that will intrigue your guests. Note that the soup and dessert are made ahead.

With the lamb you might serve big pitchers of sangria, a good California red jug wine from a top winery, or a lightly chilled Beaujolais.

MENU
[JAMES A. BEARD]

Chilled Minted Pea Soup
Grilled Boned Legs of Lamb
Hashed Brown Potatoes (see page 261)
Marinated Grilled Eggplant Slices
Summer Pudding

The Wine

Sangria, California Zinfandel or Mountain Red Burgundy,
Beaujolais Brouilly or Beaujolais Villages

CHILLED MINTED PEA SOUP

  1½ cups green split peas
   1 tablespoon salt
   8 to 12 cups chicken broth
   2 cloves garlic, crushed
   6 tablespoons sour cream
     Fresh mint, chopped

Soak peas overnight in water to cover. Add additional water needed to cover and the salt, and bring to a boil. Boil for ½ hour, drain, return to the pot, and add 8 cups chicken broth and the garlic. Bring to a boil again, reduce the heat, and simmer until peas are thoroughly cooked. If too thick, add additional broth. Purée the peas, measure, and combine with equal amount of broth. Correct the seasoning, and chill. When ready to serve, stir in 1 tablespoon sour cream per serving, and sprinkle with fresh mint. Serve very cold.

GRILLED BONED LEGS OF LAMB

   2 legs of lamb
   6 cloves garlic, slivered
     4-ounce can anchovy filets, cut in ½" pieces
     Rosemary, powdered in a mortar and pestle

¼ cup olive or peanut oil
1 cup Japanese soy sauce
½ cup finely shredded fresh ginger
½ cup sherry

Have the butcher bone the lamb and butterfly it (split the leg, but not all the way through, so it will lie flat, in one piece), leaving the shank bones intact. Make deep gashes in the meat and stuff one leg with 4 of the slivered garlic cloves, the other with the remaining slivered garlic and the pieces of anchovy. Rub both legs with powdered rosemary and place in a deep large baking dish or similar container large enough to hold the meat, preferably of pottery or enameled iron. Add the oil, soy sauce, ginger and sherry. Marinate for 3 to 4 hours, turning several times.

Grill the legs on the charcoal grill over medium-hot coals, allowing about 18 to 20 minutes per side for rare. Brush from time to time with the marinade.

To serve, cut in rather thick slices across the leg. Serve on very hot plates.

MARINATED GRILLED EGGPLANT SLICES

2 to 3 eggplants
Marinade used for lamb
Oil
Salt, pepper

Cut the unpeeled eggplant in slices about 1″ thick and marinate for half an hour. Remove from the marinade, brush with oil, and grill over coals with the lamb until nicely browned on both sides. Brush with the marinade, and season with salt and pepper to taste.

SUMMER PUDDING

Thin slices of slightly stale bread
1 quart raspberries
½ pint red currants
1 cup sugar
Heavy cream (optional)

Remove the crusts from the bread. Arrange slices overlapping in a round mold so that the fruit juice will not leak through. Save a few slices for the top. Combine fruits and sugar, and cook for about 3 to 4 minutes. (You may use equal proportions of currants and raspberries, if you prefer.) Spoon fruit into the mold, reserving some of the juice. Top with bread slices to seal completely, and cover with a plate that will fit tightly inside the mold. Weight with a 2-pound object and refrigerate for 12 to 24 hours. To serve, unmold, and pour either the reserved fruit juice or heavy cream over the pudding. This is a truly refreshing dessert for the summer months.

Fourth of July Dinner for Eight

Salmon is about as traditional as anything for the Glorious Fourth, and nothing could be more American than corn, hot dogs, and strawberry shortcake. The fact that most of this menu is cooked outdoors makes it all the more fun. If you are going to make the cucumber salad in advance, don't add the dressing until you are ready to serve or it will become too watery from the juices in the cucumber. The shortcake, of course, should be made at the last minute and eaten hot. A dry white wine is indicated with the salmon but you could, if you'd rather, serve a Grenache rosé from California, or even beer.

MENU
[PHILIP S. BROWN]

Tiny Sausages on Sticks

Spit-Roasted Salmon, Egg Sauce

Ash-Roasted Corn   *Buttered Fresh Peas*

Cucumber Salad

Bread Sticks

Strawberry Shortcake

The Wine

Pinot Chardonnay or Grenache Rosé

TINY SAUSAGES ON STICKS

Buy small-size wieners at the delicatessen or Vienna sausages in cans. For 8 people, you will need at least 2 dozen sausages, and maybe half again as many. Impale each one lengthwise on a bamboo skewer and wrap it in baking-powder-biscuit dough or yeast-roll dough, rolled very thin. Cook over a medium charcoal fire until the bread is done and golden brown and the sausage within is hot. Turn a couple of times during the cooking so that the bread will brown on all sides. Have mustard for those who want it.

SPIT-ROASTED SALMON, EGG SAUCE

> 1 small whole salmon or large center cut, about 4 to 5 pounds, skin intact
> Juice of one lemon
> Salt, pepper
> Butter
> ½ cup flour
> 1 cup consommé or fish stock
> 2 cups milk
> 1 cup light cream
> Minced fresh dill (optional)
> 6 hard-cooked eggs
> Thin slices lemon
> Parsley

Sprinkle the cavity of the salmon with the lemon juice, salt and pepper. Butter the skin liberally, then fold a piece of coarse-meshed chicken wire around the whole fish and secure it well, making a sort of basket. Spit the fish on the diagonal, and roast over a medium fire. Melt some butter and brush the salmon from time to time. When a meat thermometer inserted into the thickest part of the fish reads 160°, it will be done.

Meanwhile, prepare the egg sauce: Melt ½ cup butter, add the flour, and cook a couple of minutes. Add the consommé, milk, cream, and season with salt, pepper, and minced fresh dill if you like. Cook until thick and smooth. Slice 3 hard-cooked eggs to garnish the platter; reserve the good slices and chop the ends along with the remaining hard-cooked eggs. Add the chopped eggs to the sauce and stir.

Remove the spit and chicken wire from the salmon. If the skin is crispy (and it should be), leave it on and serve a little with each piece of salmon. Arrange your beautiful production on a platter, garnish with the lemon slices, parsley, and hard-cooked egg slices reserved from the sauce. Serve with the egg sauce.

ASH-ROASTED CORN

Allow at least 2 ears per person, with a few extra for the gluttons. Pull back the husks and remove all the silk, then replace the husks and tie the ends together. Soak the ears in cold water for at least half an hour before roasting on the coals. Lay the wet ears directly on top of the fire. Turn the ears two or three times during the roasting. They will cook in 10 to 15 minutes. When done, remove husks (wear heavy gloves for this) and stack on a platter. Serve with plenty of butter.

BUTTERED FRESH PEAS

Buy fresh peas in the pod and allow 4 pounds of unshelled peas for 8 persons, or half a pound per head. Do not shell until you are ready to cook them, and then boil briefly in a very small amount of boiling salted water until just tender. Do not overcook. Drain and toss with butter and, if you wish, sprinkle with chopped fresh mint or parsley.

CUCUMBER SALAD

For 8, buy 4 long thin cucumbers, preferably not waxed. If they are waxed, peel them; if not, leave the skins on. In either case, slice them very thin and dress with ½ cup French dressing to which 2 tablespoons grated onion have been added. Serve in lettuce cups.

STRAWBERRY SHORTCAKE

3 pints strawberries
4 tablespoons sugar
2 cups flour
2 teaspoons baking powder
¾ teaspoon salt
1 egg
  Butter
⅓ (approximately) cup milk
1 egg beaten with 1 tablespoon water
½ pint heavy cream

Wash and hull the strawberries, reserve a dozen or so nice ones for the crown of the cake, and slice the remaining strawberries. Sprinkle with 3 tablespoons sugar and keep in the refrigerator until time to put the shortcake together.

Make a biscuit dough with the flour, baking powder, the remaining 1 tablespoon sugar, salt, 1 egg, 5 tablespoons of butter, and enough milk to make a soft dough. Divide it in half and pat one half into a 10″ cake pan—this will make a rather thin layer. Brush with 1 tablespoon melted butter, pat the other half of the dough on top, brush with egg beaten with water and bake in a 450° oven for about 10 minutes, or until brown. Turn out carefully, split on the division line, and transfer the bottom half to a plate, using two spatulas and taking great care.

Spread the bottom layer with more butter, cover very generously with sliced sugared strawberries, put the top layer in place, add more sliced strawberries, and put a wreath of large perfect berries around the top. The shortcake should be eaten hot, so work quickly. Serve with thick unwhipped cream (whip it if you prefer, but it won't be as good).

Labor Day Dinner for Eight

Bring the season to a close with style—and a very special dinner of spit-roasted ribs of beef, potatoes Chantilly, and onions braised in Madeira. With this, a fine Burgundy or a California vintage Pinot Noir.

MENU

Shrimp, Latin American Style
Spit-Roasted Rib Roast of Beef
Potatoes Chantilly
Onions Braised in Madeira
Watercress Salad with French Dressing
Raspberry Trifle

The Wine

Chambertin Clos de Bèze or California Pinot Noir

SHRIMP, LATIN AMERICAN STYLE
[JAMES A. BEARD]

    2 cups olive oil
    2 pounds raw shrimp, shelled and cleaned
    2 egg yolks
    ½ cup dry white wine
    ½ teaspoon anchovy paste
    ¼ cup wine vinegar
    ¼ cup fresh lime juice
    4 pinches mace
    1 tablespoon mustard
    1 teaspoon parsley
    1 teaspoon chives
    1 teaspoon capers
    2 teaspoons tarragon
    2 teaspoons freshly ground black pepper
    2 teaspoons salt
    2 teaspoons Worcestershire sauce

Heat 1 cup of the olive oil. Toss the raw shrimp in the hot oil 2 to 3 minutes, or until pink. Drain and cool. Place the rest of the ingredients in the blender and blend only until smooth. Do not blend until the mixture turns into a mayonnaise.

Pour the marinade over the cooled, drained shrimp and let stand in the refrigerator for 24 hours before serving.

SPIT-ROASTED RIB ROAST OF BEEF
[JAMES A. BEARD]

Buy a 4- or 5-rib roast for 8 people; that way you will have some left over. If you don't like cold or reheated roast beef, buy a smaller one, but no less than 3 ribs. Have your butcher remove the chine bone and "strap" and tie a blanket of fat over the exposed end. Also have the rib ends cut off so that the bones are not more than 5″ or 6″ long. (You can use these in a short-ribs recipe.) Let the roast remain out of the refrigerator for at least 24 hours before cooking so that it will reach room temperature throughout. Balance the roast well on the spit. (Large rib roasts are usually much heavier on one side, so run the spit through on a diagonal, from the rib end to the top of the eye. This gives you better balance and your spit will turn more evenly.) Start the roast on a good brisk fire to brown the fat and seal the ends. In 15 to 20 minutes the heat will decrease by itself until a spit thermometer will ready 250° to 300°. Cook the meat to not more than 120° internal temperature (for rare), then douse or remove the fire and let it "coast" for 20 minutes or so; it will reach 130° during this time. This process develops the juices in the meat. Cooking time will be about 2 hours, but do check with a meat thermometer. The minutes-per-pound method is of little use here, as a 3-rib roast takes as long to cook as a 5-rib one. Lay the roast on a carving board, remove the spit and carve, spooning some of the savory juice over each slice.

POTATOES CHANTILLY
[ELOISE DAVISON]

> 8 medium-size Idaho potatoes
> 1 cup heavy cream
> 4 tablespoons butter
> Salt, freshly ground black pepper
> Chopped parsley
> ¾ cup grated sharp cheese

Peel potatoes and cut into thin strips as for French fries. Place one half in center of each of two large pieces of aluminum foil. Pour over the cream, dot with butter, and sprinkle with salt and pepper to taste, some chopped parsley, and the cheese. Bring foil up over potatoes and seal all edges together to make a tight package. Place on a cookie sheet or jelly-roll pan and bake in a 425° oven for 40 minutes. Serve from the foil. The potatoes will be deliciously soft with the cream and cheese practically absorbed.

ONIONS IN MADEIRA
[JAMES A. BEARD]

8 tablespoons butter
4 large onions, cut into ½″ slices
1½ teaspoons salt
½ cup Madeira

Melt the butter in a large heavy skillet or sauté pan and make a layer of the onion slices. Sprinkle with salt, cover tightly, and steam over low heat until the onions are just tender. Add the Madeira and cook a few minutes longer, then remove to an oven-proof serving dish and put in a 450° oven for 5 minutes.

RASPBERRY TRIFLE
[NIKA HAZELTON]

3 eggs
¼ cup sugar
2 cups light cream, scalded
½ teaspoon almond extract
4 ounces sponge cake cut into fingers, or lady fingers
½ cup raspberry jam
4 ounces almond macaroons, coarsely crumbled
¼ cup sweet sherry
1½ cups fresh raspberries or drained frozen raspberries
1 cup heavy cream, whipped

Beat the eggs until frothy in the top of a double boiler. Beat in the sugar. Stir in the scalded light cream gradually. Cook over hot, not boiling, water, stirring constantly, until mixture thickens and coats a silver spoon. Remove from heat and stir in the almond extract. Cool.

Line a crystal serving dish with the sponge or lady fingers. Top with the jam. Top the jam with the macaroon crumbs. Pour the sherry over the crumbs and let stand for 15 minutes.

Pour the cooled custard over all. Top with 1 cup of the raspberries and spread with the whipped cream. Decorate with the remaining berries. Chill thoroughly before serving.

Weekend Dinner for Four

Assuming that this dinner is for a couple of weekend house guests you would like to entertain well, the food is suave and imaginative and the table should be set as beautifully as though it were indoors, with fine crystal and linen, candles and flowers. It would be best not to serve appetizers before dinner; perhaps just have salted almonds of the best quality with a glass of dry sherry or a cocktail. To accompany the noisettes of lamb, choose a rather light red Bordeaux, a good Beaujolais, or a red wine from the Touraine.

MENU

Chilled Avocado Soup
Noisettes of Lamb with Herbed Sauce
Tiny New Potatoes with Butter and Chopped Chives
Green Beans with Mushrooms
Ambrosial Soufflés in Orange Cups

The Wine

A château-bottled St. Julien or a Moulin-à-Vent or Chinon

CHILLED AVOCADO SOUP

    2 ripe avocados
    1 cup chicken broth
    4 to 6 tablespoons sour cream
    4 to 6 tablespoons heavy cream
       Juice of ½ lemon
    ½ teaspoon salt
       Finely chopped shallots or onion
       Chopped cilantro or thin lemon slices for garnish

Scoop out avocado flesh, dice coarsely, and put in blender with broth, sour cream, heavy cream, lemon juice, salt, and chopped shallot to taste. Whirl until puréed. Check seasoning, and add salt if necessary. Serve in small chilled bowls and sprinkle with cilantro.

NOISETTES OF LAMB WITH HERBED SAUCE

Buy rib or loin chops cut to the thickness you prefer. Judging by the size of the eye of the chops, allow 2 or 3 chops per person. Cut around the bone with a small, sharp, pointed knife (a boning knife, if you have one), leaving the meat intact. (In the case of loin chops, this will mean using the meatiest section on just one side of the T-bone.) The outside edges of these morsels of meat should then be wrapped with either the tails of the chops or thin slices of salt pork or bacon, as a filet mignon is barded. Secure the wrapping with butcher's string.

Broil the noisettes very quickly over charcoal until they are browned on the outside and pink inside. Season with salt and pepper while broiling.

HERBED SAUCE

    5 tablespoons butter
    1 small onion, finely chopped
    5 tablespoons flour
    1 teaspoon salt
    ½ teaspoon freshly ground black pepper
    1 cup red wine

1 cup beef bouillon (canned may be used)
2 tablespoons chopped parsley
2 teaspoons chopped fresh mint or chervil

Melt the butter in a heavy saucepan and sauté the onion until just buttery yellow. Mix flour into onion, season with salt and pepper, and stir in red wine. Allow the mixture to thicken, and simmer for about 5 minutes. Add the bouillon and cook until thickened to taste. Simmer over very low heat for an additional 10 minutes. Strain through a fine sieve and keep warm.

Spoon a few tablespoons of the sauce on a hot platter and arrange the noisettes on top. Garnish with chopped parsley and mint. Pass the rest of the sauce in a sauceboat.

NOTE: If you want to present this dish even more handsomely, ask the butcher to saw several 1″ slices of beef marrow bone. Poach in beef broth, arrange on the platter, and top with the noisettes.

GREEN BEANS WITH MUSHROOMS
[PHILIP S. BROWN]

1 pound green beans, cleaned
1 cup chicken stock
½ pound mushrooms, chopped
5 to 6 tablespoons butter

French-cut each bean into 4 lengthwise strips. Cook in chicken stock until tender-crisp. This shouldn't take more than 10 minutes. If the chicken stock is well seasoned, you shouldn't need more salt. If it isn't, add salt to taste. Meanwhile, sauté the mushrooms in 4 tablespoons butter until wilted. Drain the beans and mix with the mushrooms. Add the remaining butter and toss together lightly.

AMBROSIAL SOUFFLÉS IN ORANGE CUPS
[ELAINE ROSS]

> 4 large oranges
> 2 tablespoons sugar
> 4 teaspoons flour
> ¼ cup milk
> 2 eggs, separated
> ¼ cup very finely chopped coconut
> 4 teaspoons orange or kumquat marmalade

Cut off the tops of the 4 oranges and scoop out the pulp. With a spoon, scrape out as much pith as possible to leave a clean shell. Be careful not to pierce the skin. Drain the orange pulp, reserving 4 teaspoons juice. Chop and reserve ¼ cup pulp.

Preheat the oven to 375°. Combine the sugar, flour, milk, and 4 teaspoons reserved orange juice in a small saucepan. Cook over low heat, stirring constantly, until the sauce becomes thick. Remove from the heat and stir in the egg yolks and coconut. Beat the egg whites until stiff, but not dry, and fold into the coconut mixture. Put a portion of the orange pulp and marmalade in the bottom of each shell. Spoon the soufflé mixture on top. Place the filled shells on a baking sheet and bake in a 375° oven for 17 minutes, or until puffed and lightly tinged with brown. Arrange on individual dishes and serve at once. (If some of the soufflé has baked over and spilled to one side, scoop it up with a spatula as you transfer the shells to a plate.)

NOTE: Soufflés may also be baked in buttered and sugared custard cups.

Southern-Style Dinner for Six

This dinner is really pseudo-Southern, but it is wonderfully good and satisfying. On a warm summer evening, under a full moon, you might initiate the mood by serving Sazeracs, an old New Orleans specialty, instead of the usual cocktails. For each drink, swirl a little Pernod in an Old Fashioned glass—just enough to coat the glass—and shake out any excess. Add ice cubes and 2 or 3 dashes of Peychaud's bitters, then pour in 2 ounces of bourbon or rye. As Sazeracs have a good deal of authority, moderation is in order and the shrimp biscuits are provided to temper their strength. With the ham, serve a pleasant vin rosé from France or California.

MENU
[PHILIP S. BROWN]

Shrimp Biscuits

Grilled Ham Steaks

Hominy Spoon Bread

Charcoal-Roasted Onions

Cole Slaw

Broiled Pineapple Slices

The Wine

Tavel or Anjou rosé or a California Cabernet rosé,
Grenache rosé or Zinfandel rosé

SHRIMP BISCUITS

Prepare enough baking-powder biscuit dough for an ordinary 12-biscuit recipe. Roll out the dough to ¼" thick and cut in 1" to 1½" rounds. Bake until brown and pretty, then split and butter. Insert a whole small cooked shrimp or half of a larger one, along with a sliver of green onion. Makes 3 to 4 dozen.

GRILLED HAM STEAKS

Have the ham steaks cut at least 1" thick, preferably 1½" or 2". A 2" center-cut steak should serve 6. Try to get ham that is not precooked, as the flavor is much better. Slash the fat around the edge to prevent curling, brush with melted butter, and grill over a rather slow fire for 30 to 60 minutes, depending upon thickness. Pass a good mustard for those who like it with ham.

HOMINY SPOON BREAD

> 1½ cups hominy grits
> 3 cups boiling water
> 3 eggs, separated
> ¼ cup butter
> 1 cup milk
> 1½ teaspoons salt
> 3 tablespoons minced chives
> 3 tablespoons minced parsley
> 2 teaspoons minced fresh marjoram
> Sesame seeds

Cook the grits in the boiling water for 4 minutes, stirring constantly until thick and smooth. Beat the egg yolks well and add with the butter, milk, and salt. Cook another 4 minutes, still stirring; take from the fire and stir in the minced herbs. Beat the egg whites until stiff but not dry and fold them into the mixture. Grease a casserole heavily with butter, pour in mixture, and sprinkle lavishly with sesame seeds. Bake in a 375° oven for 45 minutes, or until set. Be sure to have butter on the table, for like all hot breads, this cries for it.

CHARCOAL-ROASTED ONIONS

Allow 3 or 4 medium-size white onions per person. Peel the onions and place each one, with a pat of butter and a sprinkling of salt, on a square of foil. Wrap, sealing well, and roast in the coals, burying them around the edge of the fire so that you won't impair the cooking heat, for about ½ hour or until fork-tender (test by jabbing the fork right through the foil). The onions will be moist, sweet, and utterly delectable.

COLE SLAW

> 1 small head cabbage, core removed
> 4 to 5 green onions, chopped with some green
> 2 stalks celery, chopped
> ½ green pepper, chopped

8 to 10 radishes, chopped
1 carrot, chopped
¼ cup (approximately) French dressing
¼ cup (approximately) mayonnaise

Slice the cabbage ¼″ thick or less, then cut the slices crosswise in 3 or 4 places. Put in a bowl and add the onions, celery, green pepper, radishes, and carrot. Dress with enough French dressing to coat each piece when thoroughly mixed. Cover and let stand for a couple of hours in the refrigerator. At serving time add the same amount of mayonnaise as French dressing, mix well and serve. (Amount of dressing depends upon the size of the cabbage.)

BROILED PINEAPPLE SLICES

Cut a ripe fresh pineapple lengthwise through leaves and skin into 6 wedges. Remove sections of core from the inner edges. Brush with melted butter and broil until hot and nicely browned. Serve as is (the skin will come away easily as the slices are eaten).

California Patio Dinner for Twelve

The outdoor informality of California life is expressed in this delightful summer menu that borrows lavishly from neighboring Mexico for the refreshing seviche appetizer, the sopa seca (or dry soup) which is actually a kind of casserole, and the little pies called empanaditas. With this, of course, California wines are in order, either a white throughout or one white, one red.

MENU

[HELEN EVANS BROWN]

Avocados with Seviche

Spit-Roasted Turkey with Herb Baste

Sopa Seca de Elote

Cheese and Sesame French Bread

Bacon and Egg Salad

Empanaditas

The Wines

California Pinot Chardonnay and lightly chilled Gamay

AVOCADOS WITH SEVICHE

    1 pound firm white fish filets, such as sole
    ½ cup lime or lemon juice
    1 large tomato, peeled, seeded and chopped
    ¼ cup grated onion
    1 or 2 canned peeled green chilis, seeded and chopped
       Salt, pepper
       Minced cilantro
    6 ripe avocados

Cut the raw fish into small dice, cover with the lime or lemon juice and marinate in the refrigerator for several hours to "cook" the fish. Drain. Add the tomato, onion, chopped chilis, and salt, pepper, and cilantro to taste. Halve the avocados lengthwise, remove the pits, and fill the cavities with the seviche.

SPIT-ROASTED TURKEY WITH HERB BASTE

    15- or 16-pound turkey (dressed weight)
       Salt
    ½ cup white wine

½ cup olive oil
1 teaspoon each: chopped tarragon, chives, parsley
½ teaspoon marjoram

Wipe the turkey carefully inside, then rub with salt. Do not stuff. Truss carefully. Tie the wings close to the body, taking care that the string does not cross the breast, tie ends of drumsticks together, then push as closely as possible to the body and tie securely. Put turkey on spit so that the point enters through the back, just in front of the tail, and comes out through the very end of the breast bone (you will probably need a mallet to drive the spit through the bone, but this method of spitting makes for good balance). Attach spit to motor and start turning over a medium fire.

Blend wine, oil, and herbs, and brush turkey with this baste from time to time. It will take about 3 hours to cook to a golden juicy perfection. To test for doneness, stick a fork deep into the heaviest part of the breast and second joint. If the juices run clear, it has cooked sufficiently. Also, the joints should move easily when the leg is pulled. If you use a meat thermometer, cook to 175° to 180°. Overcooked turkey is hard to carve and too dry to be really good.

SOPA SECA DE ELOTE

¼ cup butter or oil
6 cups corn kernels, cut from fresh ears
1 cup chopped onion
1 cup chopped green pepper
1 cup milk
Salt, freshly ground black pepper to taste

Heat the butter or oil in a large skillet, add the corn, onion and green pepper and cook, stirring, until slightly browned. Add milk and salt and pepper to taste. Cover and cook quickly until the corn is tender and the liquid absorbed.

CHEESE AND SESAME FRENCH BREAD

    ½ cup sesame seeds
    2 long loaves French bread
    ¼ pound butter
    ½ cup grated Parmesan cheese

Toast the sesame seeds in a heavy, hot skillet, covering the pan and shaking it over the heat until the seeds are lightly browned. Crush the seeds in a mortar.

Split the loaves lengthwise and toast over charcoal. Combine the butter, cheese, and sesame seeds and spread thinly over the toasted bread. Wrap loaves in foil and keep hot until serving time.

BACON AND EGG SALAD

    2 large or 3 medium heads romaine
    5 hard-cooked eggs
    ½ pound bacon
    4 green onions, minced
    3 tablespoons vinegar
    Freshly ground black pepper

Wash and crisp the romaine. Chop the eggs, and cook the bacon until crisp. Drain the bacon and crumble, saving the fat.

Break the lettuce into a bowl and sprinkle with the chopped eggs, minced onions, and crumbled bacon. Heat the bacon fat, add the vinegar and pepper to taste. Pour over the salad and mix thoroughly. Taste for seasoning and add salt, if necessary. Mix again immediately before serving.

EMPANADITAS

    4 ounces cream cheese
  1½ cups flour
    6 ounces butter
    Salt
    ½ cup grated well-drained pineapple
    ¾ cup cooked mashed sweet potatoes (fresh or canned)

¼ cup grated fresh coconut
1 to 2 tablespoons Jamaica rum
Sugar
1 egg, beaten with 1 tablespoon water

Combine the cream cheese, flour, butter and ½ teaspoon salt and work with the fingers until it forms a soft ball of dough. Chill. Roll out thinly and cut into 3″ circles. Combine the pineapple, sweet potatoes, coconut, mix well, then add the rum, a few grains of salt and, if necessary, a little sugar. Put a spoonful of this filling on each circle of pastry, fold in half, moisten the edges and press them together to seal well. Brush with beaten egg mixture and bake in a 375° oven for 15 minutes, or until nicely browned. This makes about 3 dozen.

A Light Luncheon for Six on a Hot Day

This unsurfeiting, delicately balanced meal is just the thing for a hot July or August day when appetites wilt and need to be tempted. You might get everyone in the mood by serving, instead of cocktails, goblets of California Sunshine, which is nothing more than half chilled orange juice, half chilled brut champagne (add an ice cube, if you feel it is needed, to maintain the chill until the drink is gone).

Have whatever white wine you choose well chilled, and keep it in a bucket of ice and water. It's a good idea to chill the wine glasses, too, as they'll help the wine keep its cool throughout the meal. Put them in the freezer for 15 minutes or so before lunch.

MENU
[PHILIP S. BROWN]

Jellied Consommé with Caviar
Broiled Chicken Breasts Sesame
Sautéed Green Beans   Buttered Rice
Broiled Peach Halves and Toasted Angel Food

The Wine

A chilled Pouilly Fuissé, Riesling, or California Fumé Blanc

JELLIED CONSOMMÉ WITH CAVIAR

> 2 12½-ounce cans jellied consommé, or 1½ pints homemade jellied consommé, chilled until very firm
> 4-ounce jar red caviar
> ½ cup sour cream
> Chopped chives (optional)

If the weather is hot, you'll probably find it easier to use canned consommé. In the bottom of each cup put a teaspoon of red caviar, spoon on about ½ cup of the jellied consommé, and top with a good dollop (about a tablespoon) of sour cream.

You can sprinkle the top with a few chopped chives as a pleasant color contrast, if you like.

BROILED CHICKEN BREASTS SESAME

> ¼ cup butter, melted
> ¼ cup soy sauce
> ¼ cup dry white wine
> 1 teaspoon tarragon
> 1 teaspoon dry mustard
> 6 chicken breasts, boned
> Sesame seeds

Mix together the butter, soy sauce, white wine, tarragon, and mustard, and marinate the chicken breasts in that for 2 to 3 hours. Broil over a medium charcoal fire for 4 to 5 minutes on each side, starting with the skin side up, and basting with the marinade two or three times. Remove from the fire, again brush with the marinade, then roll the breasts in sesame seeds until they are well coated. Return the coated chicken breasts to the fire for a minute or two to brown the seeds.

Serve them with plain buttered rice.

SAUTÉED GREEN BEANS

> 1½ pounds young green beans
> 2 tablespoons butter
> 2 tablespoons olive oil
> 1 tablespoon chopped parsley
> 1 tablespoon chopped chives

Remove the stems and strings, if any, from the beans. If the beans are very young and small, leave them whole; if larger, cut into 3 or 4 pieces. Boil them in salted water until just barely tender, then drain well. This may be done well ahead of time. Just before serving, sauté the beans in the butter and olive oil to which the chopped herbs have been added. This will take only 4 to 5 minutes.

BROILED PEACH HALVES AND TOASTED ANGEL FOOD

Allow 1 canned cling peach half for each person. Put them hollow side down on a fine-meshed grill over a medium fire and let them heat and brown a little. Turn, and in each hollow put about ½ teaspoon butter and a sprinkling of brown sugar. Cut inch-thick slices of angel food and toast them quickly over the charcoal—it will take only a minute or two on each side. Watch carefully so that the cake doesn't burn; it should just be a lovely golden brown. When the peaches are thoroughly warmed through and broiled to a pretty brown color on the bottom, serve them with the slices of toasted angel food.

Mediterranean Luncheon for Six

This is a pleasant, easy menu for Saturday luncheon during the summer, as the salad, artichokes, dessert, and beef rolls may be prepared in the morning and the salad tossed and served while the main course is cooking. Have an Italian wine with the beef—a simple Chianti in the familiar straw-covered *fiasco*, or a lightly chilled Valpolicella.

MENU

Mediterranean Salad, Anchovy Dressing
Beef Birds Spiedini
Chilled Whole Artichokes
Melone con Frutta

The Wine

Chianti or Valpolicella

MEDITERRANEAN SALAD
[LOU SEIBERT PAPPAS]

    2 cucumbers, peeled and sliced
    3 tomatoes, cored and cut in wedges
    2 green onions, sliced
      7-ounce can white albacore tuna
    4 eggs, hard-cooked
    1 small green pepper, cut in rings
      5-ounce can pitted ripe olives
      Salt and freshly ground pepper
      Anchovy Dressing (see recipe below)

Arrange cucumbers, tomatoes, and green onions on a rimmed platter with tuna in the center. Slice eggs and place around the edge. Garnish with pepper rings and olives. Cover and chill up to 4 hours. Before serving, season to taste, add dressing, and toss gently.

ANCHOVY DRESSING

    8 anchovy filets
    2 green onions
    1 teaspoon Dijon mustard
    2 tablespoons tarragon white wine vinegar
    ½ cup olive oil

Finely chop anchovy filets and the white part of the green onions. Place in a screw-top jar and add mustard, vinegar, and olive oil. Cover, shake well, and chill thoroughly.

BEEF BIRDS SPIEDINI
[LOU SEIBERT PAPPAS]

2½ pound center-cut sirloin tip roast
Salt and freshly ground pepper
½ teaspoon ground sage
9 thin slices Monterey Jack cheese or Danish Samsoe cheese (about 6 ounces)
9 thin slices prosciutto
French bread or rolls
½ cup butter
1 clove garlic, minced

Have your butcher slice beef into 9 slices, 3/16" thick, and cut each slice in half. Lay each piece between 2 sheets of wax paper and pound lightly and evenly, to make pieces 3" x 4½". Sprinkle each with salt, pepper, and a pinch of sage. Cut cheese slices in half and lay a piece on each slice of meat. Cut prosciutto slices in half and lay on top. Roll up each from the narrow end. Cut French bread into 12 strips the size of the meat rolls (about 1¼" thick and 3" long). Melt butter with garlic and roll bread in it. Alternate meat rolls and bread strips on 6 skewers, spacing them about ¼" apart, with 3 meat rolls and 2 bread strips on each skewer. Grill over medium-hot coals, turning, about 6 to 8 minutes for rare.

MELONE CON FRUTTA
[HELEN EVANS BROWN]

For each serving, cut the top from a small cantaloupe and scoop out the insides (if you are using larger melons, cut the cantaloupes in half and allow one half per serving). Dice melon flesh and combine with a few raspberries, strawberries, chunks of pineapple, seedless grapes or diced peaches—any or all of these fruits, according to taste. Pour 1 to 2 tablespoons kirsch over all and chill. Serve in the melon shells.

Shore Luncheon for Four

Fresh salmon is one of the most glorious fish of summer, and it deserves to be served often—and with great flair. The inspired combination of flavors in the main dish for this menu will make your reputation—so don't tell your guests how easy it really is to prepare. As the steaks are thick, half will be enough for a serving. With this, have a really superb white Burgundy.

MENU

Chilled Sorrel Soup
Broiled Salmon à la Russe
Tiny Boiled New Potatoes, Sprinkled with Chopped Dill
Salad of Wilted Cucumbers, French Dressing
Raspberries with Framboise

The Wine

Chassagne-Montrachet or Meursault

CHILLED SORREL SOUP
[HARRY ROGERS]

2 cups (lightly compacted) sorrel leaves, stems and midribs removed
1 medium onion, coarsely chopped
4 mushroom caps, coarsely chopped
3 cups chicken broth, fresh or canned
1 egg yolk
½ cup medium cream
2 dashes Tabasco sauce

Cook sorrel, onion, mushrooms, and chicken broth at a slow boil for 10 minutes. Remove from heat and when slightly cooled, whirl in blender at medium speed for 30 seconds. Pour into a heavy saucepan or the top of a double boiler. Beat egg yolk lightly with cream and Tabasco and slowly stir into soup mixture. Heat gently (preferably over hot water), stirring from time to time, until mixture thickens slightly. Do not allow it to boil. Chill overnight. Serve in chilled soup bowls.

BROILED SALMON À LA RUSSE
[PHILIP S. BROWN]

> 2 salmon steaks, cut 1½" thick
> Salt, pepper
> Olive oil
> 5 anchovy filets
> 4 tablespoons sweet butter
> Paprika
> 2 tablespoons black caviar
> 1 cup Hollandaise sauce (see page 420)

Season the steaks on both sides with salt and pepper and rub with oil. Broil over charcoal, allowing about 7 minutes per side. Overcooking is the main hazard, so watch them carefully. They should be removed from the heat as soon as the flesh flakes easily when tested with a fork and has lost its translucent look in the center.

While the salmon is cooking, mash the anchovies with the butter until smooth (or whirl in the blender). Add just enough paprika to give the mixture a lovely pink color. Spread this anchovy butter over the cooked steaks. Mix the caviar into the Hollandaise and serve with the salmon.

RASPBERRIES WITH FRAMBOISE

For four, allow two pint baskets of raspberries. Serve in glass dishes, with 1½ tablespoons Framboise poured over each serving.

Creole-Style Luncheon for Ten

Spicy and sweet flavors and the unctuous blandness of spoon bread make this a departure from the usual outdoor barbecued meal. It's simple and speedy, because the game hens can be roasting while the

291

spoon bread cooks in the oven, and the first course and dessert are made in advance. A pleasantly fruity rosé wine would be better here than a white or a red.

MENU
[LOU SEIBERT PAPPAS]

Shrimp with Lime and Chili Sauce
Spit-Barbecued Game Hens, Creole-Style
Salad of Sliced Tomatoes and Cucumbers, French Dressing
Southern Spoon Bread
Praline Pie or Watermelon

The Wine

A Tavel or Grignolino rosé

SHRIMP WITH LIME AND CHILI SAUCE

Allow 6 jumbo shrimp, cooked and peeled, per serving. Arrange them in a glass dish, like a shrimp cocktail, with a tiny bowl of chili sauce for dipping and lime wedges rather than the standard lemon.

SPIT-BARBECUED GAME HENS, CREOLE-STYLE

10 Rock Cornish game hens, about 1 pound, 6 ounces each
⅓ cup melted butter
    Salt, freshly ground black pepper
    Spicy Barbecue Sauce (see recipe below)

Remove the innards from the game birds and reserve for future use. Rinse birds, pat dry, and close the openings with skewers. Roll in the butter and sprinkle with salt and pepper. Run the spit diagonally through the breastbone to the backbone just above the tail and secure with prongs, spacing birds about 1 inch apart.

With spit about 6 inches above the coals, roast for 15 minutes, then baste with spicy barbecue sauce and continue cooking about 30 minutes, basting occasionally.

SPICY BARBECUE SAUCE

    1 cup catsup
   ⅓ cup water
   ¼ cup white wine vinegar
    1 tablespoon Worcestershire sauce
    4 cloves garlic, minced
    2 tablespoons brown sugar
    2 tablespoons honey
    1 teaspoon dry mustard
   ½ teaspoon chili powder

Combine all the ingredients in a saucepan and simmer, uncovered, for 10 minutes. Makes about 1¾ cups.

SOUTHERN SPOON BREAD

  2½ cups milk
   ¼ cup butter
    1 tablespoon sugar
  1½ teaspoons salt
   ¾ cup yellow corn meal
    5 eggs, separated
  1¼ cups shredded sharp Cheddar cheese
       12-ounce can whole kernel corn

Heat milk, butter, sugar, and salt in a saucepan just to boiling. Add corn meal gradually, stirring constantly, and cook until thickened, about 3 minutes. Remove from heat and stir in slightly beaten egg yolks and cheese. Beat egg whites until soft peaks form and fold in with corn. Turn into a buttered 2½-quart casserole and bake in a 375° oven for 35 minutes, or until the top springs back when touched lightly.

PRALINE PIE

    4 eggs
    ½ cup sugar
    3 tablespoons unsifted flour
    ½ teaspoon vanilla
    ⅛ teaspoon salt
    2 cups dark corn syrup
 1½ cups pecan halves
       9-inch unbaked pastry shell
    ½ pint heavy cream, whipped and sweetened

Beat eggs slightly. Mix together sugar and flour and add to the eggs with vanilla and salt. Add corn syrup and stir until blended. Reserve 12 pecan halves for topping, coarsely chop the remainder, and sprinkle over the bottom of the pastry shell. Pour the syrup mixture into shell and lay pecan halves on top. Bake in a 425° oven for 10 minutes, reduce temperature to 325° and bake 40 minutes longer, or until set. Cool. Serve with sweetened whipped cream.

Italian Supper for Eight

An informal, easy meal for a summer evening when everyone feels relaxed and hungry. As the scampi-style shrimp are eaten with the fingers, provide large paper napkins and hot fingertip towels for the final clean-up. If you possibly can, get fresh basil for the fettucine, since the flavor is so much better.

Be sure to have plenty of everything, especially the shrimp, which will disappear fast. As true scampi don't exist here, you should use jumbo shrimp, or prawns as they are called in some parts of the country—these run about 10 to the pound.

Serve a white Italian wine, and have one more bottle chilled than you think you'll need.

MENU
[PHILIP S. BROWN]

Fresh Figs or Pears and Prosciutto
Shrimp, Scampi-Style
Fettucine with Basil and Parsley
Broiled Eggplant Slices
Garlic Olives and Cherry Tomatoes
Zabaglione

The Wine

Soave or Frascati

SHRIMP, SCAMPI-STYLE

  4 pounds raw jumbo shrimp
  8 cloves garlic, crushed in 2 tablespoons salt
  2 cups olive oil
½ cup minced parsley
  2 tablespoons lemon juice

Split the shrimp shells up the back with a sharp-pointed pair of scissors and rinse out the sand vein, but leave the shells on. Prepare a marinade by blending the remaining ingredients and marinate the shrimp for 2 to 4 hours. Broil the shrimp over a medium fire for about 3 minutes on a side (turn with tongs) and serve at once. You will need a couple of bowls for the shells, and finger bowls are a good idea.

FETTUCINE WITH BASIL AND PARSLEY

  2 pounds fettucine (narrow egg noodles)
  2 cloves garlic, crushed
  2 tablespoons minced parsley
  2 tablespoons minced fresh basil
  1 cup grated Parmesan cheese
½ cup melted butter

Boil the noodles in a large pot in plenty of boiling salted water until just tender and still firm to the tooth—*al dente*. Drain and lift with a fork or spaghetti tongs to let the steam escape. Put in a large heated bowl and add the garlic, minced herbs, 1 cup or less of Parmesan, and the butter. Toss until thoroughly mixed and serve. Pass more grated Parmesan in a bowl.

BROILED EGGPLANT SLICES

     2 medium-size eggplant
     2 cloves garlic
     1 tablespoon salt
     ¼ teaspoon oregano
     ⅓ cup olive oil
     1 tablespoon red wine vinegar

Slice each unpeeled eggplant in 8 slices. Grind the garlic with the salt, add the other ingredients and mix thoroughly. Paint the eggplant slices with the mixture and broil over a medium fire until brown on both sides and tender.

GARLIC OLIVES AND CHERRY TOMATOES

     1 pint jar ripe olives
     2 cloves garlic, crushed
     Olive oil
     1 pint basket cherry tomatoes, stems removed
     ½ cup chopped parsley

Drain the juice from the olive jar, add the garlic and fill the jar with olive oil. Cover and keep in the refrigerator for a day to a week. Put the cherry tomatoes in a bowl and add the garlic olives. Pour in a little of the garlic oil and lightly toss the tomatoes and olives so that all are coated. Add the chopped parsley, toss once more, and serve instead of salad.

ZABAGLIONE

For each person, allow 2 egg yolks, 2 teaspoons sugar, and 4 table-spoons Marsala. Beat the yolks and sugar together until they are frothy and pale in color. Stir in the Marsala and put the whole mixture into the top of a double boiler over hot but not boiling water, or into a heavy pan over a very slow fire. Stir continuously, taking great care that the zabaglione does not curdle; it must not boil. As soon as it thickens, pour it into warmed glasses and serve immediately.

Mexican Supper for Eight

Most of the preparation for this Mexican meal can be done in advance, even the tortillas, if you choose to make them yourself. With the spicy food, drink a gutsy Mexican beer rather than wine.

MENU

Carnitas con Mantequilla de Pobre
Chuletas con Salsa Fria
Frijoles Refritos   *Tortillas*
Ensalada Verde
Casos de Guayaba con Queso de Crema

The Drink

Mexican beer

CARNITAS CON MANTEQUILLA DE POBRE
[PHILIP S. BROWN]

2 pounds lean pork such as boneless butt, cut into 1″ to 1½″ cubes
  Salt, pepper, monosodium glutamate
2 medium avocados, cut into tiny cubes
2 tomatoes, cut into tiny cubes
3 tablespoons red wine vinegar
1 tablespoon salad oil

Put the pork cubes in one layer in a shallow baking pan and sprinkle with salt, pepper and monosodium glutamate. Let stand for an hour or so, then bake in a 300° oven for about 1½ hours, stirring and draining off the fat a few times.

Meanwhile, prepare the mantequilla de pobre: Combine the avocados, tomatoes, vinegar, salad oil, salt and pepper to taste. Toss gently until well mixed and let stand at least half an hour at room temperature before serving.

String the baked pork cubes on bamboo skewers that have been well soaked in water, about 3 to 4 to a skewer, and cook them over charcoal until brown and crispy. Remove from the skewers, impale each on a toothpick, and dip into the mantequilla de pobre.

NOTE: If desired, tostadas (crisp fried pieces of tortilla) may be used as scoops for the mantequilla and eaten along with the carnitas.

CHULETAS CON SALSA FRIA
[PHILIP S. BROWN]

1 pound lean ground round steak
1 cup finely chopped parsley
1 cup finely chopped onion
3 tablespoons grated Parmesan cheese
1 egg
¼ teaspoon monosodium glutamate
  Salt, pepper to taste
1½ cups fine dry bread crumbs

Mix all ingredients except the bread crumbs very well and shape the mixture into 12 to 16 balls. Now put the crumbs on a good-size board, lay the balls on top, and pat the balls into quite thin patties about 4″ in diameter, turning so that they are well covered on each side. Chill well, then cook on a well-greased fine-meshed grill for not over 3 minutes on a side. Serve them with Salsa Fria (see below).

SALSA FRIA

    1-pound, 4-ounce can solid-pack tomatoes, chopped fine
1 cup chopped sweet onion
    4-ounce can peeled green chilis, chopped
1 teaspoon chopped cilantro
1 teaspoon chopped oregano
2 tablespoons wine vinegar
2 tablespoons olive oil
    Salt, pepper to taste

Combine all ingredients well and serve very cold.

FRIJOLES REFRITOS
[ELISABETH ORTIZ]

    2 cups pinto, black, or red kidney beans
2 onions, finely chopped
2 cloves garlic, chopped
    Sprig epazote or 1 bay leaf
2 or more serrano chiles, chopped, or 1 teaspoon dried pequin chiles, crumbled
    Lard
    Salt, pepper to taste
1 tomato, peeled, seeded, and chopped

Wash beans, but do not soak. Put in cold water to cover with half of the chopped onion and garlic, the epazote or bay leaf, and chiles. Cover and simmer gently, adding more water, always hot, as needed. When beans begin to wrinkle, add 1 tablespoon lard. When beans are soft, almost done, add seasonings. Cook another half hour without adding more water; there should not be a great deal of liquid when beans are done. Heat 2 tablespoons lard and sauté the remaining chopped onion and garlic until limp. Add tomato and cook for 1 to 2 minutes, then add a tablespoon of beans and mash into the mixture, add a second tablespoon of beans without draining them so that some of the bean liquid evaporates in this cooking process. Add a third tablespoon of beans and continue to cook until you have a smooth, fairly heavy paste. Keep adding beans until all have been mashed into lard over low heat. Add lard from time to time and cook until beans are creamy and have become a heavy, quite dry paste. You may cheat a little by using the blender to purée beans, adding them to the skillet bit by bit, and frying them in the hot lard.

TORTILLAS
[ELISABETH ORTIZ]

> 2 cups Quaker Masa Harina
> 1⅓ cups warm water
> 1 teaspoon salt

Mix the ingredients to form a soft dough. Divide into balls the size of a small egg and flatten on a tortilla press between two sheets of plastic or waxed paper to a thin pancake about 4″ across. If the tortilla sticks, the dough is too moist. Scrape it off, add a little more masa harina to the dough and begin again. It does not hurt the dough to handle it.

Place ungreased comal or griddle over medium heat and cook tortillas one at a time, about 2 minutes on each side, or until the edges begin to lift and they are very slightly browned. Makes 1 dozen small tortillas.

NOTE: Tortillas can be kept warm for several hours. Preheat oven to 150°. Have ready a cloth napkin or kitchen towel wrung out in hot water. As you make the tortillas, wrap them first in paper towels and then in the napkin and put in the oven. When there are a dozen stacked up, dampen the napkin again, wrap the lot in aluminum foil, and keep in the oven until needed. Cold tortillas can be reheated over direct heat, turning them constantly. If they have become dry, pat them with damp hands.

Large tortillas, about 6″ across, are mostly eaten as bread with meat dishes, as are the small 4″ tortillas, which are also used for made-up dishes. Use a ball of masa about the size of a large egg for the 6″ tortillas.

CASOS DE GUAYABA CON QUESO DE CREMA (GUAVA SHELLS
WITH CREAM CHEESE)
[PHILIP S. BROWN]

Guava shells packed in heavy syrup in cans are available at fancy food
markets.

2 10½-ounce cans guava shells
   3-ounce package cream cheese
2 tablespoons light cream
   Toasted slivered almonds

Allow 2 shells for each person (there are 7 or 8 in each tin). Drain
them, saving the syrup, and arrange on dessert plates. Soften the cream
cheese by mixing well with the cream and fill each guava shell with
it. Sprinkle with toasted slivered almonds and drizzle some of the reserved syrup over and around them. Serve with plain rich crackers like
butter thins.

Midsummer Brunch for Six

A late breakfast or brunch is a nice informal way to entertain on a
summer Sunday, with the guests assembling around noon for libations,
and the food served at 1 o'clock. While they sip their favorite midday
drinks, you can make and serve the appetizers from the grill and bury
the potatoes in the coals to roast. Put the mushrooms on the grill before
you start the flank steak, which takes a very short time to cook. A lightly
chilled red wine is delicious with the steak on a hot day.

MENU

[PHILIP S. BROWN]

Chicken Livers and Bacon en Brochette

London Broil

Mushrooms in Foil   Roast Potatoes

Toasted Bread

Preserves

Breakfast Cheese or Brie

The Wine

Lightly chilled Beaujolais or California Gamay

CHICKEN LIVERS AND BACON EN BROCHETTE

For appetizers from the charcoal grill these are hard to beat. They may be prepared for cooking ahead of time and kept covered in the refrigerator. For each guest allow 3 chicken livers and 3 slices of bacon. Cut the livers in half and wrap each one in a half slice of bacon, then string on thin bamboo skewers that have been well soaked in water. (Or use thin metal skewers or knitting needles; you will need gloves to handle the latter.) Broil over charcoal until the bacon is crisp—it won't take too long, about 5 to 8 minutes should do it—and serve on the skewer.

London Broil

London broil is simply beef flank steak, grilled to perfection. Unless it's very large, a flank steak will serve 3 comfortably as a main course, so provide 2 Prime-grade or Choice-grade steaks for 6 people. Have the butcher remove the thin membrane that covers this piece of meat, but don't have it scored or put through the "tenderizer." Have a good brisk fire ready, brush the steaks with olive oil or French dressing, and cook for 3 minutes on a side, or a minute longer if you don't like really rare meat. (No longer, though, or it will be tough and stringy.) The steaks will contract and puff up during the cooking. Lay them on a carving board and, using a very sharp, thin-bladed knife, slice in long thin diagonal slices across the grain—the knife blade should be at an angle of 30 degrees or less to the meat. You will have lots of juice in the well of the carving board, so be sure to spoon some over each serving.

MUSHROOMS IN FOIL

> 1 pound fresh mushrooms
> 6 tablespoons butter
> Salt, pepper

Clean the mushrooms by brushing lightly under cold running water, then trimming off the tough ends of the stems. If they are big ones, cut them in 2 to 4 pieces; if small, leave whole. Cut heavy-duty foil into 6 pieces, each measuring 6" by 12". Fold the foil rectangles in half, making 6" squares. Divide the mushrooms among the squares, put 1 tablespoon of butter on each, sprinkle with salt and pepper and fold into neat packages, sealing the edges with a triple fold. Lay the packets around the edge of the coals for 10 minutes, then turn and cook another 10 minutes. Serve them in the foil, but have scissors handy for easy opening.

ROAST POTATOES

Here's an easy way to roast potatoes—a trifle messier than roasting them in foil, perhaps, but they will be just about the best potatoes you ever tasted. Select nice big Idaho russets, 1 per person, and simply bury them in the ashes as is. Let them cook until tender to the fork, about 45 to 60 minutes. The skins will be black and charred, but the insides will be fluffy and white and altogether wonderful. Have plenty of butter and salt and pepper, or sour cream and chopped chives.

TOASTED BREAD

If you're a once-a-week baker, you'll have homemade bread on hand. If not, buy the best loaf you can find. Either French bread or a good sourdough is fine toasted over the coals. Slice either one fairly thick and either lay it on the grill or impale it on a long fork and toast until nice and brown. Butter lavishly and serve with preserves—strawberry, raspberry, cherry, or what have you.

Breakfast Cheese is made by the Rouge et Noir company in Petaluma, California. If you can't get it, a fine Brie is a good substitute. Accompany it with more of the toasted bread.

Kebab Party by the Pool for Twenty-Four

A labor-saving idea for a big outdoor party, either luncheon or dinner, is to make up and marinate all kinds of kebab combinations and arrange them on a buffet table to be skewered by the guests and cooked to order. For this you'll need a couple of charcoal grills and hibachis, and plenty of skewers, so it might be smart to make this a cooperative party with your summer neighbors.

For small appetizer-type kebabs that don't take long to cook, such as anticuchos and chicken liver and heart kebabs, the thin bamboo skewers from Japan that come in packages are quite adequate and can be discarded after use. Be sure, though, to soak these wood skewers in water for a couple of hours to make them fireproof.

All you need with your kebabs would be a couple of casseroles of pilaf and individual loaves of the flat Middle East bread called pita that is hollow inside, so you can slide the contents of a skewer into the interior and eat the kebab sandwich-style. Instead of salads, which tend to wilt as they stand, have big platters of crudités (raw vegetables) with one or two flavored mayonnaises. Carafes of inexpensive California wine are best with this informal party food.

MENU

Anticuchos *Pork Sasaties* *Teriyaki Steak Kebabs*
Chicken Liver and Heart Kebabs *Scallop and Bacon Kebabs*
Duck Kebabs *Chicken en Brochette* *Wurst Kebabs*
Pilaf (see page 427)
Pita
Crudités with Flavored Mayonnaises
Curried Watermelon *Fresh Fruit* *Lime Sherbet*

The Wine

Carafes of Zinfandel and California chablis

ANTICUCHOS
[PHILIP S. BROWN]

This Peruvian specialty deserves to be better known than it is, especially if you like highly seasoned foods. A whole cleaned beef heart weighs about 3 pounds, but many markets cut them into smaller pieces before offering them for sale. Although beef steak is sometimes used for this recipe, there is no real substitute for the unique texture and flavor of the beef heart. The secret of perfectly broiled heart is to cook it very quickly, lest it become tough.

2 pounds beef heart
1 cup red wine vinegar (or more, to cover meat)
1 bay leaf, crushed
3 chili pequins, crushed
6 whole peppercorns, crushed
1 clove garlic, pressed
  Salt to taste
  Olive oil
1 tablespoon Tabasco sauce

Trim the heart of skin and fat, and cut into neat bite-size squares. Put in a bowl and add vinegar, bay leaf, chilis, peppercorns, garlic, and salt. Marinate for 24 hours in the refrigerator. At cooking time, drain the

305

meat and dry it well, string on water-soaked bamboo skewers (3 or 4 pieces to a skewer), brush with olive oil, and broil quickly over a hot fire, turning once. Add Tabasco to the marinade, heat, and serve as a dipping sauce, or simply use Tabasco or other hot sauce (if you like a really fiery dip). Serve on the skewers as appetizers.

PORK SASATIES
[PHILIP S. BROWN]

> 2 cups apricot purée (1 cup dried apricots stewed until soft and sieved, with enough water added to make 2 cups)
> ¼ cup white wine vinegar
> 2 cups chopped onion, sautéed until soft in 4 tablespoons butter
> 2 tablespoons curry powder
> 2 to 3 dashes Tabasco sauce
> Salt to taste
> 2 pounds cubed pork

Mix first 6 ingredients together well, add pork, and marinate overnight. String meat on skewers and broil; use marinade as a baste and serve as a sauce for the cooked meat.

TERIYAKI STEAK KEBABS
[PHILIP S. BROWN]

> ½ cup soy sauce
> ¼ cup dry sherry or sake
> 1 clove garlic, pressed
> 1 teaspoon powdered ginger
> 1 teaspoon sugar, or less
> 2 pounds sirloin steak, cut in strips 6″ long and ½″ thick

Combine first 5 ingredients in a bowl. Add beef strips and marinate 1 hour. Weave strips onto small bamboo skewers that have been soaked well in cold water. Grill over a hot charcoal fire for not more than 30 seconds a side—preferably less. The meat will be rare, juicy, and delicious.

CHICKEN LIVER AND HEART KEBABS
[PHILIP S. BROWN]

Buy equal quantities of chicken livers and chicken hearts. Halve the livers and wrap each piece in a half slice of thinly sliced bacon. Alternate livers on skewers with the chicken hearts and chunks of fresh or canned pineapple. Mix equal parts of soy sauce and sweet sherry and use to baste the kebabs during cooking. Broil only until bacon is crisp—the hearts will be tender and juicy; if overcooked, they become tough and hard to chew.

SCALLOP AND BACON KEBABS
[PHILIP S. BROWN]

Partially cook a slice of bacon, then weave it onto a skewer, with a scallop in between each fold of bacon (one side of each scallop is covered with bacon). Use 3 or 4 scallops to a slice of bacon. Brush with melted butter and broil, turning several times, until the bacon has finished cooking—about 5 or 6 minutes.

CHICKEN EN BROCHETTE
[PHILIP S. BROWN]

¾ cup white Burgundy wine
¼ cup olive oil
1 tablespoon dried tarragon
1 teaspoon salt
Freshly ground white pepper to taste
3 whole chicken breasts, boned and cubed
Mushroom caps, pitted ripe olives (optional)

Mix first 5 ingredients well and let stand for an hour to soften the tarragon. Add the cubed chicken and marinate for 1 to 2 hours. Skewer and grill over charcoal, brushing frequently with the marinade and turning 2 or 3 times. Mushroom caps and olives may be inserted between the cubes of chicken if desired.

DUCK KEBABS
[PHILIP S. BROWN]

> 2 ducks
> 1 cup orange juice
> ¼ cup olive oil
> 1 clove garlic, pressed or chopped
> Stuffed green olives
> Orange sections
> Salt, freshly ground pepper to taste

Remove breast and thigh meat from the ducks, leaving the skin and fat beneath it attached to the meat. Cut into pieces about 1" by 2½". Mix together the orange juice, oil, garlic, add the duck meat, and marinate for 2 hours, turning from time to time. String on skewers, alternating a piece of meat with an olive or an orange section (these may be peeled or unpeeled; if unpeeled, the rind gives an interesting flavor to the meat). Sprinkle with salt and pepper and broil, skin side toward the fire, until skin is crisp and brown. Brush with marinade, turn, and cook other side until done. Allow about 10 minutes on skin side, 5 minutes on meat side.

WURST KEBABS
[PHILIP S. BROWN]

Buy a selection of large sausages that are not too salty, such as bratwurst, knockwurst, and weisswurst. Cut them into 1" to 1½" cubes, string them on skewers, and broil until heated through and just crisp on the surface. Do not overcook.

CRUDITÉS WITH FLAVORED MAYONNAISES
[JAMES A. BEARD]

Assemble a variety of very fresh vegetables that taste good raw, such as baby carrots and turnips, scallions, radishes, rings of green pepper, thinly sliced small zucchini, cucumber strips, and various kinds of tomatoes. You might also have bowls of very young tender peas in pods and freshly gathered fava or broad beans (to be dipped in coarse salt).

As a dip for the vegetables, serve mustard mayonnaise, anchovy-garlic mayonnaise, and coarse salt and pepper. For 24 people you will need a quart of homemade mayonnaise. Add 3 tablespoons or so of Dijon mustard to 1 pint; 3 cloves crushed garlic and about 18 chopped anchovies to the other pint. If you have a blender, blend the anchovies and garlic with a small amount of oil, then stir this paste into the mayonnaise.

CURRIED WATERMELON
[ELISABETH ORTIZ]

> 3 small watermelons
> 3 tablespoons curry powder
> Juice of 6 limes
> 3 cups light cream
> Sugar to taste

Cut out the top of each watermelon so it looks like a basket with a handle. Remove seeds and cut the meat into balls or 1″ squares. Mix the curry powder with the lime juice and strain into the cream, then sweeten to taste with sugar. Pour over watermelon balls or squares and chill. Serve as quickly as possible, or watermelon tends to get mushy.

Middle East Supper for Twelve

This is an interesting menu to serve at the end of the season, when everyone has become bored with the same old summer food.

During the cocktail hour, the guests can nibble on the little hot pastries, the taramasalata and Greek olives (if you can find the cracked green variety, marinate them for a few days in olive oil with a couple of cloves of garlic and some crushed coriander seed).

With the lamb you might serve a lightly cooled Beaujolais or a rosé. Strong, sweet Turkish coffee and raki or ouzo, spirits with a strong anise flavor, would make a good digestif at the end of the supper.

MENU

Cheese Boerek   *Taramasalata with Pita*   *Greek Olives*

Charcoal Broiled Lamb Chops

Pilaf with Pine Nuts

Salad of Cucumbers in Yoghurt

Basket of Fresh Apricots or Nectarines and Grapes

Saragli

The Wine

Lightly cooled Beaujolais or chilled rosé

CHEESE BOEREK
[LOU SEIBERT PAPPAS]

   1 pint small-curd cottage cheese
½ pound Monterey Jack or mozzarella cheese, shredded
¼ pound feta cheese, crumbled
   2 eggs
   1 tablespoon chopped parsley
12 sheets filo or strudel dough, 12″ x 18″
½ cup butter, melted

Beat cheeses and eggs together until blended. Add parsley and mix well. Lay out filo on a board and cut sheets in half to make pieces 9″ x 12″. One at a time, brush a piece of filo with melted butter and spoon a ribbon of cheese across a narrow end, leaving 1″ borders. Fold over sides 1″ and roll up; place seam side down on ungreased baking sheets. Bake in a 375° oven 20 to 25 minutes, or until golden brown and puffed. Serve hot on small plates. These may be made in advance, cooled, and refrigerated or frozen. Before serving reheat at 375° until hot, about 15 minutes. Makes 24.

TARAMASALATA
[LOU SEIBERT PAPPAS]

2 egg yolks
1 teaspoon grated onion
2 tablespoons lemon juice
1 tablespoon wine vinegar
¼ cup olive oil
¾ cup vegetable oil
⅓ cup (about 3 ounces) tarama (carp roe)

Put egg yolks, onion, lemon juice, and vinegar in blender container and blend a few seconds. With cover off and motor running, gradually pour in olive oil and vegetable oil in a slow stream. When thick, add tarama and blend just until well mixed. Mound in a small bowl and chill. Serve spread on small pieces of pita (Middle East bread). Makes 1½ cups.

CHARCOAL BROILED LAMB CHOPS
[LOU SEIBERT PAPPAS]

3 tablespoons lemon juice
⅓ cup vegetable oil
⅔ cup dry vermouth or dry white wine
4 cloves garlic, minced
1 tablespoon fresh rosemary or 1 teaspoon dried rosemary
1 teaspoon salt
Freshly ground pepper
12 saddle lamb chops with kidneys, or 24 small loin lamb chops
3 lemons, cut in wedges
Fresh rosemary sprigs

Mix together lemon juice, oil, vermouth, garlic, rosemary, salt, and pepper. Place chops in a large shallow pan, pour over marinade, and turn chops to coat well. Marinate 4 hours, turning occasionally. Barbecue over hot coals, turning meat once, and basting with remaining marinade. Allow about 15 minutes for rare chops. Garnish with lemon, rosemary sprigs.

PILAF WITH PINE NUTS
[LOU SEIBERT PAPPAS]

    10 tablespoons butter
     2 cups long-grain white rice
     4 cups boiling water
     2 teaspoons salt
    ⅓ cup currants
    ½ cup pine nuts or slivered blanched almonds
     2 tablespoons chopped parsley
     1 tablespoon finely slivered orange zest

Melt 2 tablespoons butter in a large saucepan, add rice, and stir until coated with butter. Pour in boiling water, add salt, cover, and simmer 25 minutes. Add currants, fluff with a fork, and remove from heat. Melt remaining butter, add pine nuts, and heat until nuts are lightly toasted and butter starts to brown; pour over rice and mix gently. Transfer to a serving dish, sprinkle with parsley and orange zest.

CUCUMBERS IN YOGHURT
[JAMES A. BEARD]

     6 cucumbers
     2 teaspoons salt
     2 cloves garlic, finely minced
     3 tablespoons lemon juice
     3 cups yoghurt
    1½ tablespoons finely chopped dill
     2 teaspoons chopped fresh mint

Peel the cucumbers, quarter lengthwise, remove the seeds and slice thinly. Sprinkle with the salt and let stand for 15 minutes to drain. Squeeze out excess juices and pat dry on paper towels. Mix the garlic, lemon juice, yoghurt, and dill, and mix with the cucumbers. Serve sprinkled with chopped fresh mint.

SARAGLI (BAKLAVA PINWHEELS)
[LOU SEIBERT PAPPAS]

- ¾ pound blanched almonds, very finely chopped or ground
- ¾ pound walnuts, finely chopped or ground
- Sugar
- Grated peel of 1 lemon
- 2 teaspoons cinnamon
- 1 pound prepared filo dough
- 1½ cups sweet butter, melted
- Whole cloves
- 1½ cups honey
- ½ cup finely chopped pistachios

Mix together the ground nuts, ⅔ cup sugar, grated lemon peel, and cinnamon. Work with ¼ of the filo sheets and nut mixture at a time. Lay out 1 sheet of filo, brush with butter, cut in half crosswise, and place 1 sheet on top of the other. Sprinkle lightly with nuts. Then alternate single sheets of filo with the nut mixture and continue in this manner until you have used ¼ of the filo and nuts. Starting at the shorter side, roll up the pastry layers tightly, strudel fashion. Slice roll into ¾"-thick pieces with a sharp knife and lay flat on a buttered baking sheet. Skewer the ends of each pastry roll with a clove to keep each one tightly closed. Brush surfaces with remaining butter.

Repeat with remaining ¾ of the filo sheets and nut mixture, working with ¼ at a time. Bake in a preheated 350° oven for 30 minutes, or until golden brown. Meanwhile, bring ½ cup sugar and ½ cup water to a boil. Stir in the honey and let simmer a few minutes. Cool. Pour cool syrup over the hot pastries. When ready to serve, spoon a mound of pistachios in the center of each pastry. Makes about 4 dozen.

Beach Picnic for Six

A picnic at the beach is just about the simplest and pleasantest way to entertain weekend guests, who will be longing for a day of bathing and sunbathing and are sure to work up hearty appetites. This menu can be pretty well prepared ahead and transported in portable ice chests and insulated bags, which will keep the greens, dressing, fruits, and sour cream cool until the last minute.

For this shore feast, you will need a small folding charcoal grill to broil the shrimp and reheat the cioppino (take it along in big screw-topped jars, then transfer it to a casserole). This American form of bouillabaisse originated among the Portuguese and Italian fishermen of the California coast, and as it is made with red wine, it breaks the usual rule about drinking white wine with fish. It should be served in deep soup plates or bowls, eaten with forks and spoons, and partnered with plenty of good crisp bread.

MENU

[JAMES A. BEARD]

Shrimp in Beer

Tiny Rolls or Pita

Scallions and Cherry Tomatoes

Cioppino

French or Italian Bread

Tossed Green Salad

Strawberries and Blueberries with Maple Syrup and Sour Cream

The Wine

California Pinot Noir

SHRIMP IN BEER

2 pounds unshelled shrimp
1 large onion, thinly sliced
2 cloves garlic, crushed
1½ teaspoons salt
1 teaspoon Tabasco sauce
1 green pepper, finely chopped
2 to 3 cups beer
Skewers

Split the shrimp down the back with a scissors or with the special gadget designed for that purpose, removing the black vein, but leaving the shells. Place in a pan or bowl with the onion, garlic, salt, Tabasco, and green pepper. Cover with beer and marinate for 6 to 8 hours. Spear shrimp on skewers and broil over charcoal fire. Serve as an appetizer with cocktails, accompanied by tiny rolls or pita, dishes of scallions, and cherry tomatoes.

CIOPPINO

1 quart clams or mussels
1 cup wine, red or white
2 Dungeness crab (in the West) or 1 pound crabmeat (in the East)
½ cup olive oil
1 large onion, chopped
2 cloves garlic, chopped
1 green pepper, chopped
¼ pound dried mushrooms, soaked in water and drained
4 tomatoes, peeled and chopped
4 tablespoons Italian tomato paste
2 cups red wine, preferably Pinot Noir
Salt, pepper
1 teaspoon dried basil or 2 tablespoons fresh basil, finely chopped
1 sea bass or striped bass, about 3 pounds, cut into serving pieces, or thick filets of fish cut into serving pieces
1 pound raw shrimp, shelled
3 tablespoons chopped parsley

Steam the clams or mussels with 1 cup red or white wine until they open. Discard any that do not open. Remove from shells. Strain the broth through a fine cloth and reserve. If you are using Dungeness crab, break in pieces, and cut the back into sections. Heat the olive oil in a large pot and cook the onion, garlic, pepper, and mushrooms for 3 minutes. Add the tomatoes, and cook for another 4 minutes. Add the strained broth from the clams or mussels, the tomato paste, and the red wine. Season to taste, and simmer for about 20 minutes. Correct the seasoning and add first the basil, next the fish, and cook through. Finally, add the clams or mussels, the crab or crabmeat and the shrimp, and heat until the shrimp are cooked through. Sprinkle with parsley and serve.

Sailing Picnic for Twelve

Good cold food that can be eaten with the hands, and plenty of it, is the best formula for a picnic on a sailboat, where no one has time to fuss around preparing a meal. While basically sandwiches, these easy-to-manage individual loaves are infinitely more interesting. To keep them fresh and unspoiled until everyone is ready to eat, wrap them in foil and take along in an insulated bag. The vegetables can go in plastic containers, the fruit in plastic bags. As sea air makes people as thirsty as they are hungry, fill a couple of ice chests with chilled beer and white wine.

MENU
[LOU SEIBERT PAPPAS]

Individual Filled Brioches   *Swedish Lobster Buns*

Dutch Broodjes   *Roman Grinders*

Marinated Vegetables   *Cherry Tomatoes*

Cucumber and Celery Sticks

Fresh Peaches   *Seedless Green Grapes*

The Drinks

Cold beer, chilled gallon jugs of California chablis

INDIVIDUAL FILLED BRIOCHES

Buy small brioches at the bakery or buy the frozen kind and thaw them. Remove the topknot from each brioche and hollow out the inside with a sharp knife, leaving a shell ½" thick, then butter the inside lightly. Fill with any of the following fillings (each is sufficient to fill 6 brioches).

PÂTÉ FILLING

Cream ¼ pound liverwurst and a 3-ounce package cream cheese until smooth. Mix in 2 tablespoons sour cream and 2 tablespoons dry vermouth. Put filling in brioches and sprinkle with 2 tablespoons chopped salted almonds. Replace tops on brioches and chill.

CREAM CHEESE-SMOKED SALMON FILLING

Mix a 3-ounce package cream cheese with 3 tablespoons sour cream, 1 tablespoon chopped chives, and 2 teaspoons lemon juice. Spread mixture inside brioches and top with sliced smoked salmon (about ½ ounce for each brioche).

CHICKEN-CHUTNEY FILLING

Coarsely chop a 5-ounce can of boned chicken and mix with 1 tablespoon each of mayonnaise and sour cream, 1 tablespoon chutney syrup, and 3 slices crisply cooked and crumbled bacon. Spoon mixture into brioches and replace tops.

SWEDISH LOBSTER BUNS

    ½ cup Hollandaise sauce (see page 420)
    ¼ cup sour cream
    ⅛ teaspoon dried dill weed
    1 teaspoon lemon juice
    3 cups cooked lobster meat or two 7½-ounce cans Alaska king crabmeat
    ⅓ cup thinly sliced celery
    12 small round dinner buns, about 2½" in diameter
    Butter
    Boston or Bibb lettuce

Mix together the Hollandaise sauce, sour cream, dill weed, and lemon juice. Flake lobster or crabmeat and mix with dressing and celery. Split buns in half and butter generously. Fill with lobster mixture and a leaf of lettuce. Chill. Makes 12 small sandwich buns.

DUTCH BROODJES

> 3″ soft round rolls (preferably covered with sesame seeds)
> Softened butter
> Boston lettuce
> Assorted sliced cold meats and cheeses: boiled ham, liverwurst, mortadella; Thuringer, Edam, Gouda, Swiss, Kuminost
> Mayonnaise
> Dijon-style mustard

Cut rolls in half and spread with butter. Place 1 or 2 lettuce leaves on the bottom and top with at least 3 different kinds of meats and cheeses, folded over or cut to fit rolls. Spread with mayonnaise and mustard and cover with tops of the rolls. Wrap individually to carry.

ROMAN GRINDERS

Use soft sesame-seed "poor boy" buns for individual servings or long thin French bread loaves for several servings. Slice horizontally, butter bread and top the bottom half of the loaf with one of the fillings below. Cover with the top half of the bread. Wrap grinders individually for easy carrying. Cut into serving-size pieces at picnic.

1. Brush loaf with olive oil and cover with layers of anchovies, sliced tomatoes, white albacore tuna fish, capers, chopped green onions, and ripe olives.

2. Cover loaf with layers of salami, sliced tomatoes, mortadella, provolone, green pepper rings, and whole sweet red peppers.

3. Cover loaf with sliced prosciutto, sliced Gruyère, marinated mushrooms, and sliced hard-cooked eggs.

MARINATED VEGETABLES

Pack fresh sliced mushrooms, drained canned chick peas, cooked Italian green beans, and drained canned artichoke hearts in glass jars. Pour in garlic-flavored French dressing, cover, and chill.

Tail-Gate Picnic for Twelve

This could be a picnic at the beach or in the country, according to the season and your inclination. You'll need a small charcoal grill to cook the steak and sausages and warm the empanadas through in their foil packages, and ice chests and insulated bags to carry everything along. It's a good idea, with this kind of finger food, to supply small terry towels for cleanup, as well as plenty of paper napkins. Beer and inexpensive red and white jug wines are best with this simple, hearty food.

MENU

Grilled Flank Steak Sandwiches

Puerto Vallarta Empanadas   *Raclette Sausage Rolls*

Finger Salad of Raw Vegetables, Watercress

Chocolate Date Squares   *Pears and Bel Paese Cheese*

The Drinks

A *selection of imported bottled beers—*
German, Danish, Dutch, Mexican;
Jugs of California Mountain Red burgundy and chablis

GRILLED FLANK STEAK SANDWICHES
[JAMES A. BEARD]

1 flank steak
1 cup dry red wine
1 clove garlic, chopped
1 onion, sliced
1 handful chopped parsley
Salt, freshly ground black pepper
2 medium-size loaves of French bread
Butter
1 clove garlic, crushed
Thyme

Remove the tough outer membrane from the meat. Put the wine, chopped garlic, onion and parsley in a shallow bowl and let the meat marinate in this mixture for 2 or 3 hours. Keep it refrigerated and turn several times to be sure the steak is evenly bathed. Transfer the meat and the marinade to a large covered plastic container, pack in an insulated bag and take to the picnic site. Leave it in the marinade until the last minute.

Grill it quickly over charcoal, allowing only about 5 minutes to each side. It should be crusty brown on the outside and red rare in the center. Brush with the marinade as it cooks and season to taste with salt and pepper.

Split the loaves of bread the long way and spread the halves with butter mixed with crushed garlic and a little thyme. Press the loaves together again and roll in foil. Heat these on the grill as the steak is cooking.

With a very sharp knife, slice through the steak diagonally from top to bottom, cutting it into thin strips. Remove the bread from the foil, and take off the top half of each loaf. Arrange the steak slices on the bottom halves of the loaves and replace the tops. Cut the loaves into thick slices to make tasty hot and hearty steak sandwiches.

PUERTO VALLARTA EMPANADAS
[LOU SEIBERT PAPPAS]

½ pound ground beef round
½ pound ground pork
1 medium onion, finely chopped
2 tablespoons salad oil
1 teaspoon salt
1 clove garlic, minced
¼ teaspoon cinnamon
⅛ teaspoon pepper
⅛ teaspoon ground cloves
½ cup beef stock
4 tablespoons tomato paste
2 tablespoons red wine vinegar
1 teaspoon sugar

3 tablespoons each currants, sliced pimiento-stuffed olives, and chopped smoked or salted almonds
Pie pastry based on 2 cups flour or 1 large package pastry mix
1 egg beaten with 2 tablespoons milk

Brown the beef, pork, and onion in oil, stirring with a fork to make it crumbly. Add salt, garlic, cinnamon, pepper, ground cloves, stock, tomato paste, vinegar, sugar, and currants. Cover and simmer 20 minutes, cooking sauce down until liquid almost disappears. Mix in olives and almonds.

On a lightly floured board, roll out pastry very thin and cut into 6″ rounds. Place ¼ cup filling on half of each round, fold over pastry, and pinch edges together. Score edges with a fork. Brush pastries with beaten egg mixture. Bake in a 425° oven for 20 to 25 minutes, or until nicely browned. This makes 12 pastries. Remove, cool slightly, and then wrap individually in foil. Pack in an insulated bag and take to the picnic site. Reheat slightly in the foil on the grill before serving.

RACLETTE SAUSAGE ROLLS
[LOU SEIBERT PAPPAS]

1½ to 2 pounds sausages, such as garlic sausage, German veal frankfurters, old-fashioned dinner franks, wieners, or smoky links, which require little additional cooking
1 pound Muenster or Monterey Jack cheese
12 soft French rolls
Butter
1-pound jar sweet-sour red cabbage

Arrange sausages on skewers and cook over medium coals until lightly browned and sizzling. Meanwhile, place cheese on a foil or metal pan and heat at the edge of the grill until melted and slightly crusty. Split and butter rolls and warm on the grill. To serve, place 1 or 2 sausages in each roll, spread with cheese, and garnish with a spoonful of red cabbage. Serve with mustard.

CHOCOLATE DATE SQUARES
[ELAINE ROSS]

        ½ cup boiling water
        ½ cup (packed) pitted, sliced dates
        6 tablespoons butter
        ½ cup sugar
        1 egg
        ¾ cup plus 2 tablespoons flour
        ½ teaspoon (scant) baking powder
        ½ teaspoon (scant) baking soda
        ½ teaspoon vanilla
          Fine bread crumbs
        ½ cup walnuts, chopped
        ½ cup chocolate morsels

Pour the boiling water over the dates and let stand for 1 hour. Cream the butter and sugar, beat in the egg and the date mixture. Sift the flour with the baking powder and baking soda and add to the batter with the vanilla.

Grease an 8″ square pan and dust it with fine bread crumbs. Spread the batter in the pan and scatter the nuts and chocolate morsels over the surface. Bake in a preheated 350° oven for 55 minutes, or until the cake shrinks from the sides of the pan and the top springs back when pressed gently. Cool the cake in the pan and cut into 12 squares.

NOTE: The squares may be made a day ahead and stored in an airtight tin, or made even farther ahead and frozen.

Parties for Holidays and Other Occasions

Probably more parties are given between Thanksgiving and Christmas than at any other time of year, for at no other season are people so geared for gaiety and conviviality.

While the prospect of a long fling of festivities is always pleasant, there's no guarantee that a holiday party will be a success just because of the seasonal spirit. Any party is only as good as the idea behind it, the food and drink that is served, and the thoughtfulness that spells true hospitality. A measure of originality and the unexpected in a party menu can do more to keep things humming than a table laden with food or a bar that never runs dry.

Customs *do* stale and you should never hesitate to discard them when you feel they have become tired and outworn. A succulent capon, a glossy-skinned goose, or a brace of pheasant, even a standing rib roast, can be a most welcome relief from the universal Thanksgiving and Christmas turkey. Or if you do feel honor-bound to produce the traditional bird, you can always poach it and serve it with rice and totally different vegetables, or give it an unusual and exotic sauce.

Nor does holiday food have to be heavy and elaborate. Champagne is better than eggnog any day, and a really superb soup or omelettes with a choice of fillings, made to order, can taste like manna to guests surfeited with rich food and drink.

True hospitality means having the courage to break the pattern when you feel it has become a bit of a bore. James Beard, a man noted for his original and iconoclastic hostmanship, has outlawed the tedious late-late party on New Year's Eve. Instead he gives his early, from six to eight-thirty, and his guests are thankful for it. At any time during the holidays it makes good sense to have a late-day, open-house party with food served buffet-style (light dishes for those who only want to nibble, something more substantial for others who may want to make this dinner), so your friends can come whenever it fits in with their other activities.

Change is the spice of holiday entertaining—not just a change of food and a change of pace but a change of hour. Instead of the usual Christmas party, you might give a midnight supper dance on Christmas Eve, a Christmas breakfast with little gifts for everyone. Or, as most people concentrate their entertaining in the Christmas week to New Year period, why not start the season early in December with a St. Nicholas party, or close it well into January with a Twelfth Night dinner? As both of these are traditional gift-giving days, one in Holland, the other in Spanish-speaking countries, you could, for once, extend the children's holiday happiness by doling out their presents over a month.

At any time of year, parties are more fun if you liberate your thinking. We all end up giving a big cocktail party, but have you ever thought of making it a pupu party (the Hawaiian name for the finger foods they serve with drinks)? Or a cocktail supper with all kinds of good things to eat, light and substantial? Nor do you necessarily have to give a cocktail party if you want to entertain more people than you can seat at table. You might have an after-supper party of dessert and spirit-spiked coffee, or revive the old-time afternoon tea party, with rafts of delicious little sandwiches and cookies. Do whatever comes naturally to you, whatever you enjoy most, and your guests will enjoy themselves too.

Traditional Thanksgiving Dinner for Eight

For a small family dinner, a traditional menu is perfectly possible, provided you don't attempt to do too many complicated dishes. You can make the pie in the morning, and prepare the scalloped oysters while the turkey is in the oven. A robust red Rhône wine is a good choice with the bird. Instead of cranberry sauce, have a refreshing cranberry sherbet between the main course and dessert.

MENU

Tomato and Clam Consommé
Scalloped Oysters
Roast Turkey with Cornbread and Sausage Stuffing
Brussels Sprouts with Water Chestnuts
Baked Sweet Potatoes
Cranberry Sherbet
Rich Pumpkin Pie

The Wine

Côte Rôtie or Gigondas

TOMATO AND CLAM CONSOMMÉ

Heat equal parts of tomato and clam juice (for 8 servings, allow 4 cups of each) with seasoning to taste, and thin slices of lemon, each stuck with a clove. Serve in bouillon cups, with a lemon slice in each.

SCALLOPED OYSTERS
[MRS. JULE RABÓ]

> Butter
> 1⅔ cups rolled saltine crumbs (not cracker meal)
> 2 pints oysters, with ½ cup of their liquor
> Salt, pepper
> ¼ teaspoon nutmeg
> ⅔ cup heavy cream
> 1 cup coarsely rolled saltine crumbs, buttered
> Dash of Tabasco sauce

Butter a 2-quart baking dish. Cover the bottom of the dish with a layer of ⅓ of the plain cracker crumbs. Add a layer of half the oysters and season with salt, pepper, and ⅛ teaspoon nutmeg. Add ¼ cup of the oyster liquor and ¼ cup of the cream. Add another third of the cracker crumbs and dot with butter. Then add the remaining oysters, the seasonings, and finally the remaining unbuttered cracker crumbs and

325

the buttered crumbs. Add the remaining ¼ cup oyster liquor and cream and sprinkle with salt, pepper, and Tabasco. Bake in a 375° oven for about 20 to 25 minutes, or until brown on top.

ROAST TURKEY WITH CORNBREAD AND SAUSAGE STUFFING
[JAMES A. BEARD]

   ¼ pound (or more) butter
1¼ cups finely chopped onion
   1 cup finely diced celery
  ½ cup chopped celery tops
1½ teaspoons thyme
   1 pound small link sausages or chipolatas
   1 tablespoon salt or more, to taste
1½ teaspoons freshly ground black pepper
   6 to 8 cups coarse cornbread crumbs
  ¾ cup Madeira
       10-pound turkey
       Olive oil
       Bacon slices

Melt the butter in a saucepan with the chopped onion. Add the celery, celery tops, and thyme. Sauté the sausages gently or broil them. Add the salt and pepper to the crumbs and mix with the onion-celery mixture, the sausages, and the Madeira. Add more melted butter or some of the rendered sausage fat, if needed. Taste for seasoning.

Stuff the bird lightly, close the vent and truss. Rub well with olive oil. Arrange on one side on a rack in a shallow roasting pan. Cover with bacon slices and roast at 325° for 1 hour. Turn on other side and roast for another hour, then turn the bird on its back and roast with bacon over the breast and legs until bird is tender and done, basting from time to time with the pan juices, or a mixture of melted butter and white wine.

BRUSSELS SPROUTS WITH WATER CHESTNUTS
[JOSÉ WILSON]

Melt ¼ pound butter in a large heavy skillet or sauté pan, add 1½ quarts trimmed and cleaned Brussels sprouts, and toss in the hot butter until well seared. Turn the heat down, sprinkle with salt to taste, cover and simmer until the sprouts are almost tender, about 10 minutes. Drain two 5-ounce cans water chestnuts, and add the chestnuts to the sprouts. Toss well, then cover and simmer a further 5 minutes, until sprouts are just crisply cooked and water chestnuts heated through. Add a squeeze of lemon juice and serve.

BAKED SWEET POTATOES
[ELOISE DAVISON]

Scrub 8 large sweet potatoes, rub the skins with oil or butter. Bake in a 425° oven for 40 minutes to 1 hour, depending on size, or until soft. Halfway through baking time, puncture the sweet potato skin to let the steam escape and prevent the skin bursting.

When soft, remove, split in half and scoop out insides. Beat potato pulp until light with salt and pepper to taste, a pinch of mace or nutmeg and just enough hot milk to make a smooth mixture. Add 2 to 3 tablespoons Madeira and mix thoroughly. Refill potato shells, brush tops with a little melted butter, and put under a hot broiler until slightly browned.

CRANBERRY SHERBET
[MRS. JULE RABÓ]

1 tablespoon unflavored gelatin
1 pound fresh cranberries
2 cups sugar
Few grains salt
Rind of 2 oranges, shredded
Juice of 3 oranges
Juice of ½ lemon

Soak the gelatin in ½ cup cold water about 5 minutes. Cook the cranberries in 3 cups boiling water until soft. Purée the mixture by forcing it through a strainer or by whirling it in a blender. Combine with the sugar, salt, orange rind and juice, and lemon juice in a saucepan. Bring to a boil. Add the soaked gelatin and stir until dissolved. Cool. Place the mixture in two ice trays in the freezing compartment. Freeze until almost firm. Remove to a mixing bowl and beat until light. Return to ice trays and freeze until firm. Serve as a palate cleanser between the main course and dessert.

RICH PUMPKIN PIE (see page 130)

Nontraditional Thanksgiving Dinner for Four to Six

If you're not celebrating the holiday in the usual way, you might instead have a small dinner party for friends who don't have family ties. As you won't want to cook a turkey for a small group, you might have stuffed capon instead. There is red wine in the recipe, so drink a good Beaujolais.

MENU

Clam Bisque

Capon St. Hubert

Cream Dilled Shallots   *Fondant Potatoes*

Raisin Bourbon Soufflé

The Wine

Moulin-à-Vent or Juliénas

CLAM BISQUE
[JAMES A. BEARD]

    2 7-ounce cans whole or minced razor clams
    2 cups heavy cream
  ½ teaspoon salt
      Dash Tabasco sauce
    2 tablespoons cognac or 3 tablespoons dry sherry
      Finely chopped parsley

Put the undrained clams into the blender and blend for 30 seconds. Transfer to the top of a double boiler and add the cream, salt, and Tabasco. Cook over hot water until the mixture just reaches the boiling point. Taste for seasoning. Just before serving, add cognac or dry sherry. Serve in hot soup cups with a sprinkling of chopped parsley.

CAPON ST. HUBERT
[VITTORIA GRAHAM]

 ½ pound ground chuck
 ½ pound sweet Italian sausages, skinned and chopped fine
 2 eggs
 ¼ cup Parmesan cheese, grated
  Dash of cinnamon
 10 chestnuts, boiled, peeled, and chopped
  Chicken liver and giblet, boiled and chopped
  Salt, pepper
 1 capon (about 6 pounds)
 8 tablespoons butter
 3 slices bacon
 1 teaspoon sage
 1 teaspoon rosemary
 ¼ cup red wine
 1 teaspoon flour
 ½ cup chicken stock

Mix ground chuck, sausage, eggs, cheese, cinnamon, chestnuts, liver, and giblet. Add a dash of salt and pepper. Stuff capon cavity with mixture and truss bird. Melt butter in a Dutch oven and place capon in it. Brown well on all sides. Lay bacon over capon and sprinkle with sage and rosemary. Add wine. Season with salt and pepper. Cover pot, reduce heat, and continue cooking for about 1½ to 2 hours. Baste frequently, adding a little stock if necessary. When chicken is tender remove to platter, blend flour with pan juices, and add ½ cup stock. Pour over chicken.

CREAM DILLED SHALLOTS
[ALEX D. HAWKES]

 1 pound shallots, separated and peeled
 ¼ cup butter
 ¼ cup all-purpose flour
 ½ teaspoon salt
 ¼ teaspoon freshly ground black pepper
 1½ cups light cream
 1 tablespoon minced fresh dill or ½ teaspoon dried dill weed

In a heavy saucepan, cook shallots in a small amount of water, covered, until just tender. Test for doneness with a sharp fork tine. Drain, reserve about ½ cup of cooking liquid. In saucepan, melt the butter, and thoroughly blend in the flour, stirring constantly, until smooth. Stir in the salt and pepper, mix well, then gradually add the reserved liquid and cream, stirring until thickened. Stir in dill and return shallots to simmer, over low heat, stirring occasionally, for about 15 to 20 minutes.

FONDANT POTATOES (see page 145)

Double or triple recipe as required.

RAISIN BOURBON SOUFFLÉ
[JAMES A. BEARD]

⅓ cup butter
⅔ cup flour
2 tablespoons sugar
⅔ cup bourbon
½ cup raisins, blended to a purée
5 egg yolks
6 egg whites
¼ cup raisins puffed in cognac, drained

Make a roux with the butter and flour by melting the butter, gradually adding the flour and stirring until smooth. Gradually stir in the sugar and bourbon. Cook until the mixture is thickened. Add the blended raisins and egg yolks, and cook for just a moment or two longer. Cool slightly. Beat the egg whites until stiff, but not dry, and fold into the mixture. Fold in puffed raisins. Pour into a buttered and sugared 1½-quart soufflé dish and bake in a 375° oven for 25 to 35 minutes. Serve with bourbon-flavored whipped cream.

Christmas Week Dinner for Six

As a break from the regular routine of holiday feasting, serve your guests roast beef—and one of the most lusciously rich potato dishes a great chef (Auguste Escoffier) ever devised. This menu deserves two fine wines, a white and a red Burgundy.

MENU

Seafood Crêpes
Roast Sirloin Shell of Beef with Truffle Sauce
Potatoes Byron   Braised Celery
Pots de Créme au Chocolat

The Wines

Meursault, Pommard

SEAFOOD CRÊPES
[JAMES A. BEARD]

    12 crêpes (see page 425)
     4 ounces butter
     4 shallots, finely chopped
    ½ pound bay scallops
    ½ pound cooked crabmeat
    ½ pound cooked shrimp, coarsely chopped
     1 cup shelled mussels or clams
    ⅓ cup or more cognac or armagnac, warmed
     1 tablespoon chopped fresh tarragon
    ¼ cup chopped parsley
    ¼ cup white wine
     1 teaspoon salt
    ¼ teaspoon or more freshly ground black pepper to taste
     2 tablespoons lemon juice
       Grated Gruyère cheese

Make crêpes and keep warm. Melt butter in a large skillet and add shallots. Cook for 4 minutes, then add scallops. Cook for another 3 minutes, shaking the pan to keep scallops from sticking. Add crabmeat, shrimp and mussels or clams, and cook for 2 minutes. Flambé with cognac or armagnac. Add the herbs, wine, salt, pepper, and lemon juice, and cook over low heat for a minute or so. Taste for seasoning.

Fill the crêpes, roll them and arrange in a buttered dish. Sprinkle heavily with Gruyère cheese. Heat in a 400° oven just until the cheese melts.

ROAST SIRLOIN SHELL OF BEEF WITH TRUFFLE SAUCE
[TATIANA MCKENNA]

> 10-pound sirloin shell of beef
> 4 shallots
> 1 large onion
> 1 carrot
> 1 stalk celery
> 1 cup white wine
> 2 cups beef bouillon
> 1 tablespoon tomato paste
> 1 teaspoon cornstarch
> 4 to 5 truffles, minced

Roast the shell of beef with the shallots, onion, carrot and celery in a 400° oven for 20 minutes. Reduce the heat to 350° and continue roasting for another 40 to 50 minutes, or until a meat thermometer registers 130°. Halfway through the cooking time, add the white wine, but do not baste the beef. When the beef is done to taste, remove and keep warm. Add the bouillon to the pan and deglaze pan over low heat. Add the tomato paste and simmer a few minutes. Dilute cornstarch with a little cold water and add. Stir until the sauce is very slightly thickened. Strain and add the minced truffles. Serve sauce separately.

POTATOES BYRON
[JAMES A. BEARD]

6 baking potatoes
3 tablespoons butter
Salt, pepper to taste
¾ cup heavy cream
⅓ cup grated Parmesan cheese

Bake the potatoes in a 325° oven for 1 hour. Scoop out pulp and put in a bowl with the butter, salt, and pepper. Mash with a fork, working in butter thoroughly.

Place an 8″ flan ring (or top of a spring-form pan) in the center of a shallow baking dish. Fill the ring with the potato mixture, packing firmly. Slowly pour the cream over the potatoes, and allow to stand 10 minutes. Remove flan ring. Sprinkle Parmesan cheese over the top.

Bake 15 minutes in a 375° oven, then brown quickly under a hot broiler.

BRAISED CELERY
[JAMES A. BEARD]

6 celery hearts, split
Chicken or beef broth
4 tablespoons butter
Salt, freshly ground black pepper

Poach the celery hearts in broth to cover until just tender. Remove, drain, and lightly brown in the butter in a skillet, seasoning with salt and pepper to taste.

POTS DE CRÈME AU CHOCOLAT
[RUTH CONRAD BATEMAN]

> 4 ounces sweet chocolate
> 2 cups light cream (or 1 cup heavy cream, 1 cup milk)
> 3 egg yolks
> 1 whole egg
> 3 tablespoons sugar
> 1 tablespoon orange Curaçao (or 1 teaspoon vanilla extract)
> Whipped cream
> Pistachio nuts or candied violets

Melt chocolate over very low heat. Heat cream until film forms on top. Whisk chocolate into cream until completely blended. Beat yolks, egg, and sugar lightly. Gradually beat in hot cream. Blend in Curaçao or vanilla extract. Pour into 6 ceramic pots or custard cups (½-cup size). Cover with lids or foil. Set in pan of hot water ½ the depth of custards. Cook (actually you are poaching) in a 325° oven for about 25 minutes; test with a knife for doneness. Cool and chill. Top each pot de crème with a whipped cream rosette and pistachio nuts or candied violets.

Christmas Eve Buffet for Twenty-four or More

This elegant party buffet is based on the ever-popular ham and turkey, but ham and turkey with such a difference! A whole glazed Smithfield ham and a turkey en chaudfroid are delicacies you wouldn't find at the usual holiday buffet. This is not the easiest of menus to handle, but well worth the effort. Allow yourself plenty of time for preparation, which can, and should, be done ahead. This is a menu that demands superlative champagne.

MENU

Glazed Smithfield Ham   *Turkey en Chaudfroid*
Port Wine Jelly with Grapes and Kumquats
Vegetables Vinaigrette
Endive and Watercress Salad
Hot Rolls and Tiny Hot Biscuits
Chocolate Macaroon Mousse Lucullus   *Vacherin Chantilly*

The Wine

Louis Roederer Cristal; Bollinger Brut Special Cuvée

GLAZED SMITHFIELD HAM
[DIONE LUCAS]

  1 cooked Smithfield ham
  1 cup honey
  6 ounces salt butter
1½ cups brown sugar
    Grated rind of 1 lemon and 1 orange
24 whole cloves
12 thin slices boiled ham
½ pound sweet butter
½ pound liver pâté
  3 tablespoons cognac
    Salt, freshly ground black pepper
  1 large truffle, thinly sliced

Aspic:
  8 cups strong cold beef stock
10 tablespoons plain gelatin
  2 tablespoons tomato paste
¼ cup sherry
  3 stiffly beaten egg whites

Place ham on a rack. Mix honey, salt butter, sugar, lemon and orange rinds in a pan. Stir over low heat until sugar dissolves. Score diamonds on top of ham with a sharp knife and place a clove in the center of each. Carefully cover with brown-sugar mixture. Glaze under a slow broiler for 15 to 20 minutes. Remove and chill.

Cut slices of boiled ham in half. Line cornucopia molds with ham and trim ragged edges with scissors. Cream sweet butter until light and fluffy. Add liver pâté and continue beating until smooth. Add cognac, salt and pepper to taste. Put into pastry bag with large plain tube. Fill cornucopias and stick a truffle on top of each. Chill.

Put the stock, gelatin, tomato paste and sherry in a heavy pan, add the egg whites and beat over low heat until liquid comes to a boil. Draw aside and allow to stand for 15 minutes. Strain through a damp cloth. Stir over ice until on the point of setting. Put a thin coat of aspic over the truffle on top of each cornucopia. Chill again. Turn out cornucopias from molds. To serve, place ham on one side of a large platter, cornucopias on the other side. Chop some of the remaining aspic finely on wax paper. Garnish dish with chopped set aspic and watercress.

TURKEY EN CHAUDFROID
[JAMES A. BEARD]

     6 tablespoons butter
     8 tablespoons flour
     3 cups chicken or turkey broth
    1½ teaspoons salt
     1 cup heavy cream blended with 3 egg yolks
     2 envelopes unflavored gelatin dissolved in ½ cup cold water
       8- to 10-pound poached or roasted turkey, chilled
       For decorations: tarragon leaves, green tops of leeks and scallions, sliced truffles, black or stuffed olives, pimiento, green pepper, hard-cooked eggs
       Beef aspic (see previous recipe)

Melt the butter and stir in the flour over medium heat in a heavy skillet or saucepan. Gradually add the broth and stir until thickened. Add salt and simmer the sauce for approximately 4 to 5 minutes.

Add the cream-and-egg-yolk mixture and dissolved gelatin to the sauce. Stir until the ingredients are well blended and the gelatin is thoroughly melted. Do not let the sauce boil after adding the egg yolks. Allow this chaudfroid sauce to cool until it is ready to set.

Arrange the chilled turkey on a rack over a large pan. You may skin the turkey or leave the skin on. If you wish to carve the bird and put the pieces back in place before adding the decorations, remove the skin and breast filets whole, slice very carefully, and replace on the bone. You may also slice the thigh meat if you wish, but for this dish it is better to leave the thighs whole.

Spoon the chaudfroid sauce, which should be all but congealed, over the entire surface of the chilled bird, being careful to cover all visible parts.

When it is completely covered with the sauce, decorate according to your own fancy. Leaves of tarragon or leaf shapes cut from leek or scallion greens, truffle slices, flowers cut from pimiento and green pepper can be combined in effective designs. The white of hard-cooked eggs, truffles, and other decorative ingredients may be cut into fancy shapes with truffle cutters or vegetable cutters. It is best to work out the design ahead of time and lay out the ingredients you will use for decorating.

When the turkey is decorated, chill again and then brush with or carefully spoon over aspic, which should be syrupy and just about to set. Cool until serving time, arrange on a platter, and decorate the platter with chopped set aspic and any greens you desire. Tiny tomatoes stuffed with salade russe and glazed with aspic, or stuffed eggs filled with a mixture piped through a pastry bag with a rosette tube, make a pretty, edible decoration.

Serve the turkey en chaudfroid with a selection of whole vegetables vinaigrette.

PORT WINE JELLY WITH GRAPES AND KUMQUATS
[DIONE LUCAS]

    3 cups port wine
    ½ cup sherry
    ½ cup lemon, lime, and orange juice, mixed
    4 tablespoons plain gelatin
    ¼ cup red currant jelly
    ½ cup superfine sugar
    ½ cup water
    1 cup granulated sugar
    ½ teaspoon cream of tartar
      Grapes and kumquats

Place the first six ingredients in a pan and stir over low heat until just dissolved. Pour into a lightly oiled fancy mold and chill in refrigerator until set. To unmold, dip mold briefly into hot water and turn out.

Put water, granulated sugar and cream of tartar in a pan and stir over low heat until dissolved. Cook without stirring until it will spin a thread. Cool a little, then dip grapes and kumquats into this syrup and arrange in a ring around the unmolded jelly.

VEGETABLES VINAIGRETTE
[JAMES A. BEARD]

Any of the vegetables listed below may be poached in broth or salted water (peppers are best sautéed), then drained and dressed with a well-seasoned vinaigrette sauce. Make this in proportions of 3 or 4 parts olive oil to 1 part wine vinegar, with salt, freshly ground pepper to taste, herbs of your choice, and a generous portion of chopped parsley. Garlic is optional.

Asparagus, artichoke bottoms, green or wax beans, beets, broccoli, cauliflower, celery hearts, white-kernel corn, leeks, green onions, onion slices, sautéed green, red, or yellow peppers, whole small zucchini or sliced zucchini.

ENDIVE AND WATERCRESS SALAD
[DIONE LUCAS]

8 heads Belgian endive
2 large bunches watercress, stems removed
2 tablespoons olive oil
¼ cup vegetable oil
2 teaspoons salt
Grated rind of 1 lemon
1 teaspoon lemon juice
½ teaspoon Tabasco sauce
1 tablespoon red wine vinegar
1 teaspoon freshly ground pepper
2 large seedless oranges, sectioned
2 tablespoons finely chopped chives

Wash the endive and watercress and dry well. Break outside leaves of endive in two, reserve smaller ones and endive hearts. Put broken endive leaves and watercress in a glass salad bowl. Put next eight in-gredients in a screw-top jar and shake well. Pour half this dressing over the greens and toss well. Arrange on a dish in a circle, heaping up slightly. Put little sprigs of watercress around the edge and a circle of orange sections around the watercress. Carefully arrange small endive leaves and hearts in center of salad ring, spoon over rest of dressing, and sprinkle with chopped chives.

CHOCOLATE MACAROON MOUSSE LUCULLUS
[LOU SEIBERT PAPPAS]

 ½ pound semi-sweet chocolate
24 regular-size marshmallows
 ¾ cup double-strength coffee
 1 teaspoon vanilla
 4 egg whites
 ⅓ cup sugar
1½ cups heavy cream
24 almond macaroons
 ¼ cup brandy
    Whipped cream (optional)

Put chocolate, marshmallows, and coffee in the top of a double boiler and heat over simmering water, stirring occasionally, until melted and smoothly blended. Remove from heat and stir in vanilla. Chill. Beat egg whites until soft peaks form and gradually beat in sugar, beating until stiff. Fold meringue into the cool chocolate mixture. Whip cream until stiff and fold in. Dip macaroons in brandy to saturate them lightly. Spoon half the chocolate mixture into a 9" spring-form pan or freezer-proof glass bowl, then arrange a layer of macaroons, cover with remaining chocolate mixture, and arrange remaining macaroons in a decorative pattern on top.

Cover and freeze until firm. To serve, remove pan sides (if spring-form pan is used) and place on a serving platter. Pass a bowl of whipped cream to spoon over, if desired. Serves 12 for a buffet.

VACHERIN CHANTILLY
[NIKA HAZELTON]

8 egg whites, at room temperature
¼ teaspoon salt
¼ teaspoon cream of tartar
2 cups sugar
1 teaspoon vanilla or ½ teaspoon almond flavoring
2 cups heavy cream, whipped and sweetened to taste with confectioners' sugar
Candied violets or cherries, or fresh strawberries

Preheat oven to 225°. Lightly grease and flour 2 large baking sheets. Line with waxed paper. With a pencil, trace the outline of a 9″ layer-cake pan 4 times, twice on each baking sheet. There should be 4 circles. Beat egg whites until frothy. Add salt and cream of tartar and beat thoroughly. Add sugar, 1 tablespoon at a time, beating constantly. Add vanilla or almond flavoring and beat until meringue is stiff and glossy, but not dry. Divide meringue into 4 parts, one part for each of the circles. Fill pastry bag with meringue mixture. Press out a pencil-thick strip of meringue around the outer rim of each waxed paper circle. Then make a lattice by pressing 4 strips of meringue horizontally and 4 strips vertically across the waxed paper circle, touching the meringue rim. Make similar lattices on the next 3 waxed paper circles. Bake until firm and dry but still white, about 45 minutes. Cool a little, but remove from paper while still warm, using a broad spatula.

Divide whipped cream into two parts. Place one meringue lattice on serving dish. Spread lightly with whipped cream. Top with second layer and repeat process until all four layers are used, but do not spread whipped cream on last layer. Fill pastry bag with remaining whipped cream. Pipe decorative swirls on side of vacherin and a row of rosettes around top. Fill lattice cavities with candied violets, candied cherries, or with large fresh strawberries. Keep refrigerated until serving time, but serve as soon as possible after decorating with whipped cream. Serves 12 for a buffet.

NOTE: There is no limit to the fanciful ways in which a vacherin may be decorated with whipped cream. Some of the whipped cream may be darkened with a little cocoa or melted chocolate to create a checkerboard effect on the top lattice, or it may be tinted with food colorings to produce swirls and rosettes of different hues.

Christmas Breakfast for Eight

One of the pleasantest ways to entertain on Christmas morning, especially if you are going to a family dinner later in the day, is with a simple, delicious breakfast. Your party might begin at eleven with vodka drinks to sip until the food is served at noon.

MENU
[PHILIP S. BROWN]

Finnan Haddie with Cream Sauce

Scrambled Eggs with Fines Herbes or Chives

Swedish Potato Sausage

Stollen *Toasted English Muffins*

Cream Cheese *Strawberry and Peach Preserves*

The Drinks

Screwdrivers, Bloody Marys

FINNAN HADDIE WITH CREAM SAUCE

    3-pound piece finnan haddie
1 quart milk
¼ cup minced green onion
¼ cup diced green pepper
2 tablespoons butter
¼ cup diced pimientos
½ cup butter
½ cup flour
2 cups light cream
    Salt, pepper to taste
1 cup crumbs, buttered

Cover the finnan haddie with the milk and poach gently until the fish separates easily. Drain, reserving the liquid. Separate the fish into flakes and remove any bones. Arrange in a large shallow baking dish. Sauté the onion and pepper in the butter for 3 minutes. Add the pimientos. Make a roux with the butter and flour and add the light cream and 2 cups of the milk used for poaching. Cook, stirring, until thickened and smooth. Add the green onion-pepper mixture, season with salt and pepper, if needed, and pour over the fish. Sprinkle the top with buttered crumbs.

NOTE: This may be prepared the day before and reheated Christmas morning.

SWEDISH POTATO SAUSAGE

> 1 pound lean ground beef
> ½ pound fresh ground pork
> 7 cups grated potatoes
> 1 onion, finely chopped
> 1 tablespoon salt
> 2 teaspoons ground ginger
> ⅓ cup butter

Mix well all the ingredients, except the butter, and stuff the mixture loosely into sausage casings. Cover the sausages with salted water and refrigerate.

To cook these delicious sausages, remove from the brine and poach in salted water for ½ hour. Drain. Melt the butter in a large skillet and brown the sausages on all sides.

STOLLEN

> ¼ cup butter
> ⅓ cup sugar
> 2 teaspoons salt
> 1½ cups milk, scalded
> 2 yeast cakes
> 2 eggs, beaten
> 5 or more cups flour
> ½ cup each of slivered citron, quartered candied cherries, halved blanched raisins
> 1 tablespoon finely chopped candied orange peel
> Melted butter
> Confectioners' sugar or thin sugar icing

Add the butter, sugar, and salt to the scalded milk. When the mixture is lukewarm, crumble in the yeast and stir until dissolved. Add the eggs, 3 cups of the flour, the citron, cherries, raisins, and orange peel. Beat well, then add enough additional flour, about 2 cups or more, to make a soft dough, and knead until smooth. Cover and let rise until double in bulk, then knead again and divide into 3 portions. Roll each into a round shape, brush the top with melted butter, and fold over ⅓ of the dough of each round to form oval shapes with one side higher than the other. Do not press edges together. Place on a buttered baking sheet, let rise until double in size, and bake in a 350° oven for 30 minutes, or until done. Serve sprinkled with confectioners' sugar, or covered with a thin sugar icing.

Christmas Dinner for Six to Eight

Although turkey is the main course and Christmas pudding the dessert, this menu could hardly be ranked as traditional, but it is all the better for that. A light red wine, such as a Beaujolais, would be delightful with the turkey "in half mourning."

MENU

Turtle Surprises Soup
Turkey en Demi-Deuil
Steamed Rice   *Spinach and Mushrooms Gratiné*
Superb English Plum Pudding, Hard Sauce

The Wine

Fleurie

TURTLE SURPRISES SOUP
[STANLEY KUNITZ]

  2 tablespoons oil
  ½ cup chopped scallions
  ⅔ cup diced chicken breast, raw or cooked
  ⅔ cup diced baked ham
  6 large raw shrimp, shelled, deveined, and chopped, or cooked shrimp, chopped
  1 5-ounce can water chestnuts, drained and sliced
  4 13-ounce cans clear turtle soup
  2 13-ounce cans consommé madrilene
  2 tablespoons chopped parsley
     Thin, notched slices of lemon

Heat the oil in a saucepan. Add the scallions, chicken, ham, and shrimp and stir-fry 3 minutes. Add water chestnuts and continue to stir-fry 3 minutes longer or until chicken pieces are tender. Add the turtle soup and consommé. Bring to a boil and simmer 3 minutes. Serve in soup bowls, sprinkle with parsley, and float a slice of lemon on each serving.

TURKEY EN DEMI-DEUIL
[JAMES A. BEARD]

  3 pounds each turkey backs, necks, and gizzards
     Turkey giblets
  1 large fowl (optional)
     Salt, pepper
     6- to 8-pound turkey
     Black truffles, as many as possible, fresh if available
  1 cup heavy Béchamel sauce (see page 418)
 1½ cups heavy cream
  4 egg yolks
     Freshly ground white pepper

Cover the backs, necks, gizzards, and giblets with 4 to 5 quarts water and bring to a boil. Reduce heat and allow to simmer very slowly for about 4 to 5 hours. If you wish a richer broth, add a fowl for the last 2 hours. (The meat may be frozen afterward and used for crêpes, salad, or other chicken dishes.) Season to taste with salt and pepper. Strain, cool, and remove excess fat.

Clean the turkey. Slice most of the truffles, slip them under the skin of the turkey breast and thighs, and allow to stand for an hour or so.

Bring the broth to the boiling point in a large kettle or braising pan. Add the turkey and bring to the boil once more. Reduce heat and let the turkey simmer, covered, allowing about 20 to 22 minutes per pound. Cook just to the point of maximum juicy tenderness—do not overcook.

Remove the cooked turkey to a large hot platter. Reduce 4 cups of the broth to 2 cups over a brisk flame. Add the Béchamel sauce and blend thoroughly. Blend the heavy cream with the egg yolks and gradually stir into the sauce. Continue stirring over low heat until the mixture is smooth and velvety. Do not allow it to boil. Season with salt and ground white pepper and add a few finely chopped truffles.

Serve this elegant dish with a separate bowl of sauce.

NOTE: You can make this dish with white truffles as well. Canned white truffles are more pungent than the black ones and provide an exciting gastronomic treat when added to the sauce.

SPINACH AND MUSHROOMS GRATINÉ
[PEGGY HARVEY]

> 4 pounds spinach
> 12 tablespoons butter
> 2 pounds mushrooms
>   Salt, pepper to taste
> 1 cup grated Swiss cheese

Wash spinach and blanch it in a small amount of boiling, salted water. Drain it well, cool it and chop it fine. Sauté it lightly, just enough to rid it of moisture, in 3 tablespoons butter. Wash and dry mushrooms, slice caps and stems, and sauté them, seasoned with salt and pepper, in 4 tablespoons butter. Mix the spinach, mushrooms, ½ cup grated Swiss cheese, and 3 tablespoons butter. Put in a lightly buttered baking dish. Cover with ½ cup grated Swiss cheese, dot with remaining butter, and put under the broiler to brown.

SUPERB ENGLISH PLUM PUDDING
[JAMES A. BEARD]

Plum pudding is really best when made a year in advance and allowed to mellow. If you can't make it the year before, at least give it a few weeks to age.

FRUIT MIXTURE

Make this 4 days ahead.
- 1 pound seedless raisins
- 1 pound sultana raisins
- ½ pound currants
- 1 cup thinly sliced citron
- 1 cup chopped candied peel
- 1 teaspoon cinnamon
- ½ teaspoon mace
- ½ teaspoon nutmeg
- ¼ teaspoon ground cloves
- ¼ teaspoon allspice
- ¼ teaspoon freshly ground black pepper
- 1 pound finely chopped suet—powdery fine
- 1¼ cups cognac

Blend the fruits, citron, peel, spices and suet and place in a bowl or jar. Add ¼ cup cognac, cover tightly, and refrigerate for 4 days, adding ¼ cup cognac each day.

PUDDING

- 1¼ pounds (approximately) fresh bread crumbs
- 1 cup scalded milk
- 1 cup sherry or port
- 12 eggs, well beaten
- 1 cup sugar
- 1 teaspoon salt
- Cognac

Soak the bread crumbs in the milk and sherry or port. Combine with the well-beaten eggs and sugar. Blend with the fruit mixture. Add salt and mix thoroughly. Put the pudding in buttered pudding bowls or tins, filling them about two-thirds full. Cover with foil and tie firmly. Steam for 6 to 7 hours. Uncover and place in a 250° oven for 30 minutes. Add a dash of cognac to each pudding, cover with foil, and keep in a cool place.

To use, steam again for 2 to 3 hours and unmold. Sprinkle with sugar; add heated cognac. Ignite and bring to the table. Serve with hard sauce or cognac sauce. Each pudding serves 12.

HARD SAUCE

⅔ cup butter
2 cups brown sugar
½ cup cognac
¼ teaspoon salt

Cream the butter well, and add the sugar and cognac gradually. Finally add the salt. Beat the mixture to a creamy consistency. Chill. Makes about 2½ cups.

Christmas Midnight Supper for Twenty or More

When the house is decorated for Christmas, it's a good idea to give a succession of parties. One might be a small dance, with a late supper afterward (the supper would be equally good, though, after a tree-trimming party or when you and friends have gone out singing carols and come back cold and hungry, in which case you might skip the champagne and just have hot consommé and omelettes). Keep the consommé boiling hot in an electric tureen or over a spirit warmer and pour into the demitasse cups just before serving.

MENU

Double Chicken Consommé, Cheesed Melba Toast
Omelettes with Sour Cream and Caviar,
Roquefort Butter, Creamed Codfish, or Curried Beef Fillings
Tossed Green Salad
Fresh Fruits in Champagne

The Wine

Brut Champagne

DOUBLE CHICKEN CONSOMMÉ
[JAMES A. BEARD]

> 2 pounds chicken necks
> 5 pounds chicken backs
> 4 quarts water
> 1½ tablespoons salt
> 1 onion stuck with 2 cloves
> 1 or 2 sprigs of parsley
> 1 pound chicken gizzards
> 1 egg white and shell

Put the necks and 2 pounds of the backs in a kettle with the water, salt, onion, and parsley. Bring to a boil, lower the heat, and simmer 2 hours. Taste for seasoning and simmer a further ½ hour. Remove from heat and strain. Return the strained broth to the kettle with the remaining chicken backs and the gizzards. Simmer 2 hours. Strain the broth and cool. When cool, skim off all the fat.

Strain the broth through a fine linen towel. Beat egg white until frothy and put strained broth in a pan with the beaten egg white and the egg shell. Return to the heat and cook a few minutes, beating with a rotary egg beater. The egg shell and white will collect any remaining impurities in the broth, leaving it clear. Strain the clarified broth once more through the linen towel, wrung out in cold water.

Serve the soup very hot, in demitasse cups. Freshly made Melba toast, sprinkled with Parmesan cheese and heated in the oven, is a perfect accompaniment.

OMELETTES

For directions for making omelettes, see page 426.

OMELETTE FILLINGS
[MRS. JACK BAKER]

SOUR CREAM AND CAVIAR

Add a goodly helping of either red or black caviar to the omelette and top with a spoonful of sour cream. Add a bit of chopped parsley or chives if you wish.

ROQUEFORT BUTTER

Cream together ½ pound Roquefort cheese, ¼ pound softened butter, 1 teaspoon Dijon mustard, and 1 tablespoon cognac. Spoon a large spoonful into each omelette as you roll it. Makes enough for 8 to 10 omelettes.

CREAMED CODFISH

> 1 pound salt codfish
> 3 tablespoons butter
> 4 tablespoons flour
> 1 teaspoon salt
> ½ teaspoon freshly ground pepper
>   Pinch of nutmeg
> 1 cup milk
> ½ cup heavy cream blended with 1 egg yolk
> 3 hard-cooked eggs, sliced

Soak the codfish overnight or for several hours. Change the water once during the soaking. Place the fish in fresh water to cover and bring to a boil. Simmer for about 5 to 6 minutes, or until the fish flakes easily when tested with a fork. Shred and taste for salt.

Make a roux by melting the butter and blending in the flour, salt, pepper, and nutmeg. Remove pan from heat and add the milk slowly, stirring until blended. Cook, stirring constantly, until sauce thickens.

349

Stir in the heavy cream blended with the egg yolk and heat until well blended. Add the shredded codfish and sliced hard-cooked eggs. Spoon codfish filling into or over the omelettes. Makes enough filling for 6 to 8 omelettes.

CURRIED BEEF

>   1 medium onion, finely chopped
>   1 tablespoon butter
>   1 tablespoon oil
>   1 greening apple, cored and grated (skin and all)
>   ½ pound lean ground chuck
>   2 tablespoons or more curry powder
>   1 teaspoon salt
>   ¾ cup brown sauce (canned may be used)
>   ½ cup seedless raisins
>   ½ cup chopped salted peanuts
>   2 tablespoons chutney

Sauté the onion in the butter and oil and add the apple. Break up the beef and add, tossing well. Brown the meat and let it cook with the apple and onion for about 3 minutes. Add the curry powder and salt and blend. Add the brown sauce and simmer for 5 minutes. Add the raisins, nuts, and chutney and heat through. Correct seasoning. Spoon into or over omelettes. Makes enough for 6 to 8 omelettes.

New Year's Eve Party for Twenty

Not everyone wants to stay up until midnight to see the new year in, so it is both thoughtful and smart to break with tradition and give your New Year's Eve party early—from six to eight-thirty. Your guests then have the choice of spending the rest of the evening quietly at home without feeling deprived of their celebration, or going on to a late-late party well fortified by substantial food and champagne.

MENU
[JAMES A. BEARD]

Chicken Liver Pâté   *Holiday Pâté Maison*

Rare Roast Beef   *Selection of Mustards*

Cotechino (Italian Sausage), Steamed and Sliced

Crudités with Tapenade

Cherry Tomatoes   French, Pumpernickel, and Rye Breads

Crocks of Sweet Butter

The Wine

Champagne

CHICKEN LIVER PÂTÉ

      3 tablespoons butter
      1 pound chicken livers
      3 eggs
      ⅓ cup heavy cream
      ⅓ cup cognac
      ½ pound pork, freshly ground with ¾ pound pork fat
      ½ cup flour
        Salt
      ½ teaspoon freshly ground black pepper
    1¼ teaspoons thyme
        Salt pork or mild bacon, thinly sliced
      1 chicken breast, boned, skinned, well trimmed, and cut into 2
        filets

Heat the butter in a skillet, add the chicken livers, and tumble them in the butter just long enough to firm them. Blend half of the livers with the eggs in a blender, pour into a bowl; then blend the remaining livers with the heavy cream and cognac. Combine the liver mixtures with the pork ground with the pork fat, and flour. Add 1½ teaspoons salt, the pepper, and thyme. Line a loaf pan with the sliced salt pork or bacon. Add half the pâté mixture and arrange the chicken filets over it, filling them into the space carefully. Sprinkle lightly with salt. Add remaining

351

pâté mixture and shake pan to settle mixture around the filets. Place in a pan of hot water and bake in a 350° oven for 1½ hours.

HOLIDAY PÂTÉ MAISON

2 pounds pork liver, coarsely ground
2 pounds veal, coarsely ground
2 pounds pork, coarsely ground, or 2 pounds sausage meat
3 slices salt pork, cut in small bits
1½ tablespoons salt
1½ tablespoons freshly ground black pepper
1 teaspoon thyme
Dash of Tabasco sauce
2 medium onions, finely chopped
5 garlic cloves, finely chopped
5 eggs
½ cup flour
¾ cup cognac
Sliced salt pork or bacon

Mix the ground meats, salt pork bits, seasonings, onion and garlic, and blend well with your hands. Add the eggs, one at a time, and mix them in thoroughly. Finally mix in the flour and cognac. Be sure the ingredients are well blended.

Line 2 large or 4 medium-size casseroles with slices of salt pork or bacon. Fill three-quarters full with the pâté mixture. Put more slices of salt pork or bacon on the top. Cover the casseroles and place them in pans of boiling water. Bake in a 375° oven, allowing 2½ hours cooking time for small or medium casseroles, 45 minutes to 1 hour longer if the casseroles are large.

Remove the casseroles from the hot water and place on a rack in the oven to finish cooking for 15 minutes more. Remove from oven and cool for 20 minutes. Remove covers and place heavy foil on each pâté. Weight them down with bulky, heavy objects (such as canned goods) on a plate until thoroughly cooled. Chill well in the refrigerator.

CRUDITÉS WITH TAPENADE

Crudités are crisp fresh raw vegetables, cut into pieces small enough to be dunked and eaten with the fingers. Any of the following make a delightful hors d'oeuvre if arranged attractively on a large white platter.

Broccoli, tiny flowerets
Carrots, cut in strips
Cauliflower, tiny flowerets
Celery, slivers or fingers
Cucumber, long peeled fingers
Endive, single leaves
Fennel, thin strips
Green onions, tiny, ends trimmed
Green pepper, thick lengthwise strips
Mushrooms, tiny raw caps or thick slices
Radish, red or icicle, whole
Snow peas, whole, raw
Zucchini, small thick unpeeled slices

With these have a big bowl of Tapenade (see below), a sauce or dunk from Provence traditionally used for saucing vegetables and eggs.

TAPENADE

⅓ pound Italian or French black olives
1 teaspoon Dijon mustard
16 to 18 anchovy filets
½ cup capers
½ cup olive oil
Touch each of ground cloves, ground ginger
Freshly ground black pepper
Dash of cognac

Chop the olives very fine and blend in the mustard. Chop or crush the anchovy filets and add with the capers, oil, spices, pepper to taste, and cognac. Beat well until thoroughly blended.

353

New Year's Day Breakfast Party for Twelve

With the exception of the sausages and English muffins, the dishes in this menu can be prepared ahead of time and held until the guests are ready to eat—you could keep the curried egg casserole and creamed chipped beef warm in chafing dishes or on a hot tray while the milk punch is served.

MENU

Milk Punch
Curried Egg Casserole
Creamed Chipped Beef
Breakfast Sausages
Toasted English Muffins
Jule Kaga

MILK PUNCH
[PEGGY HARVEY]

6 quarts milk
3 cups cognac
2 cups Jamaica rum
Sugar to taste
Freshly grated nutmeg

Mix the milk and liquors in a large container. Add sugar to taste. Refrigerate overnight. When ready to serve, pour into a punch bowl over ice. Serve in Old Fashioned glasses and grate a little nutmeg over the top.

CURRIED EGG CASSEROLE
[PEGGY HARVEY]

2 medium onions, minced
1 clove garlic, minced
1 piece ginger root, sliced
3 tablespoons butter
1 tablespoon curry powder
3 tablespoons flour
2 cups chicken bouillon
3 cups milk
1 cup seedless raisins
1 small apple, peeled, cored and chopped
  Juice of ½ lemon
1 strip lemon peel
18 hard-boiled eggs

Sauté the onions, garlic and ginger in the butter until lightly browned. Stir in the curry powder (use more, if you like a hotter curry) and cook for a minute or two, then mix in the flour and cook that for a minute. Gradually add the chicken bouillon and milk, which have been heated together. Stir and simmer until smooth. Strain into a double boiler. Add the raisins, which have been soaked in tepid water, then drained, the apple, lemon juice and peel. Cook slowly over hot water for 10 minutes, then add seasoning to taste. Peel and slice the eggs and add them to the curry sauce. Serve on English muffins.

CREAMED CHIPPED BEEF
[PEGGY HARVEY]

½ pound dried beef
2 ounces butter
4 tablespoons flour
  Black pepper
1 quart milk or half-and-half
¼ cup pickled grated horseradish

Soak the beef in warm water for 15 minutes if it is very salty. Drain, and tear it into small pieces.

Melt the butter in a large skillet and sauté the beef until it starts to

355

brown. Sprinkle with the flour, grind some pepper over it and stir until the meat is coated with the flour. Add the milk or half-and-half slowly, and stir until thickened. Add the horseradish and cook over low heat, stirring for a few minutes. Serve on English muffins.

JULE KAGA
[JAMES A. BEARD]

        1 cup milk
    ½ cup sugar
        1 teaspoon salt
    ½ cup shortening
        2 packages yeast dissolved in ¼ cup warm water (110° to 115°)
    4½ cups sifted enriched flour
    1½ teaspoons ground cardamom
    ½ cup raisins
    ¼ cup chopped citron
    ¼ cup chopped candied cherries
    ¼ cup chopped almonds
        Plain icing, nuts, candied fruit

Scald the milk and blend in the sugar, salt, and shortening. Cool to lukewarm. Pour into the dissolved yeast and stir well. Add 2 cups of the sifted flour and beat thoroughly. Cover the bowl and set in a warm place to rise until double in bulk.

Stir mixture down, then add cardamom, raisins, citron, cherries, and almonds. Blend well and work in the rest of the flour. Turn out onto a lightly floured board and knead until smooth and elastic. Place in a greased bowl and brush top with shortening. Cover and let stand in a warm place until double in bulk. Punch the dough down and form into a round loaf. Place loaf on a greased baking sheet, cover again and let stand in a warm spot to rise a third time until double in bulk.

Bake in a 400° oven for 10 minutes, then reduce the heat to 350° and continue baking for 40 minutes. Cool the bread before frosting with plain icing. Decorate with nuts and candied fruits.

New Year's Day Soup and Spirits Buffet for Twelve to Eighteen

This is a very easy menu if you are holding open house on New Year's Day. Friends who drop in for a late lunch or an early supper anytime between three and seven can have a drink or two first and then help themselves to either of the hearty soups, which could be kept hot in chafing dishes or electric tureens at either end of the dining room table. (The menudo, the traditional Mexican "morning after" soup, is a great pick-me-up after the carousing of New Year's Eve.)

MENU

Menudo with Tostadas
Black Bean Soup
Tiny Hot Biscuits, Split and Buttered
White Fruit Cake with Aged Cheddar Cheese

MENUDO
[ELENA ZELAYETA]

> 2 calves' feet
> 5 pounds tripe
> 3 cups white hominy
> 3 onions, minced
> 4 cloves garlic, minced
> 2 teaspoons cilantro
> 1 tablespoon oregano
> Salt, pepper
> Minced green onions and minced mint leaves or hot red chile sauce

Wash the calves' feet and cook in 6 quarts water for 1 hour. Wash the tripe thoroughly and cut in 1″ by 2″ pieces. Add to the calves' feet with the hominy, onion, garlic, the herbs, tied loosely in a cheesecloth bag, and salt and pepper to taste. Simmer 6 to 7 hours. Adjust seasoning.

Serve with minced green onions and minced mint leaves to be sprinkled on top or a red chile sauce. Makes 12 servings.

NOTE: This soup can be made ahead of time and frozen.

TOSTADAS

These are tortillas that have been fried until golden brown and crisp in hot lard or oil. Make small tortillas, about 2″ in diameter, according to the directions on page 300, or buy canned tortillas and quarter them.

BLACK BEAN SOUP
[MRS. DAVID EVINS]

> 1 pint black beans
> 2 tablespoons chopped onion
> 1 clove garlic, minced
> ¼ cup fat or butter
> 1 celery root, diced
> 2 teaspoons salt
> ¼ teaspoon freshly ground pepper
>   Cayenne pepper
> ¼ teaspoon dry mustard
> 1 lemon, thinly sliced

Wash beans and soak overnight in water. Drain and rinse. Sauté onion and garlic in the fat or butter until soft. Add to beans. Add celery root and 2 quarts cold water. Cook over low heat until beans are soft. Push through a sieve, then season with salt, pepper, cayenne to taste, and mustard. Garnish with lemon slices. Makes 6 to 8 servings.

WHITE FRUIT CAKE
[CATHRINE HINDLEY]

In the nineteenth century this was called "Ladies' Cake" and was served to callers with tea or sherry. It also makes a good sweet dessert to serve with aged Cheddar.

> 1 cup blanched, shredded, very lightly toasted almonds
> 1 cup flaked coconut
> 1½ cups white or golden raisins

1 cup candied pineapple, cut in small pieces
½ cup candied citron, cut in small pieces
1 cup halved candied cherries
1 teaspoon grated lemon or ½ teaspoon grated lime rind
1 cup butter
2 cups sugar
2 tablespoons lemon juice
⅓ cup orange juice
4 cups sifted cake flour or 3½ cups sifted all-purpose flour
½ teaspoon salt
1 teaspoon soda
6 egg whites
Corn syrup for glazing (optional)

Put nuts, coconut, fruits, and lemon or lime rind in mixing bowl and toss well to combine evenly. Grease 2 loaf pans 9½″ x 5½″ x 3″ and line with buttered paper. The paper will prevent the sides and bottom of the cake from darkening.

Cream butter well, then cream in sugar gradually until very light-colored. Add juices alternately with flour that has been sifted with salt and soda. When well combined, add fruit mixture and turn over repeatedly until well blended. Beat egg whites until stiff but not dry and fold into cake batter. Immediately turn into the prepared pans. Bake in a 275° oven about 2 to 2½ hours, or until cake springs back when touched lightly in center. If cake is to be decorated, brush just before removing from oven with light corn syrup. Cool on cake rack, loosen from pan with spatula, invert on cake rack, and remove paper. Brush with light rum or brandy, if desired. When cool, slip into freezer bags and allow to age a week to 10 days before storing in the refrigerator. If the cake seems dry, before storing, brush several times with liquor.

NOTE: The fruits for white cake are not usually soaked in liquor before baking because the batter tends to darken during the baking.

New Year's Day Dinner for Eight

Goose, a much neglected and extremely succulent bird, is a good choice for a New Year's Day dinner—when everyone is apt to be fed to the teeth with turkey—and with a rich fruit stuffing this dark-meated bird tastes even more delicious. Drink a red wine with the goose, a fine bordeaux or a wine from the Rhône or Beaujolais district.

MENU

Broiled Clams with Herb Butter
Roast Goose with Prune and Apple Stuffing
Purée of Celery Root and Potatoes
Salad of Watercress and Sliced Raw Mushrooms, French Dressing
Almond Praliné Charlotte

The Wine

Médoc, such as Château Léoville-Las-Cases; Hermitage; Fleurie

---

BROILED CLAMS WITH HERB BUTTER
[JOHN CLANCY]

- ½ pound butter
- 4 tablespoons finely chopped parsley
- 4 tablespoons finely chopped chives
- ¾ teaspoon dried oregano
- ½ teaspoon salt
- ½ teaspoon freshly ground black pepper
- 2 large cloves garlic, finely chopped
- 4 tablespoons dry white wine or dry vermouth
- 2 teaspoons Worcestershire sauce
- 48 littleneck clams on the half shell
- ¾ cup fresh soft bread crumbs

Cream butter until soft, then add herbs, salt, pepper, and garlic. Gradually beat in wine and Worcestershire sauce. Be sure mixture is well blended, then chill until medium firm. Shape into a long roll, about 1″ in diameter, wrap in wax paper, and refrigerate 1 hour or until very firm.

Slice herbed butter about 1″ thick and place 1 slice on each clam. Sprinkle with bread crumbs and put in oven-proof dish. Broil 3 inches from heat for about 3 to 4 minutes, or until butter is bubbling and bread crumbs are golden brown. Serve immediately.

ROAST GOOSE WITH PRUNE AND APPLE STUFFING
[JAMES A. BEARD]

18 prunes soaked in Madeira
6 to 8 apples, peeled, cored and coarsely sliced
Salt to taste
10-pound goose
White wine
1 large onion, chopped
Beurre manié

Soak the prunes in the wine overnight. Next day, cook them in the wine until they are tender and easily pitted. Remove the pits. Combine the prunes and the apples and season with salt to taste.

Wash the goose well with hot water to remove any greasy film, and be sure to remove excess fat from the cavity. Reserve the giblets. Stuff the bird about ⅔ to ¾ full (the fruit will swell during the cooking) and close the vent securely. Rub the skin with a little salt and arrange the bird on a rack in a roasting pan. Roast in a 350° oven, allowing 18 to 20 minutes per pound, or until the internal temperature reaches 175° when tested with a meat thermometer in the thigh. Baste frequently with a fruity white wine such as an Alsatian wine, a Moselle, or a California Riesling. Prick the skin occasionally to allow the fat to run out.

While the goose is roasting, cook the gizzard and heart in well-seasoned water with a little of the basting wine added. When you have a rich broth, strain and save it. Sauté the chopped onion and the goose liver in a little of the fat from the roasting pan.

When the roast goose is tender and the skin is brown and crisp, remove the bird and place it on a hot platter. Keep warm. Skim the fat from the pan juices. Add the broth to the juices and thicken with beurre manié (small balls of butter and flour mixed). Taste for seasoning and stir in the onion and liver. Serve the sauce separately.

PURÉE OF CELERY ROOT AND POTATOES

(See recipe on page 97. Increase ingredients if necessary.)

ALMOND PRALINÉ CHARLOTTE
[RUTH CONRAD BATEMAN]

>   6 egg yolks
>   ½ cup sugar
>   1½ cups milk, scalded
>   Salt
>   2 envelopes plain gelatin
>   ½ cup Almond Praliné powder
>   2 tablespoons dark rum or rich cream sherry
>   1 teaspoon vanilla extract
>   ¼ teaspoon almond extract
>   2 cups heavy cream, whipped until softly peaked
>   12 ladyfingers, split, lightly toasted
>   Additional whipped cream, coarsely crushed almond praliné for garnish

With a whisk or beater, beat egg yolks in top of double boiler until light. Gradually beat in sugar until mixture is creamy-pale and thick. Slowly stir in hot milk and a pinch of salt, stirring constantly. Cook and stir over hot, not boiling, water just until custard thickens enough to coat the spoon and has a creamy, cooked look and taste. Do not overcook or it will curdle. Soften gelatin in ⅓ cup cold water and dissolve in the hot custard. Stir in the praliné powder, rum, and extracts. Chill until thick but not set. Gently fold in the cream. Line the sides (not the bottom) of a 2-quart charlotte or other straight-sided mold with ladyfingers, standing them upright and close together. Carefully spoon in the mousse. Cover top with more ladyfingers. Cover mold with plastic wrap and chill until set, several hours or overnight. Unmold on a plate and decorate base with rosettes of whipped cream. Sprinkle the top with coarsely crushed praliné.

ALMOND PRALINÉ

>   ½ cup granulated sugar
>   ¼ cup water
>   ⅛ teaspoon cream of tartar
>   ½ cup chopped blanched almonds

Combine sugar, water, and cream of tartar in a small heavy saucepan. Stir over moderate heat until sugar dissolves. Add almonds and boil without stirring until syrup and almonds are a rich caramel color. Turn out onto an oiled marble slab or jelly-roll pan and cool. Break into pieces, then crush either coarsely or into fine powder with a rolling pin or in the blender. Makes about 1 cup. If stored in an air-tight jar, it will keep for weeks.

New Year's Day Open House Party for a Crowd

Whether or not your friends have celebrated on New Year's Eve, they are apt to be at loose ends late the next afternoon. For those who can face no more than a cool, refreshing drink and a little light nourishment, serve champagne punch and cold sliced meats and fish. Guests who are really hungry and thirsty will appreciate heartier dishes like the braised beef with barbecue sauce, and a well-stocked bar.

MENU
[PEGGY HARVEY]

Braised Beef on Tiny Buns, Hot Barbecue Sauce
Cold Cooked Shrimp with Special Sauce
Pâté en Croûte
Celery Stuffed with Tartar Steak
Stuffed Eggs
Spicy Dunk with Breadsticks, Raw Vegetables, Cocktail
Frankfurters
Sliced Smoked Turkey, Duck, or Pheasant
Smoked Salmon and Sturgeon
Thinly Sliced Polish Rye Bread Spread with Sweet Butter
Pickled Mushrooms   *Pickled Artichoke Hearts*

The Drinks

Cocktails and Champagne Punch

BRAISED BEEF WITH HOT BARBECUE SAUCE

> 2 whole beef filets (3 to 3½ pounds each) or 6 to 7 pounds boned and trimmed sirloin
> Salt, freshly ground black pepper
> ½ pound butter
> 1 cup Madeira

Bring the meat to room temperature, season it with salt and pepper and braise it slowly in the butter in a shallow pan on top of the stove. Baste often with the Madeira. Turn the meat several times, using two spoons so that the surface of the meat is not punctured. Cook for 10 minutes to the pound. The meat should be rare and if you keep it hot, it will cook a bit more. Cut into small, fairly thin pieces to fit onto the buns, which should be the size of a half dollar. Butter the buns, keep them warm in a heater and have the beef and barbecue sauce in two other heaters. This amount of beef and sauce will make enough for 12 dozen tiny buns, which should feed about 70 or 75 people.

HOT BARBECUE SAUCE

> 2 tablespoons butter
> 1 medium onion, chopped
> 2 teaspoons dry mustard
> ½ cup sugar
> 1 teaspoon cider vinegar
> 2 cups water
> 1 teaspoon Tabasco sauce
> 1 tablespoon Worcestershire sauce
> 1 cup tomato catsup
> 2 beef bouillon cubes
> 1 teaspoon celery salt
> 1 teaspoon paprika
> 2 tablespoons arrowroot or cornstarch

Melt the butter and sauté the onion until soft and golden. Add the mustard, sugar, vinegar, 1½ cups water, Tabasco, Worcestershire, catsup, bouillon cubes, celery salt and paprika. Bring to a boil and stir in the arrowroot or cornstarch, mixed with ½ cup cold water. Simmer, stirring occasionally, for at least 1 hour.

SPECIAL SAUCE FOR COLD SHRIMP

    1 cup parsley clusters
    1 bunch watercress, leaves only
    1 cup shredded fresh spinach
    2 shallots, sliced
    1 clove garlic, sliced
    2 teaspoons dry mustard
    1 egg yolk
    1 tablespoon tarragon vinegar
       Juice of ½ lemon
   ½ teaspoon salt
       Black pepper
1¼ cups mayonnaise
  ½ cup sour cream

Put the parsley, watercress, and spinach in a blender, 1 cup at a time, and blend for six seconds after each addition. With motor off, press greens down into the blades. Add the shallots, garlic, mustard, egg yolk, vinegar, lemon juice, salt, and a grind or two of pepper. Cover and blend for 30 seconds. Add mayonnaise and sour cream. Cover and blend for 30 seconds more. Chill. This makes enough sauce for 3 to 4 pounds of shrimp.

PÂTÉ EN CROÛTE

    3 cups all-purpose flour
1¼ cups soft butter
    ½ cup cold water
    ½ pound salt pork
    ¾ pound lean veal
    ¾ pound lean pork
    ¾ pound lean ham, cut 1¼″ thick and diced
    2 tablespoons Madeira
    1 tablespoon cognac
      Pinches of thyme, rosemary, tarragon
      Black pepper
    1 tablespoon minced parsley
    2 or 3 truffles, chopped (optional)
    2 slices bacon
    1 egg yolk

First, make the pastry. Blend the flour and butter with the fingers until you have a sandy mass. Gradually add the water, mixing slowly, and work the dough into a ball. The less water used, the better. Wrap in waxed paper and refrigerate. When ready to make the pâté, roll out about ¼″ thick.

Have the salt pork, veal and lean pork ground together twice by the butcher.

Line a 1½-quart spring-form pan with ¾ of the pastry, reserving the rest for the top crust.

Mix together the ground meats, ham, Madeira, cognac, seasonings, parsley and chopped truffles (if used). Fill the mold with this mixture and put the bacon slices on top. Cover with the reserved pastry, moistening the edges to seal the top crust to the bottom. Cut slits on top for the steam to escape. Decorate the top crust with small pieces of pastry cut in star or leaf forms. Beat the egg yolk with a little cold water and paint the crust with this egg wash.

Bake in a preheated 350° oven for 1½ hours. Serve sliced.

SPICY DUNK

> 3 medium onions, chopped
> 1 clove garlic, minced
> 1 cup peanut oil
> ¼ pound butter
> 1 20-ounce can solid-pack tomatoes
> 1 teaspoon rosemary
> 1 bay leaf
> 1 pint red wine
> 1 6-ounce can tomato paste
> ½ cup pine nuts
> ¼ cup drained capers

Sauté the onions and garlic in the oil and butter until limp. Add the tomatoes, rosemary, bay leaf, wine and tomato paste. Simmer until sauce is thick and mellow. Add the nuts and capers, taste for seasoning, and simmer a half hour longer. Chill. Serve as a dunk for breadsticks, raw vegetables, cocktail frankfurters, or the cold shrimp.

CHAMPAGNE PUNCH

The night before the party, make the "mother" that is the base of the punch. Use 1 quart of it, strained, to 3 quarts of cold champagne, poured over a block of ice in a punch bowl. The punch should be served in champagne glasses, not punch cups. If you are serving this punch to seventy or more people, plan on having about 1½ cases of champagne and about 5 quarts of the "mother."

To make 1 quart "mother":
> ½ bottle cognac
> ⅔ bottle dry white wine
> 1 navel orange, sliced but unpeeled
> 1 lemon, sliced but unpeeled
> ⅕ cup Curaçao or Grand Marnier
> ⅕ cup Cointreau or Triple Sec
> ⅓ cup kirsch

Mix ingredients together in a large enamel container. Do not refrigerate.

Twelfth Night Party for Six

Twelfth Night, known as King's Day or Dia de los Reyes in Mexico and other Latin countries, traditionally winds up the holiday season. For this farewell-to-Christmas party, serve a Mexican supper and for dessert have rosca de reyes, a circular cake bread in which a small china doll, representing an infant, has been baked. Custom has it that whoever gets the figure will have good luck in the year to come. As the main dish is not fiery hot and contains wine, you could drink either beer or a white wine with it.

MENU
[ELISABETH ORTIZ]

Pollo Mestizo

Frijoles   Rice   Tortillas

Green Salad   Guacamole

Rosca de Reyes

The Drinks

Chilled beer or Bernkasteler Riesling

POLLO MESTIZO

4 tablespoons oil and butter (2 of each)
3½- to 4-pound fryer, cut into serving pieces
1 cup dry white wine
1 cup pineapple juice
Bay leaf
Salt, pepper to taste
6 small potatoes
2 medium tomatoes, peeled and seeded
2 cloves garlic

1 onion
6 canned pimientos
3 chorizos (Spanish sausages)
1 tablespoon capers
3 canned jalapeño chilis, or to taste

Heat the oil and butter in a skillet and sauté the chicken until golden. Remove the chicken to a covered casserole and add the wine, pineapple juice, bay leaf, salt, and pepper, leaving fat in skillet for later use. Simmer chicken until barely tender, about 45 minutes. Cook the potatoes in salted boiling water, drain, and reserve. Put the tomatoes, garlic, onion, and pimientos in a blender and blend until smooth, adding a little stock from the chicken if necessary. Skin and chop the chorizos and sauté in oil and butter remaining in the skillet. Drain and add to the casserole. Put the blender mixture in the skillet and cook in the remaining fat for 5 minutes, stirring constantly. Add to the casserole with the potatoes and capers. Rinse the jalapeño chilis, remove seeds, if any, cut in strips, and add to the casserole. Check seasoning, simmer for a few minutes, and serve.

GUACAMOLE

2 large ripe avocados
1 medium tomato, peeled, seeded, and chopped
1 tablespoon finely chopped onion
2 or more canned serrano chilis, chopped, or fresh hot red or green peppers, seeded and chopped
3 or 4 sprigs fresh coriander (cilantro), chopped
Salt, freshly ground pepper
Pinch of sugar

Cut the avocados in half, remove the seed. Mash in the shell with a fork, spoon out, and mix with all the other ingredients. If guacamole is not served immediately, cover with plastic wrap and refrigerate to prevent the surface turning dark.

FRIJOLES (see page 428)

ROSCA DE REYES (KING'S DAY RING)

      1 envelope yeast
   2½ cups flour
      ½ teaspoon salt
      ¼ cup sugar
      2 eggs, well beaten
      4 egg yolks
      4 tablespoons butter, at room temperature
        Grated rind of 1 lemon
   1½ cups mixed, chopped candied fruits and peels
        Tiny china doll
        Melted butter
      1 cup confectioners' sugar, sifted
      2 tablespoons light cream
        Maraschino cherries, cut in half

Soften the yeast in ¼ cup lukewarm water. Mix half the flour, the yeast mixture, salt, sugar, eggs, egg yolks, softened butter, and lemon rind in a large bowl and beat until well blended. Dust 1 cup of the fruits and peel with flour and beat into the dough, with the remaining flour. The dough should be soft, but not sticky. If necessary, add a little more flour.

Turn onto a lightly floured board and knead until smooth and satiny, about 5 minutes. Shape into a ring, tucking the china doll into the dough. Place on a greased baking sheet, cover with a cloth, and leave in a warm place until the dough is double in bulk, about 2 hours or more. Brush with melted butter and bake in a preheated 350° oven for 30 minutes. Allow to cool.

Mix the sifted confectioners' sugar with the light cream and spread over the ring. Decorate with the remaining ½ cup fruits and peels and halved Maraschino cherries. Makes enough for 12 large slices.

Easter Luncheon for Six

For a small holiday weekend luncheon party, nothing could make more exquisite eating than an ethereal mousse of fresh salmon, a specialty of the famous Paris restaurant, Le Taillevent. With this, have the simplest of first courses, a delicate salad, and good hot rolls. To partner the mousse, drink either white Burgundy or the equivalent American wine.

MENU

Jellied Clam and Chicken Consommé, Topped with Red Caviar
Mousseline de Saumon, Sauce Venitienne
Salad of Endive Spears, Cucumber Fingers, and Avocado
with Herbed French Dressing
Hot Rolls
Cassata Siciliana

The Wine

Pouilly Fuissé or Pinot Chardonnay

MOUSSELINE DE SAUMON
[RUTH CONRAD BATEMAN]

12 ounces (net weight) fresh salmon, trimmed of all skin and bone
4 ounces (1 stick) softened sweet butter
3 egg yolks
1 egg
  Salt, white pepper
1 tablespoon lemon juice
1⅓ cups heavy cream

Pound the salmon in a mortar until smooth or put through a food grinder twice, using the finest blade. Work with a wooden spoon until very smooth. Gradually work in the butter until mixture is light, then egg yolks, one by one, and finally the whole egg. Season with about 1 teaspoon salt, a generous dash of white pepper, and the lemon juice. Force through a sieve and chill at least 30 minutes, until mixture becomes very firm. Mix in the cream. Spoon into 6 small, well-buttered molds or ramekins. Place in a pan containing 1 inch of hot water. Bake in a 350° oven 25 to 30 minutes, until mousselines are firm to the touch on top. Let stand a few minutes; invert over a warm serving plate. Cover with Sauce Venitienne (see below).

371

SAUCE VENITIENNE

½ cup dry white wine
¼ cup tarragon vinegar
1 cup hot thick Béchamel sauce made with fish stock (see page 418)
4 tablespoons heavy cream
1 tablespoon sweet butter
½ teaspoon mixed chopped chervil and tarragon

Reduce wine and vinegar by half over high heat. Add the hot sauce and swirl in the heavy cream and sweet butter bit by bit. When thoroughly mixed, add chervil and tarragon.

CASSATA SICILIANA
[ELAINE ROSS]

¼ cup light rum
¾ cup sugar
½ cup finely diced mixed candied fruits
1 frozen pound cake, thawed
1 pound ricotta or cottage cheese
1 teaspoon almond extract
1 ounce unsweetened chocolate, coarsely grated
6 candied cherries, halved

Mix the rum with ¼ cup of the sugar, pour over the mixed candied fruits and marinate for ½ hour. Drain the fruits, reserving the juice. Cut the cake into 6 equal layers. Sprinkle the reserved juice over the layers. Beat the cheese with the remaining sugar until very smooth and creamy. Stir in the almond extract, and fold in the drained fruit and the chocolate. Reassemble the cake, spreading the cheese filling between each layer and on the top and sides of the cake. Garnish with halved candied cherries. Chill.

Easter Dinner for Six

The season when baby lamb is in the markets is the time to make this Provençal gigot, which requires a small, tender leg, no larger than 5 pounds. A red Bordeaux is the traditional wine for lamb, but you could serve its California equivalent, or a fine red Burgundy.

MENU

Cheese Soufflé in a Tart Shell
Gigot in the Style of the Prieuré
Leeks Provençal
French Apple Meringue

The Wine

St. Emilion or California Cabernet Sauvignon;
Bonnes Mares or Chambertin

CHEESE SOUFFLÉ IN A TART SHELL
[ELAINE ROSS]

    1 recipe Pastry #1 (see page 423)
    2 tablespoons flour
   ⅛ teaspoon nutmeg
   ½ teaspoon prepared mustard
    1 cup milk
   ¼ pound Gruyère cheese, coarsely grated
   ¼ cup freshly grated Parmesan cheese
    4 eggs, separated
      Salt to taste
   ¼ teaspoon cream of tartar

Prepare the pastry, roll it out, and fit it into a 10″ pie plate. Flute the rim and prick the surface with a fork. Bake in a preheated 450° oven for 15 minutes.

Combine the flour and nutmeg in a saucepan. Add the mustard and milk and bring to a boil, stirring constantly. Cook until the sauce thickens, and remove from the heat. Add the cheeses, replace over the heat and cook, stirring constantly, until the cheeses are melted. Remove from the heat and add the egg yolks and salt. Beat the egg whites until foamy, add the cream of tartar, and beat until stiff. Fold into the cheese sauce, and pour into the partially baked tart shell. Bake the tart in a 375° oven for 25 minutes, or until the soufflé filling is puffed and golden.

GIGOT IN THE STYLE OF THE PRIEURÉ
[JAMES A. BEARD]

6 to 8 potatoes, peeled, thinly sliced and washed
Butter
1 small leg of lamb, about 4½ to 5 pounds
1 small onion, thinly sliced
Salt, freshly ground pepper
1 cup broth
3 cloves garlic, cut into slivers
1 teaspoon rosemary
Parmesan cheese (optional)

Dry the washed potato slices thoroughly. Butter a baking dish that is at least as long as the leg of lamb. Arrange the potato slices in layers, adding the onion slices after two layers. Season with salt and pepper to taste and dot each layer with butter. Add the broth.

Trim the leg of lamb well, pierce it with small gashes and insert the garlic. Rub with the rosemary, salt, and freshly ground pepper.

Place the roast on the potatoes or on the oven rack directly over the potatoes. Roast at 325° until the lamb is pinkish rare, about 135° internal temperature, and the potatoes nicely brown and crusty.

If the potatoes should be done first, remove and continue cooking the lamb. Return the potatoes to the oven for 10 minutes before serving. Then sprinkle with grated Parmesan cheese, if you wish.

LEEKS PROVENÇAL
[JAMES A. BEARD]

2 bunches leeks
⅓ cup olive oil
2 or 3 cloves garlic, sliced

4 tomatoes, peeled, seeded, and cut in sixths
25 to 30 soft black olives (preferably Italian or Greek), pitted
6 strips lemon zest
   Salt and freshly ground pepper

Clean leeks, trim off a little of the green part, and cut into 2" pieces. Heat olive oil in a skillet and cook leeks over brisk heat for 10 minutes. Add garlic, tomatoes, olives, lemon zest, and season with salt and pepper to taste. Continue to cook, covered, for 6 minutes longer.

FRENCH APPLE MERINGUE
[RUTH CONRAD BATEMAN]

1 cup plus 6 tablespoons sugar
1 tablespoon butter
1 tablespoon lemon juice
1½ cups water
4 large apples, peeled, cored, cut in halves crosswise
   Grated peel of 1 lemon
½ cup heavy cream, whipped
   Crème Pâtissière (see recipe below)
3 tablespoons macaroon crumbs
3 egg whites (left over from Crème Pâtissière)
   Dash of salt

Combine 1 cup sugar, butter, lemon juice, and water in saucepan and simmer 5 minutes. Add half the apple halves and poach gently until just tender, about 5 minutes. Turn once during cooking; remove carefully with slotted spoon to drain. Poach rest of apples. Fold lemon peel and whipped cream into cold Crème Pâtissière and spread about ⅓ of it in buttered baking dish (a 9" or 10" round oven-proof dish). Cover with apple halves; sprinkle with half the macaroon crumbs. Spread remaining cream evenly on top and scatter crumbs over it. Beat egg whites with salt until fluffy. Gradually beat in the 6 tablespoons sugar until whites are stiffly peaked. Swirl over crème, covering it completely. Bake in a 300° oven for about 25 to 30 minutes, or until meringue is golden and tinged with brown. Cool and chill.

CRÈME PÂTISSIÈRE

> 2 cups milk
> 4 egg yolks
> ¾ cup sugar
> 6 tablespoons flour
>   Dash of salt
> 1 tablespoon butter
> 2 teaspoons vanilla extract

Heat milk to boiling. Beat yolks in heavy saucepan. Gradually beat in sugar, flour, and salt. Slowly whisk in boiling milk until well blended. Set over moderate heat and cook, stirring constantly, until mixture reaches a boil. Turn heat very low. Cook 3 to 4 minutes, stirring constantly with a whisk. If lumps form, keep stirring until cream is smooth. Remove from heat and beat in butter and vanilla. Makes about 2½ cups.

Special Cocktail Party for Ten

This is the kind of superb menu you might serve if you are having just a few friends in before a theater party, a concert, a vernissage, or any other special occasion when some sustaining but not surfeiting food and drink is in order. The perfect tipple with this would be, of course, iced Russian vodka served in tiny glasses brought straight from the freezer.

MENU

Buckwheat Crêpes with Sesame Eggplant
Russian Piroshki with Mushroom Filling
Sturgeon and Caviar Sandwiches
Smoked Salmon Spread with Toast Fingers

BUCKWHEAT CRÊPES WITH SESAME EGGPLANT
[ELAINE ROSS]

2 eggs
¼ cup buckwheat flour
¼ cup white flour
¼ teaspoon salt
¼ cup water
½ cup milk
Sesame Eggplant (see recipe below)

Beat the eggs with a whisk. Add the buckwheat flour, white flour, and salt, and beat with a whisk until smooth. Gradually add the water, beating constantly until there are no lumps. Stir in the milk. Follow directions on page 425 for making crêpes. Fold the crêpes in half, speckled side in, then fold them in half again. (Each folded crêpe should be fan-shaped.) Serve the crêpes immediately, or keep them hot in the blazer of a chafing dish over hot water.

To serve the crêpes with cocktails, let each guest place a crêpe on a small plate and help himself to a spoonful of the cold eggplant to be eaten with the crêpe. Makes about 10 cocktail servings.

SESAME EGGPLANT

1 medium eggplant
2 tablespoons lemon juice
1 small clove garlic, mashed
4 teaspoons tahini (sesame seed paste) or mayonnaise
Salt to taste
1 tablespoon minced parsley

Bake the eggplant in a preheated 400° oven for 1¼ hours, or until tender. Peel off the skin, mash the pulp, and add all the ingredients except the parsley. Place in a serving bowl, sprinkle the parsley on top, and chill.

RUSSIAN PIROSHKI WITH MUSHROOM FILLING
[KAY SHAW NELSON]

    1 cake or package yeast
    1 cup lukewarm milk
    2 teaspoons sugar
      Salt
    ¼ cup melted butter
    3 eggs, well beaten
    5 cups sifted flour
    ½ pound mushrooms
    2 tablespoons butter
    1 medium onion, chopped
      Pepper
    ¼ teaspoon paprika
    2 tablespoons chopped dill
    ¼ cup sour cream
    1 egg yolk, well beaten

Put yeast in a large bowl with 2 tablespoons of the lukewarm milk, and stir to dissolve. Add sugar, 1 teaspoon salt, melted butter, and eggs to the remaining milk and mix well. Mix in dissolved yeast. Add the flour, 1 cup at a time, stirring well after each addition. Knead well on a floured board until smooth and elastic. Form into a large ball, and place in a buttered bowl, turning over once to grease top. Let rise, covered, in a warm (80°) place for 1½ hours.

Meanwhile, wash and dry the mushrooms and cut off tough stem ends. Chop. Melt the 2 tablespoons butter in a skillet, add the onion and sauté 1 minute. Add the chopped mushrooms, salt and pepper to taste, and paprika, and sauté 4 minutes. Remove from heat and drain off any juices. Add the dill and sour cream. Mix well and cool.

Punch down the risen dough. Remove to a floured board and knead. Pinch off small pieces, large enough to flatten into a thin 3″ circle. Place 1 teaspoon mushroom filling in the center of each. Bring up dough around filling and close securely, shaping into a smooth round. Place on a greased cookie sheet and let rise for 15 minutes in a warm place. Brush with beaten egg yolk. Bake in a 400° oven for about 20 minutes, until done. Makes about 35 piroshki.

STURGEON SANDWICHES

This novel treatment of smoked sturgeon was invented for a great dinner at The Four Seasons in New York. Spread fresh caviar between two thin slices of choice sturgeon, top with paper-thin half slices of cucumber, and serve with lemon wedges.

SMOKED SALMON SPREAD
[JAMES A. BEARD]

> 1 pound smoked salmon, preferably Nova Scotia
> 1 medium onion, peeled and thinly sliced
> 1 tablespoon capers
> 2 teaspoons chopped fresh dill or 1 teaspoon dill weed
> 1 cup sour cream or ½ cup sour cream and ½ cup mayonnaise
> Freshly ground black pepper
> Chopped parsley

Cut the salmon into thin strips and mix with onion, capers, dill, sour cream, and, if you like, mayonnaise. Blend well, spoon into crocks, and top with pepper and chopped parsley. Cover and chill. To serve, arrange crocks on platters, surrounded with toast fingers.

A Small Cocktail Party for Twelve to Sixteen

At a cocktail party for a limited number of guests, the food assumes more importance, for people are more inclined to sample than just to stand around drinking and talking. This is the time to make some rather special things that would be impractical for a large group. Remember, too, always to have aperitifs, chilled white wine, and a good club soda, in addition to the usual mixed drinks and liquor.

379

MENU

Curry Cocktail Almonds   *Cheese Truffles*
Smoked Salmon Pastry Rolls
Truffled Chicken Liver Strudel
Shrimp Pâté

CURRY COCKTAIL ALMONDS
[RUTH CONRAD BATEMAN]

Heat ¼ cup butter in a skillet. Add 2 cups blanched almonds and cook, stirring often with wooden spoon, about 10 minutes. Sprinkle liberally with curry powder and cook until nuts are a rich tawny gold, about 10 minutes longer. Fish out a hot almond and break or cut it to test if it is completely, but lightly, roasted all the way through. Drain on paper towels and sprinkle while hot with coarse salt (Kosher or sea salt if available). To keep hot, place salted almonds in the dry outer or water pan of a chafing dish over a very low flame.

NOTE: Walnuts, almonds, pecans, or filberts may also be used with any of the following seasonings: chili powder, ginger, mustard, allspice, Beau Monde.

CHEESE TRUFFLES
[KAY SHAW NELSON]

    ¼ pound butter, softened
    ¼ pound grated Gouda or Edam cheese
    ¼ teaspoon paprika
       Salt, freshly ground pepper, grated nutmeg to taste
    3 to 4 slices pumpernickel

Combine the butter, cheese, paprika, salt, pepper, and nutmeg, and mix well. Chill 20 minutes. Shape into small balls. Chill 30 minutes. Toast the pumpernickel twice and whirl in a blender or crush with a rolling pin to make crumbs. Roll each cheese ball in the crumbs. Makes about 20.

SMOKED SALMON PASTRY ROLLS
[PHILIP S. BROWN]

    Pastry for 2-crust pie (see page 423)
½ to ¾ pound thinly sliced smoked salmon
½ cup minced green onion
    Freshly ground black pepper
1 egg, slightly beaten

Divide pastry and roll out into two 9″ circles. Completely cover with slices of smoked salmon, smoothing and spreading with your hands. Sprinkle evenly with the onion and grind on plenty of black pepper. Cut each circle into 16 wedges with a sharp knife. Beginning at the outside edge, roll each wedge tightly. Arrange on a lightly buttered baking sheet, and brush the rolls with the beaten egg. Bake in a 400° oven for 15 to 20 minutes, or until nicely browned. Serve hot. Makes 32 rolls.

TRUFFLED CHICKEN LIVER STRUDEL
[ELAINE ROSS]

1 large onion, diced
3 tablespoons rendered chicken fat or butter
½ pound chicken livers
    Salt, freshly ground black pepper
3 hard-cooked eggs, coarsely chopped
½ cup mashed avocado
3 tablespoons minced truffle
    Salt, pepper
1 package strudel leaves, defrosted
3 tablespoons melted butter
¼ cup fine dry bread crumbs
1 egg yolk mixed with 1 teaspoon water

Sauté the onion in the fat in a heavy skillet over medium heat for 10 minutes, or until tender. Add the livers and sauté 5 minutes longer. Remove from the heat and add ½ teaspoon salt, ⅛ teaspoon pepper, and eggs. Grind the mixture in a meat grinder, using the finest blade, or chop in a wooden bowl. Adjust seasonings.

Mix the liver, avocado, and truffle. Add salt and pepper to taste. Remove 2 strudel leaves from the package and place each leaf on a dampened cloth a little larger than the leaf. Carefully brush the surface of the leaves with melted butter and sprinkle them with bread crumbs. On one leaf place the liver filling along the edge nearest you, leaving an inch uncovered at each end. Fold the uncovered ends over the filling to enclose it. Take hold of the end of the cloth nearest you and lift it slightly. As you do so, the strudel will roll up away from you. Place a well-buttered baking sheet at the other end of the cloth so that the last roll will deposit the strudel on the sheet. Repeat with the second leaf. Brush the tops and sides of the strudels with the egg mixture and bake in a 400° oven for 15 minutes, or until golden brown. Cut each roll in 12 slices and serve immediately. Makes 24 servings.

SHRIMP PÂTÉ
[MYRA WALDO]

    2 cups beer
 1½ teaspoons salt
    1 stalk celery
 1½ pounds raw shrimp, shelled and deveined
   ¼ cup parsley
    3 tablespoons diced onion
   ½ cup diced green pepper
   ⅓ cup heavy cream
    1 tablespoon lemon juice
   ⅛ teaspoon Tabasco sauce

Bring the beer, salt, and celery to a boil. Add the shrimp; cook over low heat 5 minutes. Let cool in the beer 20 minutes. Drain.

Combine the shrimp, parsley, onion, green pepper, cream, lemon juice and Tabasco in blender and whirl until mixture is very fine and smooth. Pack into a mold and chill. Serve with crackers or toast.

Hawaiian Pupu Cocktail Party for Thirty or More

In Hawaii, the finger foods for drinks, without which no party is complete, are called pupus, and they draw on a mixed heritage—Chinese, Japanese, Korean, Polynesian, American, plus some that are purely native to the islands. They are easily made in quantity, according to the size of the party, and you might choose from a representative selection of the recipes below, based on your guest list. Pupus lend themselves especially well to a big outdoor cocktail buffet by the pool or on the terrace. You might have a long trestle table covered with tatami matting or a mantle of fresh green leaves stapled to cardboard as your buffet base.

MENU
[HELEN EVANS BROWN]

Cream Cheese Balls with Ginger and Coconut

Ham and Pineapple on Skewers   *Grab Bag Dip*   *Avocado Dip*

Shrimp Tempura   *Char Siu*   *Yakitori*   *Teriyaki*   *Sashimi*

Lomi Salmon   *Korean Meat Balls*   *Crisp Won Ton*   *Poisson Cru*

CREAM CHEESE BALLS WITH GINGER AND COCONUT

Mix a small package of cream cheese with 1 teaspoon of grated fresh ginger, ½ teaspoon of soy sauce and ½ teaspoon of sugar. Chill, form into small balls and roll in freshly grated coconut. Serve on toothpicks. This makes 10 to 12 balls.

HAM AND PINEAPPLE ON SKEWERS

Wrap chunks of pineapple with thinly sliced ham and string on skewers. Brush with teriyaki sauce (see page 386) and broil, turning and basting, until the ham browns. Roll in finely chopped macadamia nuts and serve.

GRAB BAG DIP
[YOSHIE OKAMOTO]

In a hot sauce in a chafing dish, bury all kinds of interesting tidbits: crisp little cocktail sausages, pickled mushrooms, pickled onions, meat balls, hot cooked shrimp, ripe olives, little cubes of crispy pork, cooked chicken livers (you can add whatever suits your fancy). The guests, armed with toothpicks, fish around in the sauce and spear a goody. The same sauce may be used cold, with such hidden treasures as raw scallops, cherry tomatoes, cooked shrimp, cold ripe olives, water chestnuts, raw vegetables or whatever. For the sauce, combine 2 cups of ready-made mayonnaise, ½ cup of drained prepared grated horseradish, ½ teaspoon of Ajinomoto (monosodium glutamate), 2 teaspoons of dry mustard (hot), 2 teaspoons of lemon juice, and ½ teaspoon salt. Mix all together. Of course, you can make it hotter, if you wish, or milder, according to taste, but it should have authority.

AVOCADO DIP

  1 ripe avocado
  1 teaspoon lemon juice
  1 tablespoon mayonnaise
  ¼ teaspoon puréed garlic
  ½ teaspoon salt
  ¼ teaspoon monosodium glutamate
   Dash of Tabasco sauce

Peel and mash avocado smooth. Combine with other ingredients, taste and correct seasoning to your preference. Serve with potato or corn chips, crackers or raw vegetables for dipping.

SHRIMP TEMPURA

Tempura is any food dipped in a light batter and fried in deep fat. The most popular of all in Hawaii is shrimp, which is often used as an appetizer.

  1 pound large raw shrimp
  1 cup flour
  ½ teaspoon salt
  1 egg
  ¾ cup water or milk
   Oil for frying

Shell and clean shrimp and split part way down the back. Open and flatten slightly. Lightly mix flour, salt, egg and water or milk to a medium batter. Don't overmix. Dip shrimp in batter and then deep fry at 375° until lightly browned. Drain and serve with Japanese soy sauce to which grated daikon (Japanese radish) and ginger have been added.

CHAR SIU (CHINESE RED PORK)

> 2 pounds boneless pork in one piece, 1″ thick
> ½ teaspoon Five Spices
> 1 clove garlic, crushed
> 1 tablespoon sherry
> 1 tablespoon honey
> 3 tablespoons shoyu sauce
> 2 tablespoons red bean curd (optional)
> ¼ teaspoon red coloring

The pork may be from the butt or loin, or the tenderloin may be used. It should be in one piece, preferably square or oblong. Marinate for 2 or 3 hours in remaining ingredients (if red bean curd is not used, increase amount of red food coloring). Turn once during marinating. Put 1 cup of water in a roasting pan with a rack, put pork on rack and roast in a 300° oven for 2 hours, or until a meat thermometer registers 175° to 180°, brushing two or three times with the marinade. Slice and serve hot or cold.

NOTE: Five Spices or 5-Spice Powder is available in Chinese markets.

YAKITORI

> 2-pound broiling chicken
> 1 bunch green onions (optional)
> ¼ pound chicken livers (optional)
> ½ cup Japanese soy sauce
> 1 teaspoon grated fresh ginger
> 1 tablespoon peanut or sesame oil
> ¼ cup sake or sherry
> Toasted sesame seeds

Bone chicken and cut in 1½″ pieces. If used, cut onions in 1½″ lengths and chicken livers in half. String chicken, onion and livers on small bamboo skewers, and marinate in next four ingredients. Broil over charcoal, turning and basting with the marinade once or twice. Do not overcook; the chicken should be juicy, not dry. Dip in toasted sesame seeds before eating.

TERIYAKI

> 1 cup good soy sauce
> 2 tablespoons sugar
> 1 clove garlic, puréed or grated
> 1 small piece fresh ginger, grated
> ¼ cup sherry or sake

Combine soy sauce, sugar, garlic, ginger, and simmer 5 minutes. Add sherry or sake. Cut pieces of beef or pork, trimmed of all fat, into bite-size pieces, string them on bamboo skewers and marinate in the teriyaki sauce for an hour or so. Drain and broil over charcoal, basting with the marinade, until cooked to your liking. The meat may also be cut in strips and woven on the skewers.

SASHIMI

Sashimi, which is raw fish (or sometimes chicken), is a delicious and popular pupu borrowed from Japan. Albacore (tuna), sea bass, halibut, swordfish or similar firm fish can be used. Remove the skin and any dark portion and slice diagonally about ¼" thick (the Japanese often slice it thicker, but this doesn't appeal to Occidental palates). Cut the fish in strips and on one end put a little heap of shredded vegetables. You may use lettuce, Chinese cabbage, radish, daikon, celery, or even cucumber or green onions. Chill thoroughly and serve with a dipping sauce made with ½ cup of Japanese soy sauce and 2 teaspoons of grated fresh ginger or horseradish or mustard.

NOTE: For sashimi, the fish must be absolutely fresh.

LOMI SALMON

In the early days, salt salmon was used in this dish because it was the only kind available in the Islands. It was soaked in cold water for 3 hours or more to desalt it. The same result can be had by soaking fresh salmon in salted water (1 tablespoon to 1 cup) overnight.

1 pound fresh salmon (soaked as above)
2 pounds ripe tomatoes
½ cup minced onion
1 bunch green onions
  Cherry tomatoes or cucumbers

Remove skin and bones from salmon and shred finely or "lomi" with the fingers. ("Lomi" means massage—in this case, squeezing with the hands until the fish is pulped.) Skin the ripe tomatoes and mash to a pulp or dice very fine. Combine with salmon and onion. Slice green onions thin, including tender part of green tops. Combine with salmon and add salt if needed. Chill thoroughly. (For a finer texture, the salmon, tomatoes and onion may be worked together to a purée with the hands.) To serve as pupu, scoop out cherry tomatoes or make cucumber cups and fill with lomi salmon. To make cucumber cups, peel slender cucumbers with a garnishing (fluted) knife, cut in 1″ sections, and scoop out part of the insides.

KOREAN MEAT BALLS

1 egg
2 tablespoons milk
1 teaspoon sugar
2 tablespoons soy sauce
½ teaspoon salt
¼ teaspoon monosodium glutamate
¼ teaspoon Tabasco sauce (or more, to taste)
½ cup fresh bread crumbs
1 clove garlic, puréed
¼ cup chopped onion
1 pound ground beef

Combine all ingredients and mix well. Shape into tiny cakes (about 30) and broil a minute. Turn and broil other side until done to your liking. Serve on toothpicks, with a sashimi sauce for dipping, if desired, or use in Grab Bag. Or make a vinegar sauce with 3 tablespoons each of shoyu sauce and vinegar, ¼ clove garlic, puréed, 1 tablespoon minced green onion, and 1 teaspoon of toasted crushed sesame seeds.

NOTE: For toasted crushed sesame seeds, brown the seeds in a heavy skillet, then crush to powder in a mortar with a pestle.

CRISP WON TON

Won ton squares may be purchased at Chinese stores. Or you can make them by mixing 3 cups of flour and 2 teaspoons of salt with 2 slightly beaten eggs and enough warm water to make a stiff dough. Knead well. Cover and let stand in a warm place for an hour, then roll thinner than paper, using cornstarch to keep from sticking. A Chinese method is to roll thin, sprinkle heavily with cornstarch, then roll the paste up on the rolling pin; continue to roll the pin back and forth, thus rolling 3 or 4 layers at once. Unroll and cut in 3½" squares.

FILLING FOR 100 WON TON SQUARES

    1 pound ground pork
    ½ pound ground raw shrimp
    ¼ cup minced green onions
    ¼ cup water chestnuts
    ¼ teaspoon monosodium glutamate
    2 teaspoons shoyu sauce
    1 teaspoon salt

Mix ingredients thoroughly. Put a rounded ½ teaspoon of filling in the center of each won ton square; fold diagonally, and then cross opposite points and press firmly together. Put on paper lightly sprinkled with cornstarch until all are folded. (Don't allow won ton to touch one another.) Fry in deep fat at 360° until nicely browned. Drain on paper towels and serve at once.

POISSON CRU

This is raw fish as served in Tahiti, now very popular in Hawaii.

    1 pound raw, boned corvina, red snapper, swordfish, bonito, or other fine-grained whitefish, thinly sliced or 1 pound raw bay scallops
    1 teaspoon coarse salt (Hawaiian or kosher)
    ¾ cup lime or lemon juice
    3 tablespoons minced onion

1 clove garlic, puréed
2 dashes Tabasco sauce (or more, to taste)
1¼ cups Coconut Cream (see recipe below)

Cut fish into fingers 2″ long and 1″ wide. Sprinkle with salt and cover with lime juice. Mix well, cover and refrigerate 5 to 6 hours. Pour off all but a small amount of the liquid. Add remaining ingredients, but only ¼ cup of the coconut cream. Mix again and chill. Have remaining coconut cream in a bowl. Serve fish on cocktail picks, and serve the coconut cream as a dip.

COCONUT MILK OR COCONUT CREAM

For the most part these two terms are interchangeable in the Islands. (The water inside a coconut is sometimes called coconut milk, but this is a misnomer.) Coconut milk is easily made: Grate fresh coconut until you have 4 cups; pour 2 cups of boiling water (part may be the liquid from the nut) over it and let stand ½ hour. Strain through a piece of strong white cloth, squeezing and pressing to extract all liquid. Put in a jar and store in the refrigerator.

Although many Hawaiians do not distinguish coconut cream from the milk, to some it means the thick creamy part that rises to the top of the coconut milk when it is thoroughly chilled.

Cocktail Supper for Forty to Fifty

This is the kind of all-evening cocktail party that really stands in for dinner. Begin with appetizers of the finger-food type at six o'clock, and then, for guests who are making an evening of it, serve more solid food around eight-thirty. For this you might order a roast of beef or corned beef and pastrami from a local delicatessen, to be served with mustards, horseradish, breads and butter and perhaps some homemade spiced onions. When you feel it is time to break up the party, tactfully close the bar and bring on very strong black coffee, with small cookies.

MENU

Curried Bananas and Bacon   Ginny Sausages
Celery and Raw Mushroom Caps Stuffed with Roquefort Butter
Shrimp and Raw Vegetables with Curry Dip
Roast Beef with a Selection of Mustards

or

Hot Corned Beef and Pastrami with Mustards and Horseradish
Sour Dill Pickles, Sliced in Fingers
Spiced Onions
Selection of Breads with Crocks of Sweet Butter
Coffee and Nut Crescents

CURRIED BANANAS AND BACON
[MILTON WILLIAMS]

Cut bananas into pieces the width of a strip of bacon. Roll in curry powder and a little lemon juice and wrap ½ slice of bacon around banana, attaching with a toothpick. Bake on a rack in a 375° oven until the bacon is almost cooked. Dip in chutney, return to oven for 5 to 10 minutes. Serve immediately.

GINNY SAUSAGES
[RUTH CONRAD BATEMAN]

    1 tablespoon butter
    1 pound pork link sausages (part may be small smoked links)
    3 tablespoons gin

Heat butter in a skillet. Prick sausages and place in pan. Add 2 tablespoons gin; cover and heat until sausages are plump, about 5 minutes. Remove cover and cook, turning often, until most of gin has been absorbed and sausages are browned. Pour rest of gin over sausages and flame. Serve when flames die.

To serve as appetizer, cut sausages into bite-size chunks. Spear with picks and keep hot.

ROQUEFORT BUTTER
[JAMES A. BEARD]

½ pound or more butter, to taste
1 pound cream cheese
2 pounds Roquefort cheese (with as much blue vein as possible)
⅓ to ½ cup cognac, to taste

Cream the butter with the cream cheese. Crumble the Roquefort cheese and blend thoroughly with the butter-cheese mixture. Beat in the cognac spoonful by spoonful. Finely chopped garlic or Dijon mustard may also be added, to taste.

CURRY DIP
[JAMES A. BEARD]

1 large onion, finely chopped
5 tablespoons butter
1 apple, unpeeled, cored, and finely chopped
2 ribs celery, finely chopped
1 to 2 tablespoons curry powder
Salt
1 cup tomato juice
2 tablespoons tomato paste
1 tablespoon chutney, finely chopped

Sauté the onion in the butter, add the apple and celery, and cook down for a short time, until the apple is tender. Add curry powder; the sauce should be quite hot. Add salt to taste, blend, and cook for 3 minutes. Add tomato juice and paste, and cook for another 4 to 5 minutes. Finally stir in the chutney. Makes about 2 cups.

The sauce should be served hot. It is wonderful with such things as tiny meat balls, crab legs, shrimp, scallops, and raw vegetables.

SPICED ONIONS
[JAMES A. BEARD]

> 5 pounds small white onions
> Salt
> Rock alum
> 1 pint white wine
> 1 quart cider vinegar
> 1 pint white wine vinegar
> 1½ pounds sugar
> 1 package pickling spices
> 2 bay leaves

Peel the onions and cover with water to which you have added 1½ cups salt. Allow to stand for 24 hours. Place a large lump of alum in a crock or large jar, if you are using a single container, or a small lump of alum in each of several small jars. Drain the onions well and put them in the crock or pack into the jars. Combine the wine, the vinegars, and the sugar, and bring to a boil. Add the spices and bay leaves, and boil for 5 minutes. Pour over the onions and cover with a lid. Allow to stand for at least 2 weeks. Makes about 8 pints.

NUT CRESCENTS
[ELAINE ROSS]

> ½ pound sweet butter
> 1 cup confectioners' sugar
> 1 egg
> ½ teaspoon vanilla
> 2 cups flour
> ½ teaspoon baking powder
> 1 cup walnuts, very finely chopped

Cream the butter with 6 tablespoons of the sugar. Beat in the egg and vanilla. Sift the flour with the baking powder and add to the creamed mixture with the chopped nuts. Chill the dough for 1 hour, or until firm enough to handle. Break off pieces of dough and roll between the palms of your hands into baguettes with tapered ends. (It may be necessary to flour your hands lightly.) Bend each baguette into a crescent and place on an ungreased cookie sheet. Bake in a preheated 375° oven for 12 minutes. Sprinkle a little of the remaining confectioners' sugar on a board. Place the baked cookies, close together, on the board. Sift the remaining sugar over them. Makes about 5 dozen cookies.

NOTE: These cookies may be made ahead and frozen.

Mid-Morning Coffee Party for Ten or More

A simple menu for a morning when you are having your charity ball committee or similar group over to discuss plans. You might have a choice of yoghurt cocktails for the weight-watchers and Russian fruit kissel for those who don't have to worry about the pounds.

MENU

Yoghurt Cocktails

Russian Fruit Kissel

Cinnamon Buns with Honey-Bee Topping

Coffee

YOGHURT COCKTAILS
[ALEX D. HAWKES]

Purée cold plain yoghurt with fresh, frozen, or canned fruit (raspberries, strawberries, blueberries, bananas), and blend in cold milk and, if needed, a touch of sugar. Serve in tall glasses.

RUSSIAN FRUIT KISSEL
[ALEX D. HAWKES]

Use fresh or canned fruits of your choice, perhaps in combination. Simmer until tender, purée, blend in a bit of dissolved cornstarch, and cook over medium heat, stirring constantly, until thickened and clear. Pour into glass serving dishes or stem glasses, and chill thoroughly. Top with whipped cream.

CINNAMON BUNS WITH HONEY-BEE TOPPING
[MRS. RALPH BAILEY]

 1¼ cups milk
  2 cakes compressed yeast
 4½ cups all-purpose flour, sifted
   Butter
  1 cup sugar
  2 large or 3 medium eggs
  1 teaspoon salt
  2 teaspoons grated lemon rind
   Cinnamon and sugar
  ¼ cup honey
  ½ cup crushed nuts

Heat 1 cup of the milk to lukewarm and dissolve the yeast in it. Stir in 1 cup of the flour. Cover and allow to rise in a warm place about 30 minutes. Beat 1¼ cups butter until it is soft and add ½ cup of the sugar gradually. Blend until the mixture is light and creamy. Beat in the eggs one at a time. Add the salt and lemon rind. Add the yeast sponge mixture and beat.

Gradually beat in the remaining 3½ cups of flour and continue beating for 5 minutes (an old-fashioned bread mixer is good for this). Cover the bowl with a cloth and let rise in a warm place until the dough has doubled in bulk, about 2 hours. Turn out on a floured board and roll the dough to a thickness of ¼". Melt some butter and spread generously on the dough. Sprinkle with a mixture of cinnamon and sugar. Roll the dough jelly-roll fashion and cut in 1" slices. Grease a square or rectangular roasting pan. Place each slice cut side down in the pan and let rise for ½ hour. (If you wish, you may freeze the buns at this point. Cover with freezer paper and place in the freezer. Remove 3 hours before baking.) Prepare the topping by combining the remaining ½ cup sugar, ¼ cup milk, ¼ cup butter, and the honey. Spread on the buns and top with the crushed nuts. Bake in a 350° oven for 30 minutes. Makes about 24 buns.

Coffee and Dessert Party for Twelve to Sixteen

If you want to entertain more friends than you can seat for dinner, it's a good idea to have them in for late-evening coffee, dessert, and liqueurs. For dessert shunners, Irish coffee, sweet and rich, is a satisfying substitute.

MENU

Frozen Mousse Grand Marnier   *Tortoni Tart*

Choice of Liqueurs, Cognac, White Fruit Brandies

Espresso   *Irish Coffee*   *Café Brûlot*

FROZEN MOUSSE GRAND MARNIER
[RUTH CONRAD BATEMAN]

  2 egg whites
    Salt
  6 tablespoons sugar
  1 cup heavy cream
  ¼ cup Grand Marnier liqueur

Beat egg whites with a pinch of salt until softly peaked, then gradually beat in ¼ cup sugar until meringue is stiff and shiny. With same beater, whip cream until stiff, then beat in rest of sugar. Gently blend in Grand Marnier. Fold in egg whites. Turn into a 1-quart mold or individual molds and freeze until firm, several hours. Unmold and serve with Berry Sauce (see below). Makes 4 to 6 servings.

BERRY SAUCE

Defrost a 10-ounce package of frozen strawberries and a 10-ounce package of frozen raspberries just enough to drain excess juices. Purée in a blender until smooth. Strain and add Grand Marnier to taste.

VARIATIONS: 1. Substitute any favorite liqueur—Curaçao, framboise,

395

crème de menthe, Triple Sec, Cointreau, Kahlua, or the fruit-flavored brandies—for the Grand Marnier. Adjust sugar accordingly.

2. For Tropical Rum Mousse, omit liqueur and sauce. Instead, drain and purée in blender a 1-pound can tropical fruit salad (papaya, pineapple, banana, guava). Add 2 tablespoons golden rum, 1 teaspoon lemon juice. Fold into meringue, and then fold in whipped cream.

TORTONI TART
[ELAINE ROSS]

>   1 recipe Pastry #2 (see page 423)
>   2 egg whites
>   ¼ cup sugar
> 1⅔ cups heavy cream
>   ⅓ cup confectioners' sugar
>   ½ teaspoon vanilla
>   ½ teaspoon almond extract
>   1 cup almond macaroon crumbs
>   ⅓ cup blanched almonds, finely chopped
>   Crystallized violets

Prepare pastry, roll it out and line a 9½″ or 10″ pie plate with it. Flute the rim and prick the bottom with a fork. Bake in a preheated 450° oven for 10 minutes. Reduce heat to 375°. Bake 7 to 10 minutes, or until golden. Cool completely.

Beat the egg whites until stiff. Gradually add the sugar and beat until thick and glossy. Beat the cream until thick, add the confectioners' sugar, vanilla, and almond extract, and beat until stiff. Fold in the macaroon crumbs, chopped almonds, and meringue. Freeze until the mixture starts to set around the edges, spoon into the cooled crust, decorate with crystallized violets, and replace in the freezer for 4 hours, or until firm. Remove from the freezer 5 to 10 minutes before serving. Makes 8 to 10 servings.

IRISH COFFEE

(see page 165)

CAFÉ BRÛLOT

Put 4 cubes of sugar, 2 cloves, 1 slice of lemon peel and 1 slice of orange peel, and a piece of cinnamon stick in the blazer pan of a chafing dish. Add 1½ cups cognac and heat. Warm a ladle and dip up some of the cognac, add a lump of sugar and ignite. When flaming, lower the ladle into the pan to light the rest of the brandy. Immediately pour in 3 cups very strong black coffee and blend with the spiced cognac by ladling up some of the mixture and then pouring it back. When the flames have subsided, serve the coffee in demitasse cups. Makes about 12 demitasse servings.

Garden Tea Party for Eight to Twelve

A summer tea party in the garden is one answer to the problem of how to find something to suit all age groups, from small children to grandparents, because everyone likes sandwiches, cookies, and cake. Provide milk if there are going to be children present.

MENU

Open-Face Sandwiches—Cream Cheese and Radish,
Liver Pâté with Capers, Smoked Salmon with Dill
Minced Chicken Sandwiches
Cucumber Sandwiches   *Watercress Sandwiches*
Fresh Lemon Cookies   *Shortbread Fingers*
Fruited Pound Cake

Choice of Teas

Lapsang Souchong, Jasmine, Keemun

CREAM CHEESE AND RADISH
[ELAINE ROSS]

>8 slices firm-textured white bread
> Heavy cream
>¼ pound cream cheese, softened
>1 bunch radishes, sliced paper-thin (discard end slices)

Cut 8 circles 2½″ in diameter from the bread with a glass or cookie cutter. Add enough cream to the softened cream cheese to bring it to a spreading consistency. Spread over the circles of bread. Place the radish slices, slightly overlapping, around the edge of each sandwich. Makes 8 sandwiches.

LIVER PÂTÉ WITH CAPERS
[ELAINE ROSS]

>4 squares light pumpernickel bread, trimmed
> Butter
>6 ounces liver pâté or fine liver sausage
>2 hard-cooked egg yolks
> Drained capers

Cut each slice of bread in half. Spread lightly with butter and cover with a slice of pâté or spread with liver sausage. Mash the egg yolks with enough butter to make them of spreading consistency and fill into a small pastry bag fitted with a small star-shaped opening. Pipe 2 lines, ½″ apart and crosswise, across the center of the pâté. Fill the space between with capers. Makes 8 sandwiches.

NOTE: Due to the difference in size of bread slices, the amounts of spreading ingredients given can only be approximate.

SMOKED SALMON WITH DILL
[ELAINE ROSS]

>4 square slices light or dark pumpernickel bread, crusts trimmed
> Sweet butter
>6 ounces (approximately) lightly salted smoked salmon, thinly sliced

8 thin slices lemon
16 sprigs dill, stems removed
Mayonnaise

Cut each slice of bread in half. Spread lightly with butter and cover with slices of salmon. Cut the lemon slices almost in half, twist each slice and place on the center of the salmon. Flank each twist of lemon with 2 sprigs of dill by inserting the stem end of the dill under the center of the lemon. Pipe small rosettes of mayonnaise in each corner. Makes 8 sandwiches.

MINCED CHICKEN SANDWICHES
[JAMES A. BEARD]

Make filling in proportions of ¾ cup minced chicken to ¼ cup chopped walnuts or dry salted peanuts with enough mayonnaise to bind the mixture together. Taste for seasoning and add salt, if needed, and freshly ground black pepper. Spread on slices of buttered thin white sandwich bread. Top with another buttered slice of bread, press together, trim off crusts and cut into quarters or fingers.

CUCUMBER SANDWICHES
[JAMES A. BEARD]

Peel and seed cucumbers and slice thinly. Soak in water with a little salt and sugar for an hour. Drain thoroughly and dry on paper towels. Arrange on thinly sliced buttered brown or white bread, season with salt and freshly ground black pepper. Top with another buttered slice of bread, press together, trim off crusts and cut into quarters.

WATERCRESS SANDWICHES
[JAMES A. BEARD]

Spread thinly sliced white or brown bread with sweet butter and cut into strips. Place sprigs of watercress on each strip and roll it up, so some of the leaves peek out at each end. Chill.

FRESH LEMON COOKIES
[ELAINE ROSS]

> 1 lemon, peeled and seeded
> 1 egg
> 1 tablespoon sour cream
> ¼ pound butter
> 1 cup sugar
> 1½ cups flour
> ¼ teaspoon baking soda
> ½ teaspoon baking powder
> ¼ teaspoon mace
> ⅓ cup confectioners' sugar
> 1 teaspoon lemon juice
> Candied lemon peel, cut in small squares

Cut the lemon pulp into pieces and place in the container of an electric blender with the egg, sour cream, butter, and sugar. Whirl in the blender, scraping down the sides with a rubber spatula, until the mixture is smooth. Sift the flour, baking soda, baking powder, and mace into a bowl, add butter mixture and stir until blended.

Drop rounded half teaspoons of the batter 1" apart on greased cookie sheets. Bake in a preheated 350° oven for 12 to 15 minutes, or until light brown around the edges and on the bottom. Cool on a board. Mix the confectioners' sugar and lemon juice and drop a little on the center of each cookie. Place small squares of candied lemon peel on the frosting. Allow to dry before packing in airtight tins. Store in tins for a few days. For longer storage, put these lemon cookies in the freezer. Makes about 5 dozen cookies.

SHORTBREAD FINGERS
[JAMES A. BEARD]

> 1 cup butter
> 1 cup granulated sugar
> 2 cups cake flour
> Pinch salt

Cream the butter and sugar together well, gradually add the flour and salt, and blend thoroughly. Form into squares and decorate, if you like, with bits of candied fruit. Place on a lightly buttered cookie sheet. Bake in a 350° oven until lightly browned—about 25 to 30 minutes. Cut the squares into fingers while still warm. Makes about 2 dozen.

FRUITED POUND CAKE
[CATHRINE HINDLEY]

2 to 2½ cups (1 pound) mixed candied fruits
1 cup white or golden raisins
½ cup halved candied cherries
1 cup coarsely chopped, lightly toasted pecans, almonds, walnuts, filberts, or Brazil nuts
8 standard-size eggs (1 pound), separated
2 cups (1 pound) butter
2 cups (1 pound) sugar
1 teaspoon vanilla or 2 tablespoons brandy or sherry
2 teaspoons grated orange rind
4½ cups sifted cake flour (1 pound) or 4 cups sifted all-purpose flour (1 pound)
¼ teaspoon salt
Honey or corn syrup for glazing

Combine fruits and nuts in mixing bowl, tossing lightly to mix well. Have all remaining ingredients, except eggs, at room temperature. Separate eggs while cold and place whites in medium-size bowl or small bowl of electric mixer.

Butter 2 loaf-cake pans 9½″ x 5½″ x 3″ or a 10″ tube pan and line bottom with buttered paper. Preheat oven to 300°.

Cream butter very well in an electric mixer. Gradually beat in sugar and continue beating until very fluffy. Beat in egg yolks one or two at a time. If mixing by hand, beat egg yolks until very light and pale yellow before adding to mixture. Add vanilla flavoring or brandy or sherry and rind. Sift flour with salt several times to incorporate as much air as possible and stir into creamed mixture until well combined. Beat egg whites until stiff but not dry. Fold the egg whites into the cake batter until just combined. Fold in fruits and nuts and divide between the 2 prepared loaf pans or put into the tube pan. Bake loaf pans about 1½ to 1¾ hours, or tube pan for about 2 hours. Test by touching cake center lightly. When it springs back it is done. Glaze cake with honey or corn syrup just before removing from oven, if desired. Remove to rack to cool in pans. When cool, brush with brandy or sherry or rum, if desired, and slip into freezer bags or into a tightly covered cake box. Age at least 1 week before storing in refrigerator. This cake freezes very successfully.

Big Parties with Small Price Tags

Who can afford to give a big party in these days of high food prices? All those who exercise their imagination and common sense. It is perfectly possible to entertain a large group of people quite inexpensively and not too arduously, provided you keep to good, simple food that can be prepared in quantity.

Think in terms of market bargains like chicken and turkey, hamburger and sausages, eggs and cheese, less costly meat cuts that can be boned and stuffed, and then look for interesting and appetizing ways to prepare them. The cuisines of the world offer hundreds of dishes that stretch the protein part of the menu with inexpensive ingredients such as dried beans, lentils and chick-peas, root vegetables, pasta, rice, sauerkraut, or any of the other many valuable extenders. Explore your collection of foreign cookbooks for new ideas—or find them closer to home. An excellent chili can be the best of all buffet dishes.

Cooking in quantity is easier if you have one or two really big pots, such as an 8-quart casserole or a large stock pot, and a couple of large baking dishes—the French oven-proof porcelain kind are handsome enough for table service and they'll hold all manner of things, from stuffed crêpes and baked fruit to a beef or herring salad or an escabeche of fish or chicken. You probably have these anyway, as part of your general *batterie de cuisine*. Remember, though, that big pots need big burners in order to cook properly and that one oven can only accommodate two large baking dishes, so when you plan your menu, make sure that only one food has to be baked or you'll find yourself desperately juggling times and temperatures. Last, if you want to keep cool and relaxed, choose dishes that can be done ahead and chilled, or reheated, or left alone to simmer in their own good time.

Sunday Brunch for 16 or More

Roulades, which are actually nothing more than soufflés baked flat, filled, and rolled, make marvelously economical and easy standbys for brunch parties, because you can vary them with any number of fillings. Unlike soufflés, they are not temperamental about timing. They can be made in advance and reheated—put them on a platter, loosely covered with foil, over simmering water. Although roulades are ethereal eating, two slices make a very satisfying serving, depending on the richness of the filling. The basic roulade mixture is enough for two rolls, each of which yields about 12 slices, so make as many as you need for your guest list, plus the filling or fillings you prefer. It is advisable not to attempt to make more than two roulade batches at one time, otherwise the volume is difficult to handle, and they should be baked no more than two at a time, either side by side in the middle of the oven or on two racks, with the pans staggered so the mixture bakes evenly.

MENU
[JOSÉ WILSON]

Bloody Mary Soup with Parmesan Cheese Straws
Roulades—Salmon, Curried Chicken, Creamed Mushroom
Compote of Figs and Green Grapes

The Wine

Carafes of California chablis

BLOODY MARY SOUP

Simply heat a spicy canned Bloody Mary mix, adding any other seasonings you like, such as celery salt, seasoned pepper, plus a good squeeze of lemon juice. Allow 1 cup per serving. Serve in cups, spiked with vodka, and float a thin slice of lemon on top.

BASIC ROULADE

8 tablespoons butter
1 cup flour
4 cups milk, heated
2 teaspoons salt
¼ teaspoon cayenne pepper
2 tablespoons cognac
2 tablespoons sour cream
8 eggs, separated

Melt the butter in a large saucepan and blend in the flour over low heat. Cook, stirring, until golden and bubbly. Remove from heat and gradually stir in the milk with a wire whisk, stirring constantly so the sauce does not lump. Return to heat and cook, stirring, until thick. Mix in the salt, pepper, cognac and sour cream, then the egg yolks, lightly beaten.

Preheat the oven to 325°. Butter two 10″ x 15″ x 1″ deep jelly-roll pans, line with wax paper, leaving an overhang of a couple of inches at each end, and butter the paper well.

Beat the egg whites until they stand in soft peaks, as for a soufflé. Fold about ⅓ into the sauce mixture, incorporating it completely, then lightly fold in the remainder of the egg whites. Divide mixture between the two prepared pans, spreading it evenly with a rubber spatula. Bake 40 minutes, or until golden on top.

Meanwhile, make chosen filling or fillings. When the roll is baked, remove from the oven and invert the pan onto a large sheet of wax paper. Loosen the paper from the pan, then peel it from the roll. Some of the surface may stick, but that doesn't matter as this side will be covered with filling. Loosen paper gently with the point of a paring knife at places where it sticks. Trim edges of roll with a large sharp knife.

Spread the uncovered surface of the roll with the filling, using a rubber spatula. Use the long side of the waxed paper to roll up the roulade like a jelly roll, and to transfer it to a heated serving platter.

SALMON FILLING

>   2 cups cooked or canned salmon, flaked
> ½ teaspoon freshly grated nutmeg
>   Salt, freshly ground black pepper
>   2 tablespoons lemon juice
>   2 tablespoons chopped fresh dill
>   2 cups sour cream

Season the salmon with the nutmeg, salt and pepper to taste, lemon juice and dill. Mix in enough of the sour cream to give a consistency soft enough to spread evenly. This makes enough filling for two roulades,

Serve the roulade in slices, each slice topped with 1 tablespoon sour cream and ½ teaspoon red caviar.

CURRIED CHICKEN FILLING

>   6 tablespoons butter
>   1 tablespoon curry powder
>   6 tablespoons flour
> 1½ cups hot chicken stock
>   Salt, cayenne pepper
>   1 tablespoon lemon juice
> ¾ cup yoghurt
> ½ cup chutney, finely minced
>   2 cups slivered cooked white meat of chicken

Melt the butter in a saucepan, stir in the curry powder and cook, stirring, for 2 minutes. Mix in the flour and cook over medium heat until bubbly. Gradually whisk in the hot chicken stock, season to taste with salt and about ⅛ teaspoon cayenne pepper, and cook over medium heat until thick. Mix in the lemon juice, yoghurt, chutney and chicken and just heat through—do not let the mixture boil after the yoghurt is added. This makes enough filling for 2 roulades. Use any excess as a sauce.

CREAMED MUSHROOM FILLING

 12 tablespoons butter
  1 pound mushrooms, sliced
  1 tablespoon lemon juice
   Salt, freshly ground black pepper
  6 tablespoons flour
1½ cups milk, heated
  1 cup heavy cream
 ½ cup chopped parsley

Melt 6 tablespoons butter in a heavy skillet, add the mushrooms and sauté quickly, sprinkling them with the lemon juice, salt and pepper to taste. Keep warm while making the sauce.

Melt the remaining butter in a saucepan, blend in the flour and cook over medium heat, stirring, until bubbly and golden. Whisk in the hot milk, whisking constantly so sauce does not lump, then cook over medium heat, stirring, until thick. Season to taste with salt and pepper and mix in the heavy cream and parsley. Stir in the sautéed mushrooms and just heat through. This makes enough filling for 2 roulades. Use any excess as a sauce.

COMPOTE OF FIGS AND GREEN GRAPES

FOR 16 SERVINGS ALLOW:

 4 1-pound, 1-ounce jars of whole figs in heavy syrup
 4 pounds seedless green grapes
⅔ cup Strega (Italian liqueur)
 4 tablespoons grated lemon zest

Drain the figs, reserving syrup. Combine figs and grapes in one or two large crystal bowls. Measure enough of the syrup to just cover the fruit, combine with the Strega and 3 tablespoons lemon zest and pour over fruit. Chill well before serving, then sprinkle remaining lemon zest over the fruit. Increase quantities proportionately according to number of guests.

A Simple Italian Luncheon for 24

The great merit of the main dish is that it combines inexpensive chicken with chick-peas and vegetables, so eliminating the need for a green and a starchy vegetable. All you need apart from this is a plain green salad, which you can make more interesting in texture and flavor by adding sliced anchovy-stuffed olives and drained canned artichoke hearts or marinated artichoke hearts. The chick-pea mixture (which also, on its own, makes a marvelous main-dish salad) has to marinate overnight, so you will need two large pottery or stainless steel bowls, and two or three large baking dishes for the cooking. Boned chicken breasts are easiest to eat, and most delicate, but you could also use the even cheaper legs and thighs, increasing the cooking time by fifteen minutes. The dessert, a light and fluffy coffee-flavored ricotta, can be made well ahead and chilled.

MENU
[JOSÉ WILSON]

Chicken Ceci

Green Salad with Sliced Anchovy-Stuffed Olives, Artichoke Hearts

French Bread

Coffee Ricotta

The Wine

Lightly chilled Valpolicella

CHICKEN CECI

　12　ribs celery with leaves, diced
　　3　large red Italian onions, diced
　　6　1-pound cans chick-peas, drained and rinsed
　　1　pound baked ham, diced
　　2　pepperoni sausages, skinned and diced
　　2　cups salad oil
　12　tablespoons red wine vinegar
　　3　teaspoons Italian herb seasoning
　　　　Salt, freshly ground black pepper to taste
　24　chicken breasts, skinned and boned

Mix together the celery, onion, chick-peas, ham and pepperoni, combining thoroughly. Blend the oil, vinegar and Italian herb seasoning with salt and pepper, as for a salad dressing, and pour this over the chick-pea mixture, tossing well. Let this marinate overnight in the refrigerator.

Arrange the boned chicken breasts in a single layer in 3 large baking dishes and cover them completely with the chick-pea mixture, including the oil-and-vinegar dressing. Bake in a 350° oven for 45 to 50 minutes, or until the chicken is cooked through, but still moist. Do not overcook. If the mixture seems to get dry during the baking, baste with a little chicken stock.

COFFEE RICOTTA

　　4　1-pound containers fresh ricotta cheese or creamed cottage cheese
　¾　to 1 cup sugar
　½　to 2 cups heavy cream
　¾　cup coffee-flavored liqueur (Kahlua, Tia Maria)
　　1　cup pulverized dark-roast Turkish coffee

If you use ricotta, beat it with an electric beater until fluffy, or put it through a fine sieve or food mill. If you use cottage cheese, which has a heavier texture, put it through a food mill.

For ricotta you will need only ½ cup heavy cream. For cottage cheese you may need up to 2 cups to give a light, creamy consistency. If obtainable, the fresh Italian ricotta is preferable, as the texture is lighter, fluffier and richer, but cottage cheese makes a perfectly good substitute.

Mix in the sugar, cream, liqueur and powdered coffee—don't add all the sugar at once; the amount you need depends on your taste and the sweetness of the liqueur you use. Blend thoroughly, beating until light, creamy and well mixed.

As this is a rich, though light, dessert, allow about ⅓ cup per serving. Put servings in pots de crème, tiny ramekins or other small dessert cups (Japanese or Chinese teacups are good). Chill for 2 to 3 hours. To serve, pop a coffee-bean candy on top of each serving and accompany with crisp plain wafers.

NOTE: While it is possible to use instant espresso for this dessert, the Turkish coffee is best, as it is completely pulverized and so blends in well, and has a good rich round flavor, not too bitter. It can be bought in stores that handle Middle Eastern foods.

Choucroute Supper for 24 to 30

That famous Alsatian dish, choucroute garnie, is one of the easiest of all recipes to stretch—you just keep adding more variations on the pork theme—and it looks absolutely spectacular if you are serving buffet-style. As you undoubtedly won't have one pot large enough to prepare choucroute for 24 or more, beg, borrow or buy two large covered casseroles or cooking pots of 8-to-12-quart capacity. Choucroute garnie is so hearty you don't need anything with it other than a light dessert; but should you want to have a first course, keep to something low in calories and piquant, such as vegetables à la Grecque or vinaigrette, or filets of marinated herring or mackerel with lemon and thin fingers of buttered pumpernickel.

MENU
[JOSÉ WILSON]

Choucroute Garnie
Pears or Apples Stuffed with Roquefort Cream

The Wine

Alsatian Riesling or a good imported beer

CHOUCROUTE GARNIE

FOR EACH POT:

> 2½ pounds salt pork
> 4 pounds fresh sauerkraut
> 3 cloves garlic and 10 juniper berries, tied in a cheesecloth bag
> 2 teaspoons freshly ground black pepper
> 12 to 15 pork loin chops
>   Butter
>   Chicken stock or dry white wine
> 2 large Polish kielbasy
> 6 to 8 knockwurst or 12 to 15 frankfurters

FOR SERVING:

> 24 to 30 small boiled potatoes, cooked in their jackets
>   A selection of mustards

Soak the salt pork in water to get rid of excess salt, or blanch it in boiling water. Cut two or three ½″ slices from the salt pork and arrange on the bottom of the pot. Drain the sauerkraut, wash it well under cold running water and squeeze dry. Put the sauerkraut in the pot, bury the remaining whole piece of salt pork in the center and also the garlic and juniper berries, and grate black pepper over it. Brown the pork chops on each side in butter and add to the pot, covering them with sauerkraut. Add enough chicken stock or white wine to cover all the ingredients. Bring to a boil, cover, reduce the heat and simmer gently for 2½ to 3 hours, then add the kielbasy and cook for 15 minutes. Add the knockwurst or frankfurters, cover and simmer 15 minutes longer.

Meanwhile, boil the potatoes. To serve, remove the meats to a carving board and slice the salt pork and kielbasy and the knockwurst. Arrange the drained sauerkraut (discard the cheesecloth bag) in the center of a large platter and surround it with the pork chops, sliced pork and sliced sausages (if you use frankfurters, leave them whole). Serve the potatoes in a separate dish. The contents of each pot will serve 12 to 15 people.

NOTE: Other forms of pork that can be used include roast loin of pork, sliced, pigs' feet or knuckles (which are cooked with the sauerkraut), sliced baked or boiled ham.

PEARS OR APPLES STUFFED WITH ROQUEFORT CREAM

  ½ pound Roquefort cheese or similar blue cheese
  ½ pound cream cheese
  8 tablespoons sour cream
  1 cup coarsely chopped walnuts
24 to 30 firm ripe pears or firm eating apples

Let the cheeses stand at room temperature until softened. Mash them to a smooth paste with the sour cream, then mix in the walnuts.

Core the pears or apples and stuff each one with approximately 2 tablespoons of the cheese-walnut mixture. Chill until ready to serve.

Serve with fruit knives and forks, as the fruit should be sliced crosswise, and peeled or not, according to preference.

Pasta Supper for 20 to 40

One of the most superb of all dishes for a buffet supper is the Greek pastitsio, which can be made in vast quantities, and which improves with reheating. The secret that makes this dish different from all other pasta dishes is the Béchamel sauce, enriched with egg yolks, cream and cheese, which binds the meat and macaroni and gives it a melting, moist richness. The quantity given is for twenty. It may be doubled, but should be done in two batches; and really large baking dishes, the type used for lasagna, are absolutely essential.

The salad, also Greek, a most unusual, tart and refreshing combination of carrots, capers and a mustardy French dressing, is a perfect contrast to the pastitsio. Unless your guests have acquired a taste for the turpentine flavor of Greek retsina, it is better to stick to an inexpensive California jug wine, served *en carafe*. Provide both red and white, so each person can choose what he or she prefers.

MENU

Pastitsio

Greek Carrot and Caper Salad

Lebanese Pine Nuts and Raisins, Chilled Yoghurt

The Wine

Carafes of California chablis and Zinfandel

PASTITSIO

[LEON LIANIDES]

MEAT MIXTURE

  2 tablespoons butter
  1 tablespoon oil
  3 cups finely chopped onion
  2 cloves garlic, finely minced
  4 pounds ground round steak
     Salt, freshly ground black pepper
  1 teaspoon oregano
  ½ to 1 teaspoon cinnamon
     Freshly grated nutmeg to taste
  ½ cup finely chopped parsley
  3 cups canned Italian plum tomatoes, well drained
  ¾ cup dry red wine

SAUCE MIXTURE

   6 cups light cream
   2 cups milk
  12 tablespoons butter
  1½ cups flour
      Salt, pepper to taste
  10 egg yolks
   1 cup heavy cream
   2 cups ricotta cheese

1½ pounds pasticcio macaroni (sold in Greek shops), or #2 long
    macaroni or ziti
1 cup finely crumbled feta cheese
1 cup grated Parmesan or Romano cheese

Melt the butter and oil in a 14″ sauté pan or skillet, or divide all the
meat mixture, including butter and oil, between two smaller skillets.
Add the onion and sauté until golden and soft. Mix in the garlic and
beef and cook, breaking the meat up with a wooden spoon, until all
traces of pink disappear. Season with salt and pepper to taste (about
4 teaspoons salt and ½ to ¾ teaspoon pepper), the oregano, cinnamon,
nutmeg, and add the parsley, tomatoes and wine. Mix well together and
taste for seasoning, adding what you think is necessary. Cook over high
heat until the liquid evaporates.

Meanwhile, scald the light cream and milk. Melt the 12 tablespoons
butter in a 4-quart saucepan, stir in the flour and cook, stirring, until
smooth and bubbly. Mix in the scalded cream and milk, stirring constantly. Season to taste with salt and pepper and cook, stirring, until
thick. Remove from the heat. Beat the egg yolks and heavy cream,
gradually add some of the hot sauce to temper the yolks, then stir this
into the balance of the sauce and beat in the ricotta. If ricotta is not
available, use 1 extra cup heavy cream.

Boil the macaroni rapidly in plenty of boiling salted water in a large
pot until just done, but still firm and *al dente*, about 10 minutes. Drain
thoroughly. Preheat the oven to 400°.

Liberally butter two large baking dishes measuring 18″ x 13″ x 2½″
deep, or 15½″ x 9″ x 4″. Reserve half the cream sauce for the topping.
Make layers of ingredients in the baking dishes, starting with a layer of
macaroni. Sprinkle this with ⅓ cup feta cheese and ¼ cup grated Parmesan. Spoon over this a layer of cream sauce, then ⅓ of the meat
mixture. Continue making layers, ending with macaroni. Pour remaining
sauce over the top and sprinkle with remaining grated Parmesan cheese.
Bake for 50 minutes to 1 hour, or until very hot and bubbling. This may
be baked in advance and reheated in a 250° oven, but if you reheat it do
not add the final sprinkling of cheese on the top until ready to reheat.

GREEK CARROT AND CAPER SALAD
[ONALEE COOKE]

> 4 pounds carrots, shredded (about 16 cups)
> 1½ cups drained capers, the largest available
> 2 tablespoons Dijon mustard
> 1 tablespoon salt
> 1½ teaspoons pepper
> 6 tablespoons wine vinegar
> 1½ cups olive oil

Combine the carrots and capers. Put the remaining ingredients in a screw-top jar and shake well. Taste for seasoning. Pour dressing over the salad, using enough to coat it, but not make it soggy, and toss lightly. Serve in a large bowl lined with romaine leaves, and allow about ¾ cup per serving.

LEBANESE PINE NUTS AND RAISINS

> 6 cups white raisins
> 2 cups honey
> 2 cups water
> Grated zest of 3 to 4 lemons (about 3 tablespoons)
> 2 cups pine nuts

Plump the raisins by soaking them in warm water for an hour. Drain. Combine the honey and water in a saucepan, bring to a boil and boil for 3 minutes, then add the drained raisins and lemon zest. Cook over low heat for 10 minutes. Remove from heat and pour into a bowl. Stir in the pine nuts. Chill until ready to serve.

Serve very cold. In the Middle East tradition, this is a very sweet dessert and you should serve only a small portion, with chilled yoghurt offered as a tart contrast, but the combination of raisins and pine nuts is utterly delicious and different.

Cocktail Buffet for 50 to 60

The best way to cope with a big cocktail buffet is to serve a minimum of fairly hearty dishes, choosing things that are fun to eat and piquant to the palate. This menu is good for holiday times because it enables you to use up leftover baked ham and roast turkey in an unusual and interesting way. To the recipes given you might add your own favorite pâté and raw vegetable dip.

MENU

Green Pepper Spiced Ham   *Shrimp Ball*
James Beard's Turkey in Lettuce Leaves
A Platter of Cheeses with Crackers and Sliced French Bread
A Platter of Sliced Sausages   *A Choice of Pâtés*
Raw Vegetables with Coarse Sea Salt and a Dip

GREEN PEPPER SPICED HAM
[JOSÉ WILSON]

> 2 tablespoons green peppercorns (available canned in specialty food shops)
> 8 to 10 slivers garlic
> 2 teaspoons cinnamon
> 6 ounces unsalted butter, softened
> Salt to taste
> 12 cups minced baked ham (about 6 pounds)
> 8 tablespoons Dijon mustard
> 12 tablespoons mayonnaise or enough to bind

Mash the green peppercorns well with the garlic and cinnamon in a mortar and pestle. Work in the butter until thoroughly blended. Taste for salt, and add as much as needed, depending on the saltiness of the ham. This spiced butter keeps well in the refrigerator or freezer.

Mix the ham, green pepper butter, mustard and just enough mayon-

415

naise to bind the mixture together, but not so much that it becomes sloppy. Pack into two 6-cup ring molds (any excess can be put in a small bowl and unmolded separately), that have been lightly oiled. Chill until just firm, then turn out onto serving platters. Fill the centers with tiny spiced onions on a bed of parsley. Serve with sliced French bread, crackers, or, preferably, tiny hot biscuits.

SHRIMP BALL
[ONALEE COOKE]

3 8-ounce packages cream cheese
8 4½-ounce cans tiny shrimp, drained
4 cloves garlic, mashed
Mayonnaise
Tabasco, salt
Finely chopped parsley

Mash the cream cheese. Chop the drained shrimp coarsely and add with the garlic and enough mayonnaise to hold the mixture together firmly. Add Tabasco and salt to taste. Form into two balls and roll in chopped parsley.

TURKEY IN LETTUCE LEAVES
[JAMES A. BEARD]

½ pound butter
6 cups finely chopped onion
2½ cups finely chopped green pepper
3 4-ounce cans green chili peppers, drained, seeded and chopped
6 tablespoons fresh hot green chili pepper, seeded and finely chopped
12 cups finely diced cooked turkey or chicken
4 tablespoons chopped fresh basil or 2 teaspoons dried basil
Salt to taste
2 teaspoons freshly ground black pepper
1 cup cognac
½ to 1 cup chicken broth (optional)
8 to 10 large heads iceberg lettuce
GARNISH: toasted shaved almonds, chopped parsley

Melt the butter in a 14″ sauté pan, or divide this and the turkey mixture between two smaller skillets. Add the onion and green pepper and cook until soft and wilted. Add the canned and fresh green chili peppers and the turkey, and toss well. Cover, and simmer for 5 minutes.

Add the chopped fresh or the dried basil, salt to taste and pepper. Taste for seasoning before adding the cognac. If mixture seems too dry, add some of the chicken broth. Taste again, and adjust seasoning.

Serve this hot, in chafing dishes or electric skillets, with a garnish of toasted shaved almonds and chopped parsley on top.

Chill the lettuce well and separate the heads into leaves. Arrange these on a platter by the turkey. The idea is that each person spoons some of the hot spicy mixture onto an icy lettuce leaf, rolls it up and eats it like a taco.

Basic Recipes

Sauces

BÉCHAMEL SAUCE (BASIC WHITE SAUCE)

> 4 tablespoons butter
> 4 tablespoons flour
> 2 cups hot liquid (milk, light cream, chicken, veal, fish or vegetable stock)
> Salt, freshly ground black pepper to taste
> Dash of freshly grated nutmeg

Melt the butter in a saucepan, mix in the flour and cook over low heat for 2 or 3 minutes, stirring well with a wooden spoon or spatula, until golden and bubbly. Gradually pour on the hot liquid, stirring constantly, and continue stirring over medium heat until the sauce is smooth and thickened. Season to taste with salt, pepper and nutmeg. Makes 2 cups.

SAUCE MORNAY

Add ½ cup grated Parmesan cheese to the Béchamel sauce and stir until melted.

MUSTARD SAUCE

Add 1½ tablespoons Dijon mustard, ¼ teaspoon Tabasco sauce, and ½ cup heavy cream to the Béchamel sauce.

BASIC BROWN SAUCE (SAUCE ESPAGNOLE)

- ½ pound butter
- 1 pound ham, or veal and ham, diced
- 2 onions, sliced
- 2 carrots, sliced
- ½ pound mushrooms, sliced
- ⅓ cup flour
- 2 quarts beef stock
- 1 bay leaf
- ½ cup tomato purée
- Salt, pepper
- ½ cup red wine

Melt the butter and brown the ham, onions, carrots and mushrooms. When well browned, add the flour and blend well; continue cooking until the flour starts to brown. Slowly add the stock and bay leaf, mix thoroughly, cover, and simmer for an hour. Now add the tomato purée, salt and pepper to taste, and the wine. Simmer for 30 minutes longer, then strain. You should have 2 quarts of sauce. If it has not thickened sufficiently, it may be boiled down.

SAUCE PÉRIGUEUX

    1 cup brown sauce
    1 tablespoon chopped truffles
    1 tablespoon truffle liquor
    1 tablespoon butter

Heat the sauce. Add truffles and liquor. Add butter, swirling it in until melted. Serve at once.

SAUCE DIABLE

    1 large shallot, chopped
    2 tablespoons butter
    Juice of 1 lemon
    1 teaspoon prepared mustard, Dijon-style
    1 teaspoon Worcestershire sauce
    Dash of Tabasco sauce
    2 cups brown sauce

Sauté the shallot in the butter until transparent. Add lemon juice, mustard, Worcestershire, Tabasco, and brown sauce, and cook, stirring, until smooth. If hotter sauce is desired, add more Tabasco and mustard.

HOLLANDAISE SAUCE

    3 egg yolks
    1 or 2 teaspoons water
    ¼ pound (½ cup) sweet butter, cut into small pieces
    Salt and cayenne pepper
    Lemon juice

Combine the egg yolks and water in the upper part of a double boiler and using a small wire whisk stir over hot water until the eggs are as thick as heavy cream. Gradually whisk in the butter, bit by bit. Whisk all the time, and be certain the water below does not boil. If your sauce becomes too thick, dilute it with a little water. If it curdles, you can bring it back with a little boiling water. When emulsified, add a few grains of cayenne, salt and lemon juice to taste. Makes approximately ¾ cup.

BÉARNAISE SAUCE

Put 2 tablespoons tarragon vinegar, 2 finely chopped shallots, and ½ teaspoon minced fresh tarragon in a pan and cook down until almost reduced to a glaze. Put this mixture in with the egg yolks when making the Hollandaise sauce.

BLENDER HOLLANDAISE

    4 egg yolks
    2 tablespoons lemon juice
    ½ teaspoon dry mustard
       Dash Tabasco sauce
    1 cup butter, melted and heated almost to the boiling point

Place the egg yolks, lemon juice and seasonings in the blender and blend for a second or so. Do not overblend until eggs liquefy. Remove the cover and pour in bubbling hot butter in a thin steady stream as the mixture blends. Blend until smooth and creamy, but do not overblend. Makes approximately 1½ cups.

SAUCE MOUSSELINE

Blend Hollandaise with an equal amount of salted whipped cream. Serve with asparagus or fish.

BASIC MAYONNAISE

    2 egg yolks
    1 teaspoon salt
    ½ teaspoon dry mustard
       Dash of Tabasco sauce
    1¼ cups olive oil (or half olive, half vegetable oil)
       Lemon juice

Be sure all the ingredients are at room temperature. Use a rotary egg beater, wire whisk or an electric hand beater. First beat the egg yolks, salt, mustard and Tabasco together in a bowl until the egg yolks start to thicken. Then start adding the oil, a very few drops at a time, beating it in thoroughly before adding more. If the mayonnaise starts to curdle, you are adding the oil too fast. Correct the curdling by starting over with another egg yolk and a little oil, then gradually beat the curdled mixture into this.

Continue adding oil until the mayonnaise is stiff and thick (once it has started to stiffen, you may add the oil more rapidly). Using all olive oil will give you a mayonnaise with a good strong flavor; if you like it lighter, use half vegetable oil.

When the mayonnaise is made, beat in lemon juice to taste to thin it down a little and sharpen the flavor. Makes approximately 1½ cups.

MUSTARD MAYONNAISE

To each cup of mayonnaise, add 1 tablespoon Dijon mustard, or more, to taste.

BLENDER MAYONNAISE

This is much easier than mayonnaise made by hand, and you use a whole egg, not yolks.

- 1 whole egg
- 1 teaspoon salt
- 1 teaspoon dry mustard
  Dash of Tabasco sauce
- 3 tablespoons wine vinegar
- 1 cup oil (all olive, or part olive, part vegetable)
  Lemon juice (optional)

Place the egg, salt, mustard, Tabasco, wine vinegar and ⅓ cup oil in the blender and blend at high speed for 5 seconds. Remove the cover insert and, with the blender at high, pour in the remaining oil in a steady stream as the mixture blends. Blend only until smooth and thick, do not overblend. If you like, you can add a drop or two of lemon juice for flavor, although the vinegar will have given it sufficient acidity. Makes approximately 1¼ cups.

BASIC VINAIGRETTE OR FRENCH DRESSING

For a simple, proper vinaigrette sauce or French dressing, use three or four parts good olive oil to 1 part wine vinegar with salt and freshly ground black pepper to taste. You can vary this, according to taste, by adding chopped herbs, a little Dijon mustard, a touch of garlic, or what you will, but the true vinaigrette is just a basic mixture of oil, vinegar and seasonings.

Pastries

PASTRY #1 (FOR ONE-CRUST PIE)

> 1 cup flour
> ¼ teaspoon salt
> 6½ tablespoons vegetable shortening
> 2 tablespoons cold water

Sift the flour and salt into a bowl. Cut in the shortening with a pastry blender or 2 knives until the mixture forms fine crumbs. Very gradually sprinkle the water over the crumbs, stir and press down with a fork until the dough begins to hold together. Shape into a ball with your hands. Chill until ready to use.

For a two-crust pie, use 2 cups flour sifted with ½ teaspoon salt, ⅔ cup shortening and approximately ¼ cup cold water. Follow the same procedure as for a 1-crust pie. Use slightly more than half the dough for the bottom crust.

PASTRY #2 (FOR ONE-CRUST PIE)

> 3 tablespoons cold water
> 1 cup plus 2 tablespoons flour
> ¼ teaspoon salt
> 7 tablespoons vegetable shortening

Mix the water and the 2 tablespoons flour, stir until smooth and set aside. Sift the remaining flour and salt into a bowl and cut in the shortening with a pastry blender or 2 knives until the mixture forms coarse crumbs. Add the flour-water mixture and stir with a fork, pressing down on the dough until it begins to hold together. Gather it together with your hands and shape into a ball. Chill until ready to use.

To make tart shells from either of these pastry doughs, roll out the dough approximately ⅛" thick. Cut in circles large enough to line the bottom and sides of shallow 4" fluted tart tins. Line the tins with the dough and bake in a preheated 350° oven for 20 minutes, or until light gold. Carefully remove the tart shells from the tins and cool completely. Recipes for 1-crust pie will make enough for six 4" tart tins.

To make a baked pie shell, roll out either dough to a circle about 1" larger in diameter than the pie plate. Gently ease the dough into the pie plate and trim it ½" beyond the rim of the plate. Turn under the overhanging edge and flute the rim with your fingers, or press down on the rim with the tines of a fork. Prick the surface of the pastry with a fork at 1" intervals. Bake in a preheated 425° oven for 15 to 20 minutes, or until golden.

RICH PASTRY (FOR DESSERT QUICHES)

> 2 cups unsifted flour
> 3 tablespoons sugar
> ½ teaspoon salt
> ¾ cup (1½ sticks) butter, firm but not ice cold, cut in pieces
> 1½ teaspoons grated lemon rind
> 3 hard-cooked egg yolks, sieved
> 2 egg whites
> 1 egg yolk, lightly beaten

Put the flour on a pastry board or in a large bowl. Make a well in the center of the flour and add the remaining ingredients, except the beaten egg yolk. Quickly work the center ingredients into a paste with your fingers and then incorporate the flour until the mixture will form a smooth, firm ball. Wrap in waxed paper and chill until firm enough to roll out.

Roll out to fit a 9" pie pan, or a 1½"-deep flan ring. To line pie pan, follow directions for pie pastry. To line flan ring, place the ring on a baking sheet. Drape the dough over a rolling pin, carefully lift and allow to drop into the ring so the dough falls to the bottom. Press the dough against the sides of the ring and the bottom of the baking sheet. Cut off excess dough by running the rolling pin across the top rim of the ring.

To bake, place a piece of aluminum foil, shiny side down, in the shell to form a lining, and weight down with dried beans or rice to keep the shell from puffing up. Bake in a 425° oven for 15 to 20 minutes, until the bottom is set and the edges slightly brown. Remove from the oven, take out the foil and beans and brush the bottom of the shell with the beaten egg yolk, then return to the oven for 2 minutes to set the yolk. This provides a seal for the crust and prevents its soaking up the custard mixture and becoming soggy. Cool shell slightly before adding and baking filling.

PÂTÉ SUCRÉE (FOR DESSERT TARTS OR FLANS)

¾ cup butter
⅓ cup sugar
1 egg
2 cups flour
½ teaspoon salt

Cream the butter and sugar together and add the egg. Blend well. Sift the flour with the salt and gradually blend into the sugar-butter mixture. If the paste is too stiff, add a little ice water, but this is seldom necessary. The pastry should be the consistency of a good cookie dough. Mold into a flan ring or pie shell, or roll out and fit into the pan. Chill before baking according to recipe directions.

Crêpes, Omelettes

BASIC CRÊPES

⅞ cup all-purpose flour
⅛ teaspoon salt
3 eggs
2 tablespoons melted butter
1¼ cups milk

Sift the flour and salt together. Add the eggs, one at a time, mixing well after each addition, until there are no lumps. Add the butter. Gradually stir in the milk and mix until the batter is the consistency of light cream. Refrigerate for an hour before using.

To make crêpes, heat a 6″ crêpe pan over medium-high heat, and brush with melted butter. Pour about 2 tablespoons batter into the pan and tip so that it runs over the entire surface. Cook until lightly browned on the underside, then turn and brown lightly on second side. Remove from pan and keep warm in a low oven, covered with foil, until ready to use. Makes about 16 crêpes.

NOTE: Extra crêpes may be wrapped in foil and stored in the refrigerator for several days or in the freezer for a month.

DESSERT CRÊPES

Sweeten the basic crêpe batter by sifting 1 tablespoon sugar with the flour and salt and adding 1 teaspoon vanilla with the butter and milk.

OMELETTES

For each omelette

3 eggs
1 teaspoon cold water
⅛ teaspoon salt
Unsalted butter

Break the eggs into a bowl with the water and salt. Beat with a rotary whisk until frothy.

Heat an omelette pan over medium heat until a tiny drop of water sizzles and evaporates when flicked on the surface. Add butter to hot pan and when sizzling, pour in the egg mixture. Stir with the back of a fork, at the same time shaking the pan so the eggs are constantly in motion and any holes made by the fork fill up. Stir only until the eggs begin to set, about 30 seconds for a runny omelette. Slide the fork carefully around the sides of the pan to loosen the omelette and start to roll the omelette from the edge of the pan nearest the handle. Take handle of pan in one hand and tip it so the omelette rolls up on itself and onto plate held in your other hand.

Rice, Beans

STEAMED RICE

    1 tablespoon butter
    1 cup long-grain rice
    ½ teaspoon salt
    2 cups water or stock

Melt the butter in a heavy pan with a tight-fitting cover. Add rice and stir until thoroughly coated. Add salt and water or stock and bring to a boil very quickly. Lower heat, cover pot tightly, and let rice cook very slowly until all the liquid is absorbed, about 20 to 25 minutes. Do not remove cover during cooking time. Fluff up rice with a fork and serve.

For saffron rice, add a good pinch of saffron to the boiling liquid before covering pot.

NOTE: When serving rice, estimate that 1 cup raw rice, which triples in bulk when cooked, will serve 4. The usual ratio is twice as much liquid as rice—2 cups liquid for 1 cup raw rice.

RICE PILAF

    2 tablespoons unsalted butter or olive oil
    1 onion, finely chopped (about 1 cup)
    1 cup long-grain rice
    2 cups boiling liquid (any kind of stock, combined with tomato juice, if desired)
    Salt, freshly ground pepper to taste

Melt fat in a heavy 1-quart pot with a tight-fitting cover. Add onion and cook until soft and golden. Do not allow to brown. Add rice and stir with a wooden spoon until it is coated with the fat. Pour the boiling liquid over the rice and season to taste with salt and pepper. Let liquid come back to a boil, then reduce heat, cover pot and simmer over very low heat for 20 to 30 minutes, or until the rice is tender and has absorbed all the liquid.

427

If the rice should get too soft (this may happen if the onion is very watery), remove the cover and place the pot in a 200° oven for 10 or 15 minutes longer to dry out the rice. Serves 4.

FRIJOLES (MEXICAN-STYLE BEANS)

> 2 cups pinto, black, or red kidney beans
> 2 onions, finely chopped
> 2 cloves garlic, chopped
> Sprig epazote or 1 bay leaf
> 2 or more serrano chilis, chopped, or 1 teaspoon dried pequin chilis, crumbled
> 3 tablespoons lard
> Salt, pepper to taste
> 1 tomato, peeled, seeded, and chopped

Wash beans, but do not soak. Put in cold water to cover with half of the chopped onion and garlic, the epazote or bay leaf, and chilis. Cover and simmer gently, adding more water, always hot, as needed. When beans begin to wrinkle, add 1 tablespoon lard or oil. When beans are soft, almost done, add seasonings. Cook another half hour without adding more water; there should not be a great deal of liquid when beans are done. Heat the remaining 2 tablespoons lard and sauté the remaining chopped onion and garlic until limp. Add tomato and cook for 1 to 2 minutes, then add a tablespoon of beans and mash into the mixture, add a second tablespoon of beans without draining them, so that some of the bean liquid evaporates in this cooking process. Add a third tablespoon of beans and continue to cook until you have a smooth, fairly heavy paste. Return this to the bean pot and stir into beans over low heat to thicken the remaining liquid. Serves 6 to 8.

Index